D0382639

Learners on the Autism Spectrum

Preparing Highly Qualified Educators

Edited by
Kari Dunn Buron and Pamela Wolfberg

Foreword by Carol Gray

AAPC Textbooks
A Division of

Autism Asperger Publishing Co.
P.O. Box 23173
Shawnee Mission, Kansas 66283-0173
www.asperger.net

© 2008 Autism Asperger Publishing Co.
P. O. Box 23173
Shawnee Mission, Kansas 66283-0173
www.asperger.net • 913.897.1004

All rights reserved. No part of the material protected by this copyright notice may be reproduced or used in any form or by any means, electronic or mechanical, including photocopying, recording, or by any information storage and retrieval system, without the prior written permission of the copyright owner.

Publisher's Cataloging-in-Publication

Learners on the autism spectrum : preparing highly qualified
educators / edited by Kari Dunn Buron and Pamela Wolfberg ;
foreword by Carol Gray -- 1st ed. -- Shawnee Mission, Kan. : Autism
Asperger Pub. Co., 2008.

    p. ; cm.

    ISBN: 978-1-934575-07-9

    Includes bibliographical references and index.
    Summary: This work has contributions from major experts in the
field of autism spectrum disorders (ASD). It provides an overview
of all major issues related to individuals with ASD, including current
research and teaching tips, including interventions. Includes
learner objectives, chapter review questions and answers.

    1. Autistic children--Education. 2. Asperger's syndrome--
Patients--Education. 3. Teachers of children with disabilities--
Handbooks, manuals, etc. 4. Teaching--Aids and devices. I. Buron,
Kari Dunn. II. Wolfberg, Pamela J. III. Gray, Carol, 1952- IV. Title.

LC4717.8 .L43 2008   2007935854
371.94--dc22   0806

This book is designed in Minion and Adobe Garamond.

Cover Art: Original watercolor by Kari Dunn Buron.

Printed in the United States of America.

Dedication

Dedicated to my parents, Tom and June Dunn, who possess two
of the gentlest and purest souls here on earth.
How fortunate I am to have witnessed their love of mankind.
– K.D.B.

Dedicated in loving memory of my beau-père Murray Gordon,
whose equally passionate pursuit of science and art
is an inspiration to all who teach and learn.

– P.W.

Table of Contents

About the Editors

Kari Dunn Buron, M.S., is the coordinator of an ASD certificate program for educators at Hamline University in St. Paul, MN. She received her Master of Science degree in behavior disorders and learning disorders from Illinois State University in 1980. She recently retired from K-12 special education after more than 30 years. Kari is one of the founding members of the MN Autism Network, a statewide group of Autism Resource Specialists, and a past president of the Autism Society of Minnesota. She has spent 17 years working with the Autistic Society of Trinidad and Tobago, where she travels annually to volunteer in homes and schools. In 1995, Kari developed Camp Discovery, a summer camp for youth with Asperger Syndrome. In 2003, she received a fellowship that allowed her to study social cognition and ASD from an international perspective. She is the co-author of *The Incredible 5-Point Scale* and the author of *When My Autism Gets Too Big!*, *A 5 Is Against the Law!* and *When My Worries Get Too Big!* She is the creator of *A "5" Could Make Me Lose Control*, an activity-based method of working with highly anxious students. Kari speaks nationally and internationally on topics related to ASD, social cognition, and challenging behavior. She serves on the professional advisory board for the Autism Society of Minnesota and the *Autism Asperger Digest*. For more information, visit www.5pointscale.com

Pamela Wolfberg, Ph.D., is associate professor of special education and director of the autism spectrum graduate program at San Francisco State University. She received her doctorate from the University of California, Berkeley, with SFSU in 1994. She has more than 20 years of experience as an educator, researcher, and practitioner devoted to diverse learners on the autism spectrum. Her research and practice are centered on peer relations, play, and childhood culture as related to the social inclusion of children with autism spectrum disorders. As originator of the Integrated Play Groups model and founder of the Autism Institute on Peer Relations and Play, she leads widespread efforts to develop inclusive peer play programs worldwide. Pamela has published extensively on these topics in peer-reviewed journals and books and is the author of *Play and Imagination in Children with Autism* and *Peer Play and the Autism Spectrum: The Art of Guiding Children's Socialization and Imagination*. She has an active agenda as an invited speaker at the local, national and international level. She currently serves as associate editor for *Autism: International Journal of Research and Practice* and as director of *Project Mosaic: Preparing Highly Qualified Educators to Meet the Unique Needs of Students with Autism in Diverse Settings* (U.S. Department of Education Grant No. H325K060211). Finally, she is the recipient of several distinguished awards for her scholarship, research, and service to the community. For more information, visit www.wolfberg.com.

Contributors

Tony Attwood, Ph.D., The Asperger's Syndrome Clinic, Petrie, Queensland, Australia

Simon Baron-Cohen, Ph.D., professor, Autism Research Centre, Department of Psychiatry, University of Cambridge, United Kingdom

Kari Dunn Buron, M.S., autism educational specialist, Hamline University, Minnesota

Winnie Dunn, Ph.D., OTR FAOTA, professor and chair, Department of Occupational Therapy Education, University of Kansas Medical Center, Kansas

Ofer Golan, Ph.D., assistant professor, Department of Psychology, Bar-Ilan University, Israel, and senior research associate, Autism Research Centre, Department of Psychiatry, University of Cambridge, United Kingdom

Paula Jacobsen, LCSW, BCD, private practice and adjunct clinical professor, Department of Psychiatry and Behavioral Sciences, Stanford University School of Medicine, California

Bonnie J. McBride, Ph.D., assistant professor, Developmental and Behavioral Pediatrics, University of Oklahoma Health Sciences Center

Heather McCracken, executive director, Friend 2 Friend Social Learning Society, Vancouver, B.C., Canada

Gary B. Mesibov, Ph.D., professor of psychology, Departments of Psychiatry and Psychology, University of North Carolina at Chapel Hill, and director of Division TEACCH, North Carolina

Nancy J. Minshew, M.D., professor of psychiatry and neurology, University of Pittsburgh School of Medicine, Pennsylvania

Brenda Smith Myles, Ph.D., associate professor, Department of Special Education, University of Kansas

Cathy Pratt, Ph.D., director, Indiana Resource Center for Autism, and board chair, Autism Society of America

Ilene S. Schwartz, Ph.D., professor and chair, area of special education, University of Washington

Victoria Shea, Ph.D., adjunct associate professor of psychology, Department of Psychiatry, University of North Carolina at Chapel Hill

Stephen Shore, Ph.D., autism consultant, Newton, Massachusetts, and board member, Autism Society of America

Sheila Smith, M.S. (ABD), AIM development specialist, Ohio Center for Autism and Low Incidence, Columbus, Ohio

Terri Cooper Swanson, Ms.Ed., doctoral student, University of Kansas

Diane Twachtmann-Cullen, Ph.D., CCC-SLP, executive director, Autism and Developmental Disabilities Consultation Center, Higganum, Connecticut

Tara Tuchel, M.S., CCC-SLP, autism specialist, Willow River Elementary, Hudson, Wisconsin

Diane L. Williams, Ph.D., CCC-SLP, assistant professor, Department of Speech-Language Pathology, Duquesne University, Pennsylvania

Michelle Garcia Winner, M.A., SLP, specialist for persons with social cognitive challenges, Michelle G. Winner's Center for Social Thinking, Inc., San Jose, California

Pamela Wolfberg, Ph.D., associate professor, Department of Special Education, San Francisco State University, California

Chapter Reviewers

California Team

Think Tank Leaders:
Shayla Duda
Emmy Fearne
Betty Yu

Think Tanks:
Sue Brock
Seana Corona
Caitlin Cora
Julianne Hoffman
Talya Kemper
Bridgette Malatesta
Vicki McCoy
Johanna Ploude
Suchitra Thapliyal

Seenae Chong
Bert Dyer
Jessica Fink
Yvette Gonzales
Rochelle Hooks
Kiara Lopez
Miriam Nathanson
Andrew Preston
Amy Schaller

Shi Shyuan Ba
Alex Caldwallader
Leah Felson
Helen Lara-Crea
Kathleen Madden
Rachel Manfredi
Corrina McGraw
Michelle Young

Minnesota Team

Mary Kay Bachel
Cathy Banks
Patty Bowe
Sarah Boyer
Cindy Brown Polson
Tami Childs
Patricia Cretella
Anne Dudley
Joseph Falkner
Diane Gallagher
Angela Haffner
Jan Hanson
Linda Hanson
Janet Holler
Nancy Huninghake
Nancy Jackley
Trudy Kluba
Jill Kuzma
Mary Lesch
Peggy Locke
Kathleen Lund

Lyn Malone
Sandra Manns
Susan McGill
Margie Menard
Dianna Michels
Donna Miller
Cathy Milostan
Laura Moore
Lynne Patterson
Kathy Patton
Lynn Peal
Christine Rodrick
Joyce Santo
Adele Simon
Kristine Smallfield
Mary Beth Solheim
Shelly Thomas
Theresa Urmann
Candace Vittorini
Pam Warren
Nichelle Zimmer

Foreword

This is an important textbook in the current autism renaissance. Thirty years ago the number of titles addressing autism spectrum disorders (ASD) could be counted on one hand. In the short history of autism, that was just yesterday. Today, parents and professionals have a wide variety of books to inform and guide their efforts. This book, however, isn't about autism's "yesterday" or even its "today." *Learners on the Autism Spectrum: Preparing Highly Qualified Educators* is about autism's tomorrow. It merges current thinking with insight to equip each reader with the tools he or she will need to effectively educate learners on the spectrum *in the future*. Designed specifically for university students, its purpose and quality distinguishes it from many other books in the field. In addition to university students, I believe that every educator – whether a parent of a child diagnosed with an ASD or an autism professional – will refer to this book many times for years to come.

Teaching is a social activity; to gain access to what is presented, students participate in an intricate exchange of information with their teacher. For typical students this is relatively easy. While students may occasionally divert their attention or decide not to follow a direction, most students have little difficulty understanding the meaning of what has been said or done. For learners with ASD the experience of a classroom and instruction is quite different. Meaning may be diverted, altered, or lost many times each day. On the seemingly short journey from teacher to student, peer to peer, or parent to child, words lose their intent. Gestures arrive without interpretation. Sensory information may be distorted. The result is often misunderstanding and frustration for student and teacher alike. Imagine being the educator, with a student diagnosed with an autism spectrum disorder in your care, and not knowing what to do.

Not knowing what to do is a part of autism's past. In 1977, when I was hired to teach four students with autism, I definitely did not know what to do. Sadly, my lack of knowledge was more the norm than the exception. This resource changes everything. For university students studying to work with learners with ASD, this text is a guide for their thinking and actions. The editors and authors have gathered information and gained experience over the last several years. Regardless of their titles – researcher, professional, parent, or person diagnosed with an autism spectrum disorder – they have combined their study, research, and experience to create one of the most accurate, trustworthy, and practical guides to autism and its interventions to date; the first step toward sound programming.

Information alone does not make an effective educator. It is evident that the editors and authors of *Learners on the Autism Spectrum: Preparing Highly Qualified Educators* have responded to people on the spectrum with care, creativity, and a respectful and unassuming curiosity. In between the lines of text, and directly reflected in the case examples that open each chapter and the lists of ideas that close them, is a demonstration of *how to think about* autism spectrum disorders. The result is a volume that contains a rare social competence with the potential to connect *all learners* on *or* alongside the autism spectrum – university students, professionals, parents, and learners diagnosed with ASD and their peers.

Each child has only one chance to grow and learn, a singular opportunity that is extremely critical when that child is also diagnosed with an autism spectrum disorder. There's no going back to the beginning and starting over. For years I had a short note to myself in a small frame on my desk: *These are not my children and I cannot be with them in the future.* It was a reminder to be very careful with the future of another person. In the same way, this text has a respect for the passing of time, and the importance of what educators do with it.

If I had owned this book in 1977, it would be dog-eared by now. Like a toddler's threadbare stuffed animal, its worn cover would be evidence of its continual use and timeless value. With this in mind, I bring my comments to a close with a word of caution for those still studying at university. When I was a university student, at the close of each term I would return triumphantly to the bookstore to sell my textbooks after final exams. It was a ceremony of sorts, a happy parting that brought me a step closer to graduation and "real life."

As you gather up your books at the end of the term, you may consider selling this book along with the rest. I wouldn't do that if I were you.

– Carol Gray

Acknowledgments

We wish to thank the many people who made this book possible. We are deeply indebted to our contributors, who gave so generously of their time and immeasurable expertise. We are grateful to the many educators, therapists, students, and parents, whose thoughtful reviews and reflections helped us to refine this work, including L. Lynn Stansberry-Bousnahan for helping with some of the editing legwork, Patricia Cretella and Shelly Schmitt for assisting in writing Tips for the Classroom, and Shayla Duda, Emmy Fearne, and Betty Yu for leading our think tanks in California. We extend our sincere gratitude to the AAPC team, and especially to Kirsten McBride for her meticulous editing and perseverance in seeing this work through to completion. Special thanks go to Heather McCracken for sharing the precious photograph that inspired Kari's painting for the cover of the book. Heartfelt thanks go to our families (especially our incredibly patient spouses), friends, and faithful canine companions for their unconditional support, friendship, and love throughout this endeavor. And finally, our deepest appreciation goes to the many children, families, and professionals who are living and learning with autism.

Preface

A Message from Kari Dunn Buron

In 1981, I was hired to develop a program for children with autism. My secret was that I really didn't know what I was doing. I had a master's degree in learning disabilities and emotional and behavior disorders. My training had prepared me well for assessing learning disorders and using behavior modification, but many of the strategies I thought would work did not. As I began to meet with other educators working with children with autism, I was relieved to find that nobody else seemed to know what they were doing either – at least I wasn't alone.

In 1985, I attended my first Autism Society of America (ASA) conference, and thus began my formal education in autism. I continued to work with a small group of local colleagues, and we became the metropolitan area autism consultants through a Minnesota state-funded project for low-incidence disabilities (Metro SPLISE). We met once a month to discuss the issues we faced in our classrooms, consulted with other teachers, and created training opportunities. As our project grew, the MN State Autism Project was developed, including professionals from every region of Minnesota. At that point, we were able to bring in world-class speakers to help in our continued education, and our project included early childhood autism initiatives.

Over my first 10 years of working in the field of autism, I realized that many of the strategies I had learned in school were not only ineffective, but quite possibly harmful to the children I was teaching. I watched my students grow with feelings of pride for some achievements and feelings of guilt and remorse for the gains that were not realized. I struggled to understand the core issues of autism in my effort to develop more effective teaching strategies. Through my affiliation with the Autism Society of Minnesota, Metro SPLISE, and the MN Autism Project, I continued to learn and evolve with every passing year.

At the ASA annual conference in 1994, I met a group of adults with autism, who represented the increasing number of people with autism who were speaking out and writing their stories. I asked them what support they wished they had received growing up. Overwhelmingly, they told me that they wished they had known other children like themselves. This information prompted me to work with the Autism Society of Minnesota to start Camp Discovery, a summer camp for children and adolescents with Asperger Syndrome (AS) and high-functioning autism (HFA). Once again, I did not really know what I was doing. I contacted Susan Moreno, founder and president of MAAP (More Advanced Autistic People), and asked her if she knew of a camp that I could model mine after. She did not know of another camp. I searched through ASA for other camps but could not find one that addressed this particular group of people with autism spectrum disorders (ASD).

Setting out on my own, I drew on the words of Temple Grandin, Donna Williams, and Tom McKean to guide my thoughts. I developed a camp philosophy and staff training based on Gentle Teaching,[1] from one of my early mentors, Dan Hobbs. I invited my friend Ruth Elaine Hane, an adult with ASD, to help me set up an environment that attended to the sensory needs of campers with ASD. I also hired young adults with ASD to serve as mentors during the week of camp. Camp Discovery has continued to grow and change as we acquire new information about the core issues of autism. Many campers have returned over the years, and some have reported that it is one of the most comfortable experiences they have ever had.

My interest in the campers at Camp Discovery led to an almost insatiable desire to learn more about what I recognized as their different form of logic. My study led me to Tony Attwood, Ami Klin, Simon Baron-Cohen, Patricia Howlin, and Francesca Happe. These amazing researchers and therapists were talking about ASD as being a disorder of social thinking. It all made so much sense to me. As I continued to study, I realized that the concept was largely unrecognized in the educational setting, yet the educational setting was proving to be perhaps the most socially frustrating environment for these students. For example, I was often called to consult about a student who was being suspended from his school program for behavior that seemed to me to be directly related to an inability to understand or effectively negotiate social information. I decided that I had to find out more about this theory of autism if I was going to be able to explain it to others and successfully support and advocate for these students.

Several years later, this professional dream was realized when I was awarded a Bush Leadership Fellowship, set up by Archibald Granville Bush and his wife, Edyth Bassler Bush, of Minnesota. This fellowship made it possible for me to pursue a 12-month, self-designed study of social cognition and Asperger Syndrome. My goal was to gather information from noted therapists, scientists, and educational researchers, from educational initiatives related to Asperger Syndrome, and from individuals with AS themselves to develop some promising practices related to AS and social cognition.

My study took the form of a "who's who" in the world of autism. Brenda Smith Myles at the University of Kansas, a leader in the field, graciously agreed to be my advisor. She supported my efforts and assisted me in reviewing current educational research. I spent time with Tony Attwood in Brisbane, Australia, where I was able to observe the use of cognitive behavioral approaches used in his clinic. I met with Ami Klin and Robert Schultz at Yale University and learned first-hand how functional Magnetic Resonance Imagery (fMRI) studies were conducted. (These are studies that look at the brain while the brain is functioning to pinpoint what part of the brain is being used.) I was able to ask them directly about their thoughts on education and how they hoped their research might impact the future of ASD education. Dr. Klin shared a paper with me explaining his learning theory called Enactive Mind. This theory implies that social learning must include active learning and doing to be truly effective.

---

[1] McGee, J., Menolascino, F., Hobbs, D., & Menousek, P. (1987). *Gentle teaching: A non-aversive approach to helping persons with mental retardation.* New York: Human Sciences Press.

I also met with Nancy Minshew, professor of psychiatry and neurology at the University of Pittsburgh School of Medicine, and discussed her work and possible implications for understanding autism behavior. I traveled to Emory in Atlanta, Georgia, where I met with Steve Nowicki and Marshall Duke, who have done amazing work in the area of nonverbal social communication (dyssemia). Because they are social psychologists and do not study autism per se, they were able to give me insight from a completely different perspective about an issue so connected to ASD.

As my fellowship year progressed, it was my task to pull all the information together and make sense of it for the real world of public education. I was learning so much – at times it felt contradictory and at other times it fit. I continued to frame and reframe my thoughts about social cognition and what it meant for education.

I then traveled to the United Kingdom, where I was able to meet with Simon Baron-Cohen at Cambridge University and Sarah Blackford and Daniel Glaser at the Institute of Cognitive Neuroscience. Simon Baron-Cohen did a wonderful job of clarifying his thoughts about systematic learning styles as well as explaining his approach to teaching nonverbal facial communication. Daniel Glaser was perhaps the most unexpected pleasant surprise of my year-long quest. He talked with me for hours about the science-education connection and eventually mentioned mirror neurons. After listening to his explanation of mirror neurons, I set off for the British Library to investigate. Later that day I had an "a-ha" moment. The excitement was overwhelming as the puzzle pieces of enactive mind, dyssemia, relationship building vs. systematic learning, cognitive behavior therapy, teaching mind reading and, finally, mirror neurons all came together.

Finally, I traveled to California, where I spent time with friends and formidable colleagues. I met with the people from AASCEND, a group of adults with AS, families, and professionals in the San Francisco area. I was able to visit the Orion Academy, a high school program designed specifically for students with AS. I met with Paula Jacobsen, a therapist whose work in understanding the "Asperger perspective" is inspiring. Paula introduced me to Judith Piggot, a researcher at Stanford, who met with me in the fMRI lab and shared how she was investigating the neurological basis of social cognition. I was also able to observe some of Michelle Garcia Winner's social thinking groups and discuss with her the issues involved with designing appropriate social training opportunities for students with AS.

It was on this same trip that I had an opportunity to connect with Pamela Wolfberg, a special education professor at San Francisco State University and co-founder of the Autism Institute on Peer Relations and Play. Pamela and I talked about the ASD certificate program I had developed at Hamline University in St. Paul, Minnesota. Pamela was teaching a new course on ASD at San Francisco State University. She asked me what text I was using for the Introduction to Autism class. This immediately led to a discussion about the need for a current volume that could be used as a core text in similar university programs. The idea was a flash of brilliance experienced simultaneously between Pamela and myself. The outline for the book was created that night at a small restaurant just a few blocks from Golden Gate Park.

It is our hope that this text will offer educators an opportunity to make similar connections between science, therapy, personal experience, and educational practices. The book's content and organization are designed to give the reader examples of how different issues affect students with ASD in the classroom, current information regarding theory and promising practices, combined with practical tips from fellow educators about how the information might be used in our schools to improve the quality of educational practices for individuals with ASD.

A Message from Pamela Wolfberg

When I met Kari Dunn Buron at the end of her fellowship year, it was like finding a long-lost soulmate. Having both traversed the field of special education for a number of years, we quickly discovered that we shared a historical and global perspective on issues facing learners on the autism spectrum. For my own part, my special education career began in the 1980s at a time when autism was not only considered rare in terms of incidence, but was also still largely mistaken as being a psychologically based disorder caused by poor parenting. My own education was to a large extent rooted in developmental psychology with leanings toward the psychodynamic tradition, although the behavioral tradition was also becoming prominent at the time.

My first professional position was as an educational therapist in a children's psychiatric hospital, where I taught adolescents who were identified as emotionally disturbed, several of whom would surely be diagnosed with ASD today. I recall 15-year-old Lydia, who was fascinated with the popular television program "Mod Squad." Although I was secretly flattered that she associated me with the lead female character (I happened to have the same hairstyle), Lydia's repeated references and rituals surrounding the show were interpreted by the psychiatric team as obsessive and delusional psychotic behavior. As was common at that time, Lydia's treatment comprised a combination of heavy-duty antipsychotic medication, psychotherapy, and behavioral intervention that included the use of aversive methods (i.e., confinement in an isolation room) to subdue her when agitated. In my role as educator, I was expected to defer to the medical experts and support implementation of the treatment plan in my teaching. As a young teacher, I wrestled with my conscience and only lasted a short while in this position. Disillusioned, I took a several-year hiatus to study and work around the world, only to discover that I was being pulled back into the field at the dawn of a new awakening to autism.

Although more than two decades have passed, still not a day goes by that I don't wonder how things could and should be different for the many children like Lydia who fall through the cracks because they are misdiagnosed, mistreated, or simply misunderstood. In my own varied experiences as a teacher, peer play specialist (see Chapter 8), and more recently as a professor and director of a new autism spectrum program at San Francisco State University, I am immensely grateful for the knowledge that has been accumulating over these years to refine our understanding of ASD. At the same time, however, I am acutely aware that gaps remain in the knowledge and skills of many educators and related professionals to meet the unique needs of this diverse and rapidly growing population.

The complex nature and wide spectrum of variability in autism poses challenges for preparing highly qualified educators. The result of a neurological condition, autism affects the most essential of human behaviors, including social interaction, communication, language, sensory processing, play, imagination, and peer relations. While changing over the lifespan, the presence of behaviors may manifest in a wide variety of combinations and degrees of intensity, ranging from mild to moderate to severe. Further, each person's capacity to learn, develop, and function in the world is naturally influenced by experiences with others, as well as the social, cultural, and societal contexts in which they participate.

Taking into account the unique, complex, and changing needs of each individual with autism, to date, no single educational method or treatment approach has been found to work for all individuals or for any given individual over time. Thus, knowledgeable and skilled professionals and families must carefully configure educational supports to maximize each individual's capacity to learn, develop, function independently, and participate in the full range of social, cultural, and general life experiences.

Based on the premise that successful teaching is rooted in understanding and experience, this volume responds to the critical need to prepare teachers with foundational knowledge and practical skills for educating diverse learners on the autism spectrum. This state-of-the art text brings together leading experts representing diverse disciplines and perspectives (i.e., researchers, therapists, educators, parents and adults on the autism spectrum) to cover a range of essential topics and themes. We hope that this collective effort will allow educators and others to translate the most up-to-date theory and research into effective and meaningful practice to ensure that every person on the autism spectrum receives the high-quality education that he or she deserves.

Overview of Textbook Features

The *Learners on the Autism Spectrum: Preparing Highly Qualified Educators* textbook contains the following features to help strengthen your understanding of material discussed in each chapter, as well as share this knowledge with parents and colleagues and apply it to your everyday work with children and adolescents with ASD:

- **Chapter learner objectives** – Refer to the list of learner objectives at the beginning of each chapter for a preview of the chapter's content, as well as to learn what information you are expected to understand and be able to explain after reading the chapter.

- **Vocabulary** – Note the terms included in grey boldface text within each chapter for at-a-glance reminders of key vocabulary. The definitions of these terms are included in the glossary in Appendix B.

- **Chapter highlights** – Review the main points listed at the end of each chapter to recall the main points discussed within the chapter.

- **Chapter review questions** – Answer the questions at the end of each chapter to check your understanding of and ability to explain the information discussed within the chapter. The review questions may also be used as a study guide when preparing for tests and/or exams.

- **Chapter review answers** – Refer to Appendix A to confirm your answers to the review questions that accompany each chapter.

- **Glossary** – Refer to Appendix B for an alphabetical listing of all vocabulary terms included in grey boldface text within the textbook.

- **Tips for the Classroom** – Refer to the final section of each chapter for Tips for the Classroom designed to provide you with information on how to effectively use the material learned in the chapter while in the classroom or otherwise working with students on the autism spectrum.

Learner Objectives

After reading this chapter, the learner should be able to:

- State the meaning of autism spectrum disorders (ASD)

- State signs of ASD in both early and late onset

- State and describe the five subgroups under the heading of ASD

- State the three areas used in the diagnostic criteria for determining autism

- Differentiate between high-functioning autism (HFA) and Asperger Syndrome

- State the five dimensions characterizing ASD

- Discuss why the dimensions of ASD can be considered a continuum

- Discuss the causes of ASD, both historical and current

- Discuss the psychological theories of ASD

- State gender differences in ASD

- Discuss why increasing numbers of children are being identified as having ASD

Chapter 1

An Overview of Autism Spectrum Disorders

Tony Attwood

Colton is an 8-year-old with a diagnosis of autism. He was nonverbal until age 7, when he began to speak using echoed speech, usually repeating phrases from popular cartoons on television. Colton avoids eye contact with others and has not established any friendships. He appears to be interested in books, but often looks at them upside down and seems to study the page numbers with as much interest as the pictures. He is particularly interested in the weather and spends time looking at the daily calendar in his classroom that shows the day's weather. Colton has difficulty when having to change clothing from one season to the next and often insists on wearing shorts far into the fall season. And he has difficulty each winter when boots and coats are required for going outside to recess. Colton has demonstrated disruptive and tantrum behaviors during his school day, most often during schedule changes or even daily activity changes. He is mainstreamed for part of his day, but does not participate in the academic activities of his mainstreamed classroom. During recess, Colton typically walks around the boundaries of the playground, avoiding crowded areas and interactive play activities.

Nic is a 10-year-old with a recent diagnosis of Asperger Syndrome. He has done well in school, but has recently had difficulty with reading tests that require him to predict or empathize with a character's position. Nic prefers to read nonfiction and has an above-grade-level knowledge of history and science facts. He seems to have some friends at school, but his parents report that he has never invited anyone to his house nor been invited to a birthday party. Nic seems to prefer to interact with adults and has a precocious vocabulary, sounding a bit like a little professor. Although he has not demonstrated problem behavior at school, Nic is often withdrawn at family functions and asks his parents to be excused from such events as Thanksgiving and 4th of July parties where his family typically gathers with extended family members for a large party.

This chapter offers a comprehensive introduction to the "autism spectrum," now commonly viewed as consisting of a variety of autism spectrum disorders (ASD), the various subtypes of disorders associated with the autism spectrum, and some possible causes. In the section The Autism Continuum, the spectrum is separated into five "dimensions" (social, communication, special interests, cognition, and sensory) with illustrations of how each of these dimensions might look at each end of the spectrum.

What Is Autism?

According to the diagnostic criteria of the American Psychiatric Association (APA), autism, also known as a **pervasive developmental disorder (PDD)** or an **autism spectrum disorder (ASD)**, occurs when a child has a severe qualitative impairment in reciprocal social interaction and communication skills and a restricted range of activities and interests (APA, 2000). Specifically, the child with autism does not appear to have the intuitive ability to socialize, has difficulty with verbal and nonverbal communication, and demonstrates a tendency to engage in unusual interests and ways of playing. Although not included in the diagnostic criteria, there can also be problems with **sensory perception**, an unusual profile of cognitive skills, and very subtle signs of movement disturbance.

Signs of Autism

The first signs of autism, such as sleep disturbance and feeding problems, may go unnoticed, as they are typical of many children in their first year. However, parents may become concerned that they have difficulty comforting the child, who also may not be drawn towards social activities, preferring to play alone, and who does not point to objects he wants you to notice. The child appears not to consider people as the most important aspects of daily life, preferring instead to relate to objects rather than people. Indeed, sometimes the child appears to treat a person as an object. The very young child may be fascinated and delighted by sensory experiences, such as the feeling of the wind on her face and the spinning of the wheel of a toy truck. When excited, she may literally jump for joy or have an unusual way of expressing pleasure by characteristic hand flapping and a contorted facial expression. The child may shun the approaches of a peer or adult, and be reluctant to share an activity with another child.

Also, parents may notice that the child – unlike most other children – does not imitate their actions or imitate domestic chores, or repeat an activity that caused a parent to smile or laugh. Eye contact is generally lacking, in greetings, in seeking approval or reassurance from a parent, and in noticing and being interested in what somebody else is looking at. The typical "look at me" or "look at this" actions may be rare, and the child is often content with long periods of solitude. The child clearly prefers consistency in his daily life. Surprises and changes are not enjoyed.

In sum, clinical experience indicates that parents, especially mothers, develop an intuitive feeling that something is wrong with the child's ability to relate to other people and describe the child as: "being on a different wavelength," "feeling as if we have borrowed him, as if he isn't ours," "looking through me when I try to make her smile, as if I am in the way," "playing differently from other children her age," and "not being interested in talking to me."

A variety of specialists may become involved at this point. The delay in the development of communication abilities, such as the use of gestures and speech, may lead parents to suspect that the child is deaf (since often the child does not respond when his name is called and fails to orientate to the speech of another person), and consequently seek a referral to a speech pathologist or audiologist. Delays in self-care skills, such as toilet training, and acute sensitivity to sensory experiences, such as sudden noises or various tactile sensations, may lead to a referral to an occupational therapist. Further, problems with specific aspects of play, learning, behavior, and emotion management often necessitate a referral to a developmental psychologist. Finally, general developmental delay and the presence of medical problems, such as epilepsy, may require that the child is referred to a pediatrician. These professionals may be the first to confirm the signs of autism when they conduct an assessment of a range of abilities and review the child's developmental history.

Regressive or Late-Onset Autism

We can reliably identify the signs of autism in children younger than 18 months, but some children with autism demonstrate no behaviors of concern to their parents until they are well into their second year (Moore & Goodson, 2003). Such children achieve the typical developmental milestones in motor, **linguistic**, and cognitive abilities, develop a reasonable vocabulary, take an interest in others, and develop early symbolic and imaginative play. However, over a very short period, sometimes just a few weeks, the child who otherwise had no conspicuous signs of developmental delay suddenly has developmental delay. Speech disappears, the child becomes self-absorbed, and play abilities deteriorate. By the age of 3, there may be no distinguishing features in behavior and abilities between a child whose onset of autism was apparent in his or her first year and a child who appeared to be developing normally. Early regression in autism is variably reported to be present in 20% to 40% of cases (Siperstein & Volkmar, 2004).

Different Types of Autism

As mentioned, the American Psychiatric Association (APA, 2000) has published diagnostic criteria for autism and identified five subgroups under the umbrella of PDD – **autistic disorder, Rett's disorder, childhood disintegrative disorder, pervasive developmental disorder-not otherwise specified (PDD-NOS)**, and **Asperger's disorder**.

Autistic Disorder

Autism disorder was first described by Leo Kanner (Kanner, 1943). The following are the current diagnostic criteria of the APA (2000, p. 75).

The child has a distinct impairment in **social interaction** with at least two of the following:
* Marked impairment in the use of multiple **nonverbal behaviors** such as eye-to-eye gaze, facial expression, body postures, and gestures to regulate social interaction

* Failure to develop peer relationships appropriate to developmental level

- A lack of spontaneous seeking to share enjoyment, interests, or achievements with other people

- A lack of social or emotional **reciprocity**

The impairments in **communication** have at least one of the following:
- Delay in, or total lack of, the development of spoken language

- In children with adequate speech, marked impairment in the ability to initiate or sustain a conversation with others

- Stereotyped and repetitive use of language, or idiosyncratic language

- Lack of varied, spontaneous make-believe play or social imitative play appropriate to developmental level

The restricted repetitive and stereotyped patterns of behavior, interests, and activities include at least one of the following:
- Encompassing preoccupation with one or more stereotyped and restricted patterns of interest that are abnormal either in intensity or focus

- Apparently inflexible adherence to specific, nonfunctional routines or rituals

- Stereotyped and repetitive motor mannerisms such as hand or finger flapping

- Persistent preoccupation with parts of objects

Rett's Disorder

Rett's disorder appears to occur primarily in girls, and is an X-linked dominant disorder. It is caused by mutations in the gene MeCP2 and affects early brain development. A progressive neurological disorder, Rett's disorder is characterized by loss of purposeful hand use, progressive spasticity of the lower extremities, **seizures**, acquired **microcephaly** (small head circumference), and very high support needs for daily living (Ellaway & Christodoulou, 1999). A noticeable characteristic is continuous "hand washing" movements often associated with hyperventilation. There is currently some debate among clinicians as to whether Rett's disorder should be considered an expression of autism.

Childhood Disintegrative Disorder

Childhood disintegrative disorder is rare, and is more common in boys than in girls. When it does occur, the child achieves the typical developmental milestones until he or she is 3 to 5 years old, after which there is a rapid and dramatic deterioration in language, social interest and ability, play, and self-care abilities, such as bowel and bladder control. The clinical description then resembles that of a child with a severe expression of autistic disorder, with no communication using spoken sentences, a conspicuous aversion to social interaction, and a level of function as would be found in severe intellectual disability.

Pervasive Developmental Disorder-Not Otherwise Specified (PDD-NOS)

The diagnostic term PDD-NOS has been associated with considerable confusion by both clinicians and parents. APA's diagnostic criteria for PDD-NOS are remarkably vague, differentiating PDD-NOS from autism on the basis of late-age onset, atypical or sub-threshold symptomatology, without adequately defining these criteria. This author describes PDD-NOS to parents and teachers as "fragments of autism," not enough for a clear diagnosis; the signs are not as severe as described in the criteria for autistic disorder.

Asperger's Disorder

The Viennese pediatrician **Hans Asperger**, in a paper published in 1944 (Asperger, 1991), described another expression of autism, originally using the term *autistic personality disorder*. Dr. Uta Frith was responsible for translating Asperger's work into English (1991). He described a group of children who demonstrated several common characteristics. They demonstrated impairments in the **pragmatic** aspects of language, especially conversation skills, with some children having **pedantic speech**, and unusual **prosody** that affected tone, pitch, and rhythm. Asperger noted conspicuous impairments in the communication and control of emotions and a tendency to intellectualize feelings. Empathy was not as mature as one would expect, considering the children's intellectual abilities. Their social maturity and reasoning was impaired, with difficulties making friends and a tendency to be teased or shunned by peers. Further, the children had an egocentric preoccupation with a specific topic or interest that would dominate their thinking and play. He noted that the children often needed more assistance with self-help and organizational skills from their mother than one would expect. Asperger also commented on conspicuous clumsiness in terms of gait, coordination, and handwriting, and observed that some children were extremely sensitive to particular sounds or aromas.

Asperger noted that the characteristics could be identified in some children as young as 2 to 3 years old, but in other children, the characteristics only became conspicuous some years later. He also noticed that some of the parents, especially the fathers, of these children appeared to share some of the personality characteristics of their child.

In the 1970s, Lorna Wing, a renowned British psychiatrist specializing in ASD, became increasingly aware that **Leo Kanner**'s descriptions, which then formed the basis of our understanding and diagnosis of autism in America and Britain, did not accurately describe some of the children and adults within her considerable clinical and research experience. In her paper, published in 1981, she described 34 cases of children and adults with autism, ranging in age from 5 to 35 years, whose profile of abilities had a greater resemblance to the descriptions by Hans Asperger than those by Leo Kanner, and did not easily match the diagnostic criteria for autism that were being used by academics and clinicians at the time. Lorna Wing first used the eponymous term Asperger's disorder to provide a new diagnostic category within the autism spectrum (Wing, 1981).

In 1994 Asperger's disorder was included in APA's diagnostic manual (*Diagnostic and Statistical Manual of Mental Disorders*), but the diagnostic criteria have been the subject of growing criticism by experienced specialists in Asperger's disorder and in the discussion sections of many research studies. For example, the criteria in the APA manual are not consistent with Hans Asperger's original descriptions. Thus, the four cases he portrayed in his seminal paper would today be diagnosed as having autistic disorder, and not Asperger's disorder, because of early language delay (APA, 1994; Asperger, 1991; Miller & Ozonoff, 2000). The diagnostic criteria for Asperger's disorder are still a work in progress. In this text, we will be using the terms Asperger's disorder and Asperger Syndrome interchangeably.

Asperger's Disorder vs. High-Functioning Autism

The term *high-functioning autism* (**HFA**) has been used in the past to describe children who demonstrated the classic signs of autistic disorder in very early childhood, but for whom formal testing of their cognitive skills in the elementary school years indicated a greater degree of intellectual ability, with greater social and **adaptive behavior** skills than are usual in children with autistic disorder. In other words, their clinical outcome or level of functioning was better than expected.

According to the APA, Asperger's disorder may be differentiated from HFA by an examination of the child's early development and the existence of some characteristics that are rare in children with autistic disorder. The APA considers that early language and cognitive skills are not delayed significantly in children with Asperger's disorder. There is also no clinically significant delay in age-appropriate self-help skills, adaptive behavior, and curiosity about the environment in childhood. The clinical profile of a child with Asperger's disorder is also less likely to include motor mannerisms and preoccupation with parts of objects as occur in autistic disorder, but the child can have an all-consuming special interest on which she spends a great deal time amassing information and facts.

APA also notes that the profile of social skills in children with autistic disorder includes self-isolation or rigid social approaches, whereas children with Asperger's disorder can demonstrate a motivation to socialize even if in a highly eccentric, one-sided, verbose, and sometimes insensitive manner. If the child's profile of abilities and developmental history are consistent with the criteria for both autistic disorder and Asperger's disorder, the APA states that a diagnosis of autism should take precedence.

The diagnostic criteria of the APA, which provide a differentiation between autistic disorder and Asperger's disorder, have been examined in several studies over the last five years. For example, research has been conducted on whether delayed language in children with autism can accurately predict later clinical symptoms. Three studies have cast considerable doubt over the use of early language delay as a differential criterion between high-functioning autism and Asperger's disorder (Dickerson Mayes, Calhoun, & Crites, 2001; Eisenmajer et al., 1998; Manjiviona & Prior, 1999). Any differences in language ability that are apparent in the preschool years between children who are later described as having HFA and those with Asperger's disorder have largely disappeared by early adolescence (Eisenmajer et al., 1998; Ozonoff, South, & Miller, 2000).

There is general agreement that children with Asperger's disorder may not show conspicuous **cognitive delay** in early childhood. Indeed, some are quite precocious or talented in terms of learning to read, numerical abilities, and in aspects of constructive play and memory. Children with autistic disorder can be recognized as having developmental delay in their cognitive abilities from infancy and be diagnosed as young as 18 months of age. Children with Asperger's disorder, on the other hand, are often not diagnosed until after they start school, with a mean age of diagnosis of 11 years (Howlin & Asgharian, 1999). The signs of Asperger's disorder in very young children may be subtler and easily camouflaged at home and school. On reflection, parents (especially mothers) and teachers have often been concerned about some aspects of the child's cognitive development, but their concerns may have been intuitive and difficult to describe to clinicians. It is not until the child is expected to show more advanced cognitive abilities that formal assessments indicate significant delay or an unusual profile in cognitive abilities.

Research studies have examined the cognitive profiles of children who have what may be called HFA (a diagnosis of autism where the child's intelligence quotient is within the normal range; i.e., above 70), and compared the findings with the cognitive profiles of children with Asperger's disorder who did not have a history of early cognitive or language delay. The results of such research have not established a distinct and consistent profile for each group. A recent study comparing behavioral profiles of children with HFA and AS concluded that the two groups were indistinguishable (Dissanayake, 2004).

One group of researchers, based at Yale University, have suggested, on the basis of their studies, that the neuropsychological profiles of children with Asperger's disorder are different from those of children with HFA (Klin, Volkmar, Sparrow, Cicchetti, & Rourke, 1995). However, other research on diagnostic differentiation using neuropsychological testing has not identified a distinct profile that discriminates between the two groups (Manjiviona & Prior 1999; Miller & Ozonoff, 2000; Ozonoff et al., 2000).

According to APA, children with Asperger's disorder must demonstrate no clinically significant delay in age-appropriate self-help skills and adaptive behavior. Yet, clinical experience indicates that parents, especially mothers, of children and adolescents with Asperger's disorder often have to assist or provide verbal reminders and advice regarding self-help and daily living skills. This can range from assistance where problems with dexterity are affecting activities, such as learning to tie shoelaces, to reminders regarding personal hygiene, proper dress, and time management. Clinicians have also recognized significant problems with adaptive behavior, especially with regard to anger management, anxiety, and mood (Attwood, 2003a; Farrugia et al., 2005; Sofronoff, Attwood, Hinton, & Levin, 2007; Tantam, 2000).

The Autism Spectrum

One of the most intriguing aspects of autism is the range of expression of each of the main characteristics; namely, difficulties in relating to people, problems with communication skills, unusual profiles of cognitive abilities and interests, and an increased sensitivity to specific sensory experiences. Each of these five characteristics can be considered as a dimension, a continuum, or a spectrum.

Social Dimension

At one end of the spectrum of difficulties in relating to people, especially peers, is the aloof child, who actively avoids social interactions; next is the child described as passive, who can tolerate social interaction with encouragement and can initiate social contact, but primarily to achieve access to something he or she wants. The next stage on this continuum is the "active but odd" child, who actively wants to interact with others, although usually adults, but, despite a motivation to socialize, is odd due to a lack of social understanding and range of social abilities. Interactions may not commence with conventional greetings, and may continue as if the child has a limited social script or repertoire of social behavior, such as a reliance on repetitive questions (Wing & Gould, 1979). At the upper end of the social continuum is the child who wants friends but appears to have a significant delay in social maturity, has conspicuous problems with theory-of-mind abilities (see Chapter 4), and may interact more as a miniature adult (or teacher) than a child. This is the Asperger's disorder area of the continuum (Wing & Attwood, 1987). There is evidence that students across the spectrum rarely establish long term or typical friendships (Orsmond, Krauss, & Seltzer, 2004).

Communication Dimension

The severest expression on the communication spectrum is the silent child who has a vocabulary of sounds, not of words. This child may have a greater comprehension of language than expression but does not easily replace a lack of speech with the development of a natural gesture language. Parents may notice that the child tries to speak but appears not to be able to connect thought to vocalization. This is a description of the classic silent and aloof child first described by Leo Kanner in 1943.

In the next area of the communication continuum, speech can occur but often requires an external prompt; for example, immediately echoing the utterance of someone (**echolalia**), seeing an object and being able to say the name of the object, or using sentences borrowed from a favorite TV program. The words may be appropriate for the context, but they are verbatim copies, often said in the voice of the original utterance.

In the next area on the continuum, the child can initiate original speech but has significant problems with the pragmatic aspects of language (i.e., the "art" of conversation), sometimes an unusual prosody, and a tendency to be very pedantic, often making a literal interpretation of someone's comments. There may also be challenges with **auditory discrimination** and **auditory processing**.

Finally, at the upper end of the continuum, the child has a remarkable verbal fluency, but a tendency to make limited eye contact and an inability to recognize the other person's lack of interest or boredom. This can be a description of a child with Asperger's disorder.

Cognitive Dimension

The cognitive spectrum starts with the child who has profound learning problems and whose play may be within the very early or infantile stages of development. This child is interested in the sensory rather than the functional or symbolic qualities of objects. She explores the world by touch and taste and is fascinated by perspective and order, arranging items in lines and examining objects from unusual angles.

Next, the continuum of cognitive skills includes the child who is familiar with and has relatively advanced skills in activities such as assembly and putting jigsaw puzzles together. She is fascinated by shapes and the functional use of objects. The child may display natural engineering skills with construction blocks or produce drawings with photographic realism.

When she starts school, a formal test of intellectual abilities usually identifies an uneven profile of development. This indicates that the child has an unusual learning style. Academic abilities such as reading or counting can be self-taught, and sometimes the child is precocious in these areas. In contrast, some children with autism have significant difficulties with reading and number skills, despite an IQ that suggests that such abilities are within their intellectual capacity. There can also be problems with organizational skills, working memory, and time management (Adreon & Duroucher, 2007; Williams, Goldstein, & Minshew, 2006; Verte, Geurts, Roeyersd, Oosterlaan, & Sergeant, 2006). This is the range on the cognitive continuum of Asperger's disorder.

Although autism is considered a **neuro-developmental disorder**, not all aspects of the brain functioning are necessarily affected (Herbert, 2005a). Approximately 10% of children with autism develop **savant** characteristics; that is, remarkable abilities compared to the child's overall level of ability (Hermelin, 2001). This can involve abilities in mathematics, music, drawing, and mechanics. Examples include rapid completion of mathematical computations; the ability to listen to music and to immediately play the music on another instrument – note perfect; or a very young child acquiring the ability to draw in perspective or to design machines or learn computer languages. Some children develop visual reasoning abilities that are in remarkable contrast to their verbal abilities, such as solving visual puzzles or learning to read despite having very limited speech.

While teachers and therapists are concerned about abilities that are significantly below the level expected of a typical child of the same age, we must also consider programs to improve particular talents and work on the child's relative strengths. For those who are visualizers, that is, having relatively good visual reasoning abilities, it is important to remember that "a picture is worth a thousand words" when trying to help them understand an educational concept. Developing a talent can lead to increased self-esteem and the possibility that a specific ability can be used constructively in the classroom and may become a successful career path (Grandin & Duffy, 2004).

Children with autism are known for a wide range of intense interests that can shift over the years. The continuum of interests can include those enjoyed by typical children, although often at a younger age, as well as some that are quite eccentric. The first stage is a preoccupation with parts of objects. The interest can be spinning the wheels of a toy tractor or manipulating electrical switches. The next stage on the continuum is a fascination with a specific category of objects and accumulating as many examples as possible. Sometimes collections comprise items typically acquired by other children, such as unusual stones, but some can be quite eccentric, such as drain covers or paddling pools. In this stage, the child's play can also be somewhat eccentric in that he can pretend to be the special interest; for example, a child rocked from side to side pretending to be windshield wipers. His fascination with windshield wipers led to his eagerly approaching cars waiting at red traffic lights and examining the wiper blades.

The next stage on the continuum is for children to acquire information and remember facts about a topic or concept. Common topics or concepts include transport, animals, and electronics. Some of the interests are developmentally appropriate and typical of peers, such as Thomas the Tank Engine, dinosaurs, castles, and computer games, whereas other interests can be unusual, such as vacuum cleaners and alarm systems. The reason for the interest is usually idiosyncratic, and not necessarily because the topic is popular with peers, or the "currency" between friends (Attwood, 2006). The focus of the interest invariably changes, but at a time dictated by the child, and is replaced by another special interest that is the choice of the child, not a parent or teacher. The complexity and number of interests vary according to the child's developmental level and intellectual capacity. Over time there is a progression to multiple and more abstract or complex interests, such as periods of history or specific countries or cultures. This is the domain of the child with Asperger's disorder (Attwood, 2003b).

Sensory Dimension

The continuum of sensory sensitivity is the spectrum or dimension of autism that we know least about. The autobiographies of adults with HFA and Asperger's disorder vividly describe a sensory perception that is different (Barron & Barron, 2002; Grandin, 1995; Shore, 2003). In the severest expression of sensory sensitivity, the child appears to be living in a "war zone" with sudden explosions of jarring noises, visual sensations that are blinding, and touch and aromas that are perceived as painful. The child might be hyper-vigilant in anticipation of the next sensory bombardment or sensory overload. The child has a startle response that is extremely difficult to inhibit to experiences that other children do not perceive as painful (Baranek, 2002). The noise of a chair scraping on the classroom floor, a dog barking, or the sound of small electric motors can cause the child to cover her ears, try to escape the situation, or somehow stop the sensory experience. There can be sensitivity to the degree of natural light intensity or artificial light, especially fluorescent light. The aromas of perfumes and smell of cleaning products can be overpowering, and the smell of certain foods can cause the child to vomit. Further, the taste and texture of food may be perceived as extremely unpleasant, leading to a severely restricted diet.

The continuum of sensory sensitivity can also include a lack of visible response to some sensory experiences; for example, the child may not communicate pain when injured or indicate medical problems as severe as a fracture. Some children do not appear to have any discomfort at being cold, and are able, for example, to walk into a lake in sub-zero temperatures.

When the sensory sensitivity is a dominant characteristic of autism, the child can develop maladaptive strategies to control his environment in order to avoid specific sensory experiences, such as running from a supermarket because of the noise of the refrigeration units or refusing to use the bathroom at school due to the automatic flushers. Sensory sensitivity can also lead to the development of anxiety, as the child can never be sure when a potentially terrifying sensory experience will occur (Bellini, 2006; Goldsmith, Van Hulle, Arneson, Schreiber, & Gernsbacher, 2006). Parents have used the term ***sensory meltdown*** when sensory experiences have been overwhelming and unavoidable.

Progression Along the Spectrum

When conducting a diagnostic assessment or annual educational review of a child with autism, it is important to establish a baseline and subsequently assess progress along each of the five continua. One way of understanding the autism continuum is to imagine a recording studio and the recording console with five sliding knobs, or for those who are interested in home audio entertainment, a graphic equalizer. During the assessment or review, the child's level of expression of each of the dimensions of autism is evaluated, and an explanation is given that autism itself is on a continuum, such that the expression of autism may change over time. At one point in a child's early development, autism may be the correct diagnosis, but some children with autistic disorder, which includes language delay, can show a remarkable improvement in speech, language, play, and motivation to socialize with their peers. They have moved along the continuum towards a diagnosis of Asperger's disorder (Attwood, 1998; Gillberg, 1998; Wing, 1981).

Causes of Autism

When first described from the late 1940s to the early 1970s, autism was considered to be an expression of schizophrenia or psychosis in childhood, and the cause to be due to a mother not loving her child. The term *refrigerator mother* is commonly attributed to Leo Kanner and was propagated by Bruno Bettelheim to describe an emotionally unavailable mother. The cause of autism was considered to be **psychogenic**: a reaction to rejection. The only treatment was prolonged psychoanalysis for both mother and child.

Scientific research has clearly established that the cause of autism is not faulty parenting as there is evidence of neurological impairment (Bauman & Kemper, 2003). We now consider autism a neuro-developmental disorder, with specific structures of the brain not functioning as we would expect. As a result, there is a trend towards conducting research on the possible causes of autism and examining factors that can affect brain development and functioning from conception to early childhood.

Genetics

The original studies to suggest a genetic cause of autism used identical and nonidentical twins (Hallmayer et al., 2002). The rate of autism among identical twins is between 70 and 90%, while in nonidentical twins, the rate is about 0 to 5% (Bailey et al., 1995). If a family has a child with autism, the chances of having another child with autism are about 5 to 7% (Turner, Barnby, & Bailey, 2000), but the rate of autistic disorder in the general population is less than 1%. We have yet to conduct extensive genetic studies of families that have a child with Asperger's disorder. However, recent research suggests that a similar profile of abilities, although to a lesser degree, may be identified in the relatives of a child with Asperger's disorder (Bailey, Palferman, Heavey, & LeCouteur 1998; Cederlund & Gillberg, 2004; Volkmar, Klin, & Pauls, 1998). Geneticists use the term *broader autism phenotype* to describe such individuals, and the presence of a number of the characteristics in some relatives has been one of the reasons why genetic factors have been considered as having a significant role in the etiology of Asperger's disorder.

Some specific chromosomal abnormalities have been associated with the development of the characteristics of autistic disorder, such as Fragile X syndrome (Zafeiriou, Ververi, & Vargiami, 2007). Research studies have also identified individuals with autism who have chromosomal abnormalities on one of the following chromosomes: 2, 7, 15, 16 and 19 (Rutter, 2005). These rare chromosomal abnormalities may not be inherited but affect genetic material or the "genetic blueprint" for specific aspects of brain development.

Neurology

Neurological studies of autism have focused on **neurochemistry**, **neuropathology** (i.e., the various structures of the brain), and **functional neuroimaging** (i.e., the way parts of the brain function during specific thoughts, emotions, or behavior) (Belmonte et al., in print). Findings of studies of neurochemistry suggest a dysfunction of two chemicals within the brain, the neurotransmitters serotonin and dopamine. As a result, many of the medications prescribed for children and adolescents with autistic disorder and Asperger's disorder modify the levels of serotonin and dopamine. While such medication does not provide a cure, it may have a beneficial effect on mood and emotion management.

Neuropathological studies have indicated that approximately 10% of young children with autism and 25% of young children with Asperger's disorder have a heavier and larger brain and head circumference than typical, known as **macrocephalus** (Gillberg & de Souza, 2002). The young brain is often enlarged by as much as 10% in volume. However, by later childhood, the brain size may be within the normal range. There appears to be a rapid but short-lived acceleration in the growth of the brain; typical children attain the same brain size, but later in their development (Herbert, 2005b).

Neuropathological studies have also identified structural abnormalities of the limbic system within the brain, which is associated with emotions, with reduced neuron size and increased neuron density. Further, there also appear to be structural abnormalities of the cerebellum and inferior olive (Bauman & Kemper, 1994).

Several structural **magnetic resonance imaging (MRI)** studies have also identified larger brain volumes in young children with autistic disorder, with increased amounts of white matter in the cerebellum and cerebral cortex, and increased amounts of grey matter in the cortex (Courchesne et al., 2001; Rojas et al., 2006). Having a larger and faster growing brain in early childhood with more nerve cells may not be beneficial to the development of specific abilities, such as socialization and communication skills and cognition. Something appears to have gone wrong with early brain development such that there is too much development rather than too little.

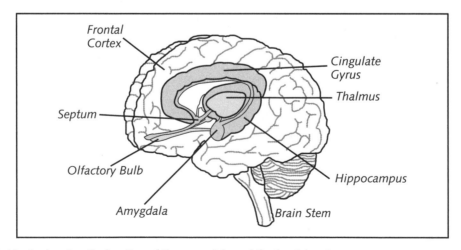

Figure 1.1. Labeled brain showing the location of the amygdala and the frontal cortex.

Studies using functional neuroimaging have suggested that the amygdala and orbitofrontal cortex (see Figure 1.1), areas of the brain associated with emotion regulation and social reasoning, are not functioning as we would expect in children with autism (Baron-Cohen et al., 1999). Thus, we now have a neurological explanation for our observations over many decades of impaired ability to understand complex social situations and to manage emotions.

Possible Errors of Metabolism

Children born with **phenylketonuria (PKN)** have a deficiency in the enzyme that converts the amino acid phenylalanine to tyrosine. A deficiency of this enzyme leads to a toxic accumulation of phenylalanine, resulting in damage to brain function that leads to intellectual disability and a behavioral profile in some children that is similar to autism. Treatment for phenylketonuria is a phenylalanine-free diet, typically involving the elimination of meat or milk, which prevents the development of intellectual disability and behavioral signs of autism (Batshaw & Tuchman, 2002). Thus, we have some evidence that one of the causes of the behaviors associated with autism is an error of metabolism.

A current debate between scientists and parents is whether autism may be caused by an error in the metabolism of gluten, which occurs in certain cereals, and casein, which occurs in dairy products. While casein- and gluten-free diets have become popular with many parents, we do not have any independent and objective studies that clearly establish the value of such diets, though there is anecdotal clinical support (Elder et al., 2006). The author has known of very young children with autism who appear to have improved in their abilities while undertaking such a diet. However, it was not possible to prove that the progress was due solely to the diet.

Infections in Pregnancy and Early Childhood

Certain viral infections have been suggested as a cause of autism. In the 1970s it was suggested that autism could be caused by congenital rubella, but a recent study has not found supportive evidence (Fombonne, 2003). Some studies have suggested that a mother contracting the herpes virus during pregnancy could be another cause of autism, and post-measles encephalitis and herpes encephalitis in early childhood may also be a potential cause (Beversdorf, 2005). One interesting theory is that immigrants may be at greater risk of having a child with autism (Gillberg & Gillberg, 1996). To date, few studies have examined the theory that moving culture and climate may affect a mother's immune system and increase the likelihood of having a child with autism, and those that have investigated this hypothesis have relied on small population samples.

Finally, the issue of immunizations causing autism has been discussed widely in the media. At present, none of the research studies has established any consistent link between the measles vaccination in which mercury is used as a preservative and the development of autism (Honda, Shimizu, & Rutter, 2005).

Psychological Theories of Autism

Three psychological theories explain some of the characteristics of autism, delayed theory of mind, weak central coherence, and impaired executive function.

Lacking Theory of Mind

The psychological term *theory of mind* means the ability to recognize and understand thoughts, beliefs, desires, and intentions of other people in order to make sense of their behaviour and predict what they are going to do next. It has also been described as "mind reading." Weak theory of mind is often referred to as "**mind blindness**" (Baron-Cohen, 1995) or, colloquially, a difficulty in "putting oneself in another person's shoes." A synonymous term is *empathy*. The child with autism does not recognize or understand the cues that indicate the thoughts or feelings of the other person at a level expected for someone of his or her age. However, we are developing strategies to teach theory of mind abilities (Attwood, 2006; Kerr & Drukin, 2004).

Weak **Central Coherence**

Children with autism can be remarkably good at attending to detail but appear to have considerable difficulty perceiving and understanding the overall picture or gist of something (Frith & Happé, 1994). A useful metaphor is to imagine rolling a piece of paper into a tube, closing one eye and placing the tube against the open eye like a telescope and looking at the world through the tube; details are visible, but the context is not perceived.

Typical children have a broader cognitive perspective than the child with autism. When learning in the classroom, the problem may not be attention, but focus. Some activities are difficult to complete on time because the child with autism has become preoccupied with the detail, focusing on parts rather than wholes (Schlooz et al., 2006). A teacher or parent sometimes needs to explain to the child where to look.

Impaired Executive Function

The psychological term *executive function* includes:
- organizational and planning abilities
- working memory
- inhibition and impulse control
- time management and prioritizing
- using new strategies

Children with autism have been recognized as having problems with executive function (Russell, 1997; Yerys, Hepburn, & Pennington, 2007). The teacher of a child with autism will soon become familiar with these characteristics and have to make adjustments to the school curriculum. In the early school years, the main signs of impaired executive function include difficulties with inhibiting a response (i.e., being impulsive), working memory, and using new strategies. Many children with autism are notorious for being impulsive in schoolwork and in social situations, appearing to respond without thinking of the context, consequences, and previous experience (Bower & Parsons, 2003; Happe, Booth, Charlton, & Hughes, 2006; Raymaekers, van der Meere, & Roeyers, 2006).

By the age of 8, a typical child is able to "switch on" and use his or her frontal lobe to inhibit a response and think before deciding what to do or say (Diamond, Kirkham, & Amso, 2002). The child with autism may be capable of thoughtful deliberation before responding, but under conditions of stress, or if feeling overwhelmed or confused, is often impulsive. It is important to encourage the child to relax and consider other options before responding and to recognize that being impulsive can be a sign of confusion and stress.

Autism in Association with Other Disorders

Autism frequently co-occurs with other disabilities (Filipek, 2005). For example, it can occur in children with Down syndrome and children with movement disorders, such as cerebral palsy and muscular dystrophy. A high percentage of children with autism or Asperger's disorder also have signs of an attention deficit disorder (Leyfer et al., 2006). Further, we have recently become more aware that children with autism may develop involuntary movements such as motor and vocal tics associated with Tourette Syndrome. Some children with tuberous sclerosis or neurofibromatosis show signs of an autism disorder that may be due to the effects of specific brain lesions, particularly in the temporal lobes. Finally, there is an association between autism and epilepsy, with bimodal peaks of onset in early childhood and with the onset of puberty. Up to 30% of children with severe autism have epilepsy (Nordin & Gillberg, 1998), which can lead to epileptic seizures.

Can the Child with ASD Develop a Secondary Disorder?

Having autism means that the child will have difficulty with social integration, communication, and cognition. This inevitably leads to stress and the possibility of developing a mood or conduct disorder (Attwood, 2003a; Bradley, Summers, Wood, & Bryson, 2002). We do not know if the development of an anxiety disorder or depression is a psychological reaction to having autism or if it is a constitutional characteristic. Research studies have confirmed that families in which there is a child with autism have a higher incidence of mood disorders. However, this is not always simply a parental reaction to having a child with autism, since treatment for a mood disorder may have occurred before the child was born. Thus, the child may have inherited a predisposition for strong emotions (Bolton, Pickles, Murphy, & Rutter, 1998; DeLong, 1994; Micali, Chakrabarti, & Fombonne, 2004).

Difficulties in developing socialization skills, coping with change, and frustration due to impaired communication and cognitive skills can lead to problems with anger management and the development of conduct problems such as oppositional and defiant behavior (Attwood, 2003a; Gadow, DeVincent, Pomeroy, & Azizian, 2004; Tantam, 2000). These secondary disorders also need to be considered when developing remedial and special education programs.

Gender and Autism

The ratio of boys to girls who have autism is about 2 to 1, and for Asperger's disorder it is 5 to 1 (Fombonne, 2005). Why the disorder is so much more common in males than in females remains unknown. In that connection, we need to determine if the clinical picture and response to treatment is different for boys than for girls with autism or Asperger's disorder. For example, clinical experience suggests that girls with Asperger's disorder are better able to camouflage their social confusion than boys and respond more positively to programs teaching social understanding in comparison to boys (Koppe & Gilberg, 1992).

Is There an Autism Epidemic?

Throughout the world, the number of children with a diagnosis of autism and Asperger's disorder is increasing. In epidemiological studies published between 1966 and 1991, the rate of autism spectrum disorders was, on average, 4.4 children in every 10,000. In studies published in the 1990s, the rate increased to 12.7 in every 10,000. In 2007, estimates of the occurrence of autism spectrum disorders ranged from one in one thousand to as high as 1 in 150 births (Centers for Disease Control, 2007; www.cdc.gov/DiseaseConditions). Why are we diagnosing more children with autism than we used to?

There are several explanations. The first is that we have widened the diagnostic goal posts. We have changed our conceptualization and broadened our definition of autism. Also, we accept that children can have more than one disorder: We no longer consider some disorders as discrete and mutually exclusive. That is, you can now have a child with several developmental disorders, including autism. Second, we have become better at diagnosing autism, especially in younger children. We are improving our ability to detect autism and to ensure fewer children escape detection. Third, in the past a child may have received a diagnosis of intellectual disability with no further diagnostic assessments conducted to determine if the child also had signs of autism. These children are now being more accurately diagnosed (Fombonne, 2005).

We may be able to prove that more children are being diagnosed because we are getting better at diagnosing them, but there remains the problem of access to resources. In this author's opinion, government agencies have been providing funding based on obsolete and inaccurate prevalence rates. Services for children with autism have recently been experiencing a three-fold increase in genuine referrals but without the proportional increase in resources. This is particularly agonizing for parents who are becoming increasingly knowledgeable about the range and success of various treatment options from information available on the Internet and literature written for parents. Politicians will need to legislate for adjustments in funding for children with autism.

Summary and Conclusions

Although we know that autism is a lifelong condition, the outcome or prognosis is much better today than in the past. We now have a better understanding of autism and how to engineer autism-friendly environments that can enable the person to achieve greater self-reliance and reduce the impact of autism on his or her quality of life. We are also achieving more success in the areas of employment, independence, and relationships.

The programs in the following chapters work: They do not propose to present a miracle cure, but outline strategies to achieve progress along the autism continuum. For many on the autism spectrum, the best outcomes would be a full-time job, leaving home, living independently, and having a lifelong relationship with a partner. A diagnosis of autism does not automatically preclude these kinds of outcomes. Any or all of these could be the eventual outcomes for a great many children. Although outcomes will inevitably vary with appropriate supports, it is possible for every child to meet his or her potential and live a happy and fulfilling life.

Tips for the Classroom

✓ In the early stages of identifying autism, it is important for educators and other professionals to listen to what parents have felt *intuitively* about their child regarding social interaction and communication.

✓ It is important to recognize that our understanding of Asperger Syndrome is still evolving, and that researchers have not yet found distinctive differences between Asperger Syndrome and high-functioning autism.

✓ Educators need to understand the history of autism and the impact that history has had and can continue to have on families.

✓ It is important for educators to understand new developments in neuroscience and how those findings can help us understand the social disorder as well as the emotional issues observed in children with autism.

✓ It is important that educators understand the implications of current psychological theories of autism as they relate to effective teaching methods.

✓ Students with autism can also have associated disorders that may complicate the student's learning profile and subsequently his needs.

✓ It can be helpful for educators to consider the continuum of autism as explained in this chapter to measure progress in areas specific to the five dimensions of autism.

✓ It is important that educators understand that special interests in a student with autism can be a window into understanding how to motivate the student to engage in educational activities.

✓ Since autism is a disorder of social relatedness, educators must make deliberate efforts to establish meaningful and mutually respectful relationships with students on the autism spectrum.

Chapter Highlights

- Autism Spectrum Disorder (ASD) is a lifelong condition.

- Autism Spectrum Disorder (ASD) consists of five subgroups or subtypes that vary in the severity and intensity of the dimensions associated with the disorder.

- The five subgroups are: Autism, Rett's Disorder, Childhood Disintegrative Disorder, Pervasive Developmental Disorder-Not Otherwise Specified (PDD-NOS), and Asperger Syndrome.

- Autism was first described by Leo Kanner in 1943.

- Children with autism are identified as having (a) severe qualitative impairment in reciprocal social interaction, (b) severe impairments in communication, and (c) restricted and repetitive range of interests and activities.

- First signs of autism include sleep disturbance, feeding problems, lack of eye contact and pointing toward objects, preference for consistency, focus on objects rather than people, reluctance to share activities with others, possible fascination with sensory experiences, and failure to imitate others' actions.

- Late-onset autism is when children demonstrate no behaviors of concern until into their second year, after having achieved typical developmental milestones. Reported in 20-40% of cases, children with late-onset autism lose abilities already developed, often over a short period of time, and, by age three, present the same as a child whose onset was early.

- Rett's disorder appears to occur primarily in girls and is a progressive neurological disorder. It is typified by loss of purposeful hand use, hand wringing, spasticity of lower extremities, microcephaly, seizures, and need for supports for daily living.

- Childhood disintegrative disorder, which typically occurs in boys, is a rare condition in which a child develops typically on all milestones until between the ages of 3 and 5. The child then experiences rapid deterioration across all areas to the point that he demonstrates significant and severe difficulties across social, communication, and intellectual skills.

- The category of pervasive developmental disorder-not otherwise specified (PDD-NOS) is somewhat vague but is generally used to refer to children who demonstrate some signs of autism but do not demonstrate a clear diagnosis. The author of the chapter describes PDD-NOS as "fragments of autism."

- Asperger's disorder/Asperger Syndrome was first identified in 1944 by Viennese pediatrician Hans Asperger, who referred to children with this diagnosis as having autistic personality disorder. In the 1970s, Lorna Wing coined the term Asperger's Disorder to describe children whose profile of autism did not match the diagnostic criteria.

- The current diagnostic criteria for children and adults with Asperger's disorder/Asperger Syndrome include lack of the significant early language and cognitive skills deficits that are commonly seen in autism, no clinically significant delay in self-help skills or adaptive behavior, and less likelihood of motor mannerisms than seen in classical autism. Asperger's Disorder may not be identified until individuals are school-aged.

- There is some controversy over the diagnostic criteria for Asperger's disorder.

- The term high-functioning autism (HFA) is used to describe children who exhibited classical signs of autism in early childhood but who demonstrated greater intellectual ability (IQ score above 70), social and adaptive skills as they got older, ultimately achieving a level of functioning better than expected.

- While the American Psychiatric Association (APA) discriminates between the classification of HFA and Asperger's Disorder, a number of studies cast doubt on this differentiation.

- The five dimensions/characteristics of ASD are social, communication, cognitive, special interests, and sensory.

- Each dimension can be represented as a continuum, with individuals having more and less significant deficits (being at different stages on the continuum). The level of deficit on the continuum can be indicative of the severity of the disorder in that individual. For example, the child with Asperger's Disorder may have a special interest that is dominant but the complexity and abstractness with regard to that interest represent greater intellectual capacity.

- From the 1940s to the 1970s, autism was thought to be an expression of schizophrenia or psychosis caused by mothers not loving their children/being emotionally unavailable. The term *refrigerator mother* was used to describe these mothers, and autism was seen as a response to this rejection.

- Autism is now considered a neuro-developmental disorder in which specific structures of the brain do not function as expected.

- Research into the causes of autism has investigated: genetics, neurology, possible errors of metabolism, and infections in pregnancy and early childhood.

- Presently, none of the research studies has established a consistent link between immunizations and autism.

- Psychological theories of autism include delayed theory of mind, weak central coherence, and impaired executive function.

- Autism can co-occur with other disorders.

- Children with ASD may develop secondary disorders such as mood and conduct disorders.

- The ratio for autism is 2:1 boys to girls, while it is 5:1 for Asperger's.

- Current estimates of occurrence of ASD range as high as 1 in 150 births.

- There are several possible explanations for why more children are being diagnosed with ASD. These include a broader definition of ASD, realization that ASD may co-occur with other disorders and better diagnostic procedures.

Chapter Review Questions

1. Give examples of signs of autism in early and late onset.

2. What is meant by the phrase autism spectrum disorders (ASD)?

3. List and describe the five subgroups under the umbrella term of ASD.

4. What are the three areas in the diagnostic criteria for autism? State and give examples of each.

5. What is the difference between Asperger's Disorder and high-functioning autism (HFA)? What is the controversy over the distinction between the two?

6. What are the five dimensions of ASD? List and describe.

7. Why can each dimension be considered a continuum?

8. What was meant by "refrigerator mother"?

9. What are currently considered to be possible causes of autism?

10. State and describe the three psychological theories of autism.

11. What are the gender differences in ASD?

12. Why does the number of children identified with ASD seem to be increasing?

References

Adreon, D., & Duroucher, J. (2007). Evaluating the college transition needs of individuals with high-functioniong autism spectrum disorders. *Intervention in School and Clinic, 42*(5), 271-279.

American Psychiatric Association. (1994). *Diagnostic and statistical manual of mental disorders. Fourth edition.* Washington, DC: Author.

American Psychiatric Association. (2000). *Diagnostic and statistical manual of mental disorders. Fourth edition, text revision.* Washington, DC: Author.

Asperger, H. (1991). Die autistischen psychopathen im kindersalter. Archiv für Psychiatrie und Nervenkrankheiten, *117*, 76-136. In U. Frith (Ed. & Trans), *Autism and Asperger Syndrome* (pp. 37-92). Cambridge, UK: Cambridge University Press (Original work published in 1944).

Attwood, T. (1998). *Asperger's syndrome: A guide for parents and professionals.* London: Jessica Kingsley Publishers.

Attwood, T. (2003a). Frameworks for behavioural interventions. *Child and Adolescent Psychiatric Clinics, 12,* 65-86.

Attwood, T. (2003b). Understanding and managing circumscribed interests. In M. Prior (Ed.), *Learning and behavior problems in Asperger Syndrome* (pp. 126-147). New York: The Guilford Press.

Attwood, T. (2006). *The complete guide to Asperger's Syndrome.* London: Jessica Kingsley Publishers.

Bailey, A., Palferman, S., Heavey, L., & LeCouteur, A. (1998). Autism: The phenotype in relatives. *Journal of Autism and Developmental Disorders, 28,* 369-392.

Bailey, A., Le Couteur, A., Gottesman, I., Bolton, P., Simonoff, E., Yuzda, F., et al. (1995). Autism as a strongly genetic disorder: Evidence from a British twin study. *Psychological Medicine, 25,* 63-77.

Baranek, G. T. (2002). Efficacy of sensory and motor interventions for children with autism. Journal of Autism and Developmental Disorders, 5(32), 397-422.

Baron-Cohen, S. (1995). *Mind blindness: An essay on autism and theory of mind.* Cambridge, MA: MIT Press.

Baron-Cohen, S., Ring, H. A., Wheelwright, S., Bullmore, E. T., Brammer, M. J., Simmons, A., & William, S.C.R. (1999). Social intelligence in the normal autistic brain: An FMRI study. *European Journal of Neuroscience, 11,* 1891-1898.

Barron, J., & Barron, S. (2002). *There's a boy in here: Emerging from the bonds of autism.* Arlington, TX: Future Horizons.

Batshaw, M. L., & Tuchman, M. (2002). PKU and other inborn errors of metabolism. In M. L. Batshaw (Ed.), *Children with disabilities* (5th ed., pp. 333-345). Baltimore: Paul Brookes Publishing.

Bauman, M. L., & Kemper, T. L. (1994). Neuroanatomic observations of the brain in autism. In M. L. Bauman & T. L. Kemper (Eds.), *The neurobiology of autism* (pp. 119-145). Baltimore: Johns Hopkins University Press.

Bauman, M., & Kemper, T. (2003). The neuropathology of the autism spectrum disorders: what have we learned? *Novartis Foundation Symp*osium, *251*, 112-122.

Bellini, S. (2006). The development of social anxiety in adolescents with autism spectrum disorders. *Focus on Autism and Other Developmental Disabilities. 21*(3), 138-145.

Belmonte, M., Mazziotta, J., Minshew, N., Evans, A., Courchesne, E., Dager, S., et al. (in press). Offering to share: How to put heads together in autism neuroimaging. *Journal of Autism and Developmental Disorders.*

Beversdorf, D., Manning, S. Hillier, A., Anderson, S., Nordgren, R., Walters, S. et al. (2005). Timing of prenatal stressors and autism. *Journal of Autism and Developmental Disorders, 35*(4), 471-478.

Bolton, P., Pickles, A., Murphy, M., & Rutter, M. (1998). Autism, affective and other psychiatric disorders: Patterns of familial aggregation. *Psychological Medicine, 28,* 385-395.

Bolton, P. F., Murphy, M., Macdonald, H., Whitlock, B., Pickles, A., & Rutter, M. (1997). Obstetric complications in autism. Consequences or causes of the condition? *Journal of the American Academy of Child and Adolescent Psychiatry, 36,* 272-281.

Bower, J., & Parsons, L. (2003). Rethinking the "lesser brain." *Scientific American, 289*(2), 50-57.

Bradley, E., Summers, J., Wood, H., & Bryson, S. (2004). Comparing rates of psychiatric and behavior disorders in adolescents and young adults with severe intellectual disability with and without autism. *Journal of Autism and Developmental Disorder, 34*(2), 151-161.

Canitano, R., & Vivanti, G. (2007). Tics and Tourette syndrome in autism spectrum disorders. *Autism: The International Journal of Research and Practice, 11*(2), 19-28.

Cederlund, M., & Gillberg, C. (2004). One hundred males with Asperger syndrome: A clinical study of background and associated factors. *Developmental Medicine and Child Neurology, 46,* 652-661.

Chawarska, K., & Volkmar, F. (2005). Autism in infancy and early childhood. In F. R. Volkmar, R. Paul, A. Klin, & D. Cohen (Eds.), *Handbook of autism and pervasive developmental disorders* (3rd ed., pp. 223-246). New York: Wiley.

Courchesne, E., Karns, C., Davis, H., Ziccardi, R., Carper, R., Tigue, Z., et al. (2001). Unusual brain growth patterns in early life in patients with autistic disorder: An MRI study. *Neurology, 57,* 245-254.

DeLong, G. (1994). Children with autistic spectrum disorder and a family history of affective disorder. *Developmental Medicine and Child Neurology, 36,* 647-688.

Diamond, A., Kirkham, N., & Amso, D. (2002). Conditions under which young children can hold two rules in mind and inhibit a prepotent response. *Developmental Psychology, 38*(3), 352-362.

Dickerson Mayes, S., Calhoun, S., & Crites, D. (2001). Does DSM-IV Asperger's disorder exist? *Journal of Abnormal Child Psychology, 29,* 263-272.

Dissanayake, C. (2004). Change in behavioral symptoms in children with high functioning autism and Asperger Syndrome: evidence for one disorder? *Australian Journal of Early Childhood, 29,* 48-57.

Dykens, M., & Volkmar, F. (1997). Medical conditions associated with autism. In D. J. Cohen & F. R. Volkmar (Eds.), *Handbook of autism and pervasive developmental disorders* (2nd ed., pp. 388-410). New York: Wiley.

Elder, J., Shankar, M., Shuster, J., Theriaque, D., Burns, S., & Sherrill, L. (2006) The gluten-free, casein-free diet in autism: Results of a preliminary double blind clinical trial. *Journal of Autism and Developmental Disorders, 36*(3), 413-420.

Ellaway, C., & Christodoulou, J. (1999). Rett syndrome: Clinical update and review of recent genetic advances. *Journal of Paediatric and Child Health, 35,* 419-426.

Eisenmajer, R., Prior, M., Leekham, S., Wing, L., Ong, B., Gould, J., & Welham, M. (1998). Delayed language onset as a predictor of clinical symptoms in pervasive developmental disorders. *Journal of Autism and Developmental Disorders, 28,* 527-533.

Farrugia, S., et al. (2005). Anxiety in adolescents with Asperger syndrome: Negative thoughts, behavioral problems, and life interference. *Focus on Autism and Other Developmental Disabilities, 21*(1), 25-35.

Filipek, P. A. (2005). Medical aspects of autism. In F. R. Volkmar, R. Paul, A. Klin, & D. Cohen (Eds.), *Handbook of autism and pervasive developmental disorders* (3rd ed., pp. 534-578). New York: Wiley.

Fombonne, E. (2003). Epidemiological surveys of autism and other pervasive developmental disorders: An update. *Journal of Autism and Developmental Disorders, 33,* 365-382.

Fombonne, E. (2005). Epidemiological studies of pervasive developmental disorders. In F. R. Volkmar, R. Paul, A. Klin, & D. Cohen (Eds.), *Handbook of autism and pervasive developmental disorders* (3rd ed., pp. 42-69). New York: Wiley.

Frith, U. (Ed.). 1991. *Autism and Asperger Syndrome.* Cambridge, UK: Cambridge University Press.

Frith, U., & Happé, F. (1994). Autism: Beyond "theory of mind." *Cognition, 50,* 115-132.

Gadow, K., DeVincent, C., Pomeroy, J., & Azizian, A. (2004). Psychiatric symptoms in preschool children with PDD and clinic and comparison samples. *Journal of Autism and Developmental Disorders, 34*(4), 379-393.

Ghaziuddin, M. (2002). Asperger syndrome: Associated psychiatric and medical conditions. *Focus on Autism and Other Developmental Disabilities, 17*(3), 138-144.

Gillberg, C. (1998). Asperger syndrome and high functioning autism. *British Journal of Psychiatry, 171,* 200-209.

Gillberg, C., & de Souza, L. (2002). Head circumference in autism, Asperger syndrome, and ADHD: A comparative study. *Developmental Medicine and Child Neurology, 44,* 296-300.

Gillberg, I. C., & Gillberg, C. (1996). Autism in immigrants: A population-based study from Swedish rural and urban areas. *Journal of Intellectual Disability Research, 40,* 24-31.

Goldsmith, H., Van Hulle, C., Arneson, C., Schreiber, J., & Gernsbacher, M. (2006). Population-based twin study of parentally reported tactile and auditory defensiveness in young children. *Journal of Abnormal Child Psychology, 34*(3), 378-392.

Grandin, T. (1995). *Thinking in pictures and other reports from my life with autism.* New York: Doubleday.

Grandin, T., & Duffy, K. (2004). *Developing talents – Careers for individuals with Asperger Syndrome and high-functioning autism.* Shawnee Mission, KS: Autism Asperger Publishing Company.

Hallmayer, J., Glasson, E., Bower, C., Petterson, B., Croen, L., Grether, J., & Risch, N. (2002). On the twin risk in autism. *American Journal of Human Genetics, 71*(4), 941-946.

Happe, F., Booth, R., Charlton, R., & Hughes, C., (2006). Executive function deficits in autism spectrum disorders and attention-deficit/hyperactivity disorder: Examining profiles across domains and ages. *Brain and Cognition, 61*(1), 25-39.

Herbert, M. (2005a). A brain disorder or a disorder that affects the brain. *Clinical Neuropsychology, 2*(6), 354-379.

Herbert, M. (2005b). Large brains in autism: the challenge of pervasive abnormality. *Neuroscientist, 11,* 417-440

Hermelin, B. (2001). *Bright splinters of the mind.* London: Jessica Kingsley Publishers.

Honda, H., Shimizu, Y., & Rutter, M. (2005). No effect of MMR withdrawal on the incidence of autism: A total population study. *Journal of Child Psychiatry and Psychology, 46*(6), 572-579.

Howlin, P., & Asgharian, A. (1999). The diagnosis of autism and Asperger syndrome: Findings from a survey of 770 families. *Developmental Medicine and Child Neurology, 41,* 834-839.

Kadesjo, B., Gillberg, C., & Hagberg, B. (1999). Autism and Asperger syndrome in seven-year-old children: A total population study. *Journal of Autism and Developmental Disorders, 29,* 327-331.

Kanner, L. (1943). Autistic disturbances of affective contact. *Nervous Child, 2,* 217-250.

Kerr, S., & Drukin, K. (2004). Understanding of thought bubbles as mental representations in children with autism: Implications for theory of mind. *Journal of Autism and Developmental Disorders, 34*(6), 637-648.

Klin, A., Volkmar, F., Sparrow, S., Cicchetti, D., & Rourke, B. (1995). Validity and neuropsychological characterization of Asperger Syndrome: Convergence with nonverbal learning disabilities syndrome. *Journal of Child Psychology and Psychiatry, 36,* 1127-1140.

Koppe, S., & Gilberg, C. (1992). Girls with social deficits and learning problems: Autism, atypical Asperger syndrome or a variant of these conditions. *European Child and Adolescent Psychiatry, 1*(2), 89-99.

Manjiviona, J., & Prior, M. (1999). Neuropsychological profiles of children with Asperger syndrome and autism. *Autism, 3,* 327-356.

Micali, N., Chakrabarti, S., & Fombonne, E. (2004). The broad autism phenotype: Findings from an epidemiological survey. *Autism, 8,* 21-37.

Miller, J., & Ozonoff, S. (1997). Did Asperger's cases have Asperger disorder? A research note. *Journal of Child Psychology and Psychiatry, 38,* 247-251.

Miller, J., & Ozonoff, S. (2000). The external validity of Asperger disorder: Lack of evidence from the domain of neuropsychology. *Journal of Abnormal Psychology, 109*(2), 227-238.

Minshew, N. J., Sweeney, J. A., Bauman, M. L., & Webb, S. J. (2005). Neurologic aspects of autism. In F. R. Volkmar, R. Paul, A. Klin, & D. Cohen (Eds.), *Handbook of autism and pervasive developmental disorders* (3rd ed., pp. 473-514). New York: Wiley.

Mind reading: The interactive guide to emotions. (2004). London: Jessica Kingsley Publishers.

Moore, V., & Goodson, S. (2003). How well does early diagnosis of autism stand the test of time? Follow up study of children assessed for autism at age 2 and development of an early diagnostic service. *Autism: International Journal of Research and Practice, 7*(1), 47-63.

National Research Council. (2001). *Educating children with autism.* Washington, DC: National Academy Press.

Nordin, V., & Gillberg, C. (1998). The long term course of autistic disorders: Update on follow-up studies. *Acta Psychiatrica Scandinavica, 97,* 99-108.

Orsmond, G. I., Krauss, M. W., & Seltzer, M. M. (2004). Peer relationships and social and recreational activities among adolescents and adults with autism. *Journal Autism and Developmental Disabilities, 34*(3), 245-256.

Ozonoff, S., South, M., & Miller, J. (2000). DSM-IV defined Asperger syndrome: Cognitive, behavioural and early history differentiation from high-functioning autism. *Autism, 4,* 29-46.

Raymaekers, R., van der Meere, J., & Roeyers, H. (2006). Response inhibition and immediate arousal in children with high-functioning autism. *Child Neuropsychology, 12*(4-5), 349-359.

Rojas, D., Peterson, E., Winterrowd, E., Reite, M., Rogers, S., & Tregellas, J., (2006). Regional gray matter volumetric changes in autism associated with social and repetitive behavior symptoms. *BMC Psychiatry, 6,* 56.

Russell, J. (1997). *Autism as an executive disorder.* Oxford, UK: Oxford University Press.

Rutter, M. (2005). Genetic influences and autism. In F. R. Volkmar, R. Paul, A. Klin, & D. Cohen (Eds.), *Handbook of autism and pervasive developmental disorders* (3rd ed., pp. 425-452). New York: Wiley.

Schlooz, W., Hulstijn, W., van den Broek, P., van der Pijll, A., Gabreels, F., van der Gaag, R., et al. (2006). Fragmented visuospatial processing in children with pervasive developmental disorder. *Journal of Autism and Developmental Disorders, 36*(8),1025-1037.

Shore, S. (2003). *Beyond the wall – Personal experiences with autism and Asperger Syndrome.* Shawnee Mission, KS: Autism Asperger Publishing Company.

Siperstein, R., & Volkmar, F. R. (2004). Parental reporting of regression in children with pervasive developmental disorders. *Journal of Autism and Developmental Disorders, 34*(6), 731-734.

Sofronoff, K., Attwood, T., Hinton, S., & Levin, I. (2007). A randomized controlled trial of a cognitive behavioural intervention for anger management in children diagnosed with Asperger syndrome. *Journal of Autism & Developmental Disorders, 37*(7), 1203-1214.

Tantam, D. (2000). Psychological disorders in adolescents and adults with Asperger Syndrome. *Autism. The International Journal of Research and Practice, 4,* 47-62.

Turner, M., Barnby, G., & Bailey, A. (2000). Genetic clues to the biological basis of autism. *Molecular Medicine Today, 6,* 238-244.

Verte, S., Geurts, H., Roeyersd, H. Oosterlaan, J. & Sergeant, J. (2006). The relationship of working memory, inhibition, and response variability in child psychopathology. *Journal of Neuroscientific Methods, 151*(1), 5-14.

Volkmar, F., Klin, A., & Pauls, D. (1998). Nosological and genetic aspects of Asperger syndrome. *Journal of Autism and Developmental Disorders, 28,* 457-463.

Williams, D., Goldstein, G., & Minshew, N. (2006). The profile of memory function in children with autism. *Neuropsychology, 20*(1), 21-29.

Wing, L. (1981). Asperger's Syndrome: A clinical account. *Psychological Medicine, 11,* 115-130.

Wing, L., & Attwood, A. (1987). Syndromes of autism and atypical development. In D. Cohen & A. Donnellan (Eds.), *Handbook of autism and pervasive developmental disorders* (pp. 3-19). New York: John Wiley and Sons.

Wing, L., & Gould, J. (1979). Severe impairments of social interaction and associated abnormalities in children: Epidemiology and classification. *Journal of Autism and Developmental Disorders, 9,* 11-29.

Yerys, B., Hepburn, S., & Pennington, B. (2007). Executive function in preschoolers with autism: Evidence consistent with a secondary deficit. *Journal of Autism and Developmental Disorders, 37*(6), 1068-1079.

Zafeiriou, D., Ververi, A., & Vargiami, E. (2007). Childhood autism and associated comorbidities. *Brain & Development, 29*(5), 257-272.

Learner Objectives

After reading this chapter, the learner should be able to:

- State the meaning of core deficit in understanding autism/ASD

- State the current most popular theories related to what are the primary impairments in ASD

- Describe why ASD can be referred to as a disorder of information processing

- Discuss what is meant by "hidden information- demands"

- State the value of the complex information processing concept

- Demonstrate an understanding of what is meant by the term *complexity*

- Define the term *central coherence*

- Define *information processing*

- State how the development of new imaging technology, specifically the fMRI, is important to the understanding of autism/ASD

- State what is different about the brains of individuals with autism/ASD that leads to differences in how they think and perceive things

- Demonstrate an understanding of compensatory strategies used by individuals with autism/ASD

- State why the chapter authors believe the diagnostic criteria of autism/ASD needs to be redefined

- Discuss why the chapter authors believe intellectual disability in autism cannot be considered a separate diagnosis

- Discuss implications of the brain basis of autism/ASD

Chapter 2

Brain-Behavior
Connections in Autism

Nancy J. Minshew • Diane L. Williams

Evan, a fifth-grade student, was extremely agitated. "They don't belong there. Make them go away," he said, pointing toward the three construction trailers taking up half of the school playground. His teacher calmly explained, "The construction men put the trailers there this summer. They needed them to put their work things in. The men will come to pick them up as soon as they have a chance." "They don't belong there. Make them go away," Evan repeated with an increasingly high pitch. His teacher once again tried to reason with him, explaining the purpose of the trailers and why they weren't moved yet. Finally, Evan threw himself onto the floor and began screaming, "They don't belong there." The teaching assistant then removed him from the room.

Evan's response might at first seem out of proportion to the problem of the construction trailers being left on the playground, but his perception of the problem was very different from that of his teacher because Evan has autism.

This chapter is about the cognitive and brain basis of autism, or what is different about the brain of individuals with autism that leads to differences in how they think and perceive things. Studies of the brains of individuals with autism provide evidence of differences in how the brain is organized, in how it functions, and even in its size. Thinking differently is not a choice in autism, but a consequence of very real differences in the brain. Understanding how people with autism think is the foundation for effective and appropriate intervention. Intervention based on an understanding of the neurocognitive aspects will help individuals with autism maximize their functioning and overall happiness.

Autism as a Disorder of Information Processing

Previously considered a psychological or behavioral disorder, autism was accepted to be of neurologic origin in the 1960s (Minshew, Sweeney, Bauman, & Webb, 2005). The search then focused on **cognition** and parts of the brain that caused the behavior that is called autism. By cause, what was meant was the deficit or alteration in thinking and in the brain that led to the abnormal behavior. Two approaches to understanding autism were subsequently pursued.

Approaches to Understanding Autism

The first approach focused on individual deficits based on the hypothesis that a single deficit causes a cascade, which results in the entire constellation of deficits in autism. The specific deficit hypothesized as "the **core deficit**" in autism has varied over the decades and from investigator to investigator. Eventually, it became apparent from accumulated research that there was evidence in autism of many such deficits. As a result, the focus shifted to emphasizing the temporal primacy of specific deficits. That is, theorists emphasized that one of the deficits preceded all others with an onset in infancy. Such hypotheses are difficult to test, and no evidence has yet substantiated the pre-existence of a single deficit in the absence of other deficits. The most popular of such theories now propose a primary impairment in the ability to shift attention (Courchesne et al., 1994), in **representational** capacity (Meltzoff & Decety, 2003), or in **social motivation** or orienting to **social stimuli** (Dawson, Webb, & McPartland, 2005; Schultz, 2005).

An alternative approach is to investigate the evidence of all simultaneously occurring impairments and intact abilities. The purpose of this line of investigation is to identify a common denominator of impairments and abilities that illuminates fundamental principles about cognition and the brain in autism. This is the traditional approach of neurologists, based on the recognition that brain abnormalities rarely result in a single impairment but rather a constellation, the pattern of which reflects the nature of the biologic disturbance. For example, the constellation of deficits resulting from acquired insults to the brain may reflect the distribution of a blood vessel, the coup-counter-coup[1] pattern of a traumatic injury, or the vulnerability profile of a metabolic insult. Similarly, the constellation of deficits resulting from a developmental disturbance may reflect the pattern of a first-trimester abnormality in the formation of the brain, a second-trimester disturbance in neuronal proliferation (increase or decrease in brain cell numbers) or migration (movement of brain cells from place of origin to final destination), or a third-trimester disturbance in neuronal organization (development of the elaborate connections of the human brain). A developmental disturbance might also reflect the impact of fetal exposure to a virus or a toxin.

Based on the perspective that many domains would be impacted by a **developmental disorder**, we approached the investigation of the cognitive basis of autism by simultaneously assessing all the common domains of neuro-psychologic functioning in samples of high-functioning children, adolescents, and adults with autism (those with Full Scale and Verbal IQ scores of 70 and above). High-functioning individuals were selected because they had all the features specific to autism without the potential nonspecific features associated with intellectual disability; they could be IQ matched to a normal control group; and they could cooperate for a comprehensive battery of tests.

---

[1] An injury in which the brain is damaged on impact with the inside of the skull at the site of impact and then suffers additional damage when the brain moves back and forth, hitting the inside of the bony skull.

Subgroup Studies of the Cognitive Basis of Autism

The principle of subgroup studies is that the subgroup is a proxy for the entire group of people with autism, even though they are not representative of the entire group. That is, even though they do not have intellectual disability with autism, they have the same disorder as individuals with autism who are mentally retarded. Therefore, principles or characteristics identified in this subgroup can be considered to be true of people with autism as a whole. Extrapolation of these characteristics or principles to more impaired individuals with autism requires consideration of their expression in a more severe form. However, the specific qualities of the disorder would remain the same, regardless of the functioning level of the affected individual.

To date, three studies, two involving adult samples and one involving children, have been completed.

Study 1 – Adolescents and adults. The first study included 33 individually matched pairs of adolescents and adults with autism compared to individually matched normal controls, all of whom had Full Scale and Verbal IQ scores of 80 and above (Minshew, Goldstein, & Siegel, 1997). The diagnosis of autism was established using the ***Autism Diagnostic Interview-Revised*** (**ADI-R**; Le Couteur et al., 1989; Lord, Rutter, & Le Couteur, 1994), a two-hour structured interview developed for research to standardize the early developmental history and current functioning in the areas of social, communication, and restricted interests and repetitive behavior relevant to the diagnosis of autism; and the one-hour ***Autism Diagnostic Observation Schedule*** (**ADOS**; Lord et al., 1989; Lord et al., 2000), a direct observation of the individual composed of a number of tasks designed to elicit social, communication, and play abilities relevant to the diagnosis of autism. All items were scored using set ratings, and the items were then scored according to the *Diagnostic and Statistical Manual, Fourth Edition* (DSM-IV) criteria for autism (American Psychiatric Association, 1994).[2] The diagnosis of autism made in this way was confirmed by expert clinical opinion. Individuals with autism with Fragile X syndrome, tuberous sclerosis, or some other identifiable cause of autism were excluded from participation in the study.

This study revealed a unique profile of impaired and intact abilities, as displayed in Table 2.1. The first principle apparent from this profile is that the acquisition of information in autism was intact. That is, the capacity to attend to (attention), perceive (elementary sensory perception), and remember (basic memory abilities) information was not impaired relative to the controls. In addition, basic or elementary skills in the other domains tested were also intact. Formal language abilities (spelling, reading words and nonwords, speaking words) were superior to those of the age- and IQ-matched controls. The capacity for learning the attributes or characteristics of objects and rules was also intact.

---

[2] In Europe this would be ICD-10 criteria (World Health Organization, 1992).

Table 2.1
Intact or Enhanced Abilities and Deficits in Adults with High-Functioning Autism

Intact or Enhanced	Cognitive Weaknesses
Attention	**Complex Motor**
Sensory Perception	Complex Memory
Elementary Motor	**Complex Language**
Simple Memory	**Concept Formation**
Formal Language	Face Recognition
Rule Learning	
Visuospatial processing	

Relative impairments were present in higher cortical sensory perception (What is the object in your hand? Are you being touched at two analogous spots on opposites sides of your body? What is the number being drawn on your fingertip?); skilled motor movements (handwriting, tying shoes, skipping); memory for complex material (a large amount of the same type of material, like word lists or material that is inherently complex like scenes or stories); higher-order language (idioms, metaphors, inferences, paragraph comprehension); flexibility (shifting strategies when one does not work in the circumstances); and concept formation (problem solving when there are no set rules; associated skills are insight and judgment).

The overriding principles of this pattern, other than the integrity of information acquisition, were not immediately apparent. It was not a pattern that had been seen before in other diseases. The principles to emerge were the following. First, the acquisition of information was intact in autism. However, information-processing capacity was reduced or constrained. This constraint disproportionately impacted higher-order information processing or the capacity to process information or material when the demands of the task or situation are high. This processing constraint occurred at a lower level than would be expected based on the individual's age and IQ.

Second, the predominance of symptoms across domains appeared to reflect the complexity of the information-processing demands. This complexity explained the preponderance of symptoms in the social, communication, and reasoning domains. However, the presence of impairments not part of the diagnostic triad and even not predicted (e.g., in memory and in motor) strongly suggested that the neurobiology or brain basis of this disorder involved a mechanism that was general to the development of brain architecture and, therefore, was not confined to the three neural systems underlying the diagnostic triad (social, language, and reasoning).

Study 2 – Children. The second study involved 56 children with high-functioning autism (HFA) and 56 typically developing children between the ages of 8 and 15 years with Full Scale and Verbal IQ scores above 80 and between 80 and 120 (Williams, Goldstein, & Minshew, 2006). These findings replicated the major principles of the initial adult study with minor differences. One particularly interesting difference was the more prominent sensory symptoms in the children with autism than in the adults, suggesting some amelioration or lessening in sensory symptoms over time.

Another difference was that the impairments in concept formation appeared more prominent in the adult study. One possible explanation for this finding is that neither the children with autism nor the typically developing controls may have reached the level of development that allowed manifestation of the reasoning impairments in autism. It is clear from our studies and the literature that abstraction abilities dependent on the frontal lobe mature in the second decade of life in typically developing children. However, adolescents with autism do not acquire these skills, and between-group differences emerge on more and more tests in the concept-formation domain (Luna, Doll, Hegedus, Minshew, & Sweeney 2006; Minshew, Meyer, & Goldstein, 2002).

Study 3 – Adults. The third study involving a second sample of adults replicated the first set of results (Minshew & Goldstein, unpublished data). Therefore, there is consistent evidence across a large age range of constraints on information processing that disproportionately impact higher-order or integrative processing. These constraints transcend domains to involve sensorimotor and memory abilities not previously appreciated to be integral elements of this syndrome. The diagnostic triad concept of autism, therefore, needs to be expanded, and the notion that this is merely or predominantly a disorder of social function or interactions must be set aside. Indeed, the difficulties with restricted and repetitive behavior, common sense, insight, and judgment are as impairing as the social impairment. These have been referred to as the non-social or cognitive aspects of autism (Minshew, Meyer, & Goldstein, 2002).

Independent Validation of the Constraints on Information Processing

One of the first concerns of a researcher upon completing a study that suggests a new principle is whether there is independent validation – a different method from a different investigator – that provides confirmation that the conclusion is correct. For example, if it is agreed that autism is a disorder characterized by a reduced capacity for information processing, then one would expect to find a decline in performance during a dual task (one that requires simultaneous processing of two types of incoming information).

A study of dual-task processing with individuals with autism was found in the literature (Garcia-Villamisar & Della Sala, 2002). This study involved 16 participants with autism with average IQ scores compared to 16 normal controls. Each group performed two tasks individually and then simultaneously. The tasks were digit recall (similar to remembering a phone number) and motor tracking (like moving a pen to keep up with a moving dot). These tasks were not demanding. When each task was performed individually, the autism group performed similarly to the control group. When the control group performed both tasks simultaneously, their performance rate on the individual tasks was unchanged from when they performed the tasks individually. However, when the autism group performed the tasks simultaneously, their performance declined about 40%. This is a dramatic example of the constraints on information processing in individuals with autism. That is, these were very simple tasks, and yet the autism group could not do them at the same time without their performance suffering substantially.

Most of everyday life entails **multitasking**. The teacher talks while she writes on the board. People speak words in combination with the tone of their voice, their facial expressions, their gaze, their gestures, and other body language. You listen to the person walking next to you while watching for the traffic in the street ahead. We are constantly managing large amounts of information and the associated allocation of processing resources. Individuals with autism have difficulty managing all of this incoming information. What we do almost without thinking about it, individuals with autism find incredibly challenging.

Though not directly tested in the dual-task study, **speed of processing** is also a variable that constrains the ability of individuals with autism to process information. That is, information-processing capacity is restricted by the amount of information presented, its complexity, and time constraints. Individuals with autism are renowned for having "one gear" that has a slower pace than others. This is another manifestation of constrained information-processing capacity in this group.

A Lesson in Hidden Information-Processing Demands

One of the first tests of language comprehension we administered was the Oral Directions subtest from the ***Detroit Tests of Learning Aptitude*** (**DTLA-2**; Hammill, 1985; Minshew, Goldstein, & Siegel, 1997). It begins with simple instructions such as "Touch the yellow circle," and then becomes steadily more complex: "Before you touch the blue square, touch the green triangle," then "Before you touch the red square, touch the purple circle, then touch the black triangle," and so on. Although high-functioning individuals with autism could readily comprehend sentences of the same length or longer that had simple grammatical construction, they had substantial difficulty understanding sentences with complex grammatical construction.

Why was there a difference when the number of words was the same? The answer is that the information-processing demands were far greater when there were clauses and phrases. When there is a clause, the brain must process the meaning of the first part of the sentence and hold it in **working memory**, then process the meaning of the second part of the sentence, and then process the meaning of the first part in relation to the second part. The information-processing demands are much higher for **complex sentences**. The language of daily life uses complex grammatical construction. Therefore, when individuals with autism are having difficulty complying with instructions, a shift to simple grammar may improve their comprehension and, in turn, compliance.

Even though the individuals with autism who participated in our studies spoke in complex sentences, they did not necessarily comprehend them when they spoke them or heard them spoken by others. And why was that? The reason was that clauses and phrases were often a single word to them. For example, in the movie *Rain Man,* when Raymond refers to the seats in his deceased father's antique car as "pitiful red," this is a stereotyped phrase that is one piece to him, not two separate words. For higher-functioning individuals with autism, longer phrases and even sentences become single encoded units that they do not fully understand. Hence, it is important to assess what individuals with autism understand by how they act – the demonstration of their understanding – and not take their words at face value. Many parents have complained, "I know he knows the rule. He says the rule while he is doing what the rule says not to do." In other words, his actions demonstrate that although he says the words, he does not know what those words mean. The parent has made the mistake of thinking that saying equals understanding. In reality, however, "doing" is the test of understanding, not saying.

The effect of increased processing demands can also be evident when individuals with autism are using expressive language. They may fail to integrate the intended message with the words and sentences that would clearly express their idea. When language is stored in chunks, those chunks must be used for spoken language, too.

The teachers were becoming very frustrated with Amanda. Day after day, she would repeatedly say, "Go swimming? Go swimming? Go swimming?" The teachers patiently told her that Tuesday was swimming day, and today was not Tuesday. They showed her the weekly picture schedule with swimming clearly indicated under Tuesday, but nothing seemed to satisfy Amanda. She persisted, "Go swimming? Go swimming? Go swimming?"

I [3] was called in to try to find a way to get Amanda to understand what her teachers were trying to communicate to her. After observing the classroom routine, I had an idea of what the problem might be. I told the teachers that the next time Amanda began saying, "Go swimming," they should answer as if she had said, "What's next?" The teachers did as instructed, and Amanda ceased her repetitive questioning. Swimming was Amanda's favorite activity. Therefore, it had strong retrieval strength for her. Whenever Amanda tried to compose a message about a school activity, the language that came "on-line" was "Go swimming?" What she really intended to say was "What are we doing next?"

As illustrated, Amanda's language had to be analyzed according to its context rather than by its content. People with autism do not always say what they mean and are dependent on their communication partners to carry the burden of interpreting their meaning.

Utility of the Complex Information-Processing Concept

The complex information-processing concept is only of value to the extent it is of help with intervention and understanding of behavior. Table 2.1, which lists the intact and impaired abilities, is an extremely useful guide for intervention in autism. Individuals with autism are generally operating on facts and rules. As a result, they need information conveyed succinctly with the fewest words possible. The bottom line needs to be stated; that is, numerous examples should not be given in hopes that they will figure out the concept or bottom line.

One case makes the application of the utility of this profile immediately apparent:

Adam was a 27-year-old young man who had been given a diagnosis of schizophrenia in early childhood, although he had never shown any signs of psychosis.[4] He lived in a rural area and had a job in a department store that he had held for 10 years. One day Adam was fired when a comment he made to a female was interpreted as sexually harassing in nature. With no job, Adam stayed in his apartment without any activities or supervision. Because he came from a religious family, he began watching evangelical shows and became preoccupied with sin and going to hell.

Adam was found by his caseworker agitated, carrying a Bible, quoting passages about going to hell. He was admitted to a psychiatric unit. The psychiatric residents were concerned that Adam was manic and thought

---

[3] DLW.
[4] This is a common misdiagnosis in verbal adults with HFA or Asperger's disorder.

he should be put on Lithium, but Adam refused to comply. For Adam, Lithium was associated with an unpleasant experience: He had taken Lithium on June 7, 1978 (17 years prior) and had gotten a stomachache. He went to the mental health clinic quite afraid that he had been poisoned and was reprimanded for coming without an appointment. He grew more agitated and soon was in physical management on the floor with several men sitting on him. No wonder he would not take Lithium again after that experience!

My advice[5] was asked, and I used what I knew of Adam's thinking. Knowing he had autism, not schizophrenia, I told the resident, "There are two forms of the medicine. One is pink, and the other is blue. Put one in each of your hands and ask which one Adam took before. When he tells you, say 'oh you took the bad pink/blue before, and now you can take the good pink/blue.'" The psychiatric resident tried this, and Adam agreed immediately to the medication. Earlier the resident had tried insight and reasoning, which Adam did not understand. Adam thinks simply in facts and concretely (show and tell).

Let's look at another case.

Stephen, a man weighing 85 lbs and near starvation, was admitted to the psychiatric unit. The resident had tried every method to persuade him to eat, but to no avail. Persuasion involves insight and higher-order language. When I met Stephen, it was 10:30 in the morning. He still had his breakfast tray and was staring at it and not eating. Through his ramblings, I gathered that his mother had told him 40 years earlier that he was getting pudgy and had better watch what he ate. So he did, by staring at it. Then someone told him that "watching what you ate" meant not eating too much. However, Stephen was now depressed and had reverted to the earlier rule of watching what he ate by staring at his food. Understanding this, we established rules of the same type to restore his eating.

More About Complexity

Complexity is a general term or concept just like learning disability or intellectual disability. It does not refer to one specific thing. Hence, a learning disability such as dyslexia is not defined absolutely as the inability to read a book, sentences, or particular words. Reading ability or disability is defined relative to a person's age and general level of function. Age-appropriate tests and norms have been developed to make such determinations. At this point in research, we have defined impairments in information processing that disproportionately impact complex abilities as resulting in poorer performance relative to age- and IQ-matched peers and below standardized norms. For example, the motor impairment in the adult profile study was not only significantly worse than in the control group but was in the moderately severe range of impairment, according to clinical norms.

---

[5] NJM.

The term *complexity* can be articulated further. Various types of information can be complex. Information can be complex by virtue of its amount – small units but many of them, such as a word list or branch points to be learned in a maze. Further, information can be complex because of its inherent structure – a complex visual scene or a story with a theme. Information can be complex because it is of multiple types and must be integrated. A good example is the need to integrate visual, vestibular, and position sense to maintain postural control. Another example of this type of complex information is skilled motor movements, where individual motor actions must be integrated into a complex sequence that is greater than the individual parts. Finally, information processing may become complex because of time constraints, multiple simultaneous processing demands, or stress or anxiety. These factors are true for all of us, but since individuals with autism have a lower capacity for information processing, these factors become limiting far sooner than for age- and IQ-matched peers.

What Is in a Name?

Once the results of the cognitive and neurologic profile studies indicated an inherent deficit in autism with the processing of complex information, the question became what to call this profile – how to characterize it?

Uta Frith (1989) had coined the term *central coherence* for a similar constellation of impairments in high-order cognitive and language abilities and strengths on tasks that required perception of details, primarily visuospatial in nature. However, this term did not accommodate the sensory, motor, or memory impairments of individuals with autism, nor did it consider the expressive deficits. Central coherence was suited to explaining the problems with comprehension – the failure to make sense of things – but individuals with autism have equal difficulty with expression, including prosody, facial expression, telling a logical story, detecting the inherent structure in material to be able to remember it, or forming signs for sign language. They also had trouble with motor skills and disturbances in sensory perception. In addition, from a brain perspective, there was no central "coherer." Therefore, we chose a descriptive terminology that was applicable to all the impairments and the intact abilities and that was standard to neurology and cognitive neuroscience: *information processing*.

The developmental neurobiologic analogue of these higher-order human abilities is well known. It is referred to as neuronal organization, or the refinement in brain circuitry that produces the abilities that are unique to human beings. Like the term *pervasive developmental disorder*, information-processing disorder has little meaning without a detailed explanation. It fundamentally means the processes whereby the brain attaches meaning to information. The distinction between simple and complex information processing was based on the observation that within domains, it was the highest-order abilities that were impacted, whereas the basic abilities were spared.

This pattern was unusual. If both simple and complex abilities had been equally affected, the result would have been a general deficit syndrome or general intellectual disability. If only simple information processing would have been affected, the result would have been a selective language impairment or learning disability such as dyslexia; however, social skills, communication, eye contact, facial expression, insight, and judgment would have been intact. Instead, unlike the general child neurology population, individuals with autism and autism spectrum disorders (ASD) have problems with higher-order skills across domains but do not have the visuospatial deficits or dyslexia common to the general child neurology patient group.

Once the concept of the selective impact on more difficult information with intact simple information is understood, the complex information-processing construct becomes a functional foundation for intervention. It is important to keep in mind that the typical predictions regarding the status of higher-order abilities based on the status of basic abilities do not hold true in autism and ASD. Hence, it is common to over-estimate the language comprehension of individuals with autism and to use reasoning rather than facts when attempting to change their behavior, as we have seen in the earlier cases studies.

The Brain Basis of Thinking in Autism

Until magnetic resonance imaging (MRI) and functional magnetic resonance imaging (fMRI) methods became available, the techniques for studying the brain in children with autism and for repeated studies were extremely limited. **Computerized axial tomography (CAT)** scans or **positron emission tomography (PET)** scans used to investigate brain disorders in adults involved radiation; thus, they could not be used in children or for repeated studies. Except for **EEG (electroencephalographic)** techniques, which yielded brain waves but not brain images, the study of the brain in autism had to wait for the emergence of magnetic resonance imaging technology.

The first application of this technology was for examining the area or two-dimensional measurements of specific brain structures (Cody, Pelphrey, & Piven, 2002). With time, computer programs and analyses were developed for three-dimensional measurements that led to more accurate volume measurements (e.g., Aylward, Minshew, Field, Sparks, & Singh, 2002; Courchesne et al., 2001; Sparks et al., 2002). The next breakthrough, and the most significant for autism, was the development of functional MRI (fMRI) methods, by which the activity of the brain during performance of cognitive or language tasks could be recorded. This became the first true window on the thinking brain in autism.

An fMRI study of sentence comprehension in 17 adolescents and young adults with HFA and 17 normal controls found the first of many important differences in brain function in autism (Just, Cherkassky, Keller, & Minshew, 2004). Compared to the control group, the autism group displayed: (a) increased brain activation in the word region of the surface gray matter; (b) reduced brain activation in the surface gray matter area that processes the meaning of sentences; (c) reduced functional connections or correlations among 10 pairs of cortical regions that participate in language function; and (d) reduced synchrony between the activity of the region pairs. This pattern means that the brain regions were not working together to support language function. When the functional connectivity was plotted for all region pairs for the autism group and the control group, the line joining the points for the autism group was parallel to, but below, the line joining the points for the control group. This suggests that the brain was organized in the same way but did not achieve the same degree of connectivity in the autism group as in the control group.

This type of fMRI study of individuals with HFA has been repeated using tasks that involve problem solving (Just, Keller, Cherkassky, Kana, & Minshew, 2007); social thinking (Kana, Keller, Williams, Minshew, & Just, 2005); and inhibiting context inappropriate behavior (Kana, Keller, Minshew, & Just, 2007). The results in all cases have been similar, suggesting a common principle of underdevelopment of the **connectivity** of the neural systems for autism.

In the brain, higher-order abilities are supported by neural systems or the collaboration of many brain regions to enable a more complex ability or function to occur. This is analogous to the collaboration that must occur between the driver, the steering mechanism, the engine, the drive train, and the axel to accomplish driving a car. The fMRI studies completed to date suggest that the neural systems of individuals with autism have fewer and smaller centers to call upon and less flexibility in doing so. Hence, when the environmental demands change and different abilities are needed to address these demands, the brain in autism has less flexibility and fewer and smaller resources to draw upon. In addition, the brain regions are not working in **synchrony** or harmony.

In summary, fMRI studies are making a substantial contribution to our understanding of the brain basis of thinking, its differences, and its limitations in autism. These can be used to guide intervention. For example, intervention might focus on alternative approaches and strategy development rather than facts and rote learning of responses.

Compensatory Strategies

The fMRI studies have also revealed that individuals with autism use different cognitive approaches to tasks – differences that are not apparent from their behavioral performance. Their alternate approach ultimately impacts their capacity, imposing limits or raising them, depending on the nature of the task. For example, in the sentence comprehension study (Just et al., 2004) described above, it was clear that individuals with autism focused on the words of the sentences rather than the meaning of the entire sentence. However, their behavioral performance was the same as controls, so it was not apparent from looking at the behavioral results that they were processing language differently.

A second fMRI study with a different type of task demonstrated the use of another type of **compensatory strategy** by the participants with autism. The task was a classic measure of working memory, called an *n*-back task. In this task, the individual is asked to monitor a string of letters presented one at a time for those that are the same when they appear two in a row (1 back) or separated by one different letter (2-back). Members of both the autism group and the control group performed similarly with respect to the behavioral results. However, the fMRI results suggested that the autism group viewed the letters as graphic figures and did not recode them into letter names as the control group appeared to have done (Koshino et al., 2005). Hence, the control group displayed brain activation in the left executive and left language areas of the brain, whereas the autism group displayed brain activation in both posterior visual areas and the right executive area. In essence, these results indicate that individuals with autism rely on lower-level visual abilities rather than higher-level abilities to perform certain tasks. Had this task involved Russian letters rather than English letters, the controls would likely have performed very poorly, and the autism group would have performed much better because the strategic use of language would not have been as readily available.

The implications of the results of the working-memory-for-letters study are that reliance on visual abilities can be either a strength or a limitation, depending on the task. This knowledge can be used in job placement, for example. Jobs such as laying tile straight, analyzing satellite surveillance maps, or screening luggage or import containers coming into the country might be potential careers for individuals with ASD that would draw on their tendency to process information visually and to perceive details.

Another study added further insight into this issue. This study involved the use of mental imagery during sentence reading (Kana, Keller, Cherkassky, Minshew, & Just, 2006). HFA and matched control groups were presented with low-imagery sentences (Addition and subtraction are mathematical operations.) and high-imagery sentences (There was a rainbow over the corn field.). The fMRI study showed that the control group activated the imagery area of the brain only for the high-visual imagery sentences. In contrast, the autism group activated the imagery area of the brain for both low- and high-visual imagery sentences. Hence, the latter appeared to think in visual pictures, presumably to enhance comprehension. This may not be true of all individuals with autism, however. Some may think in words rather than pictures. Studies like this of a much larger number of individuals with autism are needed to determine if there are different types of thinkers, as Dr. Temple Grandin (1995) suggests.

What happens when material cannot be visualized? For example, how do people with autism visualize words that are abstract, like justice or honor? **Temple Grandin** has written about her experiences with **visual thinking** (thinking in pictures). For abstract words like justice, she thinks of episodes of the TV program *Law and Order.* This dependence on already experienced situations or visual pictures (e.g., concrete examples) for comprehension highlights the limitations of comprehension even in more able individuals with autism. It also highlights the compensatory use of visual strategies for performance of many tasks that are typically performed with language or executive processes.

Using visual strategies, either pictures or written words, to communicate instructions or messages to individuals with autism serves to reduce the amount of content and compress the content to essential information. The format of these instructions should be written like the directions on a soup can – brief and to the point. As seen above, clauses and phrases add processing demands that individuals with autism may not be able to negotiate. Unnecessary words should be eliminated, and only essential facts should be included. For example, individuals with autism would greatly benefit from the software programs that extract key points from textbooks and class notes and eliminate nonessential information, clauses, and phrases. However, it is important to remember that not all individuals with autism are visual thinkers and that some think in words.

Origin of the Brain Differences

Neuroimaging studies are providing increasing evidence of the brain differences in individuals with autism, but where do these brain differences come from? Autism is currently thought to have multiple levels of causation that are assumed to originate in abnormalities in the genetic code that controls what will happen later in brain development (Rutter, 2005). Autism is a disorder that starts in utero but is only identified as development unfolds during the first years of life. The abnormal mechanisms of brain development are realized as structural and functional abnormalities of the brain. They are seen as cognitive and neurological abnormalities that are ultimately manifested as behavioral differences.

Thus, the behavioral differences that characterize the disorder we call autism result from underlying biological differences. Individuals with autism learn and act differently because their brains function differently. While the environment can influence their learning, it cannot change the underlying neurophysiological differences (not yet, at any rate). Thus, although individuals with autism cannot control the way they think about the world, we can understand better how their brains handle information. Such understanding will help us to design interventions that assist the brains of individuals with autism in handling processing challenges of increasing load and complexity of task.

Memory and Learning

Impairments of memory and learning are not included in the list of diagnostic criteria for autism or ASD but have been documented in autism in profiles of neuropsychologic functioning (Minshew, Goldstein, & Siegel, 1997). Such impairments have significant implications for the way in which individuals with autism learn and, by inference, for identifying the teaching strategies that are most appropriate for this population.

In a comprehensive study of verbal and visual information of a wide range of complexity in 52 high-functioning adolescents and adults with autism and 40 group-matched normal controls, Minshew and Goldstein (2001) found that the basic memory abilities were intact, but the capacity to learn and remember deteriorated as the complexity of the information increased. Impairments were found (a) if the amount of information of a single type was large or (b) if the inherent structure of the visual or verbal information was complex. A maze learning task documented the relationship between increasing complexity of the material and progressively worse memory impairments in the autism group. As the mazes became increasingly complex, the performance of the autism group became progressively worse relative to the controls.

In essence, the autism group had memory difficulty in both the auditory and the visual domains. Thus, the predictive factor for difficulty was not whether it was auditory or visual. Rather, difficulty occurred in both modalities if the material to be learned or remembered required a cognitive organizing structure or required the detection of organizational principles inherent in the material (Minshew & Goldstein, 2001). The flip side of this impairment was that learning and memory could be improved by presenting material to be learned or remembered in small chunks or by simplifying it (pre-processing it by providing the bottom line rather than examples from which the principle was to be extracted). In addition, memory and learning could be improved if increased time was provided, or if the material remained in sight for rehearsal at the individual's own pace.

There are two major implications of these findings. The first is, again, that the involvement of the brain in autism extends beyond the diagnostic triad and that there is a need to redefine this syndrome in DSM-IV and **ICD-10**. The second is that the brain involvement in autism extends not just to the underdevelopment of connections *within* neural systems but also to connections *between* neural systems. The observed impairment in memory and learning relates to the use of concepts and language in the service of memory and, thus, depends on interactions and connections between the memory, language, and reasoning systems of the brain.

Generalization of the Construct to More Impaired Individuals with Autism

The findings presented in this chapter are based on the study of verbal individuals with IQ scores primarily above 80 who were between 8 and 55 years old. The requirements for the participants to be verbal, over the age of 8, and to be without intellectual disability were based on the need for participants to be able to complete a large number of tests to reveal the pattern of intact abilities and impairments and be able to cooperate during functional imaging. We also wanted to match the participants with autism with a typically developing or normal IQ group. An IQ score below 80 made it impossible to find typically developing children or normal adults who matched. Intellectual disability has a variety of causes each with its own cognitive signature. Thus, the presence of intellectual disability presents a confound when looking for group differences unique to autism. Further, using mental age-matched younger children creates age disparities that present another confound when studying a developmental disorder. In brief, the use of individuals with autism with IQ scores in the average range allowed us to identify the cognitive and brain features that were unique to autism and not attributable to intellectual disability.

The study of a subgroup rather than a representative sample of the entire population of individuals with a disorder is a well-accepted scientific approach to establishing the essential features of a disorder that apply to the entire disorder. The justifications for the extrapolation to the entire disorder are based on the assumptions that all individuals have the disorder in question and that the disorder has a common **pathophysiology**.[6]

All evidence to date supports autism as being a single disorder of wide severity. Severity in and of itself has never been a justification for dividing a disorder into different conditions. Perhaps the most striking evidence of the commonality between low- and high-functioning autism is the co-occurrence of high- and low-functioning cases within the same families and even within twin pairs (Le Couteur et al., 1996). Other evidence is the shared neuropathology, family history, and severity of presentation in the early years (Rutter, 2005).

How do the findings apply to those with autism who were not tested (e.g., those who were lower functioning by virtue of age or IQ)? We cannot directly answer that question because those individuals were not tested since they cannot consistently cooperate for formal neuropsychological or fMRI procedures. Theoretically, as described in the following section, the information-processing capacity is progressively truncated to the point that no meaning is attached to sensory information, and there is no functional connectivity within the brain to attach meaning to sensory information.

Intellectual Disability in Autism Is Not a Separate Diagnosis

It is common practice for low-functioning individuals with autism also to receive a diagnosis of intellectual disability, as though there were two co-occurring diagnoses rather than a modifier to indicate level of function. As the severity of autism increases, information-processing capacity falls rapidly. The predicted consequence is intellectual disability bearing the hallmarks of the cognitive profile in autism – disproportionate impairments in higher-order sensory, motor, memory and learning, language, and abstraction abilities with preservation of elementary abilities in the same domains. When autism is at its most severe, there is essentially no capacity to attach meaning to sensory information. This progressive reduction in information-processing capacity with preservation of the autism profile (disproportionate impact on higher-order abilities and preserved simpler abilities) presents as intellectual disability. But in actuality, it is part and parcel of the cognitive impairment typical of autism. The profile is present at all levels of function in autism – in verbal individuals, it may be characterized as a learning disability, whereas in low-functioning individuals, it is characterized as intellectual disability. The brain basis of this cognitive profile is a reduction in the functional connections between the brain regions needed to perform tasks. In general, as we have seen, the brain in autism has fewer processing subregions and deploys them less flexibly to address task demands than normal controls.

---

[6] Pathophysiology should be distinguished from etiology. Pathophysiology refers to the mechanism of expression within the brain – the brain structures affected and the way in which they are affected. Etiology refers to the way in which this pathophysiology is triggered. There can be many different triggers for the same pathophysiology. If autism was not assumed to have a common pathophysiology, there would be no justification for any of the scientific studies conducted. That is, if every case of autism has a totally different brain basis, there would be no rationale for studies of groups of participants that look for a common finding or difference between those with autism and those without.

Implications of the Brain Basis of Autism

Expectations for an individual with autism cannot be based on an "intelligence score." There is a disconnection between IQ score and adaptive functioning in autism. In other words, IQ does not predict adaptive functioning. Individuals with autism will not demonstrate the same level of common sense or problem-solving ability as age peers of a similar level of intelligence. They cannot "act their age." Therefore, more immature behaviors should be expected, regardless of the overall cognitive functioning level.

A child with autism may be placed in a classroom with other fifth-graders because he can do fifth-grade-level academic work. However, his social behavior may be more like that of a kindergarten-age child. This should not be cause for alarm among the teaching staff, but should be an expected and planned-for consequence of the developmental disorder of autism. We see severe social and emotional immaturity persist into the adult years. For example, we know a middle-age woman with autism with an above-average IQ. She speaks of buildings as if they are "hunks" and talks about going on dates with them. If you close your eyes, you would think you were talking to a preadolescent with a crush on members of the latest boy band. She has combined her obsession with buildings with an adolescent or younger crush.

If individuals with autism are not doing something, such as following through on an assignment, it does not necessarily mean that they are being "uncooperative." They are just reacting to the biological response of their body. As human beings, we do the things we are good at and feel comfortable with and resist doing things we find difficult. However, typical people use executive functions to override this basic tendency. "If we don't do this, we are going to get fired, and if we get fired, we can't make our house payment." We talk ourselves into doing what we would otherwise resist.

Individuals with autism do not necessarily have the executive function, the decision-making process to override their initial tendency to resist doing a hard or unpleasant task. Besides, they do not respond to social consequences in the same way that individuals without autism do. Consequently, they are very unlikely to do something they judge to be difficult. It doesn't matter if this judgment is an accurate assessment or not. The fact that the individual with autism is resistant means that he perceives the behavior as being hard or unpleasant. The challenge is to figure out why he thinks the task is hard and to change the task so that he is able to do it.

Because individuals with autism cannot change the way they think and perceive the world, changes have to be made to accommodate them. Previously, autism was considered a "psychological" problem. Underlying this label was the notion that it had no connection to the brain; that it was in the "mind." Individuals with psychological problems are assumed to have some control over their actions (i.e., if you wanted to act differently, you could). As discussed above, we now have a much better understanding of the brain-behavior connection in autism.

Unfortunately, many people still hold to the idea that autism is a psychological problem that individuals choose to give into. For example, if a child with autism has already done a task and refuses to do it again, a teacher is likely to say, "He can do it. He just won't." However, the reason for the child's inaction may be that the environment has changed so that he doesn't recognize it as the same task. It may be that he does not understand what is expected of him. It may also be that he is thinking, "I've already done it, why should I do it again?" The child reacts in a certain way because of the information his brain gives him about the situation. He does not do it to be uncooperative or to create problems for the teacher. To get the child to do the task, the teacher must use her perceptive skills to try to determine what is a likely interpretation of the child's behavior and make changes so that the child will respond.

Summary and Conclusions: The Future in Intervention for Individuals with Autism

The current work in neuropsychological and neuroimaging research is greatly advancing our understanding of the brain-behavior connection in autism. The motivation for continuing this work is the eventual development of cognitive interventions that will promote the growth of underdeveloped brain circuitry and higher-level skills in individuals with autism. While such interventions are yet to be developed, it is our hope that teachers will use the current level of knowledge as the basis for creating intervention programs that accommodate but also challenge the brain development of their students with autism.

Tips for the Classroom

✓ Because students with autism cannot process large amounts of information efficiently, the amount of information presented to them must be reduced. Rather than expecting the student to learn large amounts of detail (something he may actually do at the expense of learning the main idea of the material), ask, "What are the main points he needs to learn from a lesson?" and focus on that material instead. Another example would be the use of a visual work task, as outlined by Gary Mesibov and Victoria Shea in Chapter 5.

✓ Because students with autism have difficulty organizing material or recognizing an implicit organization, you need to "pre-process" the information by highlighting and presenting it with an explicit organization.

✓ Because students with autism process language/information differently, they do better with language/information that is clear and concise as this reduces the processing load. They also do better when given more time to process language/information.

✓ Be careful about asking a student with autism to do several demanding tasks at once. For example, he cannot think of what to write and how to write it at the same time. Writing in stages may go smoother; that is, brainstorm the idea, write the key words needed to express the idea, and then put the key words into sentences. Visual task lists are excellent ways to break down information. A good example to remember is the soup can analogy. The label on the soup can contains very specific and precise directions (add water, heat).

✓ You can't use the level of expressive language of a student with autism to gauge the level of language input. Expressive output may represent unanalyzed language that has been learned and stored as large chunks. Therefore, you should gauge the appropriateness of your language level by the response of the child or adult. This can be particularly confusing when working with students with

Asperger Syndrome because they often use very sophisticated language but have a poor grasp of social and emotional concepts. This leads many teachers to expect more social understanding from these students.

✓ Even though a student with autism may be able to do a task, you don't know what cognitive resources she is using. Therefore, she may not be able to do a task if you increase its complexity. Remember: What is complex is defined individually and situationally.

✓ Persons with autism can do some visual processing better than auditory processing because it is reduced dynamically. However, they may have difficulty with visual processing if it is dynamic or complex, demanding more than one cognitive process or coordination of different processing areas across the cortex.

✓ Persons with autism can have difficulty with new situations and environments and demanding or socially stressful situations due to inflexible problem-solving skills. Viewing inflexibility as a neurological issue can be helpful when considering what adaptations and supports are needed. Labels like *oppositional* do little to help educational teams understand the neurological nature of inflexible thought. Inflexibility also indicates the need for skill practice in multiple environments to assist in generalization.

✓ Students with Asperger Syndrome or HFA may perform well in school in the early grades, but have increased difficulty in their teens. This may be due to the higher-level concepts used in secondary education. This confounded problem may also be seen in social interactions, as the nature of social relationships change in the teenage years.

✓ Repetitive practice of learning routines can increase both competence and motivation in students with autism. For example, if a student refuses to participate in an activity, you can assume that something about the activity is frustrating or overwhelming to him. If you can create learning routines, the student is more likely to recognize expectations early on and consequently be more willing to participate. The use of repetitive routines is also helpful in social interactions and activities.

✓ Always consider adaptive behavior scores when assessing the needs of students with autism. This is often missed, particularly if the student performs well on academic tasks.

✓ Proactively plan to support students with autism in social environments. Misinformed educators may place unreasonable expectations for "appropriate social behavior" on students who have significant delays in social maturity. For example, a student who does well in the third-grade classroom may require support from a paraprofessional or aide on the playground where social interaction is unstructured.

✓ It is important for all educators to understand the current research on social thinking and learning. Problems in this area of learning often lead to challenging behaviors in the school setting. Recognition that challenging behaviors are the result of a differently wired brain can lead parents and teachers towards more innovative and ultimately more effective long-term interventions and supports.

Chapter Highlights

- Studies of the brains of individuals with autism provide evidence of differences in how their brains are organized and function.

- In the 1960s, it was accepted that autism was of neurologic origin, rather than a psychological or behavioral disorder.

- Once autism was seen as brain-based, the focus shifted to cognition and parts of the brain involved in autism; specifically, the deficit or alteration in the brain and thinking.

- The brain-based and cognitive view of autism led to two different approaches to understanding autism: (a) the core deficit hypothesis/primary deficit and (b) a hypothesis that looks at all simultaneously occurring impairments and intact abilities in an attempt to come up with a common denominator regarding thinking and the brain in autism/ASD.

- The chapter authors discuss several studies of the cognitive basis of autism using individuals with HFA (IQ score over 70). Various intact and impaired abilities were found, demonstrating that individuals with HFA appeared to acquire information on par with neurotypical controls; however, impairments were apparent in more complex processes (see Table 2.1 for specifics).

- The pattern of impairments across domains in individuals with HFA in the studies is indicative of a reduced capability in the area of information processing, with increasing difficulties as the complexity of the task increases.

- In addition to impairments in the social, communication, and reasoning domains typical of the standard diagnostic profile in autism/ASD, the studies also showed impairments in memory and motor domains.

- Tasks requiring multitasking and increased speed of processing put constraints on the information-processing abilities of individuals with autism/ASD.

- Hidden information-processing demands refer to the ability to understand complex sentences or work with tasks that require holding multiple steps in working memory (multitasking).

- Individuals with autism/ASD may store verbal information in chunks and use it in expressive language; sometimes they appear to have greater understanding than they do. Observing actions rather than spoken words may give a better picture of actual abilities.

- The complex information-process concept is of value for intervention purposes by reminding those working with individuals with autism/ASD that it is necessary to convey information clearly and succinctly and recognize that individuals on the spectrum are generally operating in a world governed by facts and rules.

- Complexity as a concept refers to the difficulty of processing information. This difficulty can be caused by certain aspects of the task requirement such as amount of information, structure of information, time constraints on completing task, or multiple simultaneous processing demands.

- Complexity interferes with efficiency in completing tasks for everyone, but the lower capacity for information processing in individuals with autism/ASD means they become limited in this area long before age- and IQ-matched peers.

- *Central coherence* is a term coined in 1989 by Uta Frith to refer to impairments in high-order cognitive and language abilities along with strengths in detail perception and visuospatial abilities in individuals with autism/ASD. Essentially, these individuals have difficulty integrating parts into a whole.

- While the profile of central coherence is similar to the profile found by the chapter authors with regard to information processing, it does not include the sensory, motor, memory impairments, or expressive deficits. Thus, the authors determined that the difficulty for individuals with autism/ASD is better termed information processing so as to address all intact and impaired structures in brain and cognition.

- Functional magnetic resonance imaging (fMRI) allows for recording of brain activity during the performance of cognitive and language tasks. fMRI studies have allowed investigators to observe what occurs in the brains of individuals with autism during different tasks and compare that to what occurs in the brains of neurotypical counterparts.

- fMRI studies have shown that the brains of individuals with autism/ASD have underdeveloped neural pathways (also known as connectivity), less flexibility in changing and meeting different demands, fewer resources to draw on, and less synchrony or harmony in regions working together.

- fMRI studies have also found that individuals with autism/ASD appear to use compensatory strategies, or different cognitive approaches, to completing tasks. These compensatory strategies may assist or interfere with task completion, depending on the strategy and the task.

- Studies have shown impairments in memory and learning exist in individuals with autism/ASD. As in previous studies, the basic abilities appear intact but, as demands and information become increasingly complex, the capacity of individuals with autism/ASD to learn and remember deteriorated.

- Based on studies involving learning and memory, the chapter authors believe the current diagnostic criteria for autism (based on social, communication, and stereotyped patterns of behavior/interests (the diagnostic triad)) needs to be refined.

- While the studies cited in the chapter involved individuals with autism who had IQ scores above 80 and were verbal, the chapter authors believe the findings can be generalized to those with more significant impairments based on the belief that the basis for autism/ASD lies in deficits related to information processing. The progressive reduction in the ability to process information leads to increased severity in functioning, thus creating an intellectual disability.

- This intellectual disability represents what is true for all individuals with autism/ASD: reduced information-processing capacity; a specific cognitive profile. What differentiates low-functioning from high-functioning individuals on the spectrum is level of impairment in connectivity and higher order abilities.

- Implications of the brain basis of autism/ASD involve realizing that individuals with autism/ASD think and perceive the world differently. It is important that interventionists take this into account when working with such students.

Chapter Review Questions

1. What is meant by core "deficit"? Is this approach still considered applicable to identifying the cause of autism?

2. What are the most popular theories with respect to the primary impairments in autism/ASD?

3. According to the chapter authors, what is different about the brains of people with autism that leads to differences in how they think or perceive things?

4. Why is autism/ASD seen as an information-processing deficit?

5. What are "hidden information-processing demands"?

6. What is the value of the complex information-processing concept?

7. What is meant by the term *complexity*?

8. What is "central coherence"?

9. Define information processing in terms of persons with autism/ASD.

10. What is fMRI and why is it important to understanding autism/ASD?

11. How are the brains of individuals with autism/ASD different from those of neurotypical individuals?

12. What are compensatory strategies used by individuals with autism/ASD?

13. Why do the chapter authors believe that the diagnostic criteria for autism/ASD need to be redefined?

14. Why do the chapter authors state intellectual disability in autism is not a separate diagnosis?

15. Give three implications of the brain basis of autism.

References

American Psychiatric Association. (1994). *Diagnostic and statistical manual of mental disorders, fourth edition* (DSM-IV). Washington, DC: Author.

Aylward, E. H., Minshew, N. J., Field, K., Sparks, B. F., & Singh, N. (2002). Effects of age on brain volume and head circumference in autism. *Neurology, 59,* 175-183.

Cody, H., Pelphrey, K., & Piven, J. (2002). Structural and functional magnetic resonance imaging of autism. *International Journal of Developmental Neuroscience, 20,* 421-431.

Courchesne, E., Townsend, J., Akshoomoff, N. A., Saitoh, O., Yeung-Courchesne, R., Lincoln, A. J., et al. (1994). Impairment in shifting attention in autistic and cerebellar patients. *Behavioral Neuroscience, 108,* 848-865.

Courchesne, E., Karns, C. M., Davis, H. R., Ziccardi, R., Carper, R. A., Tigue, Z. D., et al. (2001). Unusual brain growth patterns in early life in patients with autistic disorder. *Neurology, 57,* 245-254.

Dawson, G., Webb, S., & McPartland, J. (2005). Understanding the nature of face processing impairment in autism: Insights from behavioral and electrophysiological studies. *Developmental Neuropsychology, 27,* 403-424.

Frith, U. (1989). *Autism: Explaining the enigma.* Oxford, UK: Blackwell Publishers.

Garcia-Villamisar, D., & Della Sala, S. (2002). Dual-task performance in adults with autism. *Cognitive Neuropsychology, 7,* 63-74.

Grandin, T. (1995). *Thinking in pictures: And other reports from my life with autism.* New York: Vintage Books.

Hammill, D. D. (1985). *DTLA-2: Detroit Tests of Learning Aptitude.* Austin, TX: Pro-Ed.

Just, M. A., Cherkassky, V. L., Keller, T. A., & Minshew, N. J. (2004). Cortical activation and synchronization during sentence comprehension in high-functioning autism: Evidence of underconnectivity. *Brain, 127,* 1811-1821.

Just, M. A., Keller, T. A., Cherkassky V., Kana R. K., & Minshew, N. J. (2007). Functional and anatomical cortical underconnectivity in autism: Evidence from an fMRI study of an executive function task and corpus callosum morphometry. *Cerebral Cortex, 17,* 951-961.

Kana, R., Keller, T., Cherkassky, V., Minshew, N., & Just, M. A. (2006). Sentence comprehension in autism: Thinking in pictures with decreased functional connectivity. *Brain, 129,* 2484-2493.

Kana, R. K., Keller, T. A., Minshew, N. J., & Just, M. A. (2007). Inhibitory control in high-functioning autism: Decreased activation and underconnectivity in inhibition networks. Manuscript submitted for publication. *Biological Psychiatry, 62,* 198-206.

Kana, R., Keller, T., Williams, D., Minshew, N. J., & Just, M. A. (2005). Attribution of mental states in high-functioning autism: Evidence for cortical underconnectivity [Abstract]. *International Meeting for Autism Research, 4,* 117.

Koshino, H., Carpenter, P. A., Minshew, N. J., Cherkassky, V. L., Keller, T. A., & Just, M. A. (2005). Functional connectivity in an fMRI working memory task with high-functioning autism. *NeuroImage, 24,* 810-821.

Le Couteur, A., Bailey, A., Goode, S., Pickles, A., Robertson, S., Gottesman, I., & Rutter, M. (1996). A broader phenotype of autism: The clinical spectrum in twins. *Journal of Child Psychology and Psychiatry, 37,* 785-801.

Le Couteur, A., Rutter, M., Lord, C., Rios, P., Robertson, S., Holdgrafer, M., et al. (1989). Autism Diagnostic Interview: A standardized investigator-based instrument. *Journal of Autism and Developmental Disorders, 19,* 363-387.

Lord, C., Risi, S., Lambrecht, L., Cook, E. H., Jr., Leventhal, B. L., DiLavore, P. C., et al. (2000). The Autism Diagnostic Observation Schedule – Generic: A standard measure of social and communication deficits associated with the spectrum of autism. *Journal of Autism and Developmental Disorders, 30,* 205-223.

Lord, C., Rutter, M., Goode, S., Heemsbergen, J., Jordan, H., Mawhood, L., et al. (1989). Autism Diagnostic Observation Schedule: A standardized observation of communicative and social behavior. *Journal of Autism and Developmental Disorders, 19,* 185-212.

Lord, C., Rutter, M., & Le Couteur, A. (1994). Autism Diagnostic Interview – Revised: A revised version of a diagnostic interview for caregivers of individuals with possible pervasive developmental disorders. *Journal of Autism and Developmental Disorders, 24,* 659-685.

Luna, B., Doll, S. K., Hegedus, S. J., Minshew, N. J., & Sweeney, J. A. (2006). Maturation of executive function in autism. *Biol Psychiatry, 61,* 474-481

Meltzoff, A., & Decety, J. (2003). What imitation tells us about social cognition: A rapprochement between developmental psychology and cognitive neuroscience. *Philosophical Transactions of the Royal Society Biological Sciences, 358,* 491-500.

Minshew, N. J., & Goldstein, G. (2001). The pattern of intact and impaired memory functions in autism. *Journal of Child Psychology and Psychiatry, 42,* 1095-1101.

Minshew, N. J., Goldstein, G., & Siegel, D. (1997). Neuropsychologic functioning in autism: Profile of a complex information processing disorder. *Journal of the International Neuropsychological Society, 3,* 303-316.

Minshew, N. J., Williams, D. L., & Goldstein, G. (2007). [Replication study of neuropsychologic functioning of adults with autism.] Unpublished raw data.

Minshew, N. J., Meyer, J., & Goldstein, G. (2002). Abstract reasoning in autism: A dissociation between concept formation and concept identification. *Neuropsychology, 16,* 327-334.

Minshew, N. J., Sweeney, J. A., Bauman, M. L., & Webb, S. J. (2005). Neurologic aspects of autism. In F. R. Volkmar, R. Paul, A. Klin, & D. Cohen (Eds.), *Handbook of autism and pervasive developmental disorders: Volume one: Diagnosis, development, neurobiology, and behavior* (3rd ed., pp. 473-514). Hoboken, NJ: John Wiley & Sons.

Rutter, M. (2005). Genetic influences and autism. In F. R. Volkmar, R. Paul, A. Klin, & D. Cohen (Eds.), *Handbook of autism and pervasive developmental disorders: Volume one, Diagnosis, development, neurobiology, and behavior* (3rd ed., pp. 425-452). Hoboken, NJ: John Wiley & Sons.

Schultz, R. T. (2005). Developmental deficits in social perception in autism: The role of the amygdala and fusiform face area. *Developmental Neuroscience, 23,* 125-141.

Sparks, B. F., Friedman, S. D., Shaw, D. W., Aylward, E. H., Echelard, D., Artru, A. A., et al. (2002). Brain structural abnormalities in young children with autism spectrum disorder. *Neurology, 59,* 184-192.

Williams, D. L., Goldstein, G., & Minshew, N. J. (2006). Neuropsychologic functioning in children with autism: Further evidence for disordered complex information processing. *Child Neuropsychology, 12,* 279-298.

World Health Organization. (1992). *International classification of diseases and related health problems* (10th ed.). Geneva: Author.

Learner Objectives

After reading this chapter, the learner should be able to:

- Explain what is meant by a "spectrum disorder"

- Discuss the importance of early intervention for children diagnosed with ASD

- Explain issues surrounding early identification of ASD, including early diagnosis and referral

- State the developmental red flags that may indicate ASD in infants and toddlers

- Discuss the importance of providing families with information on intervention services and community supports as part of the assessment process and the type of information to be provided

- List and describe the key features of effective programs for young children with ASD

- State the types of questions families need to ask when selecting intervention programs for their young children with ASD

- Describe what is meant by the term *outcome-oriented framework*

- Discuss ways in which families may decide on meaningful outcomes for their child with ASD

- Explain what a curriculum-based assessment (CBA) is and why such a tool is useful

- List and describe the components of Project DATA

- Describe the areas to which Project DATA preschool environments pay particular attention

Chapter 3

Getting a Good Start: Effective Practices in Early Intervention

Ilene S. Schwartz • Bonnie J. McBride

Eric is 2-1/2 years old and has sparkling blue eyes. He does not talk yet, but if he wants something, he pulls an adult by the hand over to what he wants and then stands and waits. Sometimes it is easy for his mother or his teacher to guess what he wants, but lately he has started crying, screaming, and falling to the ground if the adult is not able to get him what he wants right away. He will keep lying on the ground screaming until the adult figures out what he wants. It is getting harder because once he starts screaming and falling on the ground, it is difficult to calm him down even if he gets what he wants. Caregivers are beginning to avoid interacting with him because they don't want to be the ones who "start" his screaming.

Jamal is 3 years old and can climb higher and faster than any other 3-year-old around. He is already reading and can answer any question about team statistics or the starting lineup of his local baseball team. However, he cannot consistently answer simple questions from adults, interact with children his own age, or tolerate changes to his routine. His parents are extremely concerned because he and his mother have been asked to stop coming to music lessons at the local community center and to find a "more appropriate" placement than the local co-op preschool. His grandparents wonder if there is anything really "wrong" with him or whether his parents simply are overindulgent.

Serena is 30 months old and has a head full of brown ringlets. Her parents report that she used to walk around the house, point to objects, label them, and laugh. She does not do that any more. In fact, these days she rarely speaks except to request certain video tapes or preferred foods. She hardly ever looks at people or things, unless she can find something that is spinning. Then she is totally mesmerized. Her parents cannot remember the last time they heard her laugh.

These young children are some of the faces of autism spectrum disorders (ASD). The number of children with ASD is increasing dramatically. The most recent numbers released by the Centers for Disease Control and Prevention (CDC; www.cdc.gov/DiseasesConditions) in 2007 reported that the prevalence is 1 in 150. ASD is a spectrum disorder, which means that children who receive this diagnosis differ dramatically in their abilities, preferences, needs, and areas of delay. As Eric, Jamal, and Serena remind us, there is no "typical" child with ASD and there is no one "right" way of educating a child with ASD. Every child and family brings a unique story to the early intervention process, and that story must be woven into the fabric of intervention and support for the process to be successful.

The importance of early intervention in treating children with ASD has become axiomatic in the autism community. In fact, in the often confusing and contradictory world of autism, it is one of the few things that we know for sure and on which professionals, parents, and advocates agree. There is overwhelming evidence that earlier is better, both in terms of autism diagnosis and intervention (Dawson & Osterling, 1997; National Research Council [NRC], 2001; Rogers, 1999). In this chapter we provide evidence of the importance of early intervention, identify recommended practices for providing intervention services, and give examples of how to translate these recommendations into classroom practice.

Many educational and behavioral interventions have demonstrated effectiveness in improving developmental outcomes for children with ASD (e.g., Boulware, Schwartz, Sandall, & McBride, 2006; Lovaas, 1987; Ozonoff & Cathcart, 1998; Schwartz, Sandall, McBride, & Boulware, 2004; Smith, Groen, & Wynn, 2000; Strain & Hoyson, 2000). While many of these interventions are effective for children of any age, there is increasing agreement that intervention has a greater impact in younger children (Harris & Handelman, 2000; Lord, 1995; Volkmar, Lord, Bailey, Schultz, & Klin, 2004) and that the gains made in level of independence, cognitive functioning, and communication associated with early intervention can result in considerable cost savings to the family and systems that provide services for children with ASD (Jacobson, 2000).

The first step towards providing high-quality early intervention to all children with ASD and their families is to accurately identify children at the earliest age possible, regardless of cultural and linguistic diversity, class, or geography. In the following, we will look at the process of early diagnosis.

The Who, What, and Where of Early Diagnosis

ASD is a lifelong neuro-developmental disability characterized by a complex compilation of learning differences and delays in social interaction, communication, and perseverative or repetitive behaviors. Early and accurate detection is critical for early intervention. Despite leading research and advocacy groups stating that ASD can be reliably diagnosed at 2 years of age, the average age for diagnosis in the United States is much later, averaging 3-6 years (Lord, 1995; Moore & Goodson, 2003; Pinto-Martin & Levy, 2004; Stone et al., 1999; www.firstsigns.org). For children who are culturally and linguistically diverse, the diagnostic picture is grimmer, with diagnosis coming later and after many more visits to professionals (Mandell, Listerud, Levy, & Pinto-Martin, 2002). Clearly, the first step to high-quality early intervention is improved early detection and diagnosis.

Work on early detection and assessment must occur on at least two fronts: improving the accuracy of the screening and diagnostic tools used and influencing policy and practice to get these tools implemented. Some of the best work integrating the two strands of this work may be found on the web site www.firstsigns.org. **First Signs**, an organization that was started by parents of children with ASD, has been instrumental in working with the CDC and local medical education groups to get the most up-to-date information disseminated to pediatricians, family practitioners, and other medical professionals. In addition, the organization has developed an outstanding web site, public service announcements, and other media information to spread the word about the developmental red flags. Since the diagnosis of ASD is complex and cannot be tied to any individual behavior at any age, this approach encourages parents, child care providers, and others to refer children to a medical practitioner if any of the following red flags are observed:

- No big smiles, or other warm, joyful expressions by 6 months or thereafter

- No back-and-forth sharing of sounds, smiles, or other facial expressions by 9 months or thereafter

- No babbling by 12 months

- No back-and-forth gestures, such as pointing, showing, reaching, or waving by 12 months

- No words by 16 months

- No two-word meaningful phrases by 24 months

- A loss of speech or babbling or social skills at any age. (www.firstsigns.org)

To Whom Should a Child Be Referred?

One of the many confusing issues families face once they or a caregiver notice any of the red flags listed above is "What do we do now?" Most families seek initial advice from their pediatrician or primary care physician. For very young children, most pediatricians, healthcare providers, or community programs refer families to a psychologist, developmental pediatrician, psychiatrist, or neurologist for a full evaluation to determine if a child has an ASD. The most common classification system used to diagnosis ASD is the *Diagnostic and Statistical Manual of Mental Disorders* (text revision, fourth edition; DSM-IV-TR; American Psychiatric Association [APA], 2000).

A professional licensed to provide diagnoses, who has experience with ASD and is trained in administering assessments designed to detect an ASD, is the most qualified person to provide an accurate diagnosis, especially in very young children. Unfortunately, in many communities there is a shortage of professionals with these credentials. It is important for parents and professionals, such as teachers, speech therapists, or occupational therapists, who suspect a young child is at risk for ASD to be actively involved in the diagnostic process and to be encouraged to ask questions regarding the procedures used to arrive at a diagnosis.

Another avenue for a child to be identified as having an ASD is through the educational system. Included in the amendments to the Individuals with Disabilities Education Act (IDEA) is the category of autism, which qualifies a child for educational services. While the educational criteria have some similarities to those of the DSM-IV-TR, there are important differences, particularly for young children. The classification of "autism" may not be used for children under the age of 6 or 9, depending on state law, so a younger child suspected of having an ASD may have to qualify for services under a broader category such as "developmentally delayed." Also, an educational classification of ASD may not be accepted by many health or social service agencies that control access to potential services for children with ASD may access. As is the case for a clinical diagnosis of an ASD, there are shortages of professionals in school systems who have the expertise to identify ASD, particularly in very young children. Further, the instruments used by a given school district to determine eligibility for special education services may not be appropriate for detecting the kind of difficulties children with ASD experience (Dahle, 2003).

Why It Is Important to Make a Referral and Get a Diagnosis Early

The National Research Council (NRC, 2001), in a report summarizing the state of knowledge and making recommendations for practice, recommended that children begin to receive specialized, intensive early intervention as soon as they receive a diagnosis or a suspected diagnosis of an ASD. Even if a child has not received a formal evaluation or diagnosis but is suspected to be at risk for an ASD, intervention focusing on social development and communication should begin right away. This means that rather than taking a wait-and-see approach to screening and referral, parents, caregivers, the medical community, and the educational/early intervention community should refer children who demonstrate the red flag behaviors listed above as early as possible. The research is clear that early intervention is effective and can have a profound impact on the quality of the lives of children with ASD and their families. Less clear is how to determine the right amount of intervention and how to match treatment approaches to individual children and families.

Making the Transition from Assessment to Intervention – What Families Need to Know and Should Not Be Afraid to Ask

Many parents walk away from the assessment process scared and confused. One parent told us that he and his wife went home, curled up in bed with their beautiful little boy, and cried for 24 hours. Other parents decide that they are going to become ASD experts and hit the Internet, only to be stymied by 18,300,000 hits on a Google search about autism, conflicting reports in the scientific and popular press, and long waiting lists for services in their communities.

Part of the assessment process must include helping families make the transition into services in their local community. This process should include helping families identify potential service providers and providing temporary support to the family until they can enlist support and technical assistance from other professional sources.

The first referral for every child should be to the publicly funded services available in the local community. These services vary by state, but include early intervention (for children under 3) or public school services (for children 3 and above) in every state. They may also include a range of other services, such as respite care, specialized funding for intensive home programming, and wraparound services that provide support to children with ASD and their families. Information should also be provided about the characteristics of effective programming for young children with ASD (NRC, 2001); local educational programs for parents of children who have been recently diagnosed with ASD; local and national parent support groups; and web sites or books that contain clear, reliable, and accurate information. Most important, any information provided to parents at the time of diagnosis should be accompanied with written materials and followed up by a phone call or visit within two weeks to see if families have additional questions.

Another important outcome of the initial assessment and diagnosis is a clear identification of a child's strengths and challenges. For example, Eric, Jamal, and Serena, the children you met at the beginning of this chapter, have different strengths and needs. As a result, the constellation of intervention services may look very different for these three children.

Something that should not be part of the initial assessment is a statement of the child's predicted long-term prognosis. Although we know that all children will benefit from intensive early intervention, and that for some children it may mitigate many of the symptoms of ASD, families need to know that ASD is a lifelong disorder and that there is no way of predicting how an individual child will respond to intervention. Given that more children identified now with ASD are within the normal range of intelligence than previous statistics indicated, and that our intervention techniques continue to improve, there is no way to know what the future holds for a specific child with ASD and his family (Chakrabarti & Fombonne, 2001; Howlin, 2000; Tsatsanis, 2003).

What Are the Key Features of Effective Programs for Young Children with Autism?

Although there is no definitive answer to the question above, guidelines exist that can help intervention teams, including families. Two key issues seem to define the debate around effective programs for young children with ASD: (a) the amount of intervention a child should receive (i.e., number of hours) and (b) what approach or methodology is most beneficial.

In 2001, the National Research Council, as part of a comprehensive review of the research and proposed recommendations, set the benchmark of 25 hours a week of intervention for young children with ASD. These hours of intervention may be made up of a combination of center-, home-, and community-based services that provide multidisciplinary instruction in the core deficit areas associated with ASD. Other sources that may be useful in determining the level of intensity needed include information from model programs that have produced good outcomes for toddlers and/or preschoolers with ASD (Boulware et al., 2006; Schwartz et al., 2004; Strain & Cordisco, 1993). In these programs the number of hours of intervention range from 16 to 40 hours per week. Examining the individual child's and family's strengths and needs determines the appropriate level of intensity. If family priorities change, or if the child is not making progress, the level of intensity should be reevaluated.

A number of educational interventions for children with ASD have demonstrated improved outcomes for children and families. The majority of both specific interventions and comprehensive programs for ASD come from the field of applied behavior analysis (ABA) (Hoyson, Jamieson, & Strain, 1984; Schwartz et al., 2004; Smith et al., 2000). However, there is growing agreement among professionals and researchers that there is no single educational strategy that is best for all children with ASD (Dunlap, 1999; NRC 2001).

Instead of focusing the debate on what are the "best" approaches or techniques for children with ASD, some researchers have focused on what elements of programming need to be in place, regardless of the educational or treatment approach used. The key features of an effective program for young children with autism have been outlined by organizations such as the National Research Council and other professionals with extensive backgrounds in autism. The most often cited are the NRC Report (2001), Dawson and Osterling's (1997) review of programs serving children with autism, and the National Early Childhood Technical Assistance System (NEC-TAS), in partnership with the Office of Special Education Programs (OSEP), review of early intervention and autism (Hurth, Shaw, Izeman, Whaley, & Rogers, 1999).

In addition to beginning intervention as early as possible, the following are key elements in effective programs for young children with ASD:
1. Sufficient hours and intensity of services
2. Comprehensible environments with access to typical peers
3. Specialized curriculum with an appropriate scope and sequence
4. Family involvement
5. Problem-solving approach to challenging behaviors
6. Appropriate evaluation tools to monitor progress

Sufficient Number of Hours and Intensity of Services

As highlighted above, the NRC Report (2001) recommends 25 hours per week of intervention for a child with ASD. In addition to the number of hours, other dimensions of intensity are also important. These include the amount of individualized or small-group instruction that is available (some 1:1 instruction is recommended), the training and expertise of the professionals implementing the program, and the child's level of engagement in the instructional tasks (Dunlap, 1999; Wolery & Garfinkle, 2002).

Comprehensible Environments with Access to Typical Peers

Environments need to be understandable to the children (comprehensible), and children with ASD need to have access to typical peers. The physical setting must be considered when determining if the environment is understandable to the child with ASD. This includes how the physical space is arranged, how and what materials are used, and how activities are scheduled and arranged. All of these will influence a child's level of independence, opportunities for peer interaction, and child-initiated communication. For example, if a classroom is organized with distinctly defined play areas and clear traffic patterns, children are more likely to be independent at initiating play (Schwartz, Garfinkle, & Davis, 2002).

The ability to have meaningful interaction with same-age peers is another important component of a comprehensive program for children with ASD (Wolfberg, 2004). Since the primary area of difficulty for young children with ASD is social-relatedness skills, having responsive peers to interact with becomes particularly critical. However, there is strong evidence to indicate that placing children in environments with other children is not sufficient for children with autism to benefit (Strain & Schwartz, 2001). Planned opportunities for peer interaction must be provided that include adequate support from trained adults.

Specialized Curriculum with an Appropriate Scope and Sequence

An appropriate curriculum for a young child with ASD would include instruction in the core deficit areas of communication, social interaction, and play. Children with ASD have difficulty in a variety of skill areas that affect relationships and learning. For example, many young children have not learned to imitate others, either for social purposes or as a learning strategy. For children who have not mastered imitation, this should be addressed as part of the curriculum. Another important area where focused teaching should occur is communication. Many children with ASD have not developed language and may not have adequate ways to communicate their wants and needs.

Family Involvement

Family members are the most consistent influence in a child's life (Dunlap, 1999; Wang, Mannan, Poston, Turnbull, & Summers, 2004). When a child is first diagnosed with ASD, parents often experience grief and confusion over what the future will hold for their child. Especially today, family members are bombarded with new treatments and promises of a cure. It is critical that professionals actively engage parents in the intervention planning process so that family priorities are addressed and parents have an avenue for discussing treatments they may have questions about.

Family involvement also enhances **generalization** of skills. Children with ASD often show difficulties in the ability to use skills learned in one context or with one person in other contexts or with other people (Strain & Hoyson, 2000). A collaborative partnership with families enhances the effectiveness of intervention by ensuring that strategies are implemented in a variety of contexts, including the home and the community. Indeed, in a recent survey conducted by the Indiana Resource Center for Autism (IRCA; www.iidc.indiana.edu/irca), families rated their own participation as the single most effective service received. In particular, they cited how important family impact is on their child's growth (Hume, Bellini, & Pratt, 2005).

Problem-Solving Approach to Challenging Behaviors

Many young children with ASD demonstrate challenging behaviors that are more intense and pervasive than what is typical for a young child. The intensity and frequency of behaviors, such as crying, screaming, or aggression, can result in these children being excluded from childcare settings and other community activities. Often addressing these behaviors is the number-one challenge faced by schools and parents.

Fortunately, research over the past 15 years has changed the focus of how we approach these challenging behaviors (Carr & Durrand, 1985; Carr et al., 2002). Instead of addressing only how to eliminate the behavior of concern, the focus of intervention is now on understanding what **communicative** *function* the behavior has for the child. That information is then used to target proactive behaviors that can be taught to replace the challenging behavior (i.e., a problem-solving approach). For instance, if a child screams every time he sees something he wants, teaching him to ask for something instead is a proactive approach to addressing the problem behavior (screaming).

Appropriate Evaluation Tools to Monitor Progress

The purpose of evaluation tools is not to determine if a child has ASD or to determine how the child is progressing compared to other children. Rather, evaluation tools are designed to determine how much the child is learning; in other words, to compare the child's progress at Time 1 to his progress at Time 2 on a specific set of behaviors and skills.

Systematic and repeated monitoring of a child's progress is an essential component of every high-quality intervention program. Progress monitoring should be done frequently and in a manner that allows for changes to occur in the child's program, if that is needed. A variety of strategies are used to monitor progress, such as recording each occurrence of the target behavior when it is observed during teaching, video taping and then recording the occurrence of target behavior from the video-tape, a skills checklist, or a rating scale.

Several factors should be considered when selecting an evaluation tool. First, it is important to ensure that the evaluation tool adequately identifies if the child is making progress or if a change in the program is necessary. For instance, if a child with ASD is learning to use an **augmentative communication** device (i.e., pictures or a computerized system) but is not using it to initiate communication across the day, choosing an evaluation method such as an observation tool will identify what is occurring in the environment that may be interfering with the child's use of the device (e.g., it is only available at certain times of the day). This, in turn, will allow for making changes that will enable the child to communicate his wants and needs and continue to make progress. Second, the ease of use of the evaluation tool is important to ensure it will be used consistently to monitor progress. In summary, the important criterion for selecting an evaluation tool is whether or not it will provide the information that is needed to make changes to the child's program in a timely manner.

Translating Recommendations into Comprehensive Programs for Children with ASD

Once a child has received a diagnosis, families are often put in the position of trying to piece together services – some publicly funded and others funded through private insurance or out of pocket – to create a comprehensive program for their preschooler with ASD. Although the literature suggests a number of "brand name" intervention approaches (e.g., **Lovaas**, 1998; Leaf & McEachin, 1999; **TEACCH** [Treatment and Education of Autistic and related Communication-handicapped CHildren], Schopler & Van Bourgondien, 1991; **floor time**, Wieder & Greenspan, 2003), most families do not have the opportunity to implement a pure intervention. Instead, they combine service providers in their community, often with different theoretical and practical orientations, to provide an eclectic program for their child that may or may not include the program characteristics described above (Hume et al., 2005).

When we counsel parents about enrolling their child in intervention programs, we urge them to consider the following questions:

- What are your primary concerns for your child?

- Does the intervention or collection of interventions you are considering address those concerns?

- Are the procedures of the intervention acceptable to you?

- Are you convinced that these interventions are a good match for your child and your family?

- What types of evidence about the effectiveness of the intervention have you seen? Is this evidence convincing to you?

- How will the interventionists communicate with you and demonstrate the progress your child is making? Is that acceptable to you?

By asking these questions, we encourage parents to identify the desired outcome at the beginning of intervention so that appropriate methods or strategies can be built into the program. An optimal time to begin this process is when the educational team or the intervention team is developing a child's **individualized education program (IEP)** or **individualized family service plan (IFSP)**.

Adopting an **outcome-oriented framework** is not a one-time endeavor; it is a problem-solving process and should be updated as often as priorities change or as often as the child's needs change. Given the diverse needs of children on the autism spectrum and the lifelong nature of the disability, it is not unreasonable to expect that one child and family will experience many types of interventions during early childhood. For example, a family may decide to implement an intensive behavioral early intervention program to supplement an inclusive preschool program upon receiving the diagnosis, and after a year decide that their child needs less one-on-one intervention. Then, they may decrease or discontinue the intensive program and enroll their child in social skills groups supplemented by supported play dates at home after preschool. Another family may make a different choice. There is no "right" choice; there is no one right way. The only way to determine if an intervention is working is to document, through frequent data collection and ongoing data analysis, that the child is making meaningful progress towards the educational outcomes that the parents and other team members think are important.

What Are Meaningful Outcomes for Young Children with ASD?

Determining what to teach young children with ASD is an important part of planning and implementing effective early intervention programs. Almost all professionals agree on certain pivotal, fundamental skills: Young children need to learn to follow simple directions, imitate, communicate their wants and needs, and perform basic self-care skills, such as becoming toilet trained.

After that, opinions tend to diverge. Should the early intervention program focus on discrete cognitive concepts or emphasize social skills? Is it more important to help children develop friendships or conduct intensive discrete trial training? There is no easy or data-based answer to these questions. Families and other members of intervention teams must look at the strengths and needs of an individual student, the priorities of the families, and existing data to decide what is meaningful for a specific child with ASD and his or her family.

A meaningful outcome is one that adds significance or purpose to somebody's life. That is, it helps the child be more independent and achieve a better **quality of life** (Carr, 2007). Carr (2007) defined quality of life as subjective well-being consisting of "meaningful gains in the areas of material well-being, health and safety, social well-being, leisure and recreation, and autonomy" (p. 4). Although this way of looking at outcomes may be too abstract when discussing program planning for young children, it is important for families to begin early to think about the scope of intervention and the life goals and dreams they have for their children. Even when children are very young, it is important to help families consider the important outcomes (e.g., belonging, having friends, happiness, good health) that they want for their child, rather than becoming overly focused on the types of discrete skills often addressed by early, intensive behavioral intervention programs.

Identification of potential skills or outcomes for a child starts with a sound assessment to determine what the child needs to learn. A **curriculum-based assessment (CBA)** provides the type of information needed to develop a comprehensive program. A CBA identifies functional skills across multiple developmental domains (i.e., adaptive, communication, cognitive, social, and motor) that are necessary for activities common in early childhood (Bagnato, Neisworth, & Munson, 1997). Several commercially available assessments include an evaluation component that is criterion-referenced and also linked to a curriculum. An example of a CBA is the *Assessment, Evaluation, and Programming System* (AEPS; Bricker, 2002).

The use of a CBA will allow the intervention team to identify skills that are useful and immediately relevant to the child's life (Macy, Bricker, & Squires, 2005). Although CBAs exist that are developed specifically for use with students with ASD and related disorders (e.g., ABLLS; Partington & Sundberg, 1998), it is possible to use an assessment developed for a more general population as the core assessment and supplement with checklists designed to assess core deficit areas for students with ASD (e.g., Schwartz et al., 2004).

Project DATA: An Example of a High-Quality Early Intervention Program for Children with ASD

In 1997, at the University of Washington, we opened the doors to Project DATA (Developmentally Appropriate Treatment for Autism; http://depts.washington.edu/dataproj/) with the help of a Department of Education, Office of Special Education, model demonstration grant. We have been running continually since and are now funded by a combination of school district tuition and private contributions.

Project DATA was designed to meet a need that we had noticed in our community: How could we help school districts meet the needs of young children with ASD and their families in a manner that was effective, acceptable to all parties, and sustainable? The project was developed to combine the best practices from ABA behavior analysis and early childhood special education into a program that recognized the unique learning characteristics and support needs of children with ASD and also recognized that children with ASD are children first.

Integrated Early Childhood Program

Project DATA consists of five components, as illustrated in Figure 3.1. The core component is an integrated early childhood program. We want every child with ASD to have opportunities to interact successfully with typically developing children. To be successful, the interactions may need to be planned and supported systematically. This component is not just about being with typically developing children; it is about interacting with and developing relationships with typically developing children. To achieve this, preschoolers in Project DATA attend an integrated preschool classroom for about 12 hours a week.

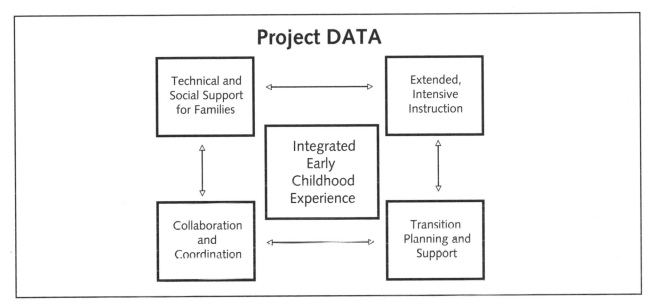

Figure 3.1. Components of project DATA.

In order to provide opportunities for the children with ASD to interact successfully with their typically developing peers, the preschool environments pay special attention to:

- Structuring the classroom environment to promote independence, participation, and successful interactions with typically developing peers

- Developing a consistent schedule and using it

- Creating the need to communicate with adults and peers

- Using children's preferred materials and activities to promote engagement

- Providing embedded and explicit instruction on valued skills

- Providing frequent reinforcement and developing effective motivation systems

Structuring the classroom environment to promote independence, participation, and successful interactions with typically developing peers. One of the primary considerations of an effective program for young children with ASD is to design the environment so as to prevent problem behaviors, promote engagement and participation, and facilitate successful interactions with typically developing peers. Because children with ASD are children first, the first step in structuring a high-quality environment is to ensure attention to the overall classroom environment, for all children.

Recommended practices for early childhood environments highlight the importance of the physical aspects of a learning environment, including the availability of developmentally and age-appropriate materials, the use of a consistent schedule of routines, and the presence of responsive adults and peers (Bredekamp & Copple, 1997; Sandall, McLean, & Smith, 2000). However, the components that comprise a high-quality early childhood environment for all young children may not be sufficient for children with ASD. Therefore, it is also important to take into consideration high-quality environments, as defined by early childhood professional groups (e.g., National Association for the Education of Young Children [www.naeyc.org] and the Division of Early Childhood of the Council for Exceptional Children [www.dec-sped.org]).

Some key characteristics of environmental design that are integrated into these classrooms include clearly defined areas of the classroom that reflect the activity to be conducted and that can be observed from everywhere in the classroom; a well-designed traffic pattern with no obvious obstacles; centers and activities that are interesting, relevant, and engaging; centers with adequate, age-appropriate materials; activities that promote and perhaps even require peer interaction; materials that are well organized and in good working order; and materials that are rotated frequently (Schwartz et al., 2002).

Developing a consistent schedule and following it. Many classrooms or intervention settings use schedules that outline the different activities children will participate in each day. In order to provide a child with ASD a comprehensible environment, a schedule of daily activities should be available in a format that is understandable to the child. For example, using pictures and symbols in addition to words may increase a child's understanding. Also, for a younger child, showing him an object that he or she associates with a common activity or routine can facilitate comprehension of what is coming next.

A schedule alone may not be meaningful to a child with ASD if the child is not taught to use it. Teachers need to refer to the schedule frequently and consistently and use it to teach the classroom routine, cue transitions, and teach children to understand changes to the routine. A variety of strategies are useful for **cueing** a child that a change is about to occur (i.e., timers, counting, singing songs, etc.). Again, whatever strategy is utilized will only be effective if the child is taught the purpose and meaning of the transition cue.

It is important to remember that schedules are not panaceas and that, used incorrectly, a schedule may end up making a child with ASD more rigid. Schedules must be used to help children navigate the environment and be independent. Children need to learn that changes to the schedule will occur and how to handle them. For example, a teacher can use a schedule to help children with ASD understand that specific activities will not be occurring on a given day (e.g., mark those activities with the international "no" symbol of a circle with a line through it) or that activities will be occurring in a different order. Schedules are instructional tools. That is, they are as useful as the instruction that accompanies them.

Creating the need to communicate with adults and peers. The classroom environment can promote opportunities and motivation to communicate. The number of opportunities that are available to help a child with ASD learn how to ask for things he wants, reject something he does not want, or initiate or respond to others is dependent on how the environment supports and, perhaps, demands those communicative behaviors.

All children who participate in Project DATA use a functional communication system. While our goal is to help all children develop functional speech, children who are not yet verbal are taught to use the Picture Exchange Communication System (PECS) (Frost & Bondy, 1994) across all school, home, and community settings. We view every classroom activity as a language-learning and -using opportunity. For instance, snack time provides an excellent opportunity for a child to learn how to ask for something he wants (i.e., favorite food), reject something she does not want (i.e., food she dislikes), and respond to the request of a peer. This can be accomplished by the use of certain strategies, such as an adult or peer regulating access to certain food items, or by providing small portions of a preferred food so that a child will have multiple opportunities to ask for what she wants. Children with ASD are also put in charge of snack items, a wonderful opportunity to work on receptive language when the child must respond to his classmates who are asking for orange slices or other snack items. Finally, across all activities, students are required to use communicative behavior to request preferred materials and activities and to control their environment. These communicative opportunities add up across the day to provide multiple opportunities to respond, which is essential in language acquisition (Hart & Risley, 1995).

Using preferred materials and activities to promote engagement. Systematically teaching children with ASD to engage in play or learning activities independently is an important goal of the preschool portion of Project DATA. To achieve this outcome, we identify materials and activities that children find interesting and make them available as part of classroom activities (McGee, Daly, Izeman, Mann, & Risley, 1991). Within the classroom, we ensure that there are preferred items for every child, and that within every activity center there is a range of materials that will engage the child with the most severe disabilities and that will challenge the most capable child.

Providing embedded and explicit instruction on valued skills. Recommended practices for young children with ASD emphasize the importance of systematic instruction on core areas of need related to autism (NRC, 2001). To promote the most optimal and generalized outcomes, such instruction needs to take place across settings, activities, people, and materials. It requires that teachers and interventionists have knowledge of different techniques to teach specific skills and are able to assess whether or not the child is making adequate progress using the selected technique so that changes can be made if progress is not sufficient.

Teachers in the preschool must plan what is going to be taught, where and how the instruction will occur, and how the child's progress will be assessed. To achieve such high frequency of instruction and data collection, teachers in the Project DATA classrooms develop an activity matrix that outlines the instructional needs for all the students in their classroom (Sandall & Schwartz, 2002). The purpose of an activity matrix is to use a grid to plan when specially designed instruction will be provided and when data collection on specific targeted skills and behaviors will occur.

Providing frequent reinforcement and developing effective motivation systems. A common characteristic of children with ASD is that they do not take advantage of the social rewards that are available to others for behaving in certain ways (Myles, 2005). They often fail to pick up important information that is communicated by adults and peers through a variety of unstated social cues or rules, and even if aware of the social rules, they may not be motivated by the social contingencies present to follow the rules. However, children with ASD respond extremely well to positive reinforcement. Therefore, systematic selection of reinforcers (i.e., reinforcer assessment) and contingent application of reinforcement to change behavior or teach new skills are necessary (Horner, Carr, Strain, Todd, & Reed, 2002).

Reinforcers come in many forms, but they always serve the same function: increasing the probability of a behavior happening again. For example, if a child with ASD points to a cup of juice, looks at the adult, and vocalizes, and the adult gives him juice, the behaviors of looking, pointing, and vocalizing are being reinforced and are more likely to happen again. However, if the child asks for juice, one teacher says no, the child begins to cry, and another teacher presents the child with juice to "help him calm down," crying is being reinforced.

When starting out in a preschool classroom, the items or activities that function as reinforcers for a child may be limited. (Remember, if an item or activity does not increase the probability of the behavior happening again, it is not a reinforcer, even if teachers think it is a preferred item.) Therefore, early in a child's preschool career, we are more likely to use more artificial (e.g., items that are unrelated to the task) reinforcers. These may include a favorite toy, stickers, bubbles, or food.

As children learn to participate in more activities and are reinforced by more items and social praise from the teacher, we attempt to use more natural reinforcers. **Natural reinforcers** are those that are logically related to the task at hand. For example, if a child wants to go outside and is standing at a closed door and says "open," opening the door and letting the child go outside is a natural reinforcer. Natural reinforcers are often the most powerful type of reinforcer because the child's motivation is high at that moment to achieve that specific outcome. Although natural reinforcers may be more acceptable in preschool classrooms, the rule in the Project DATA classroom is to use whatever type and amount of reinforcement that is needed to promote skill development and appropriate behavior.

Extended, Intensive Instruction

The second component of our program is extended, intensive instruction. Three days a week, Project DATA has extended school days. During this time children receive additional, explicit instruction on IEP objectives and on other behaviors that will help them be successful in the classroom, home, and the community. Instruction may be provided one-on-one or in small groups. The size of instructional groups and the instructional strategies used depend on the child, the objective being worked on, and the child's progress as measured by daily data collection. This component adds approximately 12 hours a week of time at school for every child. In addition, we ask parents to work with their child at home for a minimum of five hours a week.

Technical and Social Support

The third component of Project DATA is technical and social support for families. All families receive a monthly home visit and are required to participate in at least six hours of educational programming every year. Also, the first year children are in the program, parents are required to participate in a class on teaching basic skills. In subsequent years parents can participate in Project DATA-run educational classes on specific topics (e.g., play or teaching communication skills) or participate in other educational opportunities available in the community (e.g., the Autism Society of Washington conference).

Collaboration and Coordination of Services

The next component is collaboration and coordination across services. Almost every family with whom we work receives some type of family-negotiated service for their child with ASD. A family-negotiated service is defined as a therapeutic service that the school district does not pay for. Services may include speech therapy, home-based behavioral programming, or horseback-riding therapy. Once a year we attempt to hold a meeting of all the therapeutic providers for the child and the parents. The purpose of these meetings is to foster communication and collaboration, not to do joint planning or evaluation.

Transition Planning and Support

The final component of Project DATA is transition planning and support. Transitions are difficult for all children and families, but they can be especially stressful for children with ASD and their families. We work with the school district, the preschool, and the family to ensure that adequate planning occurs to facilitate a smooth transition. This may include teaching skills specific to the new environment (e.g., carrying lunch on a tray), transferring visual supports, and providing an opportunity for the child to visit the new school and meet his new teacher a few days before school starts.

Summary and Conclusions

This chapter focused on the importance of early intervention. We specifically highlighted a range of recommended intervention services and examples of how to translate these recommendations into classroom practice. Project DATA is only one example of what effective early intervention services can look like for children with ASD. Project DATA has been extremely successful. Over 50% of the children leave our program and are placed in inclusive kindergarten programs (Schwartz et al., 2004). In addition, parents and school officials have been extremely satisfied with the program, and many school districts in the state are implementing local versions of an extended-day program. The important thing to remember is that there is no one right way to educate children with ASD, and a program is only successful if a child is making progress.

Tips for the Classroom

✓ Early and accurate identification is the first step towards providing high-quality early intervention to all children with ASD and their families, regardless of cultural and linguistic diversity, class, or geography.

✓ Know the early signs or red flags of autism and don't hesitate to make a referral for assessment. A helpful resource is www.firstsigns.org

✓ Educators who suspect a child has ASD should be actively involved with parents in the diagnostic process and be encouraged to ask questions regarding the procedures used to arrive at a diagnosis.

✓ Help families make the transition into services in their local community by identifying potential service providers and providing temporary support to the family until they can enlist support and technical assistance from other professional sources.

✓ Even if a child has not received a formal evaluation or diagnosis but is suspected to be at risk for an ASD, intervention focusing on social development and communication should begin right away.

✓ An effective early intervention program for young children with ASD must include the following key elements:

- Sufficient hours and intensity of services
- Comprehensible environments with access to typical peers
- Specialized curriculum with an appropriate scope and sequence that addresses the core areas of autism
- Family involvement
- Problem-solving approach to challenging behaviors
- Appropriate evaluation tools to monitor progress through systematic data keeping
- Planned opportunities for peer socialization

✓ Fundamental skills to address in an early intervention program include teaching young children to follow simple directions, imitate, communicate their wants and needs, and perform basic self-care skills.

✓ Other skills or meaningful outcomes to address must take into consideration the individual child's strengths and challenges, priorities of the family, and existing data based on a careful assessment of learning and development across multiple domains (i.e., communication, social, cognitive, adaptive, and motor).

✓ There is no one best approach to teaching all children with ASD. However, there are many educational and behavioral interventions that have demonstrated effectiveness in improving developmental outcomes for children with ASD.

Chapter Highlights

- There is no "typical" child with ASD; there can be dramatic differences in abilities, preferences, needs, and delays.

- There is overwhelming evidence of the effectiveness and importance of early detection and intervention for children with ASD.

- While research indicates ASD can be reliably diagnosed at 2 years of age, the current average age of diagnosis in the United States is 3-6 years of age. For children who are culturally and linguistically different, diagnosis can be even later.

- First Signs, an organization started by parents of children with ASD, has been instrumental in working with the CDC and other medical groups to get the most up-to-date diagnostic information as well as inform the public, through public service announcements and a website, about ASD and early diagnosis. First Signs has also developed a list of developmental red flags that may indicate a child might have an ASD.

- For diagnosis at an early age, most families are referred to a psychologist, developmental pediatrician, psychiatrist, or neurologist for a full evaluation; however, finding professionals who are trained and experienced in diagnosing ASD is difficult in many communities.

- Another avenue for diagnosis is the educational system; however, in many cases children are classified as having a developmental delay rather than ASD.

- It is important to provide families with information on intervention services and community supports after a diagnosis of ASD.

- Parents need to be made aware that ASD is a life-long disorder and that there is no way to predict how an individual child will respond to intervention.

- There are two key issues of debate related to early intervention for children with ASD: (a) the amount of intervention a child should receive and (b) what approach or methodology is most beneficial.

- The authors suggest that, rather than focusing on what program is the "best," the focus should be on what is known about the essential elements of effective programs, including:

  - Sufficient hours and intensity of services

  - Comprehensible environments with access to typical peers

  - Specialized curriculum with an appropriate scope and sequence

  - Family involvement

  - Problem-solving approach to challenging behaviors

  - Appropriate evaluation tools for monitoring progress

- Families need to ask questions before enrolling their children in early intervention programs to ensure the program matches what they see as outcomes for the child, addresses family desires for the child, matches family comfort levels, and has proof of effectiveness.

- Outcome-oriented frameworks of intervention refer to a problem-solving process that is ongoing and based on the child's needs at any given time.

- Meaningful outcomes for children with ASD should improve the child's quality of life.

- Curriculum-based assessment (CBA) is one means of identifying potential skills or outcomes for young children.

- Project DATA, an early intervention program at the University of Washington, is an example of a high-quality early intervention program for children with ASD.

- The core component of Project DATA is an integrated early childhood program with planned and systematic interactions between children with ASD and their typically developing peers. The program emphasizes:

  ➢ Structuring the classroom environment to promote independence, participation, and successful interactions with typically developing peers

  ➢ Developing a consistent schedule and following it

  ➢ Creating the need to communicate with adults and peers

  ➢ Using preferred materials and activities to promote engagement

  ➢ Providing embedded and explicit instruction on valued skills

  ➢ Providing frequent reinforcement and developing effective motivation systems

- Other foundational components of Project DATA are as follows:

  ➢ Extended intensive instruction

  ➢ Technical and social support

  ➢ Collaboration and coordination of services

  ➢ Transition planning and support

Chapter Review Questions

1. What is meant by a "spectrum disorder"?

2. Why is early intervention so important for children diagnosed with ASD?

3. What are some of the major issues surrounding early identification of ASD (including early diagnosis and referral)?

4. What are the developmental red flags that may indicate ASD in infants and toddlers?

5. Why is it important to provide families with information on intervention services and community supports as part of the assessment process? What type of information should be shared?

6. What are the key features of effective programs for young children with ASD?

7. What types of questions do families need to ask when selecting intervention programs for their young children with ASD?

8. What is meant by the term "outcome-oriented framework"?

9. How might a family decide on meaningful outcomes for their child with ASD?

10. What is a curriculum-based assessment (CBA) and why is it useful?

11. What are the five components of Project DATA?

12. What are the areas to which Project DATA preschool environments pay particular attention?

References

American Psychiatric Association. (2000). *Diagnostic and statistical manual for mental disorders* (4th ed., text revision). Washington, DC: Author.

Bagnato, S. J., Neisworth, J. T., & Munson, S. M. (1997). *Linking assessment and early intervention.* Baltimore: Paul H. Brookes.

Boulware, G., Schwartz, I. S., Sandall, S. R., & McBride, B. J. (2006). Project DATA for toddlers: An inclusive approach to very young children with ASD. *Topics in Early Childhood Special Education, 26*(2), 94-105.

Bredekamp, S., & Copple, C. (1997). *Appropriate practice in early childhood programs* (rev. ed.). Washington, DC: National Association for the Education of Young Children.

Bricker, D. (2002). *Assessment, evaluation, and programming system for infants and young children: AEPS measurement from birth to six years.* Baltimore: Paul H. Brookes.

Carr, E. G. (2007). The expanding vision of positive behavior support: Research perspectives on happiness, helpfulness, and hopefulness. *Journal of Positive Behavior Interventions, 9,* 3-14.

Carr, E. G., Dunlap, G., Horner, R. H., Koegel, R. L., Turnbull, A. P., Sailor, W., et al. (2002). Positive behavior support: Evolution of an applied science. *Journal of Positive Behavior Interventions, 4,* 16-20.

Carr, E. G., & Durrand, V. M. (1985). Reducing behavior problems through functional communication training. *Journal of Applied Behavior Analysis, 18*, 111-126.

Chakrabarti, S., & Fombonne, E. (2001). Pervasive developmental disorders in preschool children. *Journal of the American Medical Association, 285*, 3093-3099.

Dahle, K. B. (2003). The clinical and educational systems: Differences and similarities. *Focus on Autism and Other Developmental Disabilities, 18*(4), 238-246.

Dawson, G., & Osterling, J. (1997). Early intervention in autism. In M. Guralnick (Ed.), *The effectiveness of early intervention* (pp. 307-326). Baltimore: Paul H. Brookes.

Dunlap, G. (1999). Consensus, engagement, and family involvement for young children with autism. *The Journal of the Association for Persons with Severe Handicaps, 24*, 222-225.

Frost, I., & Bondy, A. (1994). *The Picture Exchange Communication System training manual.* Cherry Hill, NJ: PECS.

Harris, S. L., & Handelman, J. S. (2000). Age and IQ at intake as predictors of placement for young children with autism: A four-to-six-year follow-up. *Journal of Autism and Developmental Disorders, 30*, 137-142.

Hart, B., & Risley, T. R. (1995). *Meaningful differences in the everyday experience of young American children.* Baltimore: Paul H. Brookes.

Horner, R. H., Carr, E. G., Strain, P. S., Todd, A. W., & Reed, H. K. (2002). Problem behavior interventions for young children with autism: A research synthesis. *Journal of Autism and Developmental Disorders, 32(5)*, 423-446.

Howlin, P. (2000). Outcome in adult life for more able individuals with autism or Asperger syndrome. *Autism, 4*, 63-83.

Hoyson, M., Jamieson, B., & Strain, P. S. (1984). Individualized group instructions of normally developing and autistic-like children: The LEAP curriculum model. *Journal of the Division for Early Childhood, 8*, 157-172.

Hume, K., Bellini, S., & Pratt, C. (2005). The usage and perceived outcomes of early intervention and early childhood programs for young children with autism spectrum disorder. *Topics in Early Childhood Special Education, 25*(4), 195-207.

Hurth, J., Shaw, E., Izeman, S., Whaley, K., & Rogers, S. (1999). Areas of agreement about effective practices serving young children with autism spectrum disorders. *Infants and Young Children, 12*, 17-26.

Individuals with Disabilities Education Act Amendments of 1997, 20 U.S.C. http://idea.ed.gov/

Jacobson, J. (2000). System and cost research issues in treatments for people with autistic disorders. *Journal of Autism and Developmental Disorders, 30*, 585-593.

Leaf, R., & McEachin, J. (1999). *A work in progress: Behavior management strategies and a curriculum for intensive behavioral treatment of autism.* New York: DRL Books.

Lord, C. (1995). Follow-up of two-year-olds referred for possible autism. *Journal of Child Psychology and Psychiatry, 36*, 1365-1382.

Lovaas, O. I. (1987). Behavioral treatment and normal educational and intellectual functioning in young autistic children. *Journal of Consulting and Clinical Psychology, 55*, 3-9.

Mandell, D. S., Listerud, J., Levy, S. E., & Pinto-Martin, J. (2002). Race differences in the age at diagnosis among medicaid-eligible children with autism. *Journal of the American Academy of Child and Adolescent Psychiatry, 41*, 1447-1453.

Macy, M. G., Bricker, D. D., & Squires, J. K. (2005). Validity and reliability of a curriculum-based assessment approach to determine eligibility for Part C Services. *Journal of Early Intervention, 28*, 1-16.

McGee, G. G., Daly, T., Izeman, S. G., Mann, L., & Risley, T. R. (1991). Use of classroom materials to promote preschool engagement. *Teaching Exceptional Children, 23*, 44-47.

Moore, V., & Goodson, S. (2003). How well does early diagnosis of autism stand the test of time. Follow-up study of children assessed for autism at age 2 and development of an early diagnostic service. *Autism, 7*, 47-63.

Myles, B. S. (2005). *Children and youth with Asperger Syndrome: Strategies for success in inclusive settings.* Thousand Oaks, CA: Corwin Press.

National Research Council. (2001). *Educating children with autism.* Committee on Educational Interventions for Children with

Autism. Catherine Lord and James P. McGee (Eds.). Division of Behavioral and Social Sciences and Education. Washington, DC: National Academy Press.

Ozonoff, S., & Cathcart, K. (1998). Effectiveness of a home program intervention for young children with autism. *Journal of Autism and Developmental Disorders, 28,* 25-32.

Partington, J., & Sundberg, M. (1998). *The Assessment of Basic Language and Learning Skills: An assessment, curriculum guide, and tracking system for children with autism or other developmental disabilities.* Danville, CA: Behavior Analysts.

Pinto-Martin, J., & Levy, S. E. (2004). Early diagnosis of autism spectrum disorders. *Current Treatment Options in Neurology, 6,* 391-400.

Rogers, S. (1999). Intervention for young children with autism: From research to practice. *Infants and Young Children, 12,* 1-16.

Sandall, S. R., McLean, M. E., & Smith, B. J. (2000). *DEC recommended practices in early intervention/early childhood special education.* Longmont, CO: Sopris West.

Sandall, S., & Schwartz, I. S. (2002). *Building blocks for teaching preschoolers with special needs.* Baltimore: Brookes Publishing.

Schopler, E., & Van Bourgondien, M. (1991). Treatment and Education of Autistic and related Communication-handicapped CHildren (TEACCH). In N. Giddan & J. Giddan (Eds.), *Autistic adults at Bittersweet Farms* (pp. 85-94). Binghamton, NY: Haworth.

Schwartz, I. S., Garfinkle, A., & Davis, C. (2002). Arranging preschool environments to facilitate valued social and educational outcomes. In M. Shinn, H. Walker, & G. Stoner (Eds.), *Interventions for academic and behavior problems II: Preventive and remedial approaches* (pp. 455-468). Bethesda, MD: National Association of School Psychologists.

Schwartz, I. S., Sandall, S. R., McBride, B. J., & Boulware, G. L. (2004). Project DATA (Developmentally appropriate treatment for autism): An inclusive, school-based approach to educating children with autism. *Topics in Early Childhood Special Education, 24,* 156-168.

Smith, T., Groen, A. D., & Wynn, J. W. (2000). Randomized trial of intensive early intervention for children with pervasive developmental disorder. *American Journal on Mental Retardation, 105*(4), 269-285.

Stone, W. L., Lee, E. B., Ashford, L., Brissie, J., Hepburn, S. L., Coonrod, E. E., et al. (1999). Can autism be diagnosed accurately in children under 3 years? *Journal of Child Psychiatry, 40,* 219-226.

Strain, P. S., & Cordisco, L. (1993). LEAP preschool. In S. L. Harris & J. S. Handelman (Eds.), *Preschool education programs for children with autism* (pp. 127-162). Austin, TX: Pro-Ed.

Strain, P. S., & Hoyson, M. (2000). The need for longitudinal, intensive social skill intervention: LEAP follow-up outcomes for children with autism. *Topics in Early Childhood Special Education: Special Issue: Early Childhood Special Education in a New Century: Voices from the Past, Visions for Our Future, Part 2, 20,* 116-122.

Strain, P. S., & Schwartz, I. S. (2001). Applied behavior analysis and the development of meaningful social relations for young children with autism. *Focus on Autism and Developmental Disabilities, 16,* 120-128.

Tsatsanis, K. D. (2003). Outcome research in Asperger syndrome and autism. *Child and Adolescent Psychiatric Clinics of North America, 12,* 47-63.

Volkmar, F. R., Lord, C., Bailey, A., Schultz, R. T., & Klin, A. (2004). Autism and pervasive developmental disorders. *Journal of Child Psychology and Psychiatry, 45,* 135-170.

Wang, M., Mannan, H., Poston, D., Turnbull, A. P., & Summers, J. A. (2004). Parents' perceptions of advocacy activities and their impact on family quality of life. *Research and Practice for Persons with Severe Disabilities, 29*(2), 144-155.

Wieder, S., & Greenspan, S. (2003). Climbing the symbolic ladder in DIR model through floor time/interactive play. *Autism: The International Journal of Research and Practice, 7,* 425-435.

Wolery, M., & Garfinkle, A. N. (2002). Measures in intervention research with young children who have autism. *Journal of Autism and Developmental Disorders, 32,* 463-478.

Wolfberg, P. J. (2004). Guiding children on the autism spectrum in peer play: Translating theory and research into effective and meaningful practice. *The Journal of Developmental and Learning Disorders, 8,* 7-25.

Learner Objectives

After reading this chapter, the learner should be able to:

- Describe what is meant by "social communication"

- State how theory of mind is involved in social language learning

- Explain what the chapter author believes can cause ineffective language intervention for individuals with autism

- Explain how interactive games assist infants in developing social communication

- Discuss why experiential learning is critical for brain development

- Describe the impact of autism on infants in terms of experiential learning and later brain development

- Define joint attention and explain its importance in developing social communication

- Explain the importance of intention reading to social-pragmatic theory

- Discuss how social-pragmatic theory provides an understanding of what goes wrong in the language acquisition process in autism

- Explain the importance of pragmatics in the acquisition of language

- Explain why social-pragmatic theory may be considered the "rule" in typical language development

- Provide examples of different pragmatic functions of words based on speaker intentions

- Define presuppositional knowledge and state how this area of pragmatics relates to communication

- List and describe the four conversational maxims

- Explain word-learning differences

- List and describe general considerations related to assessment of language development in terms of social pragmatics

- List and explain the ten principles of language intervention in autism

Chapter 4

Symbolic Communication: Common Pathways and Points of Departure

Diane Twachtman-Cullen

Several years ago I was consulting with a school district regarding a preschool child with high-functioning autism. Michael was not only very bright; he was also hyperlexic. He had a love of words for their own sake that was underscored by his favorite activity – writing strings of unrelated words on the chalkboard, which he would engage in obsessively if left on his own.

Despite his extensive vocabulary and the ability to speak, Michael rarely used his words to express his needs and desires. This prompted me to ask his teacher how he typically let her know if he wanted something. The teacher informed me that he would simply obtain whatever he wanted without asking, even if it meant having to climb on a chair to fetch something from a high shelf. Upon hearing this, a red flag immediately went up! Did Michael have a problem with obtaining attention or requesting, or both? Since these are important pragmatic functions of communication, I decided to investigate what he would do if we moved an enticing item from a lower shelf to a higher one and told him that he couldn't climb up to get it.

The first thing that Michael did was to walk over to the shelves and stare at the small letter board that he wanted. Next, he pointed to it. Although his teacher and I were close by, he neither tried to obtain our attention before pointing to the shelf, nor check back to see if we were looking at the place where he was pointing, both of which are important social-cognitive precursors to symbolic communication. In fact, Michael gave no indication whatsoever that he was intending to communicate with us. He simply continued to stare at and/or point to the letter board, as though those things alone would enable him to obtain it.

After a few moments, Michael tried to drag a chair over, in an effort to obtain the letter board himself. His teacher stopped him, saying that it was too dangerous to climb on the chair and adding that she would be happy to get the item for him. Even though he had the ability to say the words, and was prompted several times by his teacher to use his words, Michael said nothing. On a few occasions, he walked a short distance away, only to come back to resume his vigil. Finally, he left the area in apparent despair. I thought that he had given up on the letter board, since there was nothing in his behavior to suggest otherwise. Instead, Michael walked directly over to a flip chart on the other side of the room, picked up a marker, wrote something down, and promptly walked away. His teacher and I walked across the room to see what he had written. To our amazement, Michael had written the word HELP, without the slightest regard for the people in his environment who could assist him, or even the knowledge that someone would have to read (be aware of) the word in order to act on it.

This vignette poignantly illustrates the nature of the **communication deficit** commonly seen in autism – even when an individual has the ability to *say* words, in no way does that guarantee that he is able to *use* them to express his intentions (thoughts, feelings, wants, and needs). Stated differently, having lots of language (i.e., words) – as Michael clearly did – does not mean that the person with autism has the ability to use that language for **social communication** purposes; that is, to bring about an intended effect in the attentional and mental states of others so that they can act upon the perceived message.

If that has a decidedly **theory-of-mind** ring to it, it is precisely because communication and theory of mind are inextricably intertwined. That is, theory of mind may be thought of as the complex array of processes that constitute the social-cognitive underpinnings of **social language learning**. At its most basic level, it is the instinctive ability to know what is in another person's mind. According to Tomasello and Bates (2001),

> Linguistic communication is about discerning what other people intend for you to pay attention to or think about when they use a linguistic convention [symbol] and then, in complementary fashion, using those same conventions yourself to manipulate the intentional and mental states of other persons. (p. 4)

Michael could not do this, even though he had the ability to say and write words. He even chose an appropriate word to write on the easel – one that would have worked in his quest for the object if it had been directed at his teacher. What Michael's behavior demonstrated was that he lacked an understanding of the quintessential function of words; that is, that they are the purveyors of one's intentions (mental states) used for the purpose of influencing the mental states of others. In other words, Michael did not know that he could *use* his words as the "**symbolic currency**" (Sacks, 1989) to communicate his *intended* meaning to someone else. Indeed, Michael's pointing behavior was **proto-imperative** or self-referenced, as opposed to **proto-declarative** – that is, accompanied by social referencing behaviors intended to direct attention and/or share his focus of interest. Clearly, Michael did not have the basic *idea* of communication as a process by which to exchange meaning between two or more people who are engaged in the complementary enterprise of influencing each other's mental states.

Happé (1996) spoke eloquently to the linkage between theory of mind and communication when she stated that "to recognize and engage in ostensive (i.e., communicative) behavior it is vital to have some recognition of mental states such as intentions" (p. 76). Carter (1999) went even further, treating communication and theory of mind as one and the same entity by stating, "More than anything, autism is a defect of communication – an inability to share feelings, beliefs and knowledge with other people" (p. 141).

Michael's inability to use words is all the more dramatic because it stands in stark contrast to his impressive **lexicon**. His plight is all too common, albeit less obvious, among many children and adolescents with autism whose vocabularies are more meager. This is particularly true for individuals at the severe end of the autism continuum. Day in and day out, these individuals are told to *use their words,* as though the ability to do so is second nature. Or worse yet, suggesting that failure to use their words represents a willful or volitional act. Such exhortations make eminently clear a fundamental lack of understanding that the essence of language does not reside in the symbols themselves – that is, in merely having them – but in the *use* of those symbols for communication purposes (Kaye, 1982).

Recall that Michael, despite having a lexicon that was rich in **symbols**, lacked the knowledge to use those symbols to communicate his intent. Unfortunately, this lack of understanding of the difference between having symbols (words) in one's repertoire and using them to communicate sets up the individual for failure in language therapy, because unknowledgeable interventionists are likely to put the proverbial cart before the horse when it comes to the selection of language-learning targets. Specifically, they are likely to build the language "structure" by starting with the "roof" (i.e., vocabulary building), instead of constructing and fortifying the "foundation" by attending to the important social-cognitive precursors (e.g., joint attention) that set the stage for symbol use.

Joint attention may be thought of as a "meeting of minds." In other words, it is not merely two people simultaneously looking at the same thing, but two people sharing an understanding that they are attending to the same thing (Call & Tomasello, 2005). Hence, a major premise of this chapter is that inappropriate language intervention practices are largely the result of a lack of understanding of the language-learning process, in general, and a lack of awareness of how abnormalities in **interpersonal relatedness** and **social cognition** serve to restrict language development in children with autism at all functioning levels. Consequently, the goal of this chapter is to (a) examine both the relevant language-learning and autism research literature; (b) discuss the ways in which both research bases relate to one another; and (c) provide a framework for translating research into effective assessment and intervention practices that make sense for people on the autism spectrum.

The Critical Role of Experience in Communication and Language Development

It is well accepted that experience is a major player in brain development; it shapes the structure of the brain and influences connectivity (Greenough & Black, 1992; Landa, 2003; Schwartz & Begley, 2002). This, in turn, promotes learning. However, there has been a paradigmatic shift in our understanding of how experience shapes the neural architecture. Early on, the infant's brain was largely viewed as a **tabula rasa** – the so-called blank slate, as yet unaffected by the experiences that would later be etched upon it to coax brain development.

Current research into infants' brains does not support this theory, but runs in opposition to it. Specifically, it is currently held (and supported by research) that babies come into the world with an excess of **neurons** (Wingert & Brant, 2005). This creates a dual, richly textured, and crucial role for experience that directly affects **brain connectivity**. Specifically, one's experiences (involvement in activities) promote new connections by laying down pathways in those areas of the brain that fuel the action required of the activity (Schwartz & Begley, 2002). In addition, in "use-it-or-lose-it" fashion, experience also "prunes" the brain by "allowing" unused neurons in other parts of the brain to die (Landa, 2003). Schwartz and Begley (2002) refer to this process as "survival of the busiest" to articulate the way in which environmental inputs (experience) create the refined neural architecture of the developing brain. An illustration may help to shed more light on this phenomenon.

Neurotypical infants have a very active "social life," readily engaging in the games of infancy with their parents/caregivers. The word *game* belies the importance of these activities, for they are the vehicles by which babies traverse the road to **symbolic communication**. For example, games such as peek-a-boo and pat-a-cake provide rich opportunities for attention and affect sharing. These behaviors are important social-cognitive precursors to the development of social communication, and they are major contributors to the infant's emerging capacity for joint attention (Wetherby, 2006). They also involve social reciprocity – the forerunner of mature turn taking that will eventually mark two-way, dialogic exchanges. The games of infancy also enable the infant to regulate the interaction, establish predictability, and anticipate what comes next. Most of all, these games enmesh the infant in a tapestry of **interpersonal relatedness** that primes the system to eventually engage the **subjective states** of others.

There is impressive research evidence to support the role of experience in brain development in both animal and human subjects. For example, Greenough and Black (1992) found that by putting geriatric rats into enriched environments in which they were able to interact with the stimulating accoutrements of the new milieu, it was possible to increase synaptic activity. With respect to human subjects, Bell and Fox (1994) noted a direct relationship between behavior and brain activity. Specifically, they found "an increase in metabolic activity in the areas of the brain having to do with emotional regulation, interaction, and sequencing *at the time that infants are involved* [italics added] in choice making, search behavior, and reciprocal interactions" (p. 319) such as those required in the games of infancy. Schwartz and Begley (2002) strike a cautionary note, however, stating that while "experience molds the brain, it molds only an attending brain" (p. 224). In other words, passivity – or for that matter, forced participation in activities, *without active attention* – is not sufficient for brain development.

I would take this cautionary note one step further to underscore the importance of actual participation in activities. For example, regarding the Greenough and Black (1992) study, it is difficult to imagine that the rat subjects would have had an increase in synaptic activity if they had only been allowed to watch other rats experiencing the various accoutrements of the enriched environment without engaging in the action themselves.

As the above studies demonstrate, the effects of **experiential learning** on brain development are relevant to individuals with autism, given that experience fuels social cognition and communication. Hence, the impoverishment of these experiences in children with autism is likely a key factor in their social-cognitive, communicative, and language deficits. Moreover, since problems in attention are very much at issue for individuals on the spectrum, it is not uncommon to see children with autism in language-learning situations in which they are unengaged. Worse yet, it is also not uncommon to see these children in "forced" language-learning situations that cause discomfort and promote resistance.

To more fully understand the plight of the child with autism with respect to experiential learning, it is necessary to consider the issue of quality of experience, since not all experiences are created equal. It is well known that babies with autism do not readily engage in the games of infancy as do their typically developing peers (Wolfberg, 1999). Hence, they miss out on rich opportunities to engage in **emotional regulation**, affect and attention sharing, anticipation, and reciprocity with their caregivers, all of which lead to the development of joint attention and set the stage for symbolic communication.

In contrast, given their preference for sameness, babies with autism are more apt to engage in **self-stimulatory** and repetitive behaviors, such as rocking, twirling, or flapping – behaviors that are distinctly unilateral and non-social. Given that experience both powers and prunes the developing brain, it is reasonable to speculate that the neural landscape of a child with autism would likely look very different from that of a neurotypical child. Schwartz and Begley (2002) lend support to this position, stating that "the **plasticity** of the young brain is based on the overabundance of synapses, which allows only those that are used to become part of enduring circuits that underlie thinking, feeling, responding, and behaving" (p. 129). In view of the distinctly non-social behavior that fires up circuits in the brains of children with autism, and in deference to the pruning process, it is likely that the capacity for affect and attention sharing, as well as other social-cognitive behaviors, does not fare well in their brain development.

Consequently, while all of an individual's experiences have the capacity to influence brain development and learning (Schwartz & Begley, 2002), the richness and extent of that influence is related to the quality of the experience itself. For example, it is well established that when typically developing children reach early childhood and learn to play in a more sophisticated manner, children with autism lag behind (see Chapter 8). This is likely due, at least in part, to differences in the quality of their early play experiences. Consider, for example, what a neurotypical boy can take in from the simple but high-quality act of playing with a toy car. He can learn that the doors and trunk open and close; that he needs to push the car up an incline, but that he can let it go down a hill by itself. He can also learn that he can make the car go fast or slow and that he can make it bump into things or stop. Contrast these rich opportunities for brain growth and concept development with the experience of the girl with autism who turns a toy car over in her hand and repetitively spins one wheel ad infinitum. Which child do you suppose has the most appropriate brain circuits firing and the best chance for **concept development**? Or, perhaps more to the point, which child's pattern of evolving neural architecture will better prepare him or her for entry into the world of symbolic communication (Hobson, 2005)?

All in all, the interactions seen in the games of infancy involve attention and affect sharing, and provide some of the major building blocks of interpersonal relatedness. They also set the stage for joint attention and intention reading, both of which are foundational to symbol use.

The Pivotal Role of Joint Attention

Joint attention is critically important to communication and language development in typically developing children (Baldwin, 1995; Bruner, 1983; Tomasello, 2003; Tomasello & Farrar, 1986; Tomasello & Todd, 1983; Tomasello, Mannle, & Kruger, 1986). It is also well established that joint attention deficits are stable characteristics of children with autism (Leekam, 1993; Lewy & Dawson, 1992; Mundy, Sigman, & Kasari, 1990; Wetherby, Prizant, & Hutchinson, 1998). As such, there is typically either an absence or paucity of social behaviors, such as gaze following, proto-declarative (social) pointing, and showing/offering gestures in this population. Since all of these behaviors are suggestive of the child's growing awareness of the need to engage other minds, they are considered to be early behavioral indicators of the child's developing theory of mind. Hence, the absence or paucity of this type of behavior in children with autism is one of the earliest indicators of their theory-of-mind difficulty.

Recent brain research evidence supports the close relationship between joint attention and theory of mind. Specifically, Williams, Waiter, Perra, Whiten, and Perrett (2005) found that joint attention was associated with activation of an area of the brain that has consistently been shown to be activated during mental-state **attribution** tasks. This finding led these researchers to conclude that the neural substrate of joint attention also serves a mentalizing function. In other words, joint attention and the ability to read mental states (theory of mind) are housed in the same area of the brain.

Research has also revealed similarities in the way in which joint attention impacts both children with autism and those who are neurotypical. Studies of normally developing children by Tomasello and Todd (1983) and Tomasello et al. (1986) have revealed a "very high" correlation between time spent in joint attention activities with their mothers and children's vocabulary size. Further, investigating whether language and communication development in toddlers with autism was related to changes in affective and joint attention development, Landa, Holman, Sullivan, and Cleary (2005) found that not only did the children demonstrate clinically significant change in language and social domains, but the greatest language gains were observed in toddlers with the strongest pre-treatment joint attention skills. In a similar vein, Siller and Sigman (2002) noted that the presence of joint attention in children with autism in their early years had predictive value for language development in their adolescent years. According to Twachtman-Cullen and Twachtman-Reilly (2007), these findings suggest that:

> Joint attention and vocabulary size are related in children with autism in the same manner in which they are related in typically developing children, suggesting that the same principles governing language acquisition in typically developing children also govern language acquisition in children with autism. (Based on studies by Loveland & Landry, 1986; Mundy et al., 1990)

The importance of this finding cannot be overstated, since it speaks to the relevance – heretofore largely unacknowledged – of the language development literature for understanding the communication and language deficits seen in individuals with autism. Moreover, it underscores the need for intervention practices that address the crucial role of joint attention in language acquisition.

Tomasello (2003) speaks eloquently to the importance of joint attention in language development, assigning a "foundational" role to it in the establishment of **intentional communication**. According to Tomasello (2003), the joint attentional frame is the milieu within which both the child and the adult establish the "common ground" within which the child eventually learns to infer the adult's communicative intentions. (The topic of intention reading will be elaborated in the next section of this chapter.)

Hobson's (2005) affective theory of joint attention fits well with Tomasello's views, positing that joint attention involves an active process of sharing attention, rather than the passive act of simply looking at what someone else happens to be attending to at the time. Hence, the critical variable in this sharing is *awareness*. Specifically,

> The infant needs to be aware of the object or event *as* the focus of the other person's attention – and in addition, for full 'jointness,' he or she should share awareness of the sharing of the focus, something that often entails *sharing an attitude* [italics added] towards the thing or event in question. (Hobson, 2005, p. 185)

Two things come to mind with respect to this description. First, joint attention evolves over time, reaching "full jointness" only when the child becomes fully aware of the **shared focus**. This would seem to be a kind of "meta-awareness" or an awareness of the awareness. Second, this description by Hobson propels joint attention into the rarefied atmosphere of **intersubjective engagement**, or the ability to share and engage emotionally in the subjective (i.e., mental) states of others – hence, his reference to "sharing an attitude."

Recall once again the games of infancy and the rich opportunities they provide for attention and affect sharing, both of which are major contributors to joint attention and intersubjectivity. Consider, too, the missed opportunities for this type of engagement by children with autism when they "reject" such games as not enjoyable, or perhaps over-stimulating, and hence, off-putting. Given the social-cognitive competencies that such experiences inspire, and their intimate relationship to later symbol use, the impoverishment of these types of experiences in children with autism will likely set in motion a negative cascading effect with respect to their language development.

To summarize, even though different theorists have posited contradictory interpretations of joint attention, there are many points on which there is general consensus, all of which are important regarding its critical role in language acquisition. Specifically,

- Joint attention, regardless of its origins, is fueled by experience (Leekam, 2005).

- Joint attention provides a rich milieu within which relatedness and emotional sharing may take place (Hobson, 2005).

- Intersubjectivity – that is, shared understanding – has its roots in joint attention (Rogoff, 1990; Tomasello, 2003).

- Joint attention sets the stage for intention reading and is intimately related to the development of symbolic communication (Mundy et al., 1990).

- Deficits in joint attention are among the most robust behavioral findings in autism.

Before considering the important role of intention reading in communication development, intersubjectivity – the "bridge" between joint attention and intention reading – needs further elaboration. Trevarthan (1980) acknowledged the role that the two concepts play in communication by defining intersubjectivity as "both recognition and control of cooperative intentions and joint patterns of awareness" (p. 530). Rogoff (1990) asserted that "communication presumes intersubjectivity" (p. 71), which she went on to describe as "shared understanding based on a common focus of attention and some shared presuppositions [judgments] that form the ground for communication" (p. 71). I would add that intention reading itself also presumes intersubjectivity – the shared understanding that is necessary for one to be able to read the intentions of others.

Social-Pragmatic Theory and Its Relevance in Autism

According to **social-pragmatic theory**, intention reading – that is, the ability of the child to "read" the adult's communicative intent – plays a critical role in language development. Indeed, intention reading may be understood as the gateway to symbolic communication. According to Tomasello (2001), central to social-pragmatic theory is the notion that understanding people as intentional agents is necessary for language acquisition (word learning) to take place. He further argues that "learning new words is dependent on young children's ability to perceive and comprehend adult intentions, and they do this using a wide array of social-pragmatic cues" (p. 114).

Tomasello and his colleagues carried out a number of ingenious experimental studies, all of which support his contention (Akhtar & Tomasello, 1996; Tomasello & Barton, 1994; Tomasello, Strosberg, & Akhtar, 1995). Tomasello offered the age at which first words develop as support for his position that language learning depends upon **intention reading**. For example, it is well known that in typical children, language acquisition (first words) begins around the time of, or just after, the child's first birthday. According to Tomasello (2001), the timing of this developmental milestone is highly significant, because symbol use depends upon the emergence of the following social-cognitive skills: gaze following, **social referencing**, and **imitative learning**, all of which "emerge in rough developmental synchrony" (p. 124). All of these skills are necessary for intention reading and symbol use. Thus, unlike other theories of language acquisition, social-pragmatic theory provides a compelling and eminently reasonable answer to the question of why language acquisition begins when it does, and not at an earlier time.

Social-pragmatic theory also seems to best account for all the pieces of the language-learning puzzle; that is, the social-cognitive elements that underpin communication and language development (affect and attention sharing, intersubjectivity, joint attention, and intention reading), and the way in which children typically learn language (in social-interactive, cultural contexts) (Tomasello, 2003; Tomasello & Bates, 2001). This final point is particularly important, and perhaps the defining feature that distinguishes social-pragmatic theory from all other theories of language development.

Tomasello (2001) provides the most comprehensive – indeed, compelling – view of how children learn language according to social-pragmatic theory:

Young children are not engaged in a reflective cognitive task in which they are attempting to make correct mappings of word to world based upon adult input, but rather they are engaged in social interactions in which they are attempting to understand adult intentions – so as to make sense of the current situation. Having complied with adult instructions to experience a situation in a particular way in a given instance, children may then learn to produce the appropriate symbols for themselves when they wish for others to experience a situation in that same way – thus entering into the world of bi-directionally (intersubjectively) understood linguistic symbols. (pp. 112-113)

Social-pragmatic theory would also seem to provide a template for understanding what goes wrong in the language acquisition process in autism. Specifically, the social-cognitive deficits in the development of attention and **affect sharing**, joint attention, and intention reading likely give rise to the unique pattern of pragmatic impairments seen in individuals with autism. In addition, problems in the social-pragmatic realm also account for many of the communication and language deficits that individuals with autism exhibit; for example, literalness, which reflects difficulty with intentionality. To illustrate, if an individual with autism is asked, "Can you pass the salt?," she is likely to take the question literally and answer "Yes," missing entirely the speaker's intent, which is to obtain the salt.

Finally, of all the aspects of language that could be impaired – **semantic, syntactic**, or **pragmatic** – it is pragmatic impairment that constitutes the defining language deficit in autism (Lord & Paul, 1997; Wetherby, Schuler, & Prizant, 1997), cutting across age and ability levels (Tager-Flusberg, Joseph, & Folstein, 2001). Taking all of these factors into account, it seems that (a) a social-pragmatic approach to language development affords the most comprehensive understanding of the subtleties and complexities involved in the language-learning process; (b) social-pragmatic theory stands alone in offering a plausible explanation for the age of language acquisition; and (c) social-pragmatic theory has relevance for individuals with autism, given the developmental trajectory of their social-cognitive deficits and their unique pragmatic profiles. Indeed, I would argue that social-pragmatic theory fits in so well with what is known about the way in which neurotypical children acquire language that it may be construed as the "rule" in typical language development. Further, given the specific nature of the language impairment in autism – social-cognitive and pragmatically based – I would also argue that the individual with autism is the "exception" that proves the (social-pragmatic) "rule"; that is, that a social-pragmatic theory of language acquisition is a sound one for both neurotypical children and those with autism.

Pragmatics and Intention Reading in Language Acquisition

Intention reading, broadly conceived by Tomasello (2003) as theory of mind, is intimately related to pragmatics, in that there is a complementary (i.e., correlative) relationship between communicative intentions and pragmatic functions, such that when a person uses language to express a specific intent, that piece of language is said to serve a particular function (Twachtman-Cullen & Twachtman-Reilly, 2007), based upon the work of Tomasello (2003).

Function. For example, if the child intends to summon Mommy when he says "Mommy," the word would serve the pragmatic function of obtaining attention. However, if the child utters the word *Mommy* upon seeing his mother returning home from work, the intention in that situation is to take note of the event, and the function served would be that of commenting. Finally, if the child in the last situation is saying *Mommy* to someone in the room with the intent of letting that person know that Mommy is arriving home, the function would be that of either announcing or informing.

These examples illustrate some important aspects of language understanding and use. First, it is highly dependent upon the speaker's intentions with respect to his communicative goal (e.g., to comment or inform). Second, a word, in and of itself, is not sufficient to carry the intended meaning. In the examples given above, the same word (*Mommy)* was used to express three to four different intents/functions. Third, context is a critical aspect of the communicative event, particularly with respect to the derivation of intent/meaning.

Presuppositional knowledge. A second aspect of pragmatics related to theory of mind concerns **presuppositional** knowledge. This consists of the judgments that speakers must make about their listeners' needs with respect to the informational content needed and the communicative style appropriate to the situation. For example, in order to know what information to convey, the speaker must be aware of what the communicative partner already knows in addition to what information she needs to know in order to understand the message. Further, in determining which communicative style to use, one needs to make judgments related to the status of the listener. For example, one would use a different communicative style when talking to a close friend than when talking to an authority figure. One must also take context into account, since formal and informal situations require different communicative styles. The ability to make these multifaceted social judgments requires a great deal of "people knowledge," particularly an understanding that people not only have thoughts, desires, needs, and perspectives, but that they can differ from person to person (Twachtman-Cullen, 1998).

Because of the **perspective-taking** requirements and theory-of-mind knowledge involved in making assumptions about listeners' needs and situational requirements, this area of pragmatics is a veritable "mine field" even for individuals with autism who are considered more able. According to Tager-Flusberg (1997), "Even when children with autism have acquired both lexical and syntactic forms, they remain at very primitive levels of communicative competence, hampered by their inability to add new information and extend a conversational topic over several communicative turns" (p. 140). The same observation applies across age levels. With this in mind, it should be obvious that, depending upon the degree of impairment, children and adolescents at the more severe end of the autism continuum may not possess sufficient social-cognitive knowledge to enable them to make presuppositions.

Conversational maxims. The third aspect of pragmatics that shares an intimate association with theory of mind is that of conversational maxims (Grice, 1975); that is, the rules of discourse by which speakers co-operate in their conversations with one another. These, of course, apply only to verbal individuals.

The first rule is that of *quantity.* This rule requires the speaker to convey only the amount of information necessary to transmit her meaning. Saying too much or too little would violate this rule. For example, a child with more severe autism is likely to violate this rule by failing to supply enough information to get his meaning across to the listener. Contrast this with the higher-functioning individual who talks non-stop on a subject of interest to her, regardless of the social distress signals (e.g., looking at one's watch multiple times) emanating from the listener.

The second maxim is that of *quality*. This rule concerns the truth value of utterances. Lying and confabulation (i.e., saying something untrue that the speaker nevertheless believes to be true) constitute violations of this rule. For example, several years ago I was called in to consult on behalf of Jason, a child with Asperger Syndrome who had become so enmeshed in the character Kevin from the movie *Home Alone* that he had taken on the character's persona. For example, he would not answer to his actual name, and he would confabulate by introducing himself to people as Kevin.

The third maxim has to do with the *relevance* of utterances. Off-topic comments and tangential utterances constitute violations of this rule. For example, if a child or adolescent with Asperger Syndrome constantly steers conversations toward his special interest (e.g., weather phenomena), this would be a violation of the rule of relevance.

The final conversational maxim is that of *clarity*. This rule obligates the speaker to convey information in a manner that is clear and understandable to the listener. Children with autism at both ends of the spectrum violate this rule when they fail to ground the listener in the subject matter at hand, or when they use metaphoric language. I am reminded of a 14-year-old boy who violated this rule by conveying his desire to have more control over his life in the following idiosyncratic manner: "I would buy the entire school. I would grow older than my teacher."

To summarize, according to social-pragmatic theory, the social-cognitive precursors that have been discussed throughout this chapter, culminating in the theory-of-mind knowledge that fuels language acquisition, are essential elements in the development of symbolic communication. Moreover, social-pragmatic theory fits in well with the variability that is seen in autism, given that the degree of deficit in social-cognitive processes such as joint attention and intention reading is roughly proportional to the degree of pragmatic impairment seen. In other words, individuals with autism who have higher levels of social cognition manifest less impairment in symbol use than their counterparts with lower levels of social cognition. For example, highly verbal individuals with autism may be able to express themselves relatively well in simple, straightforward situations, particularly when dealing with concrete, factual information. These same individuals typically evidence greater difficulty in expressing abstract or emotionally laden information. By contrast, depending upon the degree of deficit in social cognition, the severity of pragmatic impairment at the lower end of the autism continuum can vary from a complete absence of verbal language to minimal verbal ability.

Nonetheless, I contend that there is a thread of commonality running through the entire autism spectrum such that, regardless of functioning level, individuals on the spectrum demonstrate a unique pattern of pragmatic language impairment that has its roots in social-cognitive deficits. In terms of the nonverbal individual with autism, pragmatic impairment may masquerade as aberrant behavior. Specifically, "individuals with autism who are unable to express their needs and desires in conventional ways (i.e., through language or other symbolic means) will express them in unconventional ways (i.e., through maladaptive behaviors)" (Twachtman-Cullen, 2006, p. 45). For example, an individual with autism who is unable to exercise the appropriate pragmatic function for protesting (e.g., saying or signing *no*) may express her dissatisfaction with a particular food item by throwing it across the room. Indeed, there is seminal research to support the depiction of aberrant behavior in terms of the pragmatic function it serves (Carr & Durand, 1985; Donnellan, Mirenda, Mesaros, & Fassbender, 1984).

Word-Learning Differences

As noted previously, the social-pragmatic view of language acquisition has implications for how children learn the meanings of words. According to Tomasello (2003), children learn words in a social-interactive context in which they are engaged in an active process of trying to infer adult intentions. Bloom (2000) argued, "What theory of mind does for children is enable them to establish the mapping between a word and a concept. But this presupposes the availability of the concept" (p. 86). In other words, children need to understand the underlying meaning (Bloom, 2000). For example, a 2- or 3-year-old child may overhear his parents discussing a legal matter involving a lawyer. The child may even be able to say the word *lawyer*; however, without an understanding of the concept of lawyer, the child can hardly be said to have truly learned the word. Moreover, without an understanding of the underlying concept, the child will not be able to use the word appropriately, since saying a word and using it to express one's intentions are two different parameters. Given the importance of the underlying concept to word leaning, interventionists should take care to ensure that vocabulary targets are within the individual's conceptual grasp.

Bloom (2000) also underscored the importance of context in word learning, stating unequivocally that "nobody doubts that for children to learn words they have to be exposed to them in contexts in which they can infer their meanings: this is a truism" (pp. 8-9). Unfortunately, given the de-contextualized settings in which language development occurs for many individuals with autism, this can hardly be said to be a "truism" for this population.

Last but not least, there are several important aspects of words and word learning that need to be taken into account in language intervention, including the following:

- According to Tomasello (2003), there is what he terms a "perspectival" quality to words, since one may use several different words to refer to the same noun (*carrot, food,* or *vegetable)* or event (fighting, disagreeing, or combating). The particular word selected would depend upon the communicative goal of the speaker vis-à-vis what he or she wishes the listener to perceive.

- Children learn verbs and nouns in different ways based upon the nature of each word class (Bloom, 2000; Tomasello, 1992; Tomasello & Kruger, 1992). For example, nouns are based upon the whole object, such as *dog* and *car.* Nouns are also static, as opposed to transient. Verbs, on the other hand, are based upon an aspect of a situation. For example, consider the verb *wags,* as in *the dog wags its tail.* The verb *wag* refers to one aspect of the dog – the movement of its tail. This movement may stop at any time, which points to the transient nature of verbs.

- Based upon the studies of Tomasello and Kruger (1992) and Tomasello (1992), Bloom (2000) notes that when a novel verb is used to comment on an ongoing event, it is harder for the child to connect it to the event and hence learn it (e.g., "*You're pushing the truck.*"). He goes on to state that children learn verbs better "when the verb is used immediately before the event" (p. 83). Adults typically use verbs in this manner as the following statements clearly demonstrate: *Throw the ball. Clean your room. Drink your milk.*

As in the case of vocabulary development and conceptual knowledge discussed previously, it is important for interventionists to take into account research findings regarding the different ways in which children learn different classes of words when addressing the language needs of children with autism.

Assessment Considerations

Going Beyond Traditional Assessment Approaches

While an in-depth examination of issues related to assessment is beyond the scope of this chapter, some general remarks are in order. First, it is necessary to go beyond static, traditional approaches that are merely "snapshots in time." · Some of the main reasons why traditional approaches are of limited benefit with individuals with autism are as follows: (a) It is often necessary to assess skills for which no **standardized tests** are available. (b) Since social cognition and pragmatics are inextricably intertwined with environmental events, they require dynamic assessment approaches that take into account context and other situational variables. (c) "Snapshots in time" have limited predictive value for future language performance or learning potential. (d) Standardized tests may not be appropriate for individuals at the lower end of the autistic continuum.

This is *not* to say that standardized tests are never appropriate for individuals with autism. Indeed, a good rule of thumb is to use standardized tests when they are available and appropriate to the client, but to supplement them with informal assessment procedures in contextually appropriate settings and situations.

Situated Pragmatics

In view of the critical importance of the social-cognitive precursors to symbolic communication, it is crucial that observation of attention and affect sharing, joint attention and social referencing behaviors, and intention reading all be a part of the assessment protocol for individuals with autism. Hewitt (2000) argued for a "situated pragmatics" approach that takes into account contextual variables, possible barriers to communication, and the contributions (negative and positive) of communicative interactants. This approach is felt to be particularly well suited to individuals with autism, since it recognizes that there is a shared responsibility for communicative breakdown that goes beyond the individual with the language impairment.

Lund (2000) defined four main features of this approach:
- Situated pragmatics looks at the entire interaction, including the relationship between interactants for clues regarding communicative breakdown.

- Situated pragmatics is competence- as opposed to deficit-based.

- Situated pragmatics focuses on the context in which the communicative event is taking place to determine the match between communicative expectations and ability level of the individual.

- Situated pragmatics is child-centered, as it "involves understanding what the child is intending to do within events and seeing how things make sense from the child's perspective" (p. 271).

Naturalistic Contexts

The pragmatic functions of communication should be assessed in **naturalistic contexts** with a view toward assessing the environmental variables that either help to facilitate or interfere with communication (Hewitt, 2000). This ideally involves assessment across several different contexts, since some contexts are more facilitative than others, and vice versa. One of the goals is to assess the range of functions in the individual's repertoire, since children and adolescents with autism often exhibit restrictions in the range of pragmatic functions at their disposal (Wetherby & Prutting, 1984). For example, individuals at the severe end of the autism continuum typically communicate for behavioral regulation purposes, as opposed to social ends. The assessment of the pragmatic functions of communication is especially crucial for nonverbal or minimally verbal individuals, since lacking conventional symbols to express their intents (e.g., wants, needs, and desires), they often use aberrant behavior (Twachtman-Cullen, 2006).

Conversational Maxims and Presuppositional Knowledge

It is also important to assess the **conversational maxims** and to obtain information regarding presuppositional knowledge in individuals with autism who are verbal. This is particularly important for the most able on the spectrum, inasmuch as their difficulty at the higher levels of pragmatics contrasts sharply with their functioning in other areas, causing them great difficulty in the social world. Since there are no formal measures with respect to these parameters, and given that these aspects of pragmatic functioning are both subjective and difficult to assess, observation in a variety of situations over time is needed to make judgments regarding ability level.

Vocabulary Development

Vocabulary development in verbal children with autism is also an area in need of assessment. While there are several standardized vocabulary tests on the market, it is necessary to go beyond norm-referenced tests to obtain a comprehensive view of a child's word knowledge. Hence, in addition to standardized measures, diagnosticians need to obtain information regarding vocabulary development from parents/caregivers. Last, and perhaps most important with respect to this population, informal assessment procedures such as an analysis of expressive language across different situations and settings can yield information regarding vocabulary size and diversity.

Comprehension

A final area of assessment relates to comprehension. Here again, it is necessary to go beyond formal measures and comprehension at the one-word level, given recent findings about how individuals with autism process meaning. Specifically, Just, Cherkassky, Keller, and Minshew (2004) found that in sentence comprehension tasks, individuals with autism demonstrated enhanced reliance on the processing of individual words and reduced processing of sentences. This has significant implications for comprehension, since meaning is not carried by the individual words in a sentence but by the embeddedness of those words in a communicative context (Bruner & Haste, 1987). Paul's (2000) advice regarding the assessment of comprehension takes into account both real-time discourse and theory of mind. Specifically, he notes

> To fully document the child's comprehension, we would need to look also at how the child copes with the task of understanding discourse in real time, the ability to integrate with the social context, and the ability to go beyond the spoken word, to 'read the mind' of the speaker in order to form a representation of the speaker's meaning. (p. 250)

In order to do this, Paul (2000) suggests that comprehension be carried out on two levels: the *literal* level (aimed at assessing the ability to derive an understanding of words and sentences) and the *discourse* level (aimed at both intention reading and the "integration of knowledge with the social context" (p. 250).

Intervention Considerations

A comprehensive assessment of the areas noted above should provide excellent guidance for need-based intervention. Given the variability in functioning levels that exists among individuals on the autism spectrum, extending from nonverbal or minimally verbal to highly verbal, it should be apparent that intervention needs will differ – sometimes significantly – as well. Notwithstanding, there are general principles of language intervention in autism that apply across age and functioning levels, and that flow directly from social-pragmatic theory.

Principle One

Intervention must begin where the learner is. If individuals with autism have not yet mastered the social-cognitive precursors to language acquisition, intervention should begin at the level of attention and affect sharing, with the goal being that of establishing joint attention. In investigating joint attention in children with autism between the ages of 3 and 4, Kasari (2005) found that they could not only learn to initiate joint attention, but also to maintain and generalize these skills.

Principle Two

Experience both prunes and powers the brain (Landa, 2003; Schwartz & Begley, 2002). Consequently, language-learning activities embedded in high-quality experiences provide an excellent milieu for establishing joint attention, intention reading, and concept and vocabulary development. Furthermore, building experiential learning activities around the individual's interests will help to provide motivation and foster engagement.

Principle Three

The use of augmentative means (e.g., gestures, handwriting, picture communication symbols, and particularly sign language) to direct and facilitate the child's attention and provide an additional language input channel is backed by a considerable body of research. For example, according to Mirenda (2003), studies investigating the use of manual signs with children with autism who were either nonverbal or minimally verbal resulted in the acquisition of both receptive and expressive vocabulary at faster rates and higher levels. Similarly, Daniels (2001) noted that because "inner speech and adept hand movements" are housed in one of the language centers of the brain (Broca's area), "there is an increased opportunity for the formation of a greater number of connections and patterns in the brain" (p. 126).

Principle Four

A great deal of emphasis must be placed upon comprehension, since it is the basis for meaningful expression (Savage-Rumbaugh & Lewin, 1994; Twachtman-Cullen, 2000). For individuals at the lower end of the autism continuum, this involves a focus on *linguistic comprehension,* or the understanding of the literal meanings of words. At higher levels of functioning, this will likely involve a focus on *pragmatic comprehension*, that which is rooted in the abstract and social aspects of language. Reading between the lines to get at intended meaning, making inferences, and dealing with idioms all involve pragmatic comprehension.

Principle Five

According to Bloom (2000), "It is not how often the adult says the word that matters; it is how often the child processes it" (p. 90). That is, *intake* is more important than *input*. Hence, interventionists should make every effort to ensure that the individual with autism is actively engaged in language-learning activities, since without active engagement, he or she will not be able to take in and process language input. At the same time, one is cautioned to avoid forced participation in language intervention activities, given that it can lead to anxiety and "shutdown," neither of which is conducive to learning.

Principle Six

"To learn what a word means, one needs to possess the relevant concept" (Bloom, 2000, p. 90). This is especially germane to individuals with autism, given that research has revealed a dissociation between concept formation and concept identification in this population. Consequently, they are impaired in their ability to form the concept (understand the meaning behind the word), even as they are able to identify the concept (point to the word that represents it) (Brown, Solomon, Bauminger, & Rogers, 2005; Minshew, Meyer, & Goldstein, 2002). Thus, it is important for interventionists to make sure that vocabulary targets are within the child's conceptual grasp, since true word learning requires **concept formation** as opposed to simple **concept identification**. This can best be done by (a) providing lots of "time in" with respect to basic-level words that are used to refer to things in the here and now; and (b) rooting language-learning activities in meaningful interactive experiences.

Principle Seven

Since children do not learn different classes of words (e.g., nouns/verbs/adjectives) in the same manner, intervention should not be carried out in the same manner for different classes of words (Bloom, 2000; Tomasello, 1992; Tomasello & Kruger, 1992). To illustrate, when children are asked to point to a noun (e.g., *cup*), it is the whole object that constitutes the noun. In contrast, when they are asked to point to pictures depicting verbs (e.g., "point to *running*"), they are being asked to identify a dynamic action in a static picture format in which only one aspect of the picture is relevant. Inasmuch as individuals demonstrate a predilection for stimulus overselectivity, as well as problems determining relevance, this is a more difficult cognitive task than learning the verb in a more active and meaningful format – say, in a game of *Simon Says*.

Principle Eight

Language intervention should be carried out in a context that supports meaning, since this makes the process of inferring intent easier. Furthermore, since, as noted earlier, words have a perspectival quality, whereby one object or event can be signified by several different words (Tomasello, 2003), the context in which the word is rendered can help to disambiguate its meaning. For example, context provides an excellent way for the individual to learn that toast is something you can *eat* in the morning, and *do* in the afternoon.

Principle Nine

Given that "theory of mind underlies how children learn the entities to which words refer, intuit how words relate to one another, and understand how words can serve as communication signs" (Bloom, 2000, p. 56), theory-of-mind activities should be woven into the fabric of the language-learning activities.

Principle Ten

Appropriate language use (which implies generalization to appropriate contexts) is most appropriately addressed in contextually relevant, usage-based, interactive routines that mirror the language-learning process by providing rich opportunities for inferring communicative intent and exercising the pragmatic functions of communication (Wetherby et al., 1997).

Summary and Conclusions

This chapter has considered the child's journey toward acquiring language – from the fledgling first steps in attention and affect sharing, to the more definitive stride toward joint attention and intention reading, and finally to the child's remarkable entry into the world of two way symbolic communication. It is a journey that *all* children begin, but only some complete.

The issues raised in this chapter are my attempt to examine the common pathways and points of departure that demarcate the journey for neurotypical children and their peers with autism. With findings from both the language and the autism research literature as the road map, common pathways in language development between neurotypical children and children with autism were found. Specifically, joint attention and intention reading loom large as foundational elements that guide the child toward the journey's end. Moreover, joint attention and vocabulary development were found to be related in the same way for both neurotypical children and those with autism, such that the greater the capacity for joint attention, the greater the size of the child's vocabulary, and vice versa. This is a critical common pathway in and of itself, but it is all the more remarkable for what it suggests: The principles governing language acquisition in neurotypical children also apply to children with autism. This finding underscores the relevance of the language research literature for this population. It also speaks to the importance of building the language structure by laying a strong (social-cognitive) foundation to support it, for it is at the juncture of joint attention and its progression toward intention reading that the pathway toward symbolic communication begins to diverge for children with autism.

This leads quite naturally to social-pragmatic theory. Given the nature of the pragmatic impairment in individuals with autism and the social-cognitive deficits that give rise to it, social-pragmatic theory provides a "good fit" for both explaining many of the language deficits and for addressing them. This is a view supported by research regarding the similarities governing language acquisition for neurotypical children and their peers with autism. It is also a view supported by the universality of the pragmatic impairment found across age and functioning levels in autism, beginning with the deficits in joint attention and intention reading early on. Simply stated, if a patient shows the symptoms of a heart attack, her heart would be examined. Likewise, if pragmatic deficits are the defining features of the language impairment in autism – and there is a plethora of research to support this – we should look to the social-pragmatic arena for answers.

Finally, the ability to communicate is the most difficult and remarkable feat of humankind. The fact that most people speak so effortlessly masks its complexity. Indeed, language users perform complex social-pragmatic tasks without awareness. For example, we not only make presuppositions about our listener's needs, but also the adjustments needed to accommodate them. And we do so automatically, in split-second time. It is only when something goes dramatically wrong in the development of language – as it does in autism – that we take notice of language at all.

I suggest that the ease with which most of us learn and use language blinds us to the complexities inherent in the language-acquisition process. The effect of this on intervention in autism is that many areas of language impairment slip below the "radar screen" (e.g., joint attention and intention reading), and consequently, crucial areas of pragmatic impairment go unaddressed. Worse yet, as noted early on in this chapter, a lack of understanding of the language-learning process and of the social-cognitive elements that are an integral part of it can result in language intervention practices that are ineffective and/or inappropriate. This should be kept uppermost in mind before asking the individual with autism to *use* his or her words.

In recent years, there has been an explosion of high-quality research on language development in both typically developing children and those with autism. This research can and should inform our intervention practices. I leave the reader with two thoughts: (a) In order to translate research into practice, we have to consult it and apply it; and (b) It is not enough to look only to the autism research literature for guidance when dealing with the complexities of language acquisition. We must also look to the language research literature, since one cannot deal effectively with disordered communication without some understanding of normal language development. Only by melding together relevant research findings from both literature bases will it be possible to obtain the best, most up-to-date "road map" for the crucial journey to symbolic communication.

Tips for the Classroom

✓ Remember that the communication disorder in autism affects a student's ability to form concepts and to accurately interpret concepts in the language of others. When we attempt to modify challenging behavior, we often verbalize our disapproval using complex social and emotional concepts. This can make the communication of expectations even more difficult. Using visual cues to support the intended message can make the task of comprehension much easier.

✓ To teach nonverbal social communication, either take pictures or use commercial pictures depicting different facial expressions, and then have the student practice imitating the various expressions (e.g., making a curious face while looking at a picture of a curious face). The same pictures may be used for matching similar expressions, grouping facial expressions into categories, and creating stories about what the person in the picture might be experiencing. Using a digital camera to take pictures of the students making different faces can add an element of fun to this activity.

✓ Expand on the traditional "sharing" times so that students with autism have ample opportunities to interact with others, using their special interests or talents as motivational "hooks" to engage them in the act of sharing.

✓ Use cartooning to support theory-of-mind development by helping students to visualize others' ideas, intentions, and thoughts. This can be done with picture books and using sticky notes to label what a particular character might be thinking. Commercial photographs depicting social situations may also be used.

✓ Consider another activity that supports theory-of-mind development, employing pictures of various faces (males, females, boys, girls, teens, etc.) and a set of statement cards: Students are asked to match a statement or verbal expression with the person most likely to say it. You can expand on this activity by using pictures of people who have different relationships to the student (parents, friends, teachers, strangers, the president of the United States, etc.), asking the student to match the most likely topic of conversation they might have with each of the characters. Inject some fun into this activity by using pictures of movie celebrities or cartoon characters.

✓ Allow reluctant students to observe language groups prior to participating in them. Give them the added support of visual structure to increase their chances of success and feelings of competence.

✓ Use ongoing language activities such as Idiom of the Week or Joke of the Week. Encourage families to carry out this activity at home by writing a letter to parents describing it.

✓ Use a variation on the theme of *Mad Libs* by writing a story, personalized to your student's special interests, to encourage the use of specific concepts and word categories.

✓ Using the format of the common game of charades, create cards with various emotions or social messages and have students take turns making simple gestures with hands and/or body stance to communicate the concept, emotion, or message. You can expand on this activity to work on subtlety by adding a scale of little, medium, and big so that a student might be asked to illustrate big confusion or little disappointment.

✓ During small groups, choose the person whose turn it is by just looking at him or her. This provides a predictable communication routine that requires students to attend to your face and eyes.

✓ Plan lessons jointly with the general education teacher so that she can incorporate language activities into the classroom throughout the week. For example, this is a great way to reinforce idioms, multiple meanings of words, and social concepts.

✓ A great activity to introduce the idea of "making a thinking guess" is the Magic Window, a plastic window behind which you hide pictures, gradually opening the window while students guess what the picture is. This activity can lead to making inferences. Be sure to introduce the activity by distinguishing between the concepts of "wild guess" and "thinking guess." You can add a visual element by drawing a face on a white board with many blank "thinking bubbles" to be filled in with wild guesses at first and then a big thinking guess later.

✓ Speak in a foreign language or in gibberish while giving many exaggerated nonverbal contextual clues about what you are trying to communicate. Ask the students to guess what you want or what you might do next.

✓ Teach verbs in the manner in which they are typically learned by asking students to perform actions. *Simon Says* is an ideal vehicle for this. Use a variation on this theme for older students.

✓ Encourage teachers to use manual signs for all students as prompts and (visual) attention getters. For example, the teacher can use the manual sign for *where* (shaking the index finger from side to side) to give advance notice to the student that a question about a place will be forthcoming. Similarly, he or she can use the manual sign for *who* (circling the index finger around the mouth) to indicate that a question about a person is coming next. Research shows that all students can benefit from this approach!

Chapter Highlights

- Social communication involves not only having spoken language but also having an understanding of the function of words and of what others are thinking.

- Theory of mind and communication are intertwined.

- Communication can be defined as the ability to use words to exchange meaning and influence others.

- Individuals with autism may have a rich vocabulary of words but lack an understanding of how to use them to communicate intent or meaning.

- For infants, playing games such as "peek-a-boo" provides opportunities for attention and affect sharing and social reciprocity, which helps the infant develop the interpersonal relatedness needed for later social communication.

- Experiential learning provides infants with the opportunity to develop new neural pathways and increases brain connectivity.

- Infants with autism do not engage in games as do their neurotypical peers and, therefore, miss out on opportunities for emotional regulation, attention sharing, anticipation, and reciprocity with their caregivers.

- Infants with autism tend to engage in repetitive behaviors; therefore, their opportunity to develop connectivity and the possibility that neurons are not "pruned" may lead to less capacity for social-cognitive behaviors, brain function, and concept development.

- Children with autism have deficits in "joint attention;" that is, in the behaviors suggestive of an increasing understanding of the need to engage other minds, such as gaze following, pointing, and showing/offering gestures.

- As brain research supports the relationship between joint attention and theory of mind, including that the two are located in the same region of the brain, children with autism who lack skills in the area of joint attention also have impaired ability to judge what others are thinking.

- Joint attention plays a pivotal role in establishing intentional communication as it is based on a shared awareness (intersubjectivity) and engagement.

- Research shows joint attention impacts typically developing children and those with autism in a similar way in that the amount of joint attention engaged in is highly correlated with vocabulary development and other language and social gains.

- Joint attention sets the stage for intention reading (the ability to "read" another's intent) and is related to the development of symbolic communication.

- Social-pragmatic theory holds that intention reading plays a critical role in language development.

- Social-pragmatic theory can provide a template for what goes wrong in the language acquisition process in autism; specifically, impairments in social cognition in terms of joint attention, affect sharing, and intention reading are seen as likely causes of the pragmatic impairments of individuals with autism.

- While all areas of language may be impaired in individuals with autism (semantics, syntax, pragmatics), deficits in pragmatics constitute the defining language deficit across age and ability levels.

- When a person uses language to express a specific intent, that piece of language is said to serve a particular function.

- In order to use language to serve a function, the individual must possess both pragmatic skills and intention reading.

- Presuppositional knowledge refers to making judgments about the listener such as that of an individual's prior knowledge of the topic in order to decide what information to provide and how to convey it.

- Conversational maxims refer to having an understanding of the rules of discourse.

- Word learning depends on context, knowledge of the underlying concept, the communicative goal of the speaker, word class, and level of novelty.

- Assessment of language for individuals with autism from a social-pragmatic perspective requires certain considerations, including the use of situated pragmatics and naturalistic contexts, evaluating conversational maxims and presuppositional knowledge, and assessing comprehension at both the literal and the discourse level.

- Intervention needs differ due to the variability in functioning levels that exist among individuals with ASD; however, 10 general principles apply across age and functioning levels. The principles include:

  ➤ Intervention must begin where the learner is

  ➤ Intervention should be experiential

  ➤ The use of augmentative means for communication is important

  ➤ Emphasis should be placed on comprehension

  ➤ Active engagement is important

  ➤ Vocabulary targets should be within the individual's conceptual understanding

  ➤ Different classes of words need to be taught differently

  ➤ Intervention should take place in context in order to support the learning of meaning

  ➤ Theory-of-mind activities should be included within language intervention

  ➤ Intervention that promotes generalization of language occurs in contextually relevant routines

Chapter Review Questions

1. What is "social communication"?

2. Explain how theory of mind relates to social language learning.

3. Why can autism be described as a defect in communication?

4. Why might a student with autism experience difficulties in using his or her words to communicate?

5. What do the chapter authors believe may be a cause of ineffective language intervention for individuals with autism?

6. How do interactive games assist infants in developing social communication?

7. How is experiential learning critical for brain development?

8. How does autism affect infants in terms of experiential learning and later brain development?

9. What is "joint attention" and why is it important in developing social communication?

10. How is intention reading important to social-pragmatic theory?

11. How does understanding social-pragmatic theory help account for the difficulties individuals with autism have in understanding the pragmatic aspects of language?

12. Why is pragmatics so important to the development of language?

13. Why might social-pragmatic theory be considered the "rule" in typical language development?

14. What is meant by saying that words have different pragmatic functions based on the speaker's intentions?

15. What is "presuppositional knowledge" and why is it important to communication?

16. List and explain the four conversational maxims.

17. What does research say about word-learning differences?

18. What are general considerations related to assessment of language development in terms of social pragmatics?

19. What are the principles of intervention in autism that come directly from social-pragmatic theory?

References

Akhtar, N., & Tomasello, M. (1996). Twenty-four-month-old children learn words for absent objects and actions. *British Journal of Developmental Psychology, 14,* 79-93.

Baldwin, D. A. (1995). Understanding the link between joint attention and language. In C. Moore & P. J. Dunham (Eds.), *Joint attention: Its origins and role in development* (pp. 131-58). Hillsdale, NJ: Erlbaum.

Bell, M. A., & Fox, N. A. (1994). Brain development over the first year of life: Relations between EEG frequency and coherence and cognition and affective behaviors. In G. Dawson & K. Fischer (Eds.), *Human behavior and the developing brain* (pp. 314-345). New York: Guilford Press.

Bloom, P. (2000). *How children learn the meanings of words.* Cambridge, MA: The MIT Press.

Brown, J. R., Solomon, M., Bauminger, N., & Rogers, S. J. (2005). *Concept formation and concept identification in high-functioning children with autism spectrum disorder.* Paper presented at the International Conference for Autism (IMFAR), Boston, MA.

Bruner, J. (1983). *Child's talk.* New York: Norton.

Bruner, J., & Haste, H. (Eds.). (1987). *Making sense: The child's construction of the world.* New York: Methuen.

Call, J., & Tomasello, M. (2005). What chimpanzees know about seeing, revisited: An explanation of the third kind. In N. Eilan, C. Hoerl, T. McCormack, & J. Roessler (Eds.), *Joint attention: Communication and other minds: Issues in philosophy and psychology* (pp. 45-64). New York: Oxford University Press.

Carr, E. G., & Durand, V. M. (1985). Reducing behavior problems through functional communication training. *Journal of Applied Behavior Analysis, 18,* 111-126.

Carter, R. (1999). *Mapping the mind.* London: University of California Press, Ltd.

Daniels, M. (2001). *Dancing with words: Signing for hearing children's literacy.* Westport, CT: Bergin & Garvey.

Donnellan, A., Mirenda, P., Mesaros, R., & Fassbender, L. (1984). Analyzing the communicative functions of aberrant behavior. *Journal of the Association for Persons with Severe Handicaps, 9,* 202-212.

Greenough, W. T., & Black, J. E. (1992). Induction of brain structure by experience: Substrates for cognitive development. *Developmental Behavioral Neuroscience, 24,* 155-299.

Grice, H. (1975). Logic and conversation. In D. Davidson & G. Harmon (Eds.), *The logic of grammar* (pp. 41-58). Encino, CA: Dickinson.

Happé, F.G.E. (1996). *Autism: An introduction to psychological theory.* Cambridge, MA: Harvard University Press.

Hewitt, L. E. (2000). Assessing communicative intents. *Seminars in Speech and Language, 21*(3), 257-266.

Hobson, R. P. (2005). What puts the jointness into joint attention? In N. Eilan, C. Hoerl, T. McCormack, & J. Roessler (Eds.), *Joint attention: Communication and other minds: Issues in philosophy and psychology* (pp. 185-204). New York: Oxford University Press.

Just, M. A., Cherkassky, V. L., Keller, T. A., & Minshew, N. J. (2004). Cortical activation and synchronization during sentence comprehension in high-functioning autism: Evidence of underconnectivity. *Brain, 127,* 1811-1821.

Kasari, C. (2005). *Growth in joint attention and symbolic play.* Proceedings of the International Meeting for Autism Research, Boston, MA.

Kaye, K. (1982). *The mental and social life of babies: How parents create persons.* Chicago: The University of Chicago Press.

Landa, R. (2003). *Keynote address.* Presentation at the Autism Society of America national conference, Pittsburgh, PA.

Landa, R., Holman, K. C., Sullivan, M., & Cleary, J. (2005). *Language and social change in toddlers with ASD: Early intervention.* Presentation at the International Meeting for Autism Research, Boston, MA.

Leekam, S. (1993). Children's understanding of mind. In M. Bennett (Ed.), *The development of social cognition: The child as psychologist* (pp. 26-61). New York: Guilford Press.

Leekam, S. (2005). Autism and joint attention impairment. In N. Eilan, C. Hoerl, T. McCormack, & J. Roessler (Eds.), *Joint attention: Communication and other minds: Issues in philosophy and psychology* (pp. 205-229). New York: Oxford University Press.

Lewy, A. L., & Dawson, G. (1992). Social stimulation and joint attention in young autistic children. *Journal of Abnormal Child Psychology, 20,* 555-566.

Lord, C., & Paul, R. (1997). Language and communication in autism. In D. Cohen & F. Volkmar (Eds.), *Handbook of autism and pervasive developmental disorders* (2nd ed., pp. 195-225). New York: Wiley.

Loveland, K., & Landry, S. (1986). Joint attention in autism and developmental language delay. *Journal of Autism and Developmental Disorders, 16,* 335-349.

Lund, N. J. (2000). Assessment of language structure: From syntax to event-based analysis. *Seminars in Speech and Language, 21*(3), 267-274.

Minshew, N. J., Meyer, J., & Goldstein, G. (2002). Abstract reasoning in autism: A dissociation between concept formation and concept identification. *Neuropsychology, 16*(3), 327-334.

Mirenda, P. (2003). Toward functional augmentative and alternative communication for students with autism: Manual signs, graphic symbols, and voice output communication aids. *Language, Speech, and Hearing Services in Schools, 34,* 203-216.

Mundy, P., Sigman, M., & Kasari, C. (1990). A longitudinal study of joint attention and language development in autistic children. *Journal of Autism and Developmental Disorders, 20,* 115-128.

Paul, R. (2000). Literal and discourse approaches to comprehension assessment. *Seminars in Speech and Language, 21*(3), 247-255.

Rogoff, B. (1990). *Apprenticeship in thinking: Cognitive development in social context.* New York: Oxford University Press.

Sacks, O. (1989). *Seeing voices: A journey into the world of the deaf.* Los Angeles: University of California Press.

Savage-Rumbaugh, S., & Lewin, R. (1994). *Kanzi: The ape at the brink of the human mind.* New York: John Wiley & Sons.

Schwartz, J. M., & Begley, S. (2002). *The mind and the brain: Neuroplasticity and the power of mental force.* New York: Regan Books.

Siller, M., & Sigman, M. (2002). The behaviors of parents of children with autism predict the subsequent development of their children's communication skills. *Journal of Autism and Developmental Disorders, 32*(2), 77-89.

Tager-Flusberg, H. (1997). Language acquisition and theory of mind: Contributions from the study of autism. In L. B. Adamson & M. A. Romski (Eds.), *Communication and language acquisition: Discoveries from atypical development* (pp. 135-160). Baltimore: Paul H. Brookes.

Tager-Flusberg, H., Joseph, R., & Folstein, S. (2001). Current directions in research on autism. *Mental Retardation and Developmental Disabilities Research Reviews, 7,* 21-29.

Tomasello, M. (1992). *First verbs: A case study of early grammatical development.* New York: Cambridge University Press.

Tomasello, M. (2001). Perceiving intentions and learning words in the second year of life. In M. Tomasello & E. Bates (Eds.), *Language development: The essential readings* (pp. 11-128). Oxford, UK: Blackwell.

Tomasello, M. (2003). *Constructing a language: A usage-based theory of language acquisition.* Cambridge, MA: Harvard University Press.

Tomasello, M., & Barton, M. (1994). Learning words in non-ostensive contexts. *Developmental Psychology, 30,* 639-650.

Tomasello, M., & Bates, E. (2001). General introduction. In M. Tomasello & E. Bates (Eds.), *Language development: The essential readings* (pp. 1-11). Malden, MA: Blackwell.

Tomasello, M., & Farrar, M. J. (1986). Joint attention and early language. *Child Development, 57,* 1454-1463.

Tomasello, M., & Kruger, A. (1992). Joint attention on actions: Acquiring verbs in ostensive and non-ostensive contexts. *Journal of Child Language, 19,* 311-333.

Tomasello, M., Mannle, S., & Kruger, A. (1986). Linguistic environment of one to two year old twins. *Developmental Psychology, 22,* 169-176.

Tomasello, M., Strosberg, R., & Akhtar, N. (1995). Eighteen-month-old children learn words in non-ostensive contexts. *Journal of Child Language, 22,* 1-20.

Tomasello, M., & Todd, J. (1983). Joint attention and lexical acquisition style. *First Language, 4,* 197-212.

Trevarthan, C. (1980). The foundations of intersubjectivity: Development of interpersonal and cooperative understanding of infants. In D. R. Olson (Ed.), *The social foundation of language and thought: Essays in honor of Jerome S. Bruner* (pp. 316-341). New York: Norton.

Twachtman-Cullen, D. (1998). Language and communication in high-functioning autism and Asperger syndrome. In E. Schopler, G. B. Mesibov, & L. Kunce (Eds.), *Asperger syndrome or high-functioning autism?* (pp. 199-225). New York: Plenum.

Twachtman-Cullen, D. (2000). More able children with autism spectrum disorders: Sociocommunicative challenges and guidelines for enhancing abilities. In A. M. Wetherby & B. M. Prizant (Eds.), *Autism spectrum disorders: A transactional developmental perspective* (pp. 225-249). Baltimore: Paul H. Brookes.

Twachtman-Cullen, D. (2006, Winter). Functional communication training: Where communication, behavior, and conventional wisdom meet. *Autism Spectrum Quarterly,* 42-45.

Twachtman-Cullen, D., & Twachtman-Reilly, J. (2007). Communication and language issues in less able school-age children with autism. In R. L. Gabriels & D. E. Hill (Eds.), *Growing up with autism: Working with school-age children and adolescents* (pp. 73-94). New York: Guilford Press.

Wetherby, A. (2006). Understanding and measuring social communication in children with autism spectrum disorders. In T. Charman & W. Stone (Eds.), *Social and communication development in autism spectrum disorders: Early identification, diagnosis, and intervention* (pp. 3-34). New York: Guilford Publications.

Wetherby, A. M., Prizant, B. M., & Hutchinson, T. A. (1998). Communicative, social/affective, and symbolic profiles of young children with autism and pervasive developmental disorders. *American Journal of Speech-Language Pathology, 7,* 79-91.

Wetherby, A. M., & Prutting, C. A. (1984). Profiles of communicative and cognitive-social abilities in autistic children. *Journal of Speech and Hearing Research, 27*(3), 364-377.

Wetherby, A., Schuler, A., & Prizant, B. (1997). Enhancing language and communication: Theoretical foundations. In D. Cohen & F. Volkmar (Eds.), *Handbook of autism and pervasive developmental disorders* (2nd ed., pp. 513-538). New York: Wiley.

Williams, J., Waiter, G., Perra, O., Whiten, A., & Perrett, D. (2005). Overlap between the neural substrate for joint attention, and white and grey matter volume differences in autistic spectrum disorder. *Neuroimage, 25,* 133-140.

Wingert, P., & Brant, M. (2005, August 15). Reading your baby's mind. *Newsweek,* pp. 32-39.

Wolfberg, P. J. (1999). *Play and imagination in children with autism.* New York: Teachers College Press.

Learner Objectives

After reading this chapter, the learner should be able to:

- Define what is meant by "structure" in teaching

- Explain what TEACCH is

- Explain "Structured Teaching," including theoretical foundations, as well as implications for students with ASD and their families

- Explain what is meant by the "Culture of Autism" and provide examples of characteristics

- List the five questions that Structured Teaching should answer by providing the learner with visual information and organization of the environment

- Discuss the importance of spaces, schedules, task organization, activity systems, and routines in the instruction of individuals with ASD

- Provide examples of strategies to address the five questions of Structured Teaching

- Describe and discuss the cases presented in the text in which Structured Teaching strategies are used to teach individuals at different ages

Chapter 5

Structured Teaching and Environmental Supports

Gary B. Mesibov • Victoria Shea

Anthony is a 5-year-old boy with autism who is in a special education class in his local public school. This is his first year at this school. Since the age of 3, Anthony has received special education services at a child development center, where his classmates have been children with Down syndrome, physical disabilities, hearing or vision loss, or speech/language delay.

Anthony is usually fussing when he is brought into the classroom. In fact, he is often carried into the room, crying loudly, by the assistant who meets him at the bus. He always goes immediately to the block corner, where he removes his coat and drops it on the floor. He apparently would prefer to spend the morning alone in the block corner, and he generally does not respond to his teachers' attempts to play with him or encourage him to go to a different play area. If he is physically removed from the block area, he has a tantrum. When he needs to use the bathroom (which is attached to the classroom), he generally pulls his pants down on his way across the room, and he comes out without flushing and with his pants unzipped.

Anthony willingly comes to circle time only on the days when musical instruments are passed around, but when these circle times are over, he has a tantrum when a teacher takes the instrument away. On other days, he is physically brought to circle time, but he typically gets up after a few minutes and runs back to the block corner. His two favorite activities are building tall towers and then knocking them down, and lying on his stomach watching out of the corner of his eye as he rolls a car back and forth. The teachers have found that the easiest way to interrupt him without causing a tantrum is to offer him a snack. He comes to the teacher, takes the snack, and then walks around the room eating it. Sometimes he comes to the snack table and takes food, even if it is on another child's plate. Similarly, when the other children are seated at their tables working on craft projects, he sometimes walks by and picks up some of the materials, then walks or runs around the room flapping them.

At the end of the day, Anthony does not respond when the teachers tell the children it is time to get their coats and go home, and he must often be pulled screaming from the block corner, down the hallway to the waiting school bus.

In this vignette, Anthony is not learning new skills, he is unhappy or frustrated for significant parts of the school day, and his teachers are probably also frustrated by their inability to engage or teach him. We believe that **Structured Teaching** methods would make a significant contribution to Anthony's educational plan. In this chapter, we will explain the principles and techniques of Structured Teaching, and then present vignettes demonstrating the use of Structured Teaching with students of various ages and skill levels.

What Is Structure?

Most modern special education professionals indicate that structure is an important element of effective teaching, but it is not always clear what is meant by "structure" or whether the term means the same thing to all those who use it.

We describe structure for students with autism spectrum disorder (ASD) as meaning that the teacher or other caregiver decides *what* the learning activities will be, *where* they take place, and *how long* they last. These decisions should be made based on the individual student's needs (not, for example, on the basis of convenience or the student's or teacher's preferences). The purpose of structure is to organize time and space in the learning environment. Individuals with ASD tend to be disorganized or otherwise ineffective in their approach to many materials and activities, so they need external organizational support (that is, structure) in order to be meaningfully engaged in learning.

What Is Structured Teaching?

Structured Teaching is the name of the instructional strategies and environmental supports for individuals with ASD developed by the **TEACCH** program. TEACCH, which stands for **T**reatment and **E**ducation of **A**utistic and related **C**ommunication-handicapped **CH**ildren, is the statewide autism service program in North Carolina. TEACCH, which is administratively housed in the School of Medicine at the University of North Carolina-Chapel Hill, has nine regional centers across the state that provide diagnostic evaluations, parent education, and other clinical services in addition to in-state, national, and international teacher training and consultation.

Structured Teaching as used within the TEACCH program has two different, equally important goals: (a) teach the individual with ASD as many skills as possible, given his developmental level; and (b) provide an environment that is as comprehensible as possible, so that the learner can understand the expectations and opportunities around him. In other words, this approach is both an educational technique and a method of organizing a supportive environment.

Structured Teaching can be used in all settings, including homes, schools, work sites, specialized therapy sessions, recreational activities, community errands, and so on. It can also be adapted for use with individuals with ASD of all ages and developmental levels. However, for the purposes of this chapter, we will focus on students in school from preschool to high school graduation.

Theoretical Foundations

Structured Teaching is a social-cognitive-behavioral approach applied to the neuropsychological characteristics of ASD. "Behavioral" indicates that the approach deals with observable behaviors and that the learning environment systematically incorporates meaningful, pleasurable consequences for productive learning and acceptable behavior. "Social-cognitive" reflects the additional importance we place on increasing the individual's understanding of his world, a broad concept that includes explaining and teaching social behaviors and interactions and broadening the individual's cognitive ideas and beliefs about the world.

We also emphasize organization of the environment and the ways activities are presented (also called antecedents to behavior) because of the distinctive ways that people with ASD think about, understand (or often, misunderstand), and then act on their environments. By including a focus on the social-cognitive perspective of the learner, Structured Teaching can prevent some of the misunderstanding and disorganization often demonstrated by students with ASD in typical special education and general education settings.

Structured Teaching and the Culture of Autism

We call the characteristic patterns of thinking and behavior of ASD the "**Culture of Autism**" (Mesibov, Shea, & Schopler, 2005). Although autism is not a culture in the traditional sense, we have found it helpful to use this metaphor to depict the shared neuropsychological patterns of thinking, communication, and behavior seen among individuals with ASD. Even though each student with ASD is a unique individual with unique skills, difficulties, interests, temperament, and personality, as a group they share a significant number of characteristics.

Table 5.1
Characteristics of the Culture of Autism

- Relative strength in and preference for processing *visual* information (compared to difficulties with auditory processing, particularly of language)

- Heightened attention to *details* but difficulty understanding the meaning of how these details fit together (sometimes called a deficit in central coherence; Frith, 2003)

- Difficulty with *combining or integrating* ideas

- Difficulty with *sequencing and organizing* ideas, materials, and activities

- Difficulties with *attention* (some individuals are very distractible, others have difficulty shifting attention efficiently)

- *Communication* problems; they vary by developmental level, but generally include impairments in the social use of language (pragmatics) and correct word usage (semantics), the understanding and use of nonverbal communication, relative difficulty with abstract or nuanced language, and delayed development of vocabulary and grammar (except in Asperger Syndrome/high-functioning autism; Mesibov, Shea, & Adams, 2001)

- Difficulty with concepts of *time*, including moving too quickly or too slowly and having problems recognizing the beginning, middle, or end of an activity

- Tendency to become *attached to routines*, so that activities may be difficult to transfer or generalize from the original learning situation, and disruptions in routines can be upsetting, confusing, or uncomfortable

- Very strong *interests and impulses* to engage in favored activities

- Marked *sensory* preferences and aversions (see Chapter 6)

The characteristics in Table 5.1 are not unique to ASD, as they overlap both with other developmental disabilities, such as intellectual disability, language disorders, and attention deficit/hyperactivity disorder, and with some mental health conditions, particularly anxiety disorders. It is the combination, severity, and pervasiveness of the characteristics of the Culture of Autism that distinguish ASD from other conditions. However, many individuals with ASD also have other, co-existing developmental disabilities or mental health problems (see Chapter 1).

The unique combination of these factors in each person means that there is no universal pattern of learning characteristics in ASD. As a result, there is no standardized curriculum that is appropriate, so the educational plan must be individualized for each student. Further, plans must be revised frequently based on learning and maturation, as well as additional observations and insights about how the student learns and think. Consequently, techniques that were effective when the student was in preschool may not be useful or necessary by first grade, much less in middle school or high school. Similarly, strategies that worked with last year's student with ASD will probably not be as effective with a different student this year.

Structured Teaching and Behavior Management

Traditional behavior management techniques may have limited effectiveness with individuals with ASD (Bregman, Zager, & Gerdtz, 2005; Schreibman & Ingersoll, 2005). Examples of traditional techniques include:

- Using tangible reward systems for good behavior (e.g., the student earns tokens for good behavior and can use the tokens for a toy or a treat at the end of the day or at the end of the week)

- Using response-cost systems in which students lose privileges or treats because of their behavior (e.g., because of misbehavior, a student is not permitted to go on a field trip or use the computer during free time)

- Praising students and expressing pride in their accomplishments and effort

- Having students observe and imitate the behavior of other students who are being praised

- Sending students to a time-out chair away from the group

The following factors frequently interfere with the effectiveness of these techniques with students with ASD:

- Reward and response-cost systems are often too language-based or too complex for students with ASD, requiring making cognitive connections among a large number of details (behaviors, rules, points or tokens, various prizes, etc.).

- Verbal praise may be meaningless or incomprehensible.

- Individuals with ASD often do not attend to, understand, or imitate the behavior of their peers.

- Time away from group activities may be desirable rather than punitive.

In thinking about how to teach and support appropriate behavior, Structured Teaching should be pragmatic. If a traditional technique might work, try it; if it works, use it; if something is not working, stop doing it and do something else. There is no hard and fast rule against using traditional behavior management techniques, particularly positive techniques, such as social praise and rewards. Many students with ASD can *sometimes* follow verbal directions (particularly when not under stress); they *may* be able to understand, enjoy, and respond to reward systems (although these are rarely sufficient to control their behavior in situations of sensory overload or intense impulses); *some* students may seek or respond to praise; and they *may* imitate another student occasionally. As a general rule, however, reward and response-cost systems are not as effective for students with ASD as they are for other students, and as a result they can be very frustrating for both students and teachers.

In particular, systems involving loss of privileges or treats are often too abstract for students who have both ASD and cognitive delays, but they may occasionally be helpful for high-functioning students. An example of such a system for reducing undesirable behaviors is having a student start the day with five visual symbols. Each times she engages in the undesirable behaviors, she loses one symbol, but if she has any symbols remaining at the end of the day, she is given a treat.

Structured Teaching and Families

The other factor that is integral to the TEACCH Structured Teaching approach is respect for families. In the not-too-distant past, parents were considered to be the cause of their child's autism, but the TEACCH program was founded on the principle that parents and professionals can work together collaboratively, with parents learning to be co-therapists for their children (Schopler & Reichler, 1971).

We recommend that teachers and other school professionals communicate regularly with families and value their perspectives. As illustrated in Table 5.2, a notebook that travels with the student between home and school, with both a template of information to exchange (individualized according to the student's particular needs and challenges) and space for additional notes, can be both useful and practical. The template may be completed with check marks or a few words, which is important given the time demands on both teachers and parents.

Table 5.2

Sample Home-School Communication Systems

Preschool Day _____ *(date)*

	Yes/No
Entered classroom happily?	
Ate breakfast?	
Used toilet/morning?	
Ate lunch?	
Slept at naptime?	
Used toilet/afternoon?	
Played with new toy?	
Number of crying episodes *(tally marks)*	

Notes:

School Day _____ *(date)*

	Yes/No
Good behavior on bus?	
Turned in homework?	
Did not argue with teacher?	
Played with others during recess?	
Raised hand before speaking during group times?	

Notes:

Home Life _____ *(date)*

	Yes/No
Any special family events last night?	
Slept typical time?	
Ate breakfast?	
Took medicine?	
Questions or problems?	

Notes:

Putting Principles into Practice

Structured Teaching should provide visual information and physical organization of the environment to answer five questions for the learner:

1. Where should I be?
2. What work or activity will I do?
3. How much work will I do?/How long will the activity last?
4. How will I know that I am making progress and when I have finished?
5. What will I do next?

We have found it useful and important to answer these five questions in some form for all new learning situations. That is, Structured Teaching typically designs an individualized way to provide this information for all new tasks, including those focused on cognitive, language, academic, and motor skills; social engagement; and activities of daily living (such as using the school cafeteria, bathrooms, playground, and transportation system for going to and from school).

In addition, providing answers to these five questions is useful during any activity in which the individual indicates, through words or behavior, that he is confused or having difficulty staying organized or focused on the activity. Indications that a student needs the answers to the five questions to be more visually clear include:

- The student wanders or runs around the room during the activity.
- The student asks repetitive questions during the activity.
- The student often refuses to start or end the activity.
- The student often leaves an activity before completing it.
- The student often has tantrums during an activity.

In such situations, we typically try to make the structure (that is, the answers to the five questions) more clear, in addition to ensuring that the activity is within the student's ability level. Although there may be additional factors that contribute to the problematic behaviors, increasing the visual structure is almost always an important aspect of getting the student back on track.

Answering the first question, "Where should I be?" is accomplished through the use of *schedules*. In addition, because each activity takes place in a consistent and, therefore, predictable location, a student learns the association between where he is going and generally what he will do there (such as one-on-one work with a teacher, P.E., lunch, etc.), which provides some information to answer the second question, "What work or activity will I do?" Additional information is provided visually by the *task* and the *work/activity system* (for multiple tasks), which shows the student specifically what he is being asked to do once he arrives at the designated location and how many times he is going to do it (Questions 3 and 4 – "How much work will I do?" or "How long will this activity last?" and "How will I know that I have finished?"). The final question, "What will I do next?" is typically answered by indicating visually what will follow the last item on the task or work/activity system and by teaching the student *routines* (which serve other purposes as well). These elements of answering the five questions are discussed in more detail in the next section.

Schedules

A schedule of activities is a fundamental element of Structured Teaching. The student's day should be a series of planned activities in designated locations (typically with a few minutes in a safe play/leisure area between activities). Further, each student's schedule should be individualized in terms of both content and form so it is meaningful for the student. Rarely do two or more students have identical learning styles, communication systems, attention spans, and interests, and therefore their schedules should reflect their individuality. If all students in a class are using the same schedule, it is highly likely that their schedules are not sufficiently individualized.

Schedules should be visual, and they should be accurate. Since life is not always predictable, however, predetermined schedules must be in a form that can be changed quickly as circumstances change, so that updating is quick and easy. This means that it is not efficient to print and laminate schedules. Students may be shown, as needed, that parts of the schedule are either being crossed off or removed, or that other activities are being substituted or inserted.

For the developmentally youngest learners, schedules can take the form of objects indicating "what's next." At the simplest level, the teacher hands the student an object that will be used in the upcoming activity. There is no symbolism involved, and the student is not required to "check his schedule." Instead, the schedule is brought to him, and he is guided toward the corresponding activity. Examples include giving the student

- A puzzle piece to get him to go to his work table, where the rest of the puzzle is waiting, along with one or more additional learning activities

- A cup that he will take to the snack table, where someone will pour a beverage into the cup

- A diaper or roll of toilet paper for use in the bathroom

- A spoon to take to the lunch table

- A carpet square to take to a group activity location

- Chalk or a bag of balls to take to the playground or gym

Although students must often be guided and assisted at first to go to the appropriate location with the object, the goal is to reduce that assistance as soon as possible, so that the student is as independent as possible in knowing where to go and what he is going to do there.

As students become more capable, we often move from the procedure of *handing them* the schedule object or picture to a procedure of *directing them to* their schedule. This skill represents increased independence on the student's part, and it enables the teacher to direct and supervise the transitions of several students at a time. Even students who use object schedules can learn to go to the location where objects are located (e.g., in a container on top of a small bookcase, or in a small row of cubbies mounted on a wall).

Learners who are somewhat more advanced developmentally can often find meaning in pictures, photographs, or symbols instead of needing concrete objects. The process of learning the association between a symbol and an activity is similar to learning the meaning of objects – that is, by repeatedly experiencing that the schedule symbol predicts the activity, many students learn the association. At all ages there are some students who can associate meaning with written words; for these students, typically, a written schedule may be used.

In addition to the individualized form of the schedule, the amount of information the schedule provides varies according to the student's ability to understand. Some students understand only "what's next," and if they see additional objects or symbols about later activities, they become confused. Other students appear to understand and make use of a series of objects or symbols, indicating the upcoming 2–3 activities. As students continue to develop, they can often use part-day or full-day schedules without becoming confused or distressed. Some students also find weekly, monthly, or yearly calendars of upcoming events to be helpful for anticipating activities they enjoy (such as vacations, holidays, special events, etc.).

Tasks and Work/Activity Systems

Tasks and work/activity systems visually show the student, from the very beginning of the activity, what items he is being asked to complete and how he will see that he is making progress toward being finished. Each task provides this information about the materials and steps *within* the task; the work/activity system provides this information about a *series* of tasks for students who are developmentally able to work on multiple tasks in one session.

One way to provide this information visually is to arrange the materials or directions to specify exactly how many or how much the student must do before being finished. When the activity itself does not involve a concrete number of materials, a different way to answer the question of how long an activity will last is to make the passage of time visual (see the Practical Strategies section in this chapter for examples).

Routines

Not all activities within a student's day require work/activity systems, which are primarily used for fostering independence and for situations in which the student would otherwise be confused or disorganized. Many students can master work/activity systems to the point that they become productive, independent routines, including entering a classroom and depositing jacket and backpack/homework in the correct location, going to a designated area to wait or play quietly between learning activities, using the bathroom, asking for help with the work, indicating that the work has been finished, and so on.

Practical Strategies for Teachers

More specific techniques for providing visual structure and answering the five questions are presented in this section.

1. **Where Should I Be?**

    The most typical way to provide this information visually is to have a designated place for the learner to sit (such as a chair, carpet square, the student's colored symbol or name, etc.) or to stand (such as on the student's symbol or name, a mark on the floor, an outline of footprints, carpet square, etc.). At times, it is helpful to have students sit down even when other students are typically standing (e.g., while waiting in line or while brushing teeth), because a chair provides additional boundaries and cues for indicating where the student is expected to be.

However, some students have difficulty remaining seated, preferring to pace or move throughout the room. For those students (particularly if they are younger or concrete learners), we might begin by defining a relatively large area to indicate where the student should be. To do this, we generally find it helpful to use various physical elements of the room, including pillars, walls, corners, large pieces of furniture, screens, and so on, both to define the student's space and to reduce distractions from other activity in the room.

While more developmentally advanced, abstract learners with ASD may learn the location of activities as quickly as their typical peers, they may still benefit from structure in the form of assigned seats, a daily schedule that includes the room number for each class, a map of the route between classes, and so on.

The basic principle is that if a student has difficulty locating or staying in the "right" place, the teacher uses visual means to show her where to be.

2. **What Work or Activity Will I Do?**

Specific ways to follow this general principle also vary depending on the student's developmental level, but the fundamental approach is to organize the materials and the activity in ways that let the student *see* what he is supposed to do and for how long. The emphasis here is on showing (visually) as opposed to telling (verbally). Thus, we recommend always supplementing spoken directions or explanations with visual or physical cues, such as gestures, pictures, concrete objects, written directions, and so on.

Structured Teaching makes a point of organizing materials for the student so that they are available in a logical order (typically from left to right and top to bottom) and are visually clear and physically stable. To do this, we use various office supplies to keep materials organized, such as:
- Baskets
- File folders
- Clear containers
- Velcro and tape
- Clips

We also work to highlight the most important parts of the visual or physical display of materials by techniques such as:
- Making the parts larger
- Highlighting them
- Putting a colored frame around them
- Eliminating clutter on the table or desk top

3. **How Much Work Will I Do?/How Long Will This Activity Last?**
    and
4. **How Will I Know That I Have Finished?**

Usually, the materials involved in the learning activity are organized and counted out (or listed) in advance, so that by looking at the materials, the student can get information about both what he is going to do and for how long. For example, for concrete learners there are containers for each of the "raw materials" involved in the task and a container for the finished product. For academic learners, there might be a set of file folders with an assignment on the left and a pocket for the finished product on the right.

When activities do not involve materials that provide information about "how much" or "how many," various forms of visual timers are available, such as hourglasses that use sand or colored water and timers that count down from a specified time (such as 10 minutes). Teachers can also devise individualized ways to make time visual; for example, the teacher puts out a set of objects (such as clothes pins) or symbols (such as clock faces or plain circles) when an activity begins, then takes one away every 5 minutes (or every minute, every 10 minutes, etc.), so that the student can *see* how much time is left.

Examples of Task Organization That Answer These Questions

- **Example #1 (Task for young or concrete learner).** The student is given a transparent basket of small objects (so he can see *how many* there are) and a container with a hole on top. Each of the small objects is to be put into the container. The student can see (and feel) that the basket of materials is getting emptier. When all the objects are gone, the task is *finished*.

- **Example #2 (Task for an older, concrete learner).** The student has a clear container of index cards, a clear container of envelopes, and a clear container of mailing labels (so he can see *how many* there are). The task is to put an index card into an envelope, put a mailing label on the envelope, and then put the envelope into a basket. Again, the student can see that the container of materials is getting emptier, and that the "finished basket" is getting fuller. When the materials are empty, the task is *finished*.

- **Example #3 (P.E. task).** The student has a container of objects and an empty container. The task is to run, skate, skip, and so on, to a finish line with one object and put it in an empty container, which shows her *how many* laps she will do. This setup can also be used for exercises such as sit-ups or stretches (objects are at the beginning position; the empty container representing "finished" is at the position reached doing the exercise). The student sees and feels that the basket of objects is getting emptier. When all the objects are in the other container, the task is *finished*.

Examples of Work/Activity Systems That Answer These Questions

- **Example #4 (Series of tasks for an academic learner).** The student has a checklist (or homework assignment book) of reading tasks: Read pages 9–11; answer questions on p. 12; write a paragraph using all of the words on p. 13. The student can see *how many* items are on the list, and by checking off each item as he completes it (or as he begins it), he can see that he is making progress. When all the activities have been checked off and performed, the work session is *finished*.

- **Example #5 (Series of tasks for an older vocational learner).** The student has a list consisting of a series of pictures of materials used in a housekeeping task: pail, water faucet, bottle of cleaning liquid, sponge mop, two bathrooms, sink, and storage closet. The student has already learned the tasks associated with each picture, so this list shows him *how many* tasks to perform (get pail, fill with water, add cleaning liquid, use mop on those bathroom floors, empty pail, and put away materials). He pulls each picture off the list and puts it into a small envelope next to the schedule before completing the task. When the list of tasks is empty and all the pictures are in the envelope, the work session is *finished*.

5. **What Will I Do Next?**

   For some students with ASD, it appears that simply achieving "finished" is a gratifying, positively reinforcing experience (which probably explains why being interrupted can be distressing). More typical, concrete reinforcement (such as something to eat or drink, computer time, music, or time to read or play with a favorite toy) can also be helpful for making clear to students that they have successfully completed a task.

   Between learning activities, we usually recommend teaching a student to engage in a productive or harmless activity in a safe, designated place in the classroom, so that the teacher can work with other students or prepare for the next activity. Sometimes the student quickly learns where to go and what is available to do during these leisure times. In other situations, an object or symbol is put in the workspace at the physical end of the work materials or at the end of the work time to show the students what to do next. This may include:
   - cassette or computer disk
   - picture from a box of snacks
   - card that says "When you have finished your work, choose a book and read until Mrs. Smith calls you over to check your work."

Application of Structured Teaching at Different Ages

Any educational content can be taught using Structured Teaching strategies and supports, ranging from toilet training of a preschool child, to learning to read in elementary school, to college preparatory or vocational classes in high school. Presented below are some examples.

Brett – A Preschool Child with Autism and Moderate Intellectual Disability

Brett attends a preschool special education classroom with four other students. None of the other children has ASD, but the teachers have put physical and programmatic adaptations in place to accommodate Brett's need for Structured Teaching. Brett is very active and easily distracted.

Spaces. At the entrance to the classroom, Brett has a cubby with a hook to hang up his coat and backpack. The inside of the cubby is covered with purple construction paper, because that is his favorite color, and it may serve to highlight this area for him. The teachers also put a purple beanbag chair in the play area with some of Brett's favorite toys (dinosaurs). Also in the classroom is a small table with two chairs, where the teacher works individually with Brett. When it is his turn to work there, the teacher puts a purple tablecloth on the table. There is also a larger table with enough chairs for all the students and teachers. This is where the students eat their snack and lunch, and it is also where they have group activities, since being seated at the table is a familiar and organizing experience, which the teachers have found works better for this particular group of students than sitting in a circle on the floor. Seats at this table are assigned, using colors, symbols, or names according to each student's understanding, but the assignments are periodically changed so the children don't become too attached to a particular seating arrangement. The other main area of importance for Brett's class is the bathroom. (Each child is at a different stage of toilet training. Brett is taken to the bathroom approximately 10 minutes before the most typical times when he wets his diapers.)

Schedule. During the first week of school, Brett spent most of his time either running around the perimeter of the classroom or tapping on all the windows in sequence until he was led to an activity. Although he reportedly understands a few words in context at home, at school he did not appear to understand any verbal directions. His teachers have started a "what's next" object schedule. They began by approaching him with a cup to be used at snack and lunch, and they have noticed that he already independently takes his cup to the seat with the purple cover at the snack table. He also shows an emerging understanding that a computer disk means that he can play on the computer, and that his backpack means it is time to go home. Several times, Brett has followed the teachers to the cabinet where they keep his objects, so next week they will begin putting each upcoming object on a purple tray on top of the bookcase and will lead Brett there to find his "schedule."

Task organization. During one-on-one work sessions with a teacher, Brett works on a single task at a time. Over the course of a day, he works on many different tasks (all "put-ins" or "take aparts"), but each is presented to him on a purple tray, with one container for the materials to put in or take apart, and one container for the results of his work. Brett has quickly mastered the routines of pulling the tray toward him, working on the task, and then, when the container of materials is empty, putting the tray into a large "finished" basket on the floor beside his chair. He has no difficulty with the actual tasks, so the teachers will begin introducing a two-task work session with a work/activity system consisting of two purple trays on his desk. The developmental complexity of the tasks will also be increased over time as Brett progresses. In addition, teachers will begin using the purple tray to teach Brett to give napkins to other students at snack time and lunch time. (The tray will have baskets with a napkin for each student – when all the baskets are empty, and all the napkins are on the placemats, the task is finished.)

Routines. Brett does not yet have many productive routines in the classroom and must be guided through each step of his day. However, for the past three days, he has headed straight for his beanbag chair as soon as he has been assisted in hanging up his coat and backpack, suggesting that he is beginning to learn this routine. His teachers are also helping him to go to this area at the end of each activity on his schedule.

Learning activities in place or upcoming. In terms of expressive communication, Brett is being taught an object exchange system during snack and lunch (cup for beverage, plate for food). A next step will be teaching him to make choices between two beverages and between two food items. During his individual instructional sessions, the teachers will introduce an element of sorting colors. Motor development activities, each structured to show Brett how much or how many items to complete, include squeezing play dough balls, picking up small objects and depositing them into containers, finger painting, jumping off low heights, and running to a goal. Socially, he is already handing napkins to his classmates at meals; a next step will be having him sit next to another student and work on a parallel task that is familiar to him. He is participating in the toileting routine by carrying his diaper into the bathroom, handing a wipe to the teacher, putting his soiled diaper in the trash, and washing his hands. An important play/leisure goal is staying in a designated area (in this case, the play area) with his favorite toys (dinosaurs) until the timer sounds. This goal is very important to his family, because Brett's hyperactivity means that he requires constant supervision, and family life would be much improved if he could at times remain safely and happily in a designated location in the home.

Carlos – A Preschool Child with High-Functioning Autism/Asperger Syndrome

This is Carlos's second year at a typical preschool; he has only recently been diagnosed with an ASD. Based on recommendations from the diagnostic team, the teachers have added elements of Structured Teaching to the situations that previously caused Carlos the most difficulty.

Spaces. The preschool classroom has typical areas (play centers, small tables for snacks and lunch, a large carpeted area for group time with the teacher, etc.). The teachers have put a carpet square in the group area to provide a visual cue to show Carlos where to sit. This physical cue also serves as a boundary to keep him and the other students from touching each other or intruding on each other's space during group (previously Carlos liked to touch other children's hair, but became very upset if other children bumped his knees during circle time). Another adaptation in the class is a screened-off area in one corner of the room, outfitted with a small cot and headphones for a small music player. This space is available to Carlos when he is overstimulated or distressed during classroom activities.

Schedule. Carlos has difficulty following verbal directions given to the whole class, but he is one of the few children in the class who are beginning to read, so his teachers have designed a schedule using written words paired with symbols. The individual word/symbol items are on cards that have been laminated and have Velcro on the back. They are used with a strip of Velcro mounted near his cubby. The teacher puts up three pictures at a time to indicate the upcoming activities. During transitions, after giving the other students verbal directions, a teacher tells Carlos, "check your schedule." He goes to the schedule, takes the card for the next activity, and brings the card to the appropriate location. Carrying the card to his destination helps make the transition more meaningful and, therefore, smoother for him. At each location, there is a small library pocket with a matching picture; he puts the card into the pocket and begins the activity. If plans change, a teacher takes Carlos to his schedule, shows him the card that is being removed, and puts up a different card (e.g., a card for indoor play instead of the "outside" card, if it begins to rain). The use of a visual schedule has almost eliminated Carlos's arguing and tantrums during transitions because it provides structure and predictability.

Work/activity system. Carlos participates in the same activities as the other students, but structure has been added to each activity to show him how much he should do and when he is finished. For example, instead of an indefinite period of playing with puzzles, which he loves, he is shown a digital timer that counts down from 15 minutes and then rings. This has eliminated tantrums when he is told that puzzle time is over. During craft activities (which he does not enjoy and used to resist), the materials and activity are organized for him. For example, there is an array of small baskets, each containing one item: a sheet of paper with a picture, a pair of scissors, a crayon, and a glue stick. Carlos has a list of directions such as "cut on the line, color the dog, glue the dog on the paper, write your name." When the baskets are empty and the finished product is in the "finished" basket, the task is over, and Carlos can leave the craft table. Carlos learned this work/activity system (working from left to right with baskets of materials) during individual sessions with the teacher, and he is now able to complete most tasks using this system independently and without resistance.

Routines. Carlos has learned that when he has finished required activities, he can either get a book or go to his quiet place until a teacher tells him, "check your schedule" to begin another activity. He has also learned, after individual instruction using a work/activity system, to follow verbal directions for routine activities, such as washing his hands, getting his cot for naptime, and putting his disposable snack cup and plate in the trash.

Learning activities in place or upcoming. Carlos does not have special goals in cognitive or pre-academic skills, because he is developing very well in these areas. He still needs work on personal hygiene, however, and has work/activity systems in place to assist him in wiping himself after using the toilet and in brushing his teeth after lunch. Socially, he is learning to take turns in simple board games (he used to have difficulty with this). So far, he has learned to play *Go Fish* with a teacher, and next week he will begin playing that game with another student with a teacher's supervision. Eventually, as he learns additional structured games, teacher supervision will be faded. He will also be taught some routines for less structured play, such as building with blocks, playing with small cars and trucks, and playing in a toy kitchen.

Demetrius – A Fourth-Grade Student with Moderate Intellectual Disability

Demetrius spends most of his day in a special education classroom for students with autism, but he goes to music with the regular fourth grade because he is very talented in singing and playing the piano, and he participates well in that class.

Spaces. In Demetrius's classroom, there is a table for individual work with the teacher, and each student also has a private work space for practicing the skills they have learned with the teacher. There is no group space in the room, because each student's program is so different and because the students don't learn well in a group. However, there is a leisure area where two students can play or relax together (sometimes joined by a teacher).

Schedule. Demetrius has progressed from an object schedule to a schedule that uses photographs of objects and/or activities. These photographs have been laminated and are attached by paperclips to a sheet of paper on a wall in the classroom. The sequence of photographs, running from left to right, forms a full-day schedule. When a teacher hands Demetrius a card with his name, he takes it to the schedule, slides it under a paperclip at the top of the paper, and then takes the photograph to the far left. Demetrius is still learning this system, so before he goes to look at his schedule, a teacher places a large red arrow under the picture at the far left to give Demetrius an additional cue of where to look. Eventually, the arrow will no longer be needed and will be faded out.

Work/activity system. During his individual work with his teacher, Demetrius is learning to use an advanced work/activity system that involves getting a task from a shelf near his work space, completing the task, and then getting the next task, for a total of four different tasks. Each task is contained in a large box with several smaller containers for materials inside. Demetrius knows which box to select by matching the number of the box to a series of numbers paper-clipped to his work table (e.g., 2, 1, 4, 3). Demetrius takes the containers out of the box, completes the task (such as sorting colors, shapes, sizes, objects, or plastic letters), puts the completed task back into the box, and puts the whole thing into a large "finished" basket on the floor by his work table.

Demetrius has almost learned the process of this work/activity system, which will soon be transferred to his independent work area for additional practice. He will continue to use the four-box work/activity system as he learns new tasks in individual sessions with his teacher. In the future, the work boxes will be moved to a more distant location in the room to give Demetrius experience with staying focused on his tasks even as he moves around the room to get materials.

Routines. Demetrius is quite independent in a number of school routines, including going to the leisure area after each activity, walking from the bus to his classroom, getting his home-school notebook out of his backpack and handing it to a teacher, giving the teacher a card when he wants to go to the bathroom down the hall, managing his tray after lunch in the cafeteria, and walking to the music room independently when music class is on his schedule.

Learning activities in place or upcoming. In addition to learning more complex schedules and work/activity systems, Demetrius is also working on matching sight words, writing his name, and matching quantities to written numbers. His expressive language is limited, but when he gives pictures to teachers to make requests, he is beginning to imitate some of the verbal labels they use (such as *juice*, *milk*, *outside*, *music*, and *cheese*). Teachers will continue to support and stimulate verbal imitation, while enabling Demetrius to use the picture communication system that is so functional for him. Other learning goals include tying his shoes, cutting his own meat and using a knife for spreading, using a variety of office tools (such as stapler, scissors, and tape), and learning to play tag with other students.

Edward – A Fourth-Grade Student with High-Functioning Autism/Asperger Syndrome

Edward has always been fully included in general education classes. He is currently in the fourth grade with Structured Teaching supports provided by the classroom teacher.

Spaces. Edward has a "solo" desk rather than the four-student shared work space used by his classmates, because he is distracted and occasionally annoyed when he works facing other students. He knows that he can go to a little room off the school office (where an adult is always present) for 10 minutes whenever he needs to calm down or get away from the noise in his busy classroom.

Schedule. Edward's schedule is a written list of the day's activities. At the beginning of the year, his teacher emailed his mother a template for the schedule, which Edward's mother goes over with him in the morning. If the teacher knows there will be changes, she emails that information to the mother the evening before, and the mother shows Edward what activities will be crossed out or added. She then puts the schedule in the front of Edward's notebook, where he can refer to it throughout the day. He also understands that the teacher may write in additional changes during the day. Edward likes to cross off each activity as he completes it, so that he can see that he is getting closer to computer time at the end of the day, which he loves.

Work/activity system. On Edward's desk is a set of colored folders with left and right pockets. There is one folder for each subject. The teacher puts a sheet with a written assignment (paper-clipped to additional materials as needed) on the left, and after Edward completes the work, he puts it in the right pocket and then takes the folder to a basket on the teacher's desk. Over the course of the day, he sees the pile of file folders on his desk getting smaller, and when all the folders are gone, he knows that he has completed his classwork for the day.

Edward is not yet consistent or reliable about bringing home an assignment book or the necessary materials, so most of his teachers email the assignment to his family (one teacher has a web site where all the students can check the assignment). Edward's mother prints out the assignments and puts each in a homework folder (of the same design as the classwork folder) and Edward completes his homework using the same work/activity system.

Edward also has a version of a work/activity system for recess, which had been the most challenging and frustrating part of the day for him. He used to wander along the fence for the entire recess, not interacting with any of the other students and not getting any exercise. His teacher devised a written checklist of activities for him to do, and one of the inclusion facilitators spent a few sessions with him practicing the activities privately. The activities included kicking a ball to each of the corners of the playground, running two laps around the playground, asking one child to catch a ball with him, and jumping off the jungle gym three times. At first, the teacher helped Edward mark off each activity on the checklist, but he now knows the routine and completes it without protest (although he still does not enjoy recess).

Routines. As described, Edward has learned the routine of doing his classwork, turning it in, and returning to check his schedule independently. After several months of prompts, he has also learned to turn in all his homework folders as soon as he arrives at school in the morning. He knows that during free time he can either choose a book or put his name on the waiting list for 5 minutes of computer time.

Learning activities in place or upcoming. Edward is excelling in science and math, but struggles with language arts. Reading comprehension is becoming more challenging as more inferential reading is required, but his teacher is supporting him through the use of repeated practice with a systematic approach to analyzing written material. Edward's greatest academic challenges have been handwriting and learning to write paragraphs. His teachers have supported these skills by allowing him to write about his favorite topics (Japanese animated characters), and he is now much more willing to write on a daily basis and at greater length.

Twice a week Edward eats lunch with a speech-language therapist and a group of students working on pragmatic language and social skills. These sessions have an overall goal of helping students have fun together, rather than formal instruction in specific social behaviors such as making eye contact and giving compliments. Using visual structure to help the students take turns, the speech-language therapist has helped the students learn to play several board games without squabbling over cheating and whose turn it is. She has also had students practice using the telephone to call each other to ask for information about homework assignments and to invite someone over to play. She is going to send home with Edward information about what games he has learned, how they were structured, and how to contact the families of other students in the group as a way of facilitating play dates outside of school.

Frannie – A 10th-Grade Student with Moderate Intellectual Disability

Frannie spends the morning working on various tasks in the school cafeteria. She spends some afternoons in her special education classroom and some afternoons on community errands and outings (such as grocery shopping and swimming).

Spaces. For most activities, Frannie is either seated or she stands on a small piece of colored cloth – she needs these cues to keep her from drifting away from the correct location. (Several of the colored cloths come with her on community outings and are used to show her where to stand in cashier's lines, at bus stops, etc.).

Schedule. Frannie can follow a full-day sequence of symbols for her schedule. However, she tended to try to rearrange the symbols, look on the teacher's desk for symbols for her favorite activities, and in general treat her schedule like a choice board or expressive communication tool. Her teachers, therefore, added to Frannie's schedule several colored squares, representing opportunities to choose her own activities. The available choices were posted nearby on a sheet of paper of the same color as the square on the schedule. For example, "music" and "play with a teacher" were always available, and sometimes choices such as "go for a walk," "go roller skating," and "computer time" were also available. The schedule pictures were put into a frame (using the removable plastic binders from report covers) so that it was relatively difficult for Frannie to rearrange the pictures or skip over her less-preferred activities.

Work/activity system. Frannie has long since mastered work/activity systems using containers of materials while seated at a table, so now she is learning tasks that involve larger materials and tasks that require her to move around a work site. As long as her work materials are laid out from left to right, she stays organized and focused on the tasks. For each new task, her teacher or instructor plans ahead the organization of materials and sequence of steps. Then Frannie stands next to an instructor, watches one or two demonstrations of how to use the materials, and then proceeds independently. The instructor watches for mistakes, confusion, disorganization, or unanticipated problems, and modifies the work/activity system accordingly. Frannie has already learned to refill condiment containers in the cafeteria, restock the containers of eating utensils, wipe tables, sweep the floor, and put trash bags into trash cans.

Routines. Frannie enjoys structured activities more than unstructured time, so she generally works for 2-1/2 to 3 hours without a break. When she does have downtime between activities on her schedule, she works on a 1,000-piece jigsaw puzzle on her table in the classroom. With specific instruction and practice, she has also learned routines such as putting on a smock and cap to work in the kitchen and going to a supervisor with a card that says "Help, please."

Learning activities in place or upcoming. Frannie speaks in short phrases and enjoys talking with her teachers about certain topics, so a conversation time is part of her daily schedule. Although Frannie will always need some degree of supervision, she is learning several life skills, including washing dishes, doing laundry, ordering a meal in a restaurant when the available items are described to her, and assisting with grocery shopping. Leisure goals include bowling, swimming, and playing *Bingo*. She is making progress in managing menstrual hygiene independently, using a very structured system for changing and disposing of pads on a schedule.

George – A 10th-Grade Student with High-Functioning Autism/Asperger Syndrome

George is taking college preparatory classes and a study skills class. He is so advanced in math that during his senior year he will have the option of taking a class at the local college. His parents think this will provide valuable experience with aspects of college while he is still living at home.

Spaces. George's classes are scattered around a large campus, so at the beginning of each semester, his advisor walks him through the route he will take from one class to the next. The advisor points out directional signs, landmarks, and room numbers to assist George in learning and feeling comfortable with the route. (When

George was in middle school, his mother used to do this, but when George moved up to high school, he said that he wanted someone else to do it, and a teacher volunteered).

Schedule and work/activity system. George is learning to use his own integrated schedule and work/activity system, which is incorporated into a notebook that also includes his class schedule, a place to list assignments and needed materials, and a calendar that shows when assignments and projects are due. This system was initially devised by his mother, and although George protested and initially resisted using it, he has seen that he is more successful when he uses it. He is becoming increasingly independent in using it, and has begun recording last-minute assignments, anticipating how long various assignments will take, and thinking about what materials to bring home at night.

Routines. George is very familiar and comfortable with all the routines at his high school; it is noticeable, however, that he is at first tense and silent in new situations. The autism specialist has encouraged school staff to provide George with written descriptions of new activities that answer the five questions (see page 166). This was successfully done prior to driver's education class and a field trip to Washington, DC. The autism specialist also provided George with a written description and explanation of the chess club and the photography club, and George is no longer protesting that he is not interested in joining any clubs.

Learning activities in place or upcoming. George is studying the driver's education manual and is on the waiting list for the driver's education class. He occasionally drops into the guidance counselor's office after frustrating experiences. He typically calms down within a few minutes and listens to advice or additional explanations of the complex social world of high school.

Summary and Conclusions

The preceding case examples demonstrate the range of cognitive and language skills, academic and vocational potential, and other personal characteristics of students with ASD. Structured Teaching and environmental supports provide students with lifelong, individualized arrangements that facilitate understanding, learning, and adaptive functioning in the school, home, and community.

Anthony, the kindergarten student from the beginning of this chapter, will be taught by teachers who use Structured Teaching principles and techniques. His teachers, having observed his interests and talked with his family about his skills and behavior at home, have designed the following initial plan:

Spaces
Anthony will have a play area on the opposite side of the room from the block area, separated by various physical and visual barriers. This was decided because it is so difficult for him to make the transition from playing in the block area to any other activity. He will also have a three-sided work table (to encourage him to stay seated), where he has brief individual work sessions with a teacher. This table is near his leisure area and also near the bathroom, so that the route to both is short and direct.

Schedule

Anthony will begin with a "what's next" object schedule that starts in the parking lot when his school bus arrives. There he will be greeted by a teacher or assistant, who will give him the object for the first activity of the day, a work session with his teacher. His day will consist of many sequences of work sessions with a teacher, alternating with free time in his leisure area, along with time on the playground, snack, lunch, nap, trips to the bathroom, and brief participation in a group activity with the other children. All transitions to new activities will be done using an object that is part of the upcoming activity. This is expected to reduce Anthony's confusion about what he is being asked to do and his resulting distress during transitions.

Task Organization

The object used to indicate work sessions will be a block that Anthony will bring to his work table. For this introduction to Structured Teaching, at the table will be a container of blocks and a container with a lid. Anthony's task will be to put each block in the container (with the teachers using the fewest number of gestures and prompts needed to accomplish this). Once all the blocks are in the container, the work session is finished, and Anthony is guided back to his leisure area (where there are musical instruments and some toy cars, both of which were chosen based on the observation during the first week that he liked them). The task (putting blocks in a container) is very simple and well within Anthony's ability – it was chosen to capitalize on his interest in blocks while teaching him a completely new set of skills: completing a task selected by a teacher in a location determined by the teacher. Once he begins to show some emerging understanding and spontaneous participation in the activity, a similar "put-in" activity will be introduced, using some of the material from craft activities that Anthony previously grabbed and used to flap. This was decided in order to introduce him to a more productive way to use that material.

The object used to indicate snack and lunch (both of which take place in the classroom) is a small paper plate. Anthony is guided to a chair at the table with the other children during snack time, and snack foods are put on his plate. At the beginning, he will not be required to hand his plate to the teacher, but eventually she will begin to position herself slightly farther away, with snack food in her hand to encourage Anthony to extend the plate in his hand toward her. If Anthony gets up from the table, his plate and food will be removed – after several minutes, the teacher will again approach him with the plate and guide him to sit at the table. This will be done as needed, three times for each snack or meal.

To teach Anthony the first steps of participating in group time, the teachers considered having music every day and using a part of a musical instrument as the object on his schedule. However, they worried that Anthony might develop a strong attachment to this routine, making it difficult to eliminate music as the first activity of group time. So instead, they decided that Anthony's task would be to come to the group once the other children were settled and to hand each child an object from a basket that the teacher holds. When the basket is empty, Anthony's task is finished, and he is free to leave the group and go to his leisure area (although there is a chair for him if he chooses to stay with the group). The objects in the basket will vary from day to day; they will be used with the other students during a group song or activity. Sometimes musical instruments will be used; Anthony will pass those out also. When the musical activity is finished, Anthony may have the job of taking the basket around the circle to collect the instruments, putting the basket into the closet, and helping to close the closet door (which will highlight for him that the activity is finished). Eventually, Anthony will be required to sit in his chair for another time-limited, visually based, or physical activity with the group, but for now the first step in integrating Anthony into a group activity will be a simple task in which the materials indicate how much he has to do.

During free time, Anthony sometimes is allowed to play alone in his leisure area, but sometimes a teacher comes into the area with him and sits near him, singing, imitating his play, or using "floor time" techniques (Greenspan & Wieder, 1998) to engage him in simple, playful social interactions.

Routines

Anthony's teacher will work on both establishing productive routines and on interrupting unacceptable ones. For example, after all activities are completed, he will be guided through the routine of going to his leisure area. His schedule is arranged so that he enters the class with an object that leads him to his first activity. Eventually, he will probably go to that location and activity with minimal supervision. His routines of pulling down his pants before arriving at the bathroom and leaving the bathroom before he has zipped up will be prevented through close supervision and physical guidance during these times, until he has learned more socially appropriate routines.

Tips for the Classroom

✓ Incorporating a student's special interests into learning activities makes them more interesting or palatable (for example: counting helicopters, writing about license plates, reading about computers, purchasing and preparing ingredients to make purple cookies).

✓ Many students with ASD benefit from occupational therapy (particularly with a sensory integration focus) and/or speech/language therapy (particularly with a focus on pragmatics).

✓ Parents are almost always their child's most passionate and knowledgeable caregivers. Their understanding of and love for their child can be a source of energy and support for teachers. Parents may be very busy or have additional stresses that teachers do not know about, but teachers should do everything they can to connect with parents and respect their input, their wishes, and their perspectives about their child (see Chapter 13).

✓ Incorporating choices of activities into the student's schedule can strengthen his communication and language skills, improve his mood, and increase his sense of self-worth and personal satisfaction at school.

✓ When you encounter a challenging behavior, look first at the structure. Does the student need more visual information, more physical structure, or other supports?

Chapter Highlights

- Structure for students with ASD involves the teacher or caregiver deciding what the learning activities will be, where they will occur, and how long they will last.

- Structured Teaching refers to environmental strategies and environmental supports for individuals with ASD developed by the TEACCH program, a statewide program for individuals with autism in North Carolina.

- Structured Teaching has two main goals: (a) teach the individual with ASD as many skills as possible, given his developmental level; and (b) provide an environment as comprehensible as possible, so the learner can understand the expectations and opportunities around him.

- Structured Teaching is a social-cognitive-behavioral approach applied to the neuropsychological aspects of ASD.

- The "Culture of Autism" refers to the shared neuropsychological patterns of thinking, communication, and behavior commonly seen among individuals with ASD.

- Integral to Structured Teaching is respect for families.

- Five central questions need to be considered and answered for each individual with ASD within Structured Teaching.

- Schedules, task organization, work/activity systems, and routines are integral to Structured Teaching.

  - Schedules are important as they allow individuals with ASD to know where they are supposed to be and what they are to be doing at a given time and allow for predictable environments with knowledge of what will come next. Schedules should be individualized, visual, accurate, and easy to alter should the need arise.

  - Task organization and work/activity systems provide a visual representation of what the student is to do each step of the way during a task or activity.

  - Routines are consistent daily activities for students. A student who has reached independence or mastery on an activity can be considered to have developed a routine (for example, placing completed work in a folder or washing hands before snack time).

- Practical strategies for teachers, including providing visual structure, organizing materials, sharing information, and creating schedules, are integral to Structured Teaching.

- The authors provide multiple examples demonstrating the use of Structured Teaching at different age and ability levels.

Chapter Review Questions

1. What is meant by "structure" in teaching?

2. What is TEACCH?

3. Explain Structured Teaching, including theoretical foundations, as well as implications for students with ASD and their families.

4. What is meant by the "Culture of Autism" and what are some examples?

5. What are the five questions Structured Teaching should answer by providing the learner with visual information and organization of the environment?

6. What is the importance of each of the following in the instruction of individuals with ASD: schedules, task organization, work/activity systems, and routines?

7. For each of the five questions of Structured Teaching, provide two or three examples of strategies.

References

Bregman, J. D., Zager, D., & Gerdtz, J. (2005). Behavioral interventions. In F. Volkmar, R. Paul, A. Klin & D. Cohen (Eds.), *Handbook of autism and pervasive developmental disorders* (3rd ed., pp. 897-924). Hoboken, NJ: John Wiley & Sons.

Frith, U. (2003). *Autism: Explaining the enigma* (2nd ed.). Oxford, UK: Blackwell.

Greenspan, S. I., & Wieder, S. (1998). *The child with special needs.* Boston: Addison-Wesley.

Mesibov, G. B., Shea, V., & Adams, L. W. (2001). *Understanding Asperger Syndrome and high-functioning autism.* New York: Kluwer Academic/Plenum Press.

Mesibov, G. B., Shea, V., & Schopler, E. (with Adams, L., Burgess, S., Chapman, S. M., Merkler, E., Mosconi, M., Tanner, C., & Van Bourgondien). (2005). *The TEACCH approach to autism spectrum disorders.* New York: Plenum/Kluwer Academic.

Schopler, E., & Reichler, R. J. (1971). Parents as cotherapists in the treatment of psychotic children. *Journal of Autism and Childhood Schizophrenia, 1,* 87-102.

Schreibman, L., & Ingersoll, B. (2005). Behavioral interventions to promote learning in individuals with autism. In F. Volkmar, R. Paul, A. Klin, & D. Cohen (Eds.), *Handbook of autism and pervasive developmental disorders* (3rd ed., pp. 882-896). Hoboken, NJ: John Wiley & Sons.

Learner Objectives

After reading this chapter, the learner should be able to:

- Define sensory processing

- List and describe the systems involved in sensory processing

- Explain modulation and thresholds in terms of sensory input to the brain

- State the purpose of sensory systems transmitting information to the brain

- Give examples of arousal/alerting and discrimination/mapping descriptors

- Explain why incorporating various sensory inputs into therapeutic programs might be useful for students with autism spectrum disorders

- Explain Dunn's conceptual model for understanding patterns of sensory processing

- Explain sensory processing differences in individuals with ASD as compared to neurotypical peers

- Describe each of the four sensory processing patterns

- State the goal of a sensory processing framework for intervention.

- Give examples of sensory processing interventions that address each type of pattern and that support student learning.

Chapter 6

Sensory Processing: Identifying Patterns and Support Strategies

Winnie Dunn

Bradley is a slow starter at school. His teacher says he lies all over his desk, leans on people, walls, and furniture, and is very slow at responding to questions and directions in class. Many times when the class has already begun an activity, Bradley requires additional personal attention to get him to participate. The teacher says it is like Bradley is in another world; he doesn't pick up the cues that something is about to happen. In these situations, the teacher moves toward Bradley, bends down to get in front of him, looks him directly in the eyes, and calls his name. She brings the appropriate materials with her and hands items to Bradley as she explains what the class will be doing. She has learned that tapping Bradley's shoulder to get his attention is a bad strategy. Even though he seems oblivious, when she touches him, he lurches, screams, and pushes her away. She gets his attention, but it is not the kind of attention she wants from Bradley for classroom work. She has learned that after Bradley gets upset in this way, it takes a while to get him settled back down, thus disrupting more of the school day.

*The teacher talks with the interdisciplinary team members at the school to get additional ideas about how to handle Bradley more effectively throughout the school day. They agree that the occupational therapist (OT) on the team will be the most helpful. The OT subsequently interviews the teacher and observes Bradley during the morning work session to get more detailed information about Bradley's reactions. She sends home the **Sensory Profile** (Dunn, 1999) for Bradley's parents to complete and asks the teacher to comlete the Sensory Profile School Companion (Dunn, 2007a). She suspects that Bradley is responding to sensory experiences differently than classroom peers, and that this might be contributing to his challenges with participating in school activities.*

*Bradley's Sensory Profile (Dunn, 1999) and School Companion (Dunn, 2007a) results verified what the OT suspected based on her interviews and observations: Bradley is missing information and is slow to respond to stimuli in the environment (called **low registration**). Consistent with the teacher's comments about Bradley's heightened reactions to touch, the Sensory Profile measures also indicated that Bradley notices touch input much more quickly than peers and reacts negatively to this particular type of input (called **sensitivity**).*

The OT explained to the teacher about Bradley's overall need for more intensity of input (due to low registration) so that he can notice and respond to cues. The teacher and OT brainstormed ways to increase Bradley's sensory input during the school day. The teacher decided to create daily routines for Bradley to get him up and moving around the classroom more often. For example, she assigned him the task of passing out worksheets, collecting assignments from other students, refilling materials bins when they were getting low, obtaining books for reading groups, and wiping the board throughout the day. The OT suggested giving Bradley "smelly" markers for seatwork, explaining that the extra input from the fragrance would keep Bradley attentive to the worksheet for a longer time. They also discussed giving Bradley a Walkman with earphones so he could listen to music while working, but the teacher was skeptical about the impact of this strategy on the rest of the class. She also thought this might make Bradley more oblivious to her classroom instruction. Instead, they decided to move his desk near the window so he would get more natural light at his work area and be able to hear the traffic going by during the day. The OT also created color-coded covers for books and materials so Bradley could find materials that go together for a classroom activity. This setup allowed for all of Bradley's supplies to be more noticeable, which met his need for extra visual information.

Then they turned their attention to Bradley's sensitivity to touch, which had the potential to disrupt many activities throughout the day. The teacher had been using a safe spot in the classroom for all the children. The children could go, or the teacher could prompt them to go, to the safe spot whenever they needed to regroup. The teacher and therapist talked about how to design the safe spot so that it would provide a comforting place for Bradley. They put a beanbag chair, a heavy quilt, and some extra-oversized heavy pillows in the safe spot so Bradley could bury himself. The OT explained that firm pressure on the skin provides a calming input, and thus could help Bradley calm down more quickly. When the OT showed Bradley how to create a cocoon around his body while in the safe spot, he smiled when trying it. After a few weeks, Bradley began going into the cocoon in the safe spot on his own when he got upset in the classroom.

Anyone who has a classroom of students will get to know a student like Bradley. Bradley is an above-average student academically, but his ways of responding to sensory experiences during the school day are interfering with his ability to demonstrate his knowledge and skills in the classroom.

In this chapter, we will explore an important aspect of student behavior: **sensory processing**. Sensory processing is a person's way of noticing and responding to sensory events that occur during everyday life. We know from research that there are particular patterns (Dunn, 1997a) of sensory processing (as introduced in Bradley's story), and that these patterns affect how people respond in situations. We also know that people who have autism spectrum disorders (ASD) have more intense reactions than their peers, which may be one of the contributing factors to their differences in responding in particular situations. When professionals and families understand the relationship between a student's sensory processing patterns and the behaviors he exhibits (Dunn, 1997a), we can adjust activities, directions, expectations, and other aspects of the school day to support the student's participation.

We all have sensory processing patterns. We might miss a lot of sensory cues, as Bradley was doing, yet be sensitive to certain sensory inputs (in Bradley's case, he was sensitive to touch). When you want the TV turned down, add

Tabasco to your food, have a favorite lotion, only purchase one brand of undergarments, and choose yoga as your preferred exercise, you are illustrating your individual sensory processing patterns. When you find yourself in a situation in which you cannot get your **sensory needs** met (either by increasing sensory input or by decreasing it), you may become irritable or unhappy. The specific patterns identified from research are explained below in more detail.

An Introduction to Sensory Processing Concepts

The sensory systems provide information to the brain (Kandel, Schwartz, & Jessell, 2000). We learn about our bodies from touch and body position senses (called **somatosensory** and **proprioceptive** systems), and this information builds the body scheme. We learn about the environment from seeing, hearing, smelling, and tasting (i.e., visual, auditory, olfactory, and gustatory systems), thus forming maps of the world. And we learn how our bodies interact with the environment from the movement sensations (i.e., **vestibular** system) (Dunn, 1991a, 1997b). The brain holds maps that are formed from this information, and these maps guide us so we are oriented in space and time and can make accurate decisions about how to react in particular situations.

Ayres (1972, 1979) originally proposed how to apply knowledge about sensory systems and the brain to understand the behaviors of children with learning challenges. Over the last three decades, scholars in occupational therapy and other disciplines have continued to study sensory processing concepts, expanding both knowledge and application of the knowledge in service to children and adults who have challenges in everyday life (Dunn, 2001a).

This research can help us understand the behaviors and needs of children with ASD. For example, when someone touches a child, the child typically looks toward the person before deciding what to do; looking adds visual input to the touch input so that the child can respond with the most information possible, not just based on one sensation (Dunn, 1991b). Children who have ASD sometimes react too quickly in such a situation, perhaps because they are responding without the benefit of multiple sensory inputs.

Many of the behaviors we observe in children with ASD can be attributed to an imbalance, or poor modulation, of sensory input in the brain. Children who are sensitive to many sensory inputs cannot complete classroom tasks because there are so many stimuli in the classroom environment. Other children fixate on one sensory input (e.g., the sound of rustling papers) while they are oblivious to other input, such as someone calling their name (Dunn, 1997b).

Another aspect of balance in the brain is related to something called **thresholds** (the point at which the system responds). When thresholds are too low, children respond too frequently to stimuli and can be distracted from everyday tasks by all the sensory input. Conversely, when thresholds are too high, children miss important cues about what is going on around them and can, therefore, seem oblivious or self absorbed (Dunn, 1997b).

Each sensory system transmits information to the brain for two reasons: (a) to generate awareness (i.e., arousal/alerting) and (b) to gather information for the brain to make maps of self and environment (i.e., discrimination/mapping) (Dunn, 1991a). These two reasons complement each other in most situations. However, in children who have ASD, arousal input frequently overpowers discriminating input, which then creates unusual behaviors as they try to manage distorted information. Table 6.1 provides a summary of the arousal and discriminating aspects of each sensory system; and Table 6.2 provides examples of how to use these sensory inputs for a therapeutic purpose.

Table 6.1
Description of the Aspects of the Sensory Systems

Sensory system	Arousal/alerting descriptors	Discrimination/mapping descriptors
For all systems	**Unpredictable:** The task is unfamiliar; the child cannot anticipate the sensory experiences that will occur in the task	**Predictable:** Sensory pattern in the task is routine for the child, such as diaper changing – the child knows what is occurring and what will come next.
Somatosensory	**Light touch:** Gentle tapping on skin; tickling (e.g., loose clothing making contact with skin). **Pain:** Brisk pinching; contact with sharp objects; skin pressed in small surface (e.g., when skin is caught in between chair arm and seat). **Temperature:** Hot or cold stimuli (e.g., iced drinks, hot foods, cold hands, cold metal chairs). **Variable:** Changing characteristics during the task (e.g., putting clothing on requires a combination of tactile experiences). **Short-duration stimuli:** Tapping, touching briefly (e.g., splashing water). **Small body surface contact:** Small body surfaces, as when using only fingertips to touch something.	**Touch pressure:** Firm contact on skin (e.g., hugging, patting, grasping). Occurs both when touching objects or persons, or when they touch you. **Long-duration stimuli:** Holding, grasping (e.g., carrying a child in your arms). **Large body surface contact:** Large body surfaces include holding, hugging; also include holding a cup with the entire palm or surface of hand.
Vestibular	**Head position change:** The child's head orientation (e.g., pulling the child up from lying on the back to sitting). **Speed change:** Movements change velocity (e.g., teacher stops to talk to another teacher when pushing the child to the bathroom in his wheelchair). **Direction change:** Movements change planes, such as bending down to pick something up from the floor while carrying the child down the hall. **Rotary head movement:** Head moving in an arc (e.g., spinning in a circle, turning head side to side).	**Linear head movement:** Head moving in a straight line (e.g., bouncing up and down, going down the hall in a wheelchair). **Repetitive head movement:** Movements that repeat in a simple sequence (e.g., rocking in a rocker).
Proprioception	**Quick stretch:** Movements that pull on the muscles (e.g., briskly tapping on a muscle belly). **Shifting muscle tension:** Activities that demand constant change in the muscles (e.g., walking, lifting, and moving objects).	**Sustained tension:** Steady, constant action on the muscles pressing or holding on the muscle (e.g., using heavy objects during play).
Visual	**High intensity:** Visual stimulus is bright (e.g., looking out the window on a bright day). **High contrast:** A lot of difference between the visual stimulus and its surrounding environment (e.g., cranberry juice in a white cup). **Variable:** Changing characteristics during the task (e.g., a TV program is a variable visual stimulus). **Competitive:** The background is interesting or busy (e.g., the junk drawer, a bulletin board).	**Low intensity:** Visual stimulus is subdued (e.g., finding objects in the dark closet). **High similarity:** Small differences between visual stimulus and its surrounding environment (e.g., oatmeal in a beige bowl).
Auditory	**Variable:** Changing characteristics during the task (e.g., a person's voice with intonation). **High intensity:** The auditory stimulus is loud (e.g., siren, high-volume radio). **Competitive:** The environment has a variety of recurring sounds (e.g., the classroom, a party).	**Rhythmic:** Sounds repeat in a simple sequence/beat (e.g., humming, singing nursery songs). **Constant:** The stimulus is always present (e.g., a fan noise). **Noncompetitive:** The environment is quiet (e.g., the bedroom when all is ready for bedtime). **Low intensity:** The auditory stimulus is subdued (e.g., whispering).
Olfactory/ gustatory	**Strong intensity:** The taste/smell has distinct qualities (e.g., spinach).	**Mild intensity:** The taste/smell has nondistinct or familiar qualities (e.g., Cream of Wheat).

From "The Sensorimotor Systems: A Framework for Assessment and Intervention," by W. Dunn, 1991c, In F. P. Orelove & D. Sobsey (Eds.), *Educating Children with Multiple Disabilities: A Transdisciplinary Approach* (2nd ed., p. 42). Baltimore: Paul H. Brookes. Reprinted with permission.

Table 6.2
Reasons for Incorporating Various Sensory Qualities into Integrated Intervention Programs

Sensory system	Arousal/alerting descriptors	Discrimination/mapping descriptors
For all systems	**Unpredictable:** To develop an increasing level of attention to Keep the child interested in the task/activity (e.g., change the position of the objects on the child's lap tray during the task).	**Predictable:** To establish the child's ability to anticipate a programming sequence or a salient cue; to decrease possibility of being distracted from a functional task sequence (e.g., use the same routine for diaper changing every time).
Somatosensory	**Light touch:** To increase alertness in a child who is lethargic (e.g., pull cloth from child's face during peek-a-boo). **Pain:** To raise from unconsciousness; to determine ability to respond to noxious stimuli when unconscious (e.g., flick palm of hand or sole of foot briskly). **Temperature:** To establish awareness of stimuli; to maintain attentiveness to task (e.g., use hot foods for spoon eating and cold drink for sucking through a straw). **Variable:** To maintain attention to or interest in the task (e.g., place new texture on cup surface each day so child notices the cup). **Short-duration stimuli:** To increase arousal for task performance (e.g., tap child on chest before giving directions). **Small body surface contact:** To generate and focus attention on a particular body part (e.g., tap around lips with fingertips before an eating task).	**Touch pressure:** To establish and maintain awareness of body parts and body position; to calm a child who has been overstimulated (e.g., provide a firm bear hug). **Long-duration stimuli:** To enable the child to become familiar and comfortable with the stimulus; to incorporate stimulus into functional skill (e.g., grasping the container to pick it up and pour out contents). **Large body surface contact:** To establish and maintain awareness of body parts and body position; to calm a child who has been overstimulated (e.g., wrap child lightly in a blanket).
Vestibular	**Head position change:** To increase arousal for an activity (e.g., position child prone over a wedge). **Speed change:** To maintain adequate alertness for a functional task (e.g., vary pace while carrying the child to a new task). **Direction change:** To elevate level of alertness for a functional task (e.g., swing child back and forth in arms prior to positioning him or her at the table for a task). **Rotary head movement:** To increase arousal prior to functional task (e.g., pick child up from prone [on stomach] facing away to upright facing toward you to position for a new task).	**Linear head movement:** To support establishment of body awareness in space (e.g., carry child around the room in fixed position to explore its features). **Repetitive head movement:** To provide predictable and organizing information; to calm a child who has been overstimulated (e.g., rock the child).
Proprioception	**Quick stretch:** To provide additional muscle tension to support functional tasks (e.g., tap muscle belly while providing physical guidance to grasp). **Shifting muscle tension:** To establish functional movements that contain stability and mobility (e.g., prop and reach for a top; reach, fill, and lift spoon to mouth).	**Sustained tension:** To enable the muscle to relax, elongate, so body part can be in more optimal position for function (e.g., press firmly across muscle belly while guiding a reaching pattern; add weight to objects being manipulated).
Visual	**High intensity:** To increase opportunity to notice object; to generate arousal for task (e.g., cover blocks with foil for manipulation task). **High contrast:** To enhance possibility of locating the object and maintaining attention to it (e.g., place raisins on a piece of typing paper for prehension activity). **Variable:** To maintain attention to or interest in the task (e.g., play rolling catch with a clear ball that has movable pieces inside). **Competitive:** To facilitate searching; to increase tolerance for natural life circumstances (e.g., obtain correct tools from equipment bin).	**Low intensity:** To allow the visual stimulus to blend with other salient features; to generate searching behaviors, because characteristics are less obvious (e.g., find own cubbyhole in back of the room). **High similarity:** To establish more discerning abilities; to develop skills for naturally occurring tasks (e.g., scoop apple sauce from beige plate).

Table 6.2 (continued)

Auditory	**Variable:** To maintain attention to or interest in the task (e.g., play radio station after activating a switch). **High intensity:** To stimulate noticing the person or object; to create proper alerting for task performance (e.g., ring a bell to encourage the child to locate the stimulus). **Competitive:** To facilitate differentiation of salient stimuli; to increase tolerance for natural life circumstances (e.g., after child learns to look when his or her name is called, conduct activity within busy classroom).	**Rhythmic:** To provide predictable and organizing information for environmental orientation (e.g., sing a nursery rhyme while physically guiding motions). **Low intensity:** To allow the auditory stimulus to blend with other salient features; to generate searching behaviors if stimulus is less obvious (e.g., give child a direction in a normal volume). **Constant:** To provide a foundational stimulus for environmental orientation; especially important when other sensory systems (e.g., vision, vestibular) do not provide orientation (e.g., child recognizes own classroom by fan noise and calms down). **Noncompetitive:** To facilitate focused attention for acquiring a new and difficult skill; to calm a child who has been overstimulated (e.g., move child to quiet room to establish vocalizations)
Olfactory/ gustatory	**Strong intensity:** To stimulate arousal for task (e.g., child smells spaghetti sauce at lunch).	**Mild intensity:** To facilitate exploratory behaviors; to stimulate naturally occurring activities (e.g., smell of lunch food is less distinct, so child is encouraged to notice texture, color).

From "The Sensorimotor Systems: A Framework for Assessment and Intervention," by W. Dunn, 1991c, In F. P. Orelove & D. Sobsey (Eds.), *Educating Children with Multiple Disabilities: A Transdisciplinary Approach* (2nd ed., p. 42). Baltimore: Paul H. Brookes. Reprinted with permission.

A Conceptual Model for Sensory Processing

Based on the brain knowledge summarized above, Dunn (1997a) proposed a conceptual model for understanding patterns of sensory processing. Figure 6.1 contains a diagram of this model; the vertical axis shows the brain thresholds and the horizontal axis shows the **self-regulation** continuum. High thresholds require a lot of sensory input, and low thresholds require very little sensory input to react. Children who have high thresholds respond infrequently, because it takes a great deal of sensory input in order to activate these thresholds. Children who have low thresholds, on the other hand, respond to many stimuli very easily. The self-regulation continuum shows how the person manages input. Children with active self-regulation strategies work to control their own input, whereas children with passive self-regulation strategies let things happen and then respond to them (Dunn, 2001b). The threshold and self-regulation parts of this diagram intersect to create four patterns of sensory processing (see Dunn, 1997a, for original presentation of this work): low registration, sensitivity, seeking, and avoiding.

A series of studies have validated and standardized measures of sensory processing (*Sensory Profile for Children, SP, Infant/ Toddler Sensory Profile*, ITSP; *Adolescent/Adult Sensory Profile*, AASP; and *Sensory Profile School Companion*), and other researchers have provided additional evidence regarding performance in disability groups (Brown,

Tollefson, Dunn, Cromwell, & Filion, 2001; Dunn & Bennett, 2002; Dunn, Myles, & Orr, 2002; Ermer & Dunn, 1998; Kientz & Dunn, 1997; Miller et al., 1998; Myles et al., 2004; Watling, Dietz, & White, 2001).

Findings across these studies illustrate links between sensory processing and particular disabilities, relationships between sensory processing and brain function, and associations between behavior and sensory processing patterns (Dunn, 2001b). Further, studies across the life span support Dunn's model of sensory processing (Brown & Dunn, 2002; Dunn, 1999; Dunn & Daniels, 2001). While people without disabilities exhibit these patterns of sensory processing, people with various disabilities seem to exhibit more extreme patterns.

	Self-Regulation Strategies	
Neurological thresholds	PASSIVE	ACTIVE
HIGH	Low Registration	Seeking
LOW	Sensitivity	Avoiding

Figure 6.1. Dunn's model of sensory processing.

Adapted from "The Impact of Sensory Processing Abilities on the Daily Lives of Young Children and Families: A Conceptual Model," by W. Dunn, 1997a, *Infants and Young Children, 9*(4), 23-25. Reprinted with permission.

Researchers have found that people with disabilities have unique sensory processing patterns, including children with attention deficit hyperactivity disorder (ADHD) (Dove, 2003; Dunn & Bennett, 2002), Fragile X Syndrome (Miller et al., 1998), autism (Kientz & Dunn, 1997; Watling et al., 2001), and Asperger Syndrome (Dunn et al., 2002; Myles et al., 2004). Children with these disorders have significantly different patterns of sensory processing when compared to their peers without disabilities and to each other (Ermer & Dunn, 1998; Myles et al., 2004).

Children with ASD are more likely to be sensitive to touch, as well as auditory and oral sensory processing (Dunn, 1999, 2000; Ermer & Dunn, 1998; Kientz & Dunn, 1997; Watling et al., 2001). They also have significantly different scores on low registration and avoiding. It may seem conflicting to have both low registration (i.e., fails to notice stimuli that others notice) and avoiding (i.e., detects and withdraws from stimuli) at the same time. However, children with ASD often seem oblivious to the environment (i.e., low registration) up until a certain point. Then they notice a stimulus (e.g., a sound, a touch) and immediately become threatened or overwhelmed, withdraw, or have a tantrum (i.e., avoiding). This scenario leaves little room for adaptive responses and learning, which is a major dilemma. We learn when we notice a stimulus and interact within the experience across time. Therefore, we want to design strategies that enable the child to notice stimuli without feeling threatened or overwhelmed.

Children with Asperger Syndrome have been found to display significant differences on virtually all of the areas of sensory processing (Dunn et al., 2002). In a follow-up study comparing children with autism and children with Asperger Syndrome, Myles et al. (2004) found that both groups were significantly different from peers in sensory processing, suggesting that sensory processing may need to be included in assessment of ASDs. Additionally, children with Asperger Syndrome were significantly more sensitive to certain types of sensory input than children with autism, challenging the notion that Asperger Syndrome is a mild form of autism.

Most recently, the Sensory Profile School Companion has become available (Dunn, 2007a). Teachers complete the School Companion about the students' behaviors and responses in school. Findings suggest that, using this tool, teachers identify unique patterns of students' responsiveness to environmental stimuli and, when combined with the therapist's data, it provides a complete picture that can be used to guide evidence-based intervention planning. As with the other *Sensory Profile* measures, students with Asperger Syndrome and autism exhibit significantly different patterns of sensory processing and school behaviors than peers (i.e., they engage in behaviors more frequently than peers).

Not every child with ASD has the exact pattern of sensory processing illustrated in group research studies. Each child is unique, so we need to understand his or her personal patterns for individualized planning to be effective. Let's look at each pattern specifically.

Seeking

Seeking reflects high thresholds and active self-regulation. Children who fall into this category add movement, touch, sound, and visual stimuli to every life event. Seekers make noises, fidget in their seats, touch everything, feel objects, touch and hang on to others, or chew on things. Each of the actions intensifies the sensory input, which, in turn, increases the child's chances of meeting high thresholds. Children might lack caution in play, display excitability, and engage in impulsive behavior in an attempt to increase sensory input (Dunn, 1997a).

Low Registration

Low registration reflects high thresholds and passive self-regulation. Children in this group do not notice what is going on around them, so they may seem dull, uninterested, or oblivious (Dunn, 1997a). Further, they might seem withdrawn, difficult to engage, or self-absorbed; they may also be easily exhausted and appear apathetic (National Center for Clinical Infant Programs/Zero to Three [NCCIP], 1994). The brain is not activating enough to cue the child about what is going on. These children need highly salient sensory input to get their attention so they can participate in school activities.

Sensitivity

With sensitivity, children have low thresholds and passive self-regulation strategies. They tend to be hyperactive, distracted, and easily upset because they notice more things than peers (Dunn, 1997a). Not surprisingly, children with sensitivity have difficulty completing tasks as new stimuli capture their attention repeatedly during the day. They may also have difficulty learning from their experiences because routines are disrupted so often that they cannot complete tasks and learn (NCCIP, 1994).

Avoiding

Avoiding reflects low thresholds and active self-regulation. Children in this group actively work to reduce input. They are resistant and unwilling to participate in activities, particularly unfamiliar ones. They experience discomfort quickly, and to keep from feeling discomfort, they reduce their activity and withdraw. For example, a student may feel overwhelmed during independent work time because of all the unpredictable sounds and movements around him; a student might become irritable or aggressive as a way to get someone to take him out of this setting, thereby reducing the unmanageable visual and auditory input.

Developing rituals is a predominant strategy for dealing with sensory input. Rituals provide comfort, because they stimulate a familiar sensory input pattern, reducing the possibility of triggering low thresholds. Changes in rituals, on the other hand, increase sensory stimulation, which generates anxiety, since triggering thresholds may be uncomfortable. Students who are avoiders appear stubborn and controlling. They might seem inattentive to some stimuli, while being preoccupied with others. These behaviors control sensory input, but may be perceived by adults as self-absorption (NCCIP, 1994). The self-absorption is related to the vigilance required to keep control over possible "assaults" from unfamiliar sensory inputs.

Designing Sensory Processing Interventions to Support Students

Our goal in serving students in schools is to improve their active participation in their education. When applying a sensory processing approach, we must identify the student's sensory processing patterns from observations, interviews, and assessments. We want to determine the exact ways that sensory processing patterns might be supporting or interfering with the student's participation. Occupational therapists are the experts on sensory processing. They focus on the student's needs in school and consider how sensory processing patterns might affect areas of concern. For example, if a student has difficulty completing seatwork, the OT can observe, interview the teacher, and conduct assessments to determine what might be interfering with seatwork time. For a student with sensitivity to sound, small groups create noise as they talk, and this interferes with concentration. If a student has low registration, small-group work would not interfere with seatwork, but perhaps the seatwork sheet is long and repetitive, making it hard for the student to keep at the task.

When using a sensory processing framework for intervention, the goal is to improve participation, not to change the sensory processing patterns. People with all types of sensory processing can have successful lives. We do not want to "cure" a student of sensation seeking; we want to make sure that sensation seeking works for learning.

Sensory experiences are part of every activity, so interventions take advantage of these naturally occurring opportunities during the school day. We don't create special circumstances to provide sensory processing interventions; we give the student more chances to participate successfully, thus improving school performance.

When possible, incorporate strategies that use the student's strengths. For example, teachers can provide a card or handout with the steps to complete the work for the day to take advantage of visual strengths. We also want to minimize challenging areas. To that end, teachers can provide foam ear plugs or set up a removed work area for a student who is sensitive to sounds.

Ways to Address Seeking

Seeking interferes with school when a student stops work to get sensory input another way (e.g., running, making noises). In this case, we design interventions that provide the extra sensory input during schoolwork, as suggested in Table 6.3.

When students demonstrate a seeking pattern of sensory processing, they *enjoy sensory experiences*. Because these students enjoy sensory input, you might observe that they move more, hum, or rub their hands on things throughout the day. They might also point out interesting sensory events throughout the day. Students' interest and pleasure in sensory events might also lead to difficulties with task completion because they may get distracted with new sensory experiences and lose track of daily tasks.

Students with a seeking pattern can *profit from more opportunities* to have sensory experiences as part of school work so they don't have to stop working to get the extra sensory input they desire. With more opportunities for sensory input, these students can continue to pay attention during daily life activities and therefore stick with them for a longer time.

Some children with ASD seek movement input by rocking, running, and jumping, but these actions interfere with school work and social interactions. Therefore, we want to reconstruct school activities so the child gets high-intensity sensory input while continuing to participate and complete work. For example, place books and materials on the floor next to the student's desk so she has to bend down to get the items (bending moves the head upside down, which provides the vestibular system with very strong input). For social interactions, pair the student with a friend to erase the chalkboards and encourage jungle gym play at recess. These tasks enable the student to receive movement input without having to stop ongoing interactions with peers.

Table 6.3

Activities That Can Provide Input for a Sensory-Seeking Student

Offer chewy, crunchy snacks	Allow student to chew gum or hard candy if quiet
Provide worksheets on colored paper	Change fonts on computer
Embed cues with visual interest (e.g., moving parts, colorful words, complex pictures)	Tape record stories in character voices, add sound effects within story, set script to a song
Dramatize the scenario with jumping, skipping, holding heavy objects during scenes	Videotape story, or make a pop-up book
Place a textured cushion on the student's seat	Encourage the student to wear highly textured socks, shirts
Encourage student to add accessories, such as head bands, wrist bands, belts	Provide variety in texture, flavor and temperature in food options
Add textures to finger paint	Add texture to handles and other work surfaces
Allow the student to change work positions (sitting, standing, different parts of the room)	Provide a textured rug mat under the student's chair so the student can rub feet on the mat while working
Allow student to use the chalkboard for some assignments	Provide textured blankets of student's choice for safe spots
Create longer routes to recess, lunchroom, library	Send this student on errands throughout the day
Have student help with tasks such as moving furniture, pushing milk carts and erasing the board	Create recess games that require climbing, crawling, hopping, running, etc.
Color code work materials using bright colors	Put posters/other pictures up at student's eye level
Provide lively music background or in a walkman for the student's work time	Use contrasting mats on work areas so papers and supplies are easier to see
Discuss things with the student as you do them	Have student look for things as you move about the school
Provide extra, colored lighting in this student's work areas	Hum/sing to songs, make up new verses
Open windows to enable ambient sound to enter near the student's desk	Provide scented lotions so the student can come to a designated area in the room and use it on the hands
Allow the student to take shoes off during class	Allow student to use scented lip balms during class
Clean toys with scented cleaners	Have student stand up to work and eat

From *The Sensory Profile Supplement*, by W. Dunn, 2007b, San Antonio, TX: Psychological Corporation. Adapted with permission.

We must be very careful to properly determine which behaviors are actually seeking behaviors. Seeking creates pleasure from sensory experiences. Some children who have ASD engage in a high rate of certain behaviors (e.g., rocking) because they are familiar for the child. When a familiar behavior has a more "driven" quality, it is likely to be an avoiding behavior because it keeps out new sensations (see below).

Noah is a middle school student who seeks deep pressure and tactile input throughout the day. When he was younger, he stopped working to rub his arms and body and then would knock things off his desk. He now wears snuggly fitting undershirts and his favorite stretchy jacket every day, which gives him extra pressure on his skin during classes; he says he pays attention better that way (VandenBerg, 2001). Now that Noah's sensory-seeking needs are being met, he gets his class work done nearly every day.

Tracey is a fourth-grader who keeps getting up from the table to run around the room. While she is getting her sensory needs met that way, this behavior keeps her from interacting with other children at the table. The teacher assigns Tracey the job of handing out the supplies. She stacks the materials on the floor so Tracey has to bend down to get them, adding more movement input. These adjustments in the small-group activity provide Tracey movement input AND social participation.

Ways to Address Low Registration

When children have low registration, they don't notice things, and, as a result, cannot focus on tasks. These behaviors can also interfere with school work, because they cause students to miss directions or other cues.

Because these students notice less, you might observe that they are more easy-going than other students, and aren't bothered by things that bother others in the classroom. However, not noticing can also mean the students don't respond when you call them, may drift away during activities, and have a harder time getting tasks completed in a timely manner.

Students with a low registration pattern can *profit from more intensity* in sensory experiences, as suggested in Table 6.4. With more intensity of sensory input, these students can continue to pay attention during daily life activities and, therefore, stick with them for a longer time.

The plan for students with low registration is to provide enough continuous and intense sensory input so that they can persist in their work. Bradley, our case study at the beginning of the chapter, has low registration. For this student, place work materials on very high or very low shelves to increase reaching and bending. Construct a flow chart for more complex tasks that the student checks off.

We need to find ways to intensify the sensory input available within the activities and environments around the child. When we do this, the brain gets more information and, therefore, has a better chance of reaching the high thresholds. Some children who have ASD may seem "out of it" because their high thresholds keep them from recognizing stimuli that other children routinely notice and respond to.

To address low registration needs, increase the contrast and reduce the predictability of events as this creates more opportunities for the sensory systems to meet high thresholds and send input to the brain. Make objects weigh more, change an item's color or the background color, or add a movement to the assignment. For example, if a student like Bradley is lethargic, we might break his seatwork assignments into smaller parts so he has to get up and turn in the parts several times during the seatwork period. We might also give the student construction paper to write on (increasing the texture) and scented markers for certain assignments. Each change adds sensory input to the seatwork task (i.e., movement, touch, smell, visual inputs, respectively), and the accumulation of inputs increases the chances that the student will reach thresholds and become more responsive.

Table 6.4
Strategies for Students Who Have Low Registration

Add rough and varied textures on handles, seats, and work surfaces	Have scented lotion available that the student can rub on hands and arms
Encourage the student to wear highly textured socks, shirts	Encourage variety in texture, flavor, and temperature in food options
Create opportunities for the student to play on different surfaces (e.g., linoleum, carpet)	Have student hand out books to class and move items for teacher to provide additional input to body
Arrange it so the student can bend down to obtain supplies from lower shelves	Offer a rocking chair in the back of the classroom
Provide a bin of materials the student can manipulate while working (such as a stress ball, a key ring)	Use textured paper for individual work when writing.
Place classroom materials out of easy reach so the student has to reach, walk and move to get to them	Have student carry books, work materials, and other heavy items to table
Be aware of safety measures when the student is moving about (may not notice objects, stairs, changes in terrain)	Select bright mats for student's work surface
Make mirrors available at floor level	Add colored tape to edges of work areas in classroom so student can easily see the edges
Turn on bright lights, or make a more focused desk lamp available for the student's work space	Point out things you pass by so student can stay engaged as the class moves from place to place
Provide lively music background, or a walkman with lively music during seatwork time	Talk about what the student/you are doing as you do it
Talk with varying voice intonation	Point out sounds you hear and name the sounds
Clean materials for the student with scented cleaners	Use spritzer scents in designated work areas for the student
Practice a routine a lot with the student; add visual cues about what to do next	Teach the student how to get clues from watching other students
Have student stand up to eat or do seatwork	Select heavier objects for the student to play with

From *The Sensory Profile Supplement*, by W. Dunn, 2007b, San Antonio, TX: Psychological Corporation. Adapted with permission.

Ways to Address Sensitivity

When students notice everything, the enormous amount of sensory input they take in can interfere with school work because the students are so distracted. Because these students notice more, you might observe that they are more easily distracted than other students and are bothered by things that others might not even notice. Students who notice more pick up more details in life and may notice changes in setting or mood very quickly. However, noticing more can also mean that students are distractible, and therefore get interrupted from getting tasks completed in a timely manner.

Students with a sensitivity pattern can profit from *more structured patterns of sensory experiences* during daily life. With more structure of sensory input, these students can continue to pay attention during daily life activities and therefore stick with them for a longer time. See Table 6.5.

Table 6.5
Strategies for Students Who Have Sensory Sensitivity

Place a rubber mat underneath the desk that provides a steady grip for the student's feet when doing seatwork	Encourage form-fitting clothing and undergarments that do NOT have tight spots or bunching
Identify favorite food flavors, textures, and temperatures and stick with them	When the student likes/dislikes a texture, name it for him/her. Then continue to use these words
Provide a buffer space for the student to play without getting bumped easily	Identify preferred surface textures and make them available to this student
Make heavy blankets available	Remove blowing vents/fans from student's location
Use firm pressure on skin to calm	Create a comfortable seating structure for the student
Place materials at chest level in drawers/ shelves so student does not have to bend over	Provide a rocker for calming when the student gets upset
Create a blank area for individualized work	Serve foods in a compartment tray
Place sheets over shelving areas to reduce visual distractions	Remove overhead light sources from room and replace with lamps and more focused lighting
Run water before the student enters the bathroom to reduce the startle from the sound of the water	Tell student what to do, and then be quiet
Provide written or taped instructions	Allow students to place books on lap to work
Organize classroom discussions so that one person is talking at a time	Use plastic utensils and paper plates to reduce noise in lunch room
Allow student to move to a more remote location for work	Play even-tempo background music during work time
Provide ear plugs/ear muffs/earphones during work time	Give student opportunities for moving ahead of or after other students when changing rooms or activities
Limit the amount of time the student must spend in loud public places	Be careful about using scents in hair products, perfumes, and lotions; these might upset this student
Tell student name of aromas of flavors/ foods	Use unscented cleaners in the classroom for this student
Create routines and stick with them	Have student wear back pack

From *The Sensory Profile Supplement,* by W. Dunn, 2007b, San Antonio, TX: Psychological Corporation. Adapted with permission.

———————————

Emphasize the organizing aspects of the sensory systems with children who have sensitivity (see Dunn, 1991a; Dunn & DeGangi, 1992) because these sensory inputs provide the brain with information without increasing arousal. Tables 6.1 and 6.2 outlined which features of each sensory system are more organizing. Touch-pressure stimuli (i.e., firm contact with the skin) provides organizing information without increasing arousal and distractibility (Dunn, 1991a). When we can provide more organizing (i.e., not arousing) input for these children, we increase their chances for completing tasks and learning from them. Teachers, parents, and other professionals must be flexible yet systematic because these children are more sensitive to the sensory information around them than other children.

Students with ASD are often sensitive to touch. Light touch can occur many times in a day (e.g., clothing, hair, people moving around) and can make the student more and more upset. We can recommend form-fitting clothing, which presses evenly on the skin. With firm pressure on the skin, it is harder to get light touch. Bradley is sensitive to touch, and the cocoon is very helpful to him when he is bothered.

Ways to Address Avoiding

Some students withdraw from situations to reduce the sensory input they have to contend with. When sensation avoiding interferes with school participation, identify what sensory input is O.K. and what is negative for the student.

When students demonstrate an avoiding pattern of sensory processing, they notice and are bothered by things much more than others. They may be more interested in being alone or in very quiet places. When environments are too challenging, these students may withdraw and, therefore, may not complete work.

Students with an avoiding pattern participate better when there is less sensory input available in the environment. When the environment is "quiet," these students can continue daily life activities for a longer time (see Table 6.6).

Table 6.6
Strategies for Supporting Students Who Are Sensory-Avoiding

Encourage family to select form-fitted undergarments	Arrange for lunch and snacks to be served at room temperature
Guide student to select foods with even textures	Identify work and play areas with space away from other students
Keep fans or vents from blowing on the student	Allow the student to hold books on lap while working
Keep student out of crowded spaces	Gather work materials for student in one place
Select an assigned seat for the student away from traffic patterns to prevent bumping	Allow student to use the library for work and getaways
Identify routines for the class and stick with them	Remove other work materials from the work surface
Keep shades drawn or move the student to a more remote location	Allow student to have one food at a time on plate
Serve plate to student rather than having student carry own tray	Cover cubby holes to decrease distractions
Create "blinders" for the student's work area	Run fan (that does not blow on student) to create "white" background noise to drown out unpredictable noises
Find closed-in, quiet places for the student to play/rest	Limit large unstructured time for the student
Use unscented materials with the student	Remove air fresheners from this student's areas
Craft alone-time for the student and recognize it is GOOD	Use very heavy blankets for safe spots
Have student carry/wear a backpack	Braid hair to increase firm pressure and decrease light touch
Have student hold the heavy doors while others file out	Wear clothing that covers well and is fitted
Use trips to the bathroom or errands to give student a break from intense environments	Educate others to use visual cues rather than touching to gain student's attention

From *The Sensory Profile Supplement*, by W. Dunn, 2007b, San Antonio, TX: Psychological Corporation. Adapted with permission.

We have to be careful not to push students into overwhelming sensory situations. Once the student has a "fight or flight" response (i.e., the response of fear or danger in which the child will become aggressive [fight] or retreat [flight] to protect self), learning is not possible, because the brain is in a protective mode. If the student's rituals are just quirky, we can leave the behavior alone.

For example, many children with ASD only eat one or two foods, which can interfere with their health. Sammy would only eat chicken broth (e.g., no noodles, no bits of meat). The team was concerned over his nutrition. The OT blended the chicken broth to adjust the texture a little without adding anything to it. Sammy squealed when he noticed the texture change, but then he continued to eat the broth. The OT then blended in a few flecks of parsley; Sammy immediately noticed them, picked them out, and ate the broth. When the OT added a few very well-cooked noodles, Sammy separated out the noodles and ate the broth. When the amount of broth was reduced, Sammy then ate the noodles. Each systematic step can set the stage for improved diet. If the team took the broth away, Sammy would likely not eat at all.

We must recognize the discomfort these students experience. Through careful observation, we can identify the sensory features of their rituals (i.e., what do they include or exclude from the ritual). Some frames of reference might suggest that we bombard these children with input so they "get used to it." However, such a strategy can lead to more and more withdrawal (Dunn, 2007b), as the children attempt to maintain some sense of control. From a sensory processing viewpoint, we recognize that ritual and control indicate a need to manage input.

Some rituals can be left alone (e.g., the way a student takes off her coat, the way the student eats a sandwich); others may need to be adjusted to support the student in learning at school (e.g., managing the sounds of the classroom and continue to work). When identifying a ritual that needs to be expanded, study the characteristics of the ritual to expand it in some small way so that there is a blending of familiar and new stimuli (Dunn & DeGangi, 1992). This enables the child to incorporate the challenging sensory inputs into a familiar ritual. For example, many students with ASD have strong food preferences, including strategies for eating and preparing the food. In order to improve nutritional circumstances, it is sometimes necessary to expand the eating patterns with the student. If the student is focused on the taste of the food, we can add a color or texture to the food to broaden the sensory qualities (e.g., we can add food coloring to pudding, or we can add finely ground nuts). By doing this, we create an opportunity for the student to arouse to the new stimulus and perhaps accept it into her ritual, broadening the ritual without causing an aggressive or withdrawing response. If we disrupt a ritual too quickly, the student will object more strongly, which usually leads to more avoidance behaviors and further decline of functional performance (Dunn, 1997a). There is a great risk of entering into power struggles (NCCIP, 1994).

Children who avoid sensation may appear disengaged, which can be confused with low registration. However, there is a difference. Children who avoid sensory experiences notice and withdraw from activities, whereas children with low registration are not aware of what is going on around them. Children with sensation-avoiding display anxiety and hypervigilance, while children with low registration seem unaware and unconcerned.

Combining Educational and Sensory Processing Strategies

Interdisciplinary teams need to integrate effective educational strategies and sensory processing knowledge to best serve children who have ASD. Dunn, Saiter, and Rinner (2002) summarize this integration for students who have Asperger Syndrome. Using priming, working independently, Social Stories™, home base, and visual supports as effective educational strategies, the authors describe how sensory processing knowledge can enhance the effectiveness of these teaching approaches. Please see the original reference for more detailed explanations and case studies applying these ideas within children's stories.

Summary and Conclusions

Understanding sensory processing enables us to better understand student behavior and planning school strategies. Evidence indicates that students with ASD notice less sensory input than others (i.e., low registration) and withdraw more quickly than others (i.e., avoiding). Effective intervention focuses on adjusting sensory demands so the student can participate in school more effectively.

This chapter illustrated how sensory processing difficulties can lead to challenging behaviors, including work avoidance, class disruption, aggression, and even explosive outbursts. It would follow that a sensory inventory is an important tool to use in a functional behavior assessment. Many of the strategies listed in this chapter can be used to effectively reduce unwanted behaviors in the classroom while leading to increased student participation.

Tips for the Classroom

✓ A first step to addressing the sensory needs of any given student with ASD is to consult with members of the team who have expertise in this area (e.g., occupational therapist) as well as have knowledge of the particular student.

✓ Strategies that may potentially help to support students who seem to seek out sensory stimulation include:

- Provide colored worksheets or colored sheet protectors to highlight the work.

- Have some healthy, chewy snacks available either in the student's desk or in a special container in the teacher's desk.

- Allow the student to change work positions or stand to do his work, as needed. It may also be helpful to allow the student to do his work on the chalkboard.

- Arrange for the student to sit on a move-n-sit cushion or a t-stool that will allow for movement while sitting.

- Send the student on errands around the school, such as to the office, to get him out of the classroom and moving.

- Have the student wear a wrist band, head band, or belt.

- Adjust the lighting in the student's work area.

- Allow the student to take off his shoes while he is in the classroom. Make sure to establish guidelines so the student is aware that shoes are required to be worn in the hallways, the cafeteria, etc.

- Make sure that visual materials are at eye level.

✓ Strategies that may potentially help to support students who seem to have low registration of sensory information include:

- Allow the student to have appropriately scented lotion in his desk to put on throughout the day.

- Arrange jobs for the student, such as handing out materials and books.

- Provide a rocking chair in the back of the classroom and allow the student to request using it between activities.

- Provide a variety of work surfaces with different textures and density.

- The student may not be aware of dangerous objects in the environment, so monitor his movement.

- Use bright lighting in the student's work areas.

- Allow the student to listen to music using an iPod during work time to help keep him alert.

- Be sure to provide plenty of visual supports and repetitive routines when teaching this student.

✓ Strategies that may potentially help to support students who seem to have sensitivity include:

- Provide a rubber mat underneath the student's desk that can provide a steady grip for his feet while working.

- Provide a cafeteria tray with divided areas to help the food from mixing and for easy identification.

- Allow the student to leave the class a bit early or stand at the beginning or end of the line while leaving the room to avoid bumping into classmates.

- Be aware that the student might startle from unexpected or sudden noises, so it is best to prepare for noises whenever possible.

- Avoid using repetitive verbal directives. After giving a single directive, be quiet and/or display a visual support.

- Limit the amount of time the student has to spend in loud or crowded spaces.

- Provide ear plugs for times when you anticipate a louder environment. Prepare the student prior to the event with a story and instructions of how to use the ear plugs.

- Directly teach the student about his sensory sensitivities. Help him to identify scents and sounds and to advocate for himself when the environment becomes unbearable.

✓ Strategies that may potentially help to support students who seem to be avoiding:

- Create predictable routines within the classroom.

- Break down tasks using a visual sequence when teaching the steps of an activity, such as toothbrushing, to create a routine that can be followed repetitively.

- Be aware that the student may have a very limited diet due to his sensitivity. Identify favorite foods and textures and help the student to choose these foods at lunch. In some cases, it may help to introduce new foods in a systematic and gradual way. For example, have the student work on just looking at the new food, then tolerate smelling it prior to ever actually tasting it.

- Arrange for lunch food to be served at room temperature.

- Be careful that fans or vents are not blowing directly on the student.

- Have the student's desk or work space out of the main traffic areas.

- Find quiet spaces within the school environment where the student can work without distracting the other students.

- Arrange for the student to go on errands to other areas of the school building to give him a break from the noise of the classroom environment.

- Be aware that the student might be highly anxious in crowded or loud assemblies as well as gym due to the movement and echoes of the gymnasium. Be sure to prepare the student in advance of these events and activities.

Chapter Highlights

- Sensory processing is a person's way of noticing and responding to sensory events that occur during daily life.

- Sensory systems provide information to the brain, which then forms maps that guide our spatial and temporal orientation, as well as how we react to different situations.

- Sensory processing systems includ: touch (somatosensory), body position (proprioceptive), sight (visual), hearing (auditory), smell (olfactory), taste (gustatory), and movement (vestibular).

- Many behaviors observed in children with ASD can be attributed to an imbalance, or poor modulation, of sensory input in the brain.

- Thresholds, or the point at which a particular sensory system responds, can create difficulties: when too low, children may respond too frequently and be distracted; if too high, children may miss important cues.

- In individuals with ASD, arousal input often overpowers discrimination which, in turn, can create unusual behaviors as they try to manage distorted information.

- Sensory systems transmit information to the brain to (a) generate awareness (arousal/alerting) and (b) gather information for brain mapping and discrimination.

- Dunn's conceptual model for understanding patterns of sensory processing combines brain thresholds with self-regulation to create four patterns: low registration, sensitivity, seeking, and avoiding.

- When using a sensory processing framework for intervention, the goal is to improve participation, not change the sensory processing patterns.

- For each of the four sensory processing patterns, the author provides specific information about the pattern, as well as ways educators and others can plan interventions to support student learning based on individual sensory needs.

Chapter Review Questions

1. What is sensory processing?

2. List and describe the systems involved in sensory processing.

3. What are modulation and thresholds in terms of sensory input to the brain?

4. What is the purpose of sensory systems transmitting information to the brain?

5. Give examples of arousal/alerting and discrimination/mapping descriptors.

6. Why is it useful to incorporate various sensory inputs into therapeutic programs?

7. Explain Dunn's conceptual model for understanding patterns of sensory processing.

8. How do individuals with ASD differ from neurotypical peers in terms of sensory processing?

9. What is the goal of a sensory processing framework for intervention?

10. Give examples of sensory processing interventions that address each type of pattern and that support student learning.

References

Ayres, A. J. (1972). *Sensory integration and learning disorders.* Los Angeles: Western Psychological Services.

Ayres, A. J. (1979). *Sensory integration and the child.* Los Angeles: Western Psychological Services.

Brown, C., & Dunn, W. (2002). *The Adult Sensory Profile.* San Antonio, TX: Psychological Corporation.

Brown, C., Tollefson, N., Dunn, W., Cromwell, R., & Filion, D. (2001). The Adult Sensory Profile: Measuring patterns of sensory processing. *American Journal of Occupational Therapy, 55,* 75-82.

Dove, S. (2003). *Sensory processing in children with specific learning disabilities.* Unpublished master's thesis, University of Kansas.

Dunn, W. (1991a). Assessing human performance related to brain function. Neuroscience foundations of human performance. *AOTA Self-Study Series, 12,* 3-38.

Dunn, W. (1991b). Motivation. Neuroscience foundations of human performance. *AOTA Self-Study Series, 7,* 3-36.

Dunn, W. (1991c). The sensorimotor systems: A framework for assessment and intervention. In F. P. Orelove & D. Sobsey (Eds.), *Educating children with multiple disabilities: A transdisciplinary approach* (2nd ed.). Baltimore: Paul H. Brookes.

Dunn, W. (1997a). The impact of sensory processing abilities on the daily lives of young children and their families: A conceptual model. *Infants and Young Children, 9*(4), 23-25.

Dunn, W. (1997b). Implementing neuroscience principles to support habilitation and recovery. In C. Christiansen & C. Baum (Eds.), *Occupational therapy: Enabling function and well-being* (pp. 182-233). Thorofare, NJ: Slack.

Dunn, W. (1999). *The Sensory Profile Manual.* San Antonio, TX: Psychological Corporation.

Dunn, W. (2000). *The Infant Toddler Sensory Profile.* San Antonio, TX: Psychological Corporation.

Dunn, W. (2001a). The sensations of everyday life: Theoretical, conceptual and pragmatic considerations. *American Journal of Occupational Therapy, 55*(6), 608-620.

Dunn, W. (2007a). *Sensory Profile School Companion.* San Antonio, TX: The Psychological Corporation.

Dunn, W. (2007b). *The Sensory Profile Supplement.* San Antonio, TX: The Psychological Corporation.

Dunn, W., & Bennett, D. (2002). Patterns of sensory processing in children with attention deficit hyperactivity disorder. *Occupational Therapy Journal of Research, 22*(1), 4-15.

Dunn, W., & Daniels, D. (2001). Initial development of the Infant Toddler Sensory Profile. *Journal of Early Intervention, 25*(1), 27-41.

Dunn, W., & DeGangi, G. (1992). Sensory integration and neurodevelopmental treatment for educational programming. *AOTA Self-Study Series, 2,* 5-55.

Dunn, W., Myles, B., & Orr, S. (2002). Sensory processing issues associated with Asperger Syndrome: A preliminary investigation. *American Journal of Occupational Therapy, 56,* 97-102.

Dunn, W., Saiter, J., & Rinner, L. (2002). Asperger Syndrome and sensory processing: A conceptual model and guidance for intervention planning. *Focus on Autism and Other Developmental Disabilities, 17*(3), 172-185.

Ermer, J., & Dunn, W. (1998). The Sensory Profile: A discriminant analysis of children with and without disabilities. *American Journal of Occupational Therapy, 52,* 283-290.

Kandel, E., Schwartz, J., & Jessell, T. (2000). *Principles of neural science.* New York: McGraw-Hill.

Kientz, M. A., & Dunn, W. (1997). Comparison of children with autism and typical children using the Sensory Profile. *American Journal of Occupational Therapy, 51*(7), 530-537.

Miller, L., McIntosh, D., McGrath, J., Shyu, V., Lampe, M., Taylor, A., Tassone, F., Neitzel, K., Stackhouse, T., & Hagerman, R. (1998). Electrodermal responses to sensory stimuli in individuals with fragile X syndrome: A preliminary report. *American Journal of Medical Genetics, 83*(4), 268-279.

Myles, B. S., Hagiwara, T., Dunn, W., Rinner, L., Reese, M., Huggins, A., et al. (2004). Sensory issues in children with Asperger Syndrome and autism. *Education and Training in Developmental Disabilities, 3*(4), 283-290.

National Center for Clinical Infant Programs/Zero to Three. (1994). *Diagnostic classification of mental health and developmental disorders of infancy and early childhood.* Arlington, VA: Author.

VandenBerg, N. (2001). The use of a weighted vest to increase on-task behavior in children with attention difficulties. *American Journal of Occupational Therapy, 55*(6), 621-628.

Watling, R., Dietz, J., & White, O. (2001). Comparison of sensory profile scores of young children with and without autism spectrum disorders. *American Journal of Occupational Therapy, 55*(4), 416-423.

Learner Objectives

After reading this chapter, the learner should be able to:

- State the definition of a crisis management approach and the advantages and disadvantages of using such an approach

- Discuss shifting behavioral perspectives and the set of assumptions that accompany this shift in thinking, including the specifics of each assumption

- List the members of the behavioral support team and their roles

- State the components of a functional behavioral assessment

- Discuss the issues involved in defining behaviors of concern

- Provide examples of behaviors that are observable and measurable

- State the goal of a functional behavioral assessment

- Explain the importance of antecedents and consequences in maintaining or diminishing behavior

- List and describe the types of questions that must be asked to determine the true function of a behavior

- Explain why collecting information is an ongoing process in functional behavioral assessment and positive behavior support

- Explain what hypothesis statements are and what they are based on

- Discuss the importance of looking at problem behavior pathways to determine how to support appropriate behavior

- State the focus of positive behavior support approaches

- List and describe curricular, classroom management, and instructional considerations involved in implementing interventions

- Explain the role of applied behavior analysis in intervention

- Discuss why behavior support plans may not be successful and the importance of monitoring implementation and outcomes

Chapter 7

Teaching a Different Way of Behaving: Positive Behavior Supports

Cathy Pratt

Matthew is a 7-year-old child with a diagnosis of autism. He was diagnosed when he was 22 months old. Up until 19 months of age, he had been developing seemingly normally but then began losing language and becoming much more introverted. When left by himself, he preferred to sit alone engaging in self-stimulatory behavior. Upon diagnosis, he was enrolled in the state's early intervention program and began working with a speech clinician, an occupational therapist, and an educational therapist in his home. His parents augmented these services with private therapy focused on behavior and communication.

Today, Matthew attends a program in a public school. Matthew remains nonverbal. In the past two years, parents and staff have noticed an increase in behavioral incidents. When requested to perform certain tasks, Matthew becomes anxious and attempts to destroy instructional materials. At recess, he either wanders the playground or pushes others off the swings. When directed to return, he refuses. His parents note that he has difficulty sleeping at night and that he is a very picky eater. He also struggles with chronic diarrhea.

Aside from these behavioral difficulties, Matthew can be a very affectionate child. He loves to crawl up on the lap of adults and be hugged tightly. He is easily entertained at times, and can sit for a period of time and play with his trains. This play is somewhat inappropriate and involves ritualistic play (e.g., spinning the wheels repeatedly of the train). He has an engaging smile and infectious laugh.

In his current program, Matthew is primarily in an early intervention classroom for students with various disabilities. The focus of the program is on teaching academic, functional, communication, and social/play skills. When working on functional/academic skills, staff report that it is difficult to keep Matthew focused on the task at hand. They often have to position a staff person close by him to continually prompt him to work on a task.

*For communication, the staff and family have chosen a **Picture Exchange Communication System (PECS)** (Frost & Bondy, 1994). Matthew has access to this system three times a week during therapy sessions. PECS is used inconsistently at home and school. Staff and family state that they understand what Matthew wants by watching his gestures and facial expressions. With strangers, he has no functional way to communicate. To teach play skills, the staff work to position Matthew in close proximity to other students in hopes that he will model their behavior.*

Matthew appears to have some sensory processing challenges. He likes to lick book pages and then play with his saliva; he becomes upset at certain noises; and he prefers to wear only certain types of clothing. As a result, Matthew works with an occupational therapist weekly on sensory-based activities. At this point, no sensory activities have been embedded into his day.

While Matthew has made some progress, there is much more to do. Overall, staff will be focusing on the following areas: initiation, joint attention, play skills, toilet training, and following directions.

Students with autism spectrum disorders (ASD) who engage in challenging behaviors (e.g., aggression, self-injurious behavior, withdrawal, refusal) place a tremendous stress on the family members and professionals who support them. This stress may be unduly increased when those involved lack training or understanding of the strategies for assessing, understanding, and addressing problem behaviors.

The purpose of this chapter is to provide some basic information about **functional behavioral assessment** approaches and **positive behavior supports**. The hope is to present information that can be easily used to ensure that programs are adopted and supports utilized that can lead to long-term behavioral change by creating positive learning environments and teaching alternative behaviors.

While this is the only chapter in this book that mentions behavior specifically in the title, behavior is involved in every topic discussed. This is for two reasons. First, the outcome of a sound behavior support plan is that an individual learns more socially appropriate ways of responding. Second, behavioral challenges are automatically reduced when programming is solid and when the individual lives and learns in supportive environments.

Role of Crisis Management

Let's begin by talking about **crisis management**. When individuals on the autism spectrum engage in behavior that threatens the safety of themselves or of others, family members and professionals want to know how to implement immediate behavior change. The question is typically framed as, "What do we do when ...?" The goal is to find an approach that will have an immediate impact in a difficult or a crisis situation.

In reality, those who ask these questions in such situations will only find a short-term solution. The response is referred to as crisis management. The goal of a crisis management plan is to diffuse or interrupt a potentially dangerous situation. While it may prove effective in the immediate situation, crisis management is a quick fix with no long-term educational benefit. In other words, the individual does not learn an alternative prosocial response.

The other danger in using a crisis management approach is that our response may strengthen a given behavior. For example, if we restrain a student who loves deep pressure, she may be reinforced for her negative behavior. If we place a student in timeout who prefers to spend time alone, we may be providing him with a vacation from the stresses of the school setting. If the behavior is related to stress or anxiety, confrontation may escalate the problem and decrease the ability to think clearly. And if we respond emotionally to a problematic situation, students may enjoy the attention and excitement their behavior elicits. Thus, we continually run the risk of reinforcing behavior through our actions.

When an individual is in the midst of a behavior, this is not the time to lecture or teach. The goal is to minimize the situation. When somebody is upset, she has less capacity to learn. Lecturing or talking to her may only serve to intensify the behavior. Instead, keep words to a minimum and always respond with a neutral affect. The goal is not to have the "last word" or to make your point heard; the goal is to keep everyone safe.

At times punishment and exclusion are considered as means to control behavioral situations. Both of these approaches also have limitations. First, many students on the autism spectrum prefer to spend time at home rather than at school, so being sent home is not punishment to many of our students. Further, once they are sent home for problematic behaviors, sometimes we must struggle to convince them to return to school. In other words, what started out as a strategy to punish or make a point has become a reward for the child.

Punishment also has limitations, in that students do not learn appropriate behaviors by being told "no" or by losing privileges. While such strategies may work in the presence of someone who physically intimidates the student or who has the stature to control, this type of control does not create a relationship of trust conducive to maximum learning. We are serving as continual role models for students. Resorting to punitive approaches as the primary means of behavior change does not teach students how to respond in a more proactive fashion in the future. In other words, the focus of a behavior support plan should be on teaching alternative behaviors and creating positive learning environments, not on gaining control or punishing students.

We now realize that learning problems associated with difficulties in executive function, central coherence, and theory of mind (see Chapter 1) may impact behavior and that the old consequence-focused strategies may not be logical approaches to behavior change. In other words, simply addressing behavior change by applying powerful consequences to decrease certain behaviors is not sufficient. Specific teaching strategies that address the core deficits of ASD will need to be applied.

Despite the many disadvantages, there is still a role for a crisis management plan. We cannot allow students to harm themselves or others. The critical word here is *plan*. Each person involved with the student must know how to respond with the goal of minimizing the situation. After an event occurs, staff and/or family members should talk about how well the plan worked and what should happen next time. When the child is not in crisis, the real work of behavior change can occur. In other words, the best time to address behavior is when behavior is not occurring. This requires a shift in thinking about behavior and the role of behavior plans, as discussed below.

Shifting Behavioral Perspectives

Today, there is a focus away from solely manipulating consequences to designing positive behavior support plans. That is, instead of designing behavior support plans that focus on consequences, behavior support plans today focus on teaching individuals socially valid ways of responding. With this approach comes a set of assumptions or beliefs about behavior. These include the following:

- *Behavior is influenced by or governed by context.* This simply means that environments provide clues about expected behaviors and set an individual up for behavioral challenges or successes. It also means that students' behavior will improve or deteriorate in various settings. For example, it is not unusual for students on the autism spectrum to behave better at home than at school. In a home setting, the student typically will have more time to regroup, and more accommodations can be made. In a school setting, there are more demands, and more stimulation. The challenge becomes one of making the school setting conducive to learning without making it so sterile that the student becomes overwhelmed when out in real-world settings.

- *Behavior is functional, purposeful, and meaningful to the individual.* It may not hold meaning for us, but for the individual with ASD there may be a sound reason for a given behavior. Our challenge is to understand his or her perspective. In addition, behavior is tied to communication challenges (Reichle & Wacker, 1993). Whether a student is verbal or nonverbal, he will use behavior when his communication system does not allow him to adequately express stress, concern, confusion, anger, or other emotions.

- *Behavior is affected by internal events, including emotional states* (e.g., *anxiety, depression*) *and biological conditions* (e.g., *gastrointestinal difficulties, seizures, ear infections*). Students cannot perform at their very best when they are not healthy. For students who have chronic ear infections, gastrointestinal difficulties, or other conditions, it is important to address health issues before expecting them to learn maximally. Likewise, many students on the autism spectrum suffer from poor self-esteem, anxiety, and/or depression. These emotional states also have a dramatic impact on behavior, and hence, learning.

- *Behavior is influenced by factors outside the immediate environment, including relationships, opportunities for engaging in various activities, and lifestyle issues.* Students on the autism spectrum who have a better overall quality of life are less prone to problematic behaviors (Carr, 2007). Sometimes parents or staff make statements such as, "until Kyle behaves, we cannot let him go into the community or be around other students." That is, they make participation in a meaningful life contingent upon perfect behavior. Instead, we need to recognize that students who are in a situation that allows them a meaningful life have fewer behavioral incidents. For example, some students do better in a general education as opposed to a special education setting because the classroom provides more stimulation and excitement.

- *Behaviors will change as people mature and develop new competencies.* One only has to mention the word *puberty* to know that this statement is true. With various ages and grade levels, certain behavioral difficulties may occur or disappear.

- *Behavioral supports are guided by a strong value base.* Our values about behavior and how we were raised will impact our response. Each of us needs to engage in self-examination to determine how our values impact our reactions. Are we more focused on quality-of-life issues and teaching the person self-control, or are we more punitive in our approach and focused on controlling the situation?

The process of examining our attitudes and belief systems must be ongoing. This is important because our values and beliefs will determine our role and the contribution we make in working as members of a team involved in an individual's life.

Putting Together a Team

The goal of any behavior support approach for a student with ASD should be long-term behavior change. While there may be a need for a short-term crisis management, as mentioned, this should never be the sole or even the primary approach used. In order to effect long-term behavior change, those involved must learn to understand the function or purpose of a given behavior. This process of gathering information is referred to as a functional behavioral assessment. While conducting a functional behavioral assessment has for many years been considered "best practice," it is now articulated in federal legislation via the Individuals with Disabilities Education Improvement Act. Likewise, this strategy is tied to national school-wide discipline and positive behavior supports initiatives.

A student enters your classroom with a history of challenging behaviors. While the first few days are calm (the so-called honeymoon period), soon you begin to see behaviors occur. These behaviors are interfering with the student's learning and the education of others. Before a behavior plan is designed, the process of conducting a functional behavioral assessment must start.

The first step in conducting a functional behavioral assessment is to identify the behavior support team who will meet to problem solve, support, and guide this process. Potential participants include family members, educators, paraprofessionals, therapists, private therapists, and the student on the autism spectrum him/herself. In other words, the team should include members from all environments in which the student interacts, people who know him well, members who know about various community support options, and members who can allocate personnel and resources. Decisions impacting the student must be made within the team structure. If other professionals (e.g., physicians, private therapists) wish to make recommendations that impact the program, they should be willing to sit as a member of the team. Programming decisions made in isolation fragments a team and lead to ineffectual planning and, ultimately, poor outcomes.

Once the team has been identified, members are responsible for (a) defining the behavior of concern, (b) gathering information, (c) developing hypothesis statements, (d) creating a behavior support plan, (e) implementing interventions, and (f) monitoring implementation and outcomes. The rest of this chapter is devoted to these steps.

Step One: Defining the Behavior of Concern

Before the behavioral assessment starts, agreement must be reached on the specific behavior of concern. The behavior then must be described and written in a measurable and observable format. That is, the behavior should be described so that everybody is clear about what the behavior looks like. For example, descriptors such as the "the student tantrums" or "the student is noncompliant or aggressive" are open to interpretation. Instead, descriptors such as "the student hits, kicks, and refuses to do work presented to her" or "the student screams" are clear and easily identified by all.

Information should also be gathered on whether a specific behavior occurs with other behaviors. For example, if a student hits, can staff also expect her to use profane language? Or if the student begins to engage in self-stimulatory behavior or self-talk, is this an indicator of anxiety and a warning that a problematic behavior is likely to occur? Again, the behavior must be described in an observable and measurable fashion.

Using the vignette at the start of this chapter, the following represents poor and good descriptors of Matthew's behavior. You will notice that by providing an observable and measurable description of the behavior, we begin to get insight into potential contributing factors.

Poor Descriptors	Measurable/Observable Descriptors
Aggressive	Pushes others off swing on the playground
Destructive	Tears instructional materials when presented
Noncompliant	On playground, does not come when called

Before an elaborate assessment is conducted, the student's instructional team should first determine whether the behavior is truly a problem or merely an annoyance. Each of us has varying levels of tolerance for specific behaviors. Although agreement can easily be reached on behaviors such as engaging in self-abuse or attacking other students, other behaviors (e.g., chewing gum, taking off one's shoes in the classroom, self-stimulation) are more benign and may actually be accelerated by our reaction.

Measures such as **frequency**, **duration**, and **intensity** may be used to determine the significance of a behavior. However, equally important is considering the long-term impact of a behavior on a child's adult options. That is, regardless of the age of the individual, programming must keep in mind where we are ultimately aiming for. In the example of Matthew, staff may find it endearing that he crawls on their laps. However, at some stage, this behavior will not be tolerated, and staff will have to break habits they have created with Matthew. If the hope is that the individual will live and work in the community, various behaviors need to be modified and alternative behaviors need to be taught early.

Step Two: Gathering Behavioral Information

Once the target behavior is determined, we must examine the relationship between the challenging behaviors and conditions in the student's life. This process is referred to as a functional behavioral assessment. Two points are important to remember here.

First, conducting a functional behavioral assessment is a team process. No one individual can determine the function without gaining input and information from the team. While a single person may be assigned to guide the process, information should be gathered using multiple people in multiple situations. This is a team fact-finding and problem-solving process that requires each team member – family and school alike – to be honest about the behavior and their possible contribution to the situation.

Second, the goal of a functional behavioral assessment is to identify the underlying causes of the behavior exhibited by the student. Crisis management strategies typically deal with symptoms. Symptoms can include hitting, kicking, screaming, cursing, and similar behaviors. However, these are signals that something else is happening. Potential underlying causes include lack of a communication system, health issues, skill deficits, and an unsupportive environment. There are many other potential causes, and our job becomes one of digging until we can identify those causes with some degree of confidence. Specifically, our focus becomes one of identifying antecedents (what happens before) and consequences (what happens after the behavior) that maintain behavior.

Antecedents. There are two potential types of **antecedents: slow triggers** (setting events) or **fast triggers** (immediate antecedents). Typically, there is a greater focus on immediate triggers because these are immediately evident and can often be easily identified. However, setting events play a critical role in increasing the likelihood that a behavior will occur.

Slow triggers, or setting events, such as schedule changes, staff changes, medication changes, illness, irregular sleep patterns, missed meals, excessive temperatures, fights with classmates, difficulties on the bus, or skill deficits can make the student less able to cope. So, on a certain day when Michael is required to do a task, he does it perfectly. The very next day, the same request is given, and he acts out. This behavior is probably not in response to the task, but reflects the occurrence of a setting event. Setting events "chip away" at a student's tolerance and ability to perform. This is especially true for students on the autism spectrum.

In this connection, it is important to remember that much of what is bothering a student at the moment may not be apparent or related to the immediate situation. In the example at the beginning of the chapter, potential setting events for Matthew include an inconsistent communication system, a social skills deficit, sensory challenges, biomedical issues related to diarrhea, lack of sleep, and poor diet. On any given day, these factors in Matthew's life may increase the possibility of a challenging behavior occurring.

Fast triggers, or immediate antecedents, are events that are directly related to the challenging behavior or that immediately precede it. Potential fast triggers include asking a student to do a nonfavored task, a certain noise (e.g., vacuum cleaner), the behavior of others, being interrupted during preferred activities, transitions, or being bullied. Immediate antecedents are more easily identified than setting events. In the opening vignette, immediate antecedents for Matthew include lack of structure on the playground and certain instructional materials.

Consequences. **Consequences** are responses that follow a behavior and that maintain behavior. We continue to engage in behavior because it allows us to get something we want or to escape something undesirable. There are a couple of important points to remember about consequences.

First, we often use the word *consequences* in the negative. Instead, we should think of consequences in terms of those things that sustain behavior. Second, we continually reinforce behaviors, whether we realize it or not. As a result, each of us must continually examine our own behavior to determine the role we might be playing in the behavior of students on the autism spectrum. And finally, consequences must be viewed from the perspective of the individual child. For example, we may find being screamed at as punishing. However, for a student with autism, being screamed at may be entertaining and provide some source of amusement. In the vignette, a possible consequence for destroying instructional materials is that Matthew escapes doing work that is too difficult or boring to him.

Data collection. Although it is important to keep data on behaviors, traditional **data-collection** procedures can present a limited perspective of a behavior. For example, simply counting behavior incidents or determining the duration of a behavior may not provide sufficient insight into factors related to the behavior. Conditions related to problem behaviors can be very complex and difficult to detect.

Functional behavioral assessments questionnaires can provide a broader insight into why a student behaves in a certain manner under specific conditions and what professionals can do to support students to behave in a way that is more socially acceptable. While there are many formal and informal instruments (e.g., *Motivation Assessment Scale* [Durand & Crimmins, 1998], *Functional Behavioral Assessment Form* [O'Neill et al., 1997]) available to uncover important information, there is no specific instrument that includes all the questions that may need to be asked to determine why a behavior is occurring.

As educators, our challenge is to begin to identify the range of questions that can lead to a better understanding of the student and issues surrounding the behavior. By asking critical questions, the educational team can begin the detective work of identifying what is happening in the student's life to maintain the problem behaviors. The questions below are based on the work of O'Neill and colleagues (1997). In determining the true function of the behavior, additional questions may be necessary.

1. **What is the history of the undesirable behavior?**

   By gathering information about the history of the student's behavior, educators can begin to determine effective and ineffective approaches. This information will also provide insight into the student's learning history. The questions to address within this category include: How long has the student engaged in the behavior? What strategies have been used in the past? Which strategies were effective? Which strategies were ineffective?

2. **Under what conditions does the student do well? During what times or activities is she most successful?**

   Often one of the questions that provide the greatest insight into programming is related to those events, interactions, situations or activities that are in place when the student with ASD is the most successful. By identifying the conditions under which an individual does her very best, the team can begin to piece together a program that has a greater opportunity for supporting the student to be successful. For example, if the student does best with staff who give exact and clear directions, then this strategy should be practiced by all. If the student does best on days when physical activity is involved, then physical activities should be infused into each day. If the student excels in math, then math should be used to build momentum for other activities and perhaps as an activity to calm the student.

3. **What are areas of strength for the student? Are these strengths being reinforced?**

   Too often, educational programs for students with ASD are based on students' deficits rather than on strengths. Instead, areas of interest and strength should be used as the foundation for teaching other skills. When meeting on behalf of a student who is exhibiting behavioral difficulties, the first questions asked should refer to areas of strength and interests. Potential questions include: What does the student seem to enjoy? In what courses does the student seem to excel? What are his fixations or intense areas of interest?

By planning in this manner, family members and professionals can begin to determine a course of action that will promote student success. For example, if a student loves to talk about NASCAR, perhaps giving the student 5 minutes to speak on the subject could be a powerful reinforcement. If a student knows all the state capitals, perhaps a unit could be developed that requires all of his classmates to learn the capitals. That way, the student on the autism spectrum automatically becomes a key source of information for classmates, and her self-esteem is boosted as a result.

If strengths and interests are avoided, the student may become more fixated and anxious in an effort to gain access to something that is highly preferred. Instead, by building them into the day, the student can have a clear picture of when access is available and, ideally, alleviate anxiety. At the same time, it is important to ensure that the reinforcement schedule is set up so that the student can reasonably earn the reinforcer. If the student is continually denied access to a highly preferred item, behaviors may accelerate.

4. **In what type of curriculum is the student currently engaged? Does this curriculum seem to be a good match and does it engage the student in meaningful activities?**

Questions related to curriculum address the functionality or usefulness of the curriculum from the perspective of the student with ASD. Today, with the focus on accountability and state standards, the challenge is to make sure that the curriculum is relevant for the individual. Many of us are willing to take courses or to participate in curriculum that may seem to hold no real, immediate purpose because we know that the course or class is a step towards a degree, better job, higher salary, or greater job satisfaction. That is, we are able to understand the long-term results of engaging in sometimes unpleasant events. However, many students, especially those on the autism spectrum, are less engaged if they do not see the immediate utility or relevance of a course or an activity. Students are more interested in learning content that holds meaning for current life circumstances or future life goals. Therefore, making curriculum relevant requires us to relate it to current or future goals with a focus on outcomes.

5. **According to the student's schedule, is the majority of her school day spent engaged in instruction? Are there extensive periods of unstructured or downtime?**

Professionals should calculate the number of minutes students are actively engaged in instruction or other activities during the school day. Time spent waiting for instruction, transitioning between activities, or waiting for others to complete an activity can provide students with opportunities to engage in problematic behavior. Likewise, activities such as physical education, lunch, recess, music, morning circle, and other less structured activities may increase the chances that a student with ASD will engage in a difficult behavior unless these activities are structured in some fashion. The standard is that students should spend 80% of their school day engaged in instruction. For students on the autism spectrum, this time should be spent on activities related to their individualized education program (IEP) or on the typical curriculum.

6. **Are there specific activities or courses during which the student is more likely to engage in problem behavior? Are there specific instructors who are more or less successful with the student? Does the student have a tendency to engage in problem behaviors during certain times of the day?**

Answers to these and similar questions begin to determine activities or periods of the day when students may be more or less frustrated, and when they may be more or less prone to engage in challenging behaviors. Begin to look at time periods during the day in which the student is more likely to engage in challenging behaviors. You may see a pattern that begins to tell you that the student needs periodic breaks, more support when learning certain course content, or a different instructional approach.

7. **Are varied instructional approaches used in the classroom (e.g., several shortened activities within a lesson, teaching using various modalities)?**

Students are more likely to be engaged in lessons that are varied and that accommodate various learning styles. For students on the autism spectrum, concrete and hands-on activities are often useful. Specific lessons or courses should be observed to determine whether modifications or adaptations are necessary. For example, students who are expected to sit quietly and listen to a lecture for an hour may be at greater risk for engaging in challenging behavior than if they are involved in varied and shorter tasks, including lecture, group activity, and hands-on instruction.

8. **Does the behavior serve a purpose for the student?**

It is commonly believed (O'Neill et al., 1997) that students engage in problem behavior because there is a payoff, including attention, escape, or fulfillment of a physiological/sensory need. If the student did not get something from engaging in the problem behavior, the belief is that the behavior would diminish or stop. Questions to probe this area might include: Does he get attention, or escape an unpleasant situation by engaging in a difficult behavior? What is unpleasant about the situation that causes him to escape? For example, students who engage in challenging behaviors to garner a reaction from someone may be engaging in the same behavior to escape work that is too difficult. And for students who engage in behavior for attention, many will not care if the attention is positive or negative.

9. **What is the student's primary means of communication?**

There appears to be a direct link between a student's ability to communicate and the occurrence (Reichle & Wacker, 1993) of problem behavior. Even if a student on the autism spectrum is highly verbal, she may not have the ability to truly express frustrations, needs, and other feelings. If nonverbal, an augmentative communication system must be in place and readily available that allows that student to communicate important messages. If highly verbal, a student may still require the opportunity to write out feelings or may need visuals to support his ability to communicate difficult topics. Often, a family member or professional who has a good rapport with the individual is able to elicit conversation. Team members should examine how students communicate across settings. For example, Matthew in the vignette is nonverbal. He may be throwing instructional materials in an effort to tell us that the work is too hard, too easy, too boring, or not preferred.

10. **Does the student have any medical problems or take any medications? If so, could this be affecting behavior? Is there a possibility of substance abuse (e.g., drugs, alcohol)?**

Conditions such as asthma, allergies, chronic diarrhea, gastrointestinal difficulties, sinus infections, seizures, and other chronic illnesses can lead to periods of problem or off-task behaviors. Likewise, many medications can affect a student's behavior. Be sensitive to dramatic behavior changes that may be indicators of illness, adverse reactions to medications, or some form of substance abuse. Communicate with family members about sudden behavioral changes or about the impact of medication changes. Also realize that some students may be self-medicating with either drugs or alcohol.

11. **Does the student have difficulty with sleeping and/or eating? Are the student's nutritional needs being met?**

    Students who are having difficulty satisfying basic life needs may have greater problems learning and acting appropriately. Gather information from parents concerning these issues. In addition, realize that if the child is not sleeping, neither are her parents. Be aware and understanding of the stress that lack of sleep may place on the entire family.

12. **Does the student have opportunities to engage in a range of activities outside of school? In other words, what is the student's life like outside of school? Are there conditions inside the home that may be troubling the student (e.g., divorce, death, marital stress, financial difficulties, abuse)?**

    The final set of questions addresses a student's home life. At times, behaviors reflect conditions at home. We must be careful not to blame parents for their child's condition or behavior. Most of us have not experienced the emotional, financial, and physical stresses that can result from having a child on the autism spectrum. The vast majority of parents would do anything to improve the quality of life for their child and family. However, diminished quality-of-life issues outside of school can have a dramatic impact on school performance and behavior. Similarly, poor school conditions can have an impact on the home.

Information about a student's life outside of school can provide valuable insight into the conditions surrounding problem behaviors. If there are financial or other difficulties in the home, outside help from various social service agencies may be needed. A student's home life should never be used as the foundation for "giving up" on a student. It is the responsibility of school personnel to ensure that all is being done to create a positive climate that is conducive to learning and to use a curriculum that is worth being taught.

When conducting a functional behavioral assessment, school personnel need to realize that collecting information is a never-ending process. As the student's life and educational circumstances change, conditions surrounding the behavior may change. For example, the onset of puberty is usually a time when behaviors shift. In addition, family members must be involved in gathering data. As the lifelong advocate for their son/daughter with autism, they can present a longitudinal picture of the behavior.

Various instruments can be used in gathering information. These include the *Motivation Assessment Scale* by Durand and Crimmins (1988), a scatter plot (Touchette, MacDonald, & Langer, 1985), and the functional behavior assessment form developed by O'Neill et al. (1997) to determine situations that may be enhancing problematic behaviors.

A **scatter plot** is a quick tool for recording the frequency of behaviors in various contexts across the school day. While a form that simply looks at the antecedent-behavior-consequence is typically suggested, this type of instrument can be difficult for educators and families to complete because it requires ongoing and intensive observation. Videotaping can be used to perform a more in-depth analysis of the sequence of activities. Videotaping also allows one to observe situations that may go unnoticed during the rush of the day.

A functional behavior assessment should be conducted whenever a student has a history of challenging behaviors. Do not relax if the student begins the year on a positive note. You may be in a honeymoon period, and the honeymoon will end. Start early in the school year. At all costs, avoid having to start the process under time constraints or in the middle of crisis. Emotions often run too high during times of intense behavior problems to gather objective information, and typically those involved want to focus solely on crisis strategies. Also, in the beginning, realize that your initial efforts may not provide the depth of information needed. Keep searching for that underlying cause.

Step 3: Developing Hypothesis Statements

A functional behavioral assessment has been accomplished when you can begin to develop some hypothesis statements about the behavior and can list potential underlying causes. In truth, a functional behavioral assessment is done when you have gathered sufficient information so that a trend in the behavior begins to emerge and a behavioral support plan logically evolves.

Hypothesis statements are informed guesses about the underlying causes of a behavior. It is based on information that has been gathered through the functional behavioral assessment process. A **problem behavior pathway** (see Figure 7.1) can be developed that outlines setting events, triggering antecedents, problem behavior, and maintaining consequences. In the opening vignette, the following behavior pathway could have occurred.

Typically, behavior support plans focus on antecedents and consequences. A common reaction may be to consider how to make the consequences more aversive to stop the behavior from occurring. However, in the diagram depicted in Figure 7.1, it becomes apparent that a skills deficit and the lack of a communication system are contributing to the problem behavior. Until these issues are addressed, manipulating consequences will not result in appropriate behaviors. So, the focus of programming should be on building a communication system that is useful at recess, on teaching the student how to play with classmates, and on teaching the student to communicate the desire for a turn.

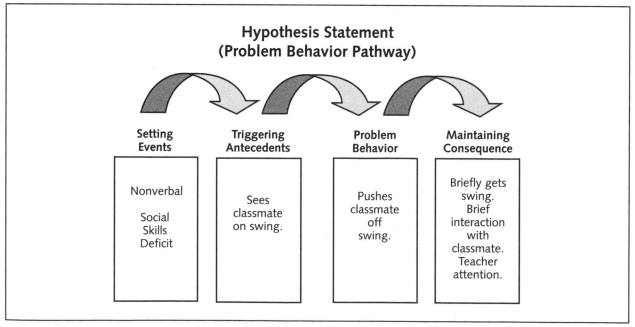

Figure 7.1. Sample problem behavior pathway.

Step 4: Creating a Behavior Support Plan

Behavior support plans should evolve from the hypotheses you develop through the functional behavioral assessment process. The type of form used in developing a behavior support plan is not important. What is important is that the plan is clearly written and that it defines how an environment will be altered in an effort to change behavior and how the student will be taught an alternative way of responding. These alternative skills should be articulated in the student's IEP.

Too often behavioral goals are written in the negative in terms of what students will stop doing; for example, the student will stop hitting, kicking, and so forth. Instead, behavioral IEP goals should be written in the positive and articulate what the student will do. Potential alternative skills relate to problem-solving skills, choice-making ability, anger control, relaxation training, self-management, communication, and social skills. Once the alternative skill is identified, it becomes important to put together a plan that includes positive behavior support approaches.

Positive behavior supports. It is important to make a distinction between positive behavior support approaches and traditional disciplinary actions or punishment procedures. As discussed earlier in this chapter, disciplinary action or punishment procedures are immediate responses to a difficult situation. In other words, they comprise short-term interventions or crisis management strategies to avoid or divert problem behavior. As such, they do not address long-term systems of support or quality-of-life issues, nor do they teach students other ways of responding in difficult or stressful situations.

Positive behavior support approaches, on the other hand, focus on creating positive learning environments and teaching students alternative ways of behaving. For some students on the autism spectrum, it may not be possible for them to generate behavioral options that have the same effect as the problem behavior or that serve the same purpose/function. For others, behaviors perceived as challenging by professionals may be appropriate or necessary for the student's survival in other settings. Our job is to expand their repertoires of acceptable options by teaching alternative behaviors.

Alternative behaviors, such as interacting with peers, waiting, participating in a conversation in a mannerly fashion, taking turns, standing at a distance from the speaker to respect personal space, and responding to adults in a positive fashion, may have to be taught. When choosing an alternative behavior, professionals and family members must consider the total person. Identify skills needed for school, home, work, and other community activities by gathering information through the functional behavioral assessment process and from conversation with family members and the student him/herself. If an appropriate alternative behavior that accomplishes the individual's purposes is not taught, she may find a replacement behavior that is less desirable than the initial behavior. Teaching alternative skills requires more effort on the part of all involved, but the beneficial outcomes will be longer lasting.

Step 5: Implementing Interventions

Once desired behavioral outcomes are identified, it becomes our job to design an instructional program that both supports and teaches the student. Below are some suggestions for creating a positive learning environment and teaching alternative behaviors, categorized under the headings of curricular considerations, classroom management and instruction, and applied behavior analysis approaches. The chapters in this book contain more information for programming or insight into autism spectrum disorders. The following are just a few ideas.

Curricular considerations. Consider the curriculum in which the student is engaged. Upon graduation, some students will attend college; others will not. Many educational programs focus on academics, rather than on career development. For many students on the autism spectrum, their high school years should be spent on preparation for employment. When choosing curriculum options and potential career paths, remember that students are more willing to learn skills and engage in activities that relate to their lives, interests, and strengths. Simply enrolling an interested student in a welding program, rather than creative writing, can begin to create an environment that attracts the student to learning. Use areas of interest to draw individuals to new situations and to ease learning activities that are challenging.

As part of the curriculum, identify alternative or replacement behaviors for the challenging behavior. Alternative behaviors should address the function of the behavior and yield the same payoff. For example, if the student engages in problem behavior as a means of gaining attention, teach a more appropriate strategy that is as effective for getting attention (and teach those involved in the student's life to listen and to respond appropriately). For example, the student may be taught to raise his hand to be called on in class instead of blurting out. If the replacement behavior is to truly replace the problem behavior, it must be as efficient and as effective as the problem behavior. In other words, when the student raises his hand, the teacher or other adult must show him proper attention.

Be specific in stating hoped-for changes. Curricular goals such as "being happy," "behaving correctly," or "being totally compliant" are open to diverse interpretations. Likewise, goals that highlight behaviors to be eliminated do not provide information about what to teach. Write goals that are specific, such as helping a student handle being teased in the hallway or moving from one class to another without an altercation. Identifying specific goals requires that those involved in the student's life examine the situation from the student's perspective and consider how best to facilitate change.

When making programming decisions, do not assume a readiness model. That is, appropriate behavior should not be a prerequisite for engaging an individual in settings or activities that may positively influence behavior.

Classroom management and instruction. Classroom structures and instructional approaches can serve as either a positive or a negative context for behavior change. Below are recommendations for structuring classroom environments and delivering instruction in the most positive and effective way.

- **Actively engage students in systematic instruction in which teaching is clearly planned.** When students have free or unstructured time, they have more opportunity to engage in difficult behaviors. Keep students busy in meaningful activities. Develop a schedule that includes varying tasks and activities to minimize fatigue, boredom, and frustration. Some students learn best when exercise or physical activity is available throughout the day. Others may need downtime to regroup.

- **Create behavioral momentum in the day.** Within the first 10 minutes of a school day or class period, we either capture or lose students' attention. When students enter an instructional situation, they need to be engaged as soon as possible. This requires instructors to be organized and prepared.

- **Intersperse easy and difficult tasks and courses to ensure that the student experiences some successes each day.** Often students who engage in problem behavior have developed a history of failures. It is critical that each student is involved in some activity in which she will be successful and be acknowledged for that success.

- **Embed opportunities for students to make choices within the context of the day.** When all control is removed, students will engage in problem behavior as a means of recapturing that control. Teaching them to control their environment in acceptable ways often results in increases in participation and skills acquisition, and contributes to decreases in the occurrence of problem behavior.

- **When a new material or a new activity is introduced, allow the student to rehearse.** Rehearsal of new materials in a classroom or resource area might involve allowing the student a sneak preview of future work. Rehearsal for a new activity might involve allowing the student to read about the activity, discuss with others, visit a new location, or view a videotape of someone else's experience. These strategies will prepare the student to be successful.

- **Clearly articulate expectations for instruction and interaction.** This assists students in knowing the expectations and helps to prevent confusion, anxiety, or anger. Clearly articulating and visually demonstrating instructions also decreases the possibility of the student engaging in inappropriate behaviors that result in negative feedback and corrective modes of interaction.

- **Assess the quality of your interactions with students.** The single most important and influential thing that school staff do in teaching students with ASD is to interact with them. At times, the majority of interactions may involve negative exchanges, such as corrective feedback or task demands. Positive exchanges should outnumber negatives. Be sure to reinforce, instruct, and converse with students in a positive fashion.

- **Establish rapport.** While this suggestion is related to the one above, it is so important that a separate bullet is necessary. If you enjoy a student and enjoy what you do, the student will read that attitude. The relationship you develop with students will promote trust and enhance their willingness and ability to learn from you.

- **Teach rules, limits, and boundaries clearly and visually and through repeated rehearsals.** Involve students in determining rules for the classroom, and for them. Behavior contracts are helpful for some. If a behavior contract is used, it should state in positive terms what you want the student to do. Once the rules have been determined, school personnel must use them consistently. You may have to teach students the rule. Do not assume that a student truly understands the rules just because he can rotely recite them verbatim. Also, students who serve as the "rule police" need to be taught flexibility and the "grayness" of situations.

- **Remember that routines are an important part of our lives.** Whether morning routines, bedtime routines, or routines when we enter the work place, routines provide comfort and ease. This is also true for students on the autism spectrum. When establishing routines, be careful not to make the student overly rigid. For example, doing the same thing every day may make the student more comfortable, but it will also make him more rigid. Build in changes periodically to help the student be more flexible. Support changes by having a visual schedule in place that highlights schedule changes and allows the student to rehearse daily events. For some students, it may be helpful to teach the routine and then gradually add variety to shape the child's tolerance for change.

- **Consider the student's learning styles.** Present prompts and instruction that acknowledge individual learning styles (e.g., kinesthetic, visual, auditory). Presenting information in a format that matches students' learning style can promote learning and ease them through uncomfortable changes. If tasks, activities, or instruction seem to be misunderstood, simplify the response requirements or present them in some other way. Allow time for students to process information. Vary the pace of instruction to meet the needs of the individual.

- **Teach strategies for coping with and negotiating the stress of daily demands.** For example, some students need to learn relaxation or other self-control strategies. The goal of self-management is to assist students in achieving greater independence and autonomy. Teaching relaxation and self-management is a long-range goal that will take time and patience, but it is well worth it.

Applied behavior analysis approaches. How does **applied behavior analysis (ABA)** fit into all of this? ABA has a long-standing and rich tradition that extends beyond the field of autism. The technology of positive behavior supports includes and is an extension of ABA. The technology of ABA should be part of any teaching situation for both students with and without ASD.

ABA approaches include discrete trial format, **chaining** and prompting procedures, shaping, and many others. **Shaping** or reinforcement of **successive** approximations of preferred behavior is particularly useful for individuals with ASD, who may become anxious if unable to perform a task with immediate perfection. Individuals may have learned inappropriate behaviors through years of practice and successful use with others in their environment. Therefore, recognize and reinforce successive approximations of the preferred behavior.

Another approach involves the use of **extinction** or **planned ignoring**. Using this strategy, professionals and family members simply ignore negative behaviors and only respond in the presence of positive behaviors. Care must be taken when using this approach, however. If you choose to ignore problem behavior, you must be prepared and able to ignore it even when the student is behaving out of control. And it must be a behavior that will not harm the student or others. If you give into the behavior after it has accelerated to a high level, you have taught the student the level she must behave at in order to get your attention in the future.

Two other approaches include redirection and consequences. Sometimes it is better to redirect students when they begin to engage in challenging behaviors. Focusing on behaviors can enhance their power and serve to intensify basically benign actions. For example, when you notice that the student is beginning to become anxious or to accelerate his behavior, redirect him to a favored activity. Consequences should be assessed in terms of what motivates a specific individual. Observe fixations as a source of uncovering potential consequences or motivators. Finally, remember that what serves as a reward may differ from person to person.

Step 6: Monitoring Implementation and Outcomes

The primary reason why a behavior support plan may not be successful is simply that it is not implemented. Behavior support plans are sabotaged when the entire team has not reached agreement about a plan, when team members refuse to implement the agreed-upon plan, when a plan is developed in isolation from the team (e.g., a consultant develops a plan without involving the team), when the plan is not doable within the various contexts in the student's life, and when the outcomes are not agreed upon by the team. So, once a plan is developed it should include a procedure for continually monitoring and improving upon the plan. As part of this monitoring process, the team must determine if there is a reduction in behavior, but more important, there needs to be a focus on enhancing positive behaviors.

Summary and Conclusions

Those who work with students on the autism spectrum who engage in difficult behavior face special challenges. There is no cookbook or recipe for handling problem behaviors. No single intervention or approach works with all students. Even if districts adopt model behavioral programs or treatment packages, many of these programs are not appropriate or effective for a student on the autism spectrum. Those involved in establishing behavior support plans must address each student individually. In other words, develop a plan based on a thorough assessment of each student's behavior. Again, the outcome of a good behavior support plan is not that students end a certain behavior, but that they begin to respond in a socially positive manner.

Learning a new way of responding takes repetition, patience, flexibility, consistency, and commitment by all. Do not give up if the student does not learn the alternative behavior quickly. The challenging behavior probably has a long history.

Finally, perhaps the hardest issue surrounding positive behavior support approaches is the realization that often it is the behavior of professionals and family members that needs to change to eliminate or decrease the student's problem behavior. For some, this realization is perceived as control being given to the student. When dealing with students with problem behaviors, thinking of behavioral reduction in terms of controlling students is a losing proposition for all involved. As educators, our goal should be to instruct. If our behavior does not change, in all likelihood, the student's behavior will not change either.

Tips for the Classroom

✓ Think prevention, rather than reaction, when it comes to dealing with problem behavior.

✓ Minimize unstructured and downtime to avoid problem situations.

✓ Consider and take into account the link between an individual's ability to communicate and the occurrence of problem behaviors.

✓ Recognize that crisis management is only a short-term solution to problem behavior.

✓ Know that in order to be maximally effective, a behavior support plan should evolve from a thorough assessment of both the problem behavior and the context in which it occurred.

✓ Bear in mind that in order for behavior support plans to work, they must be followed!

✓ Make the teaching of alternative responses an integral part of your behavior plan.

✓ Accept the fact that there is no single recipe for handling problem behavior; each individual and situation is different.

✓ Remember that behavior serves a purpose for the individual and that it is our job to figure out that purpose.

✓ Realize that effective behavioral change may require that all involved in the child's life change their behavior as well.

Chapter Highlights

- Crisis management refers to a short-term solution to immediately manage potentially dangerous behavior. While crisis management may play a role in terms of dealing with immediate problems, it does not teach the student a prosocial response or appropriate alternate behavior.

- Punishment, which is typically how crisis management is managed (by definition, punishment procedures decrease an undesirable behavior), does not teach appropriate behavior or create an environment of trust and learning.

- Exclusion, another way crisis situations are typically managed, also has limitations in that it may be reinforcing (and thus increase the undesired behavior) if the individual prefers not to be a part of a given activity.

- Perspectives on how to manage behavior have changed from looking at only consequences (reinforcement and punishment) to evaluating the student (including strengths, needs, desires) and the environment (including instruction, classroom management, classroom structure and routines) to design support plans to teach the individual socially valid ways of responding. The set of assumptions on which this change is based include:

  ➤ Behavior is influenced by context

  ➤ Behavior is functional, purposeful, and meaningful

  ➤ Behavior is affected by external events, including emotional and biological conditions

  ➤ Behavior is influenced by factors outside the immediate environment

  ➤ Behaviors will change as people mature and develop new competencies

  ➤ Behavioral supports are guided by a strong value base

- The goal of positive behavior support should be long-term behavior change based on identifying the function or purpose the behavior serves for the individual. This process is called a functional behavioral assessment (FBA).

- Before conducting an FBA, a behavior support team is created to problem solve, support, and guide the process.

- An FBA should lead to intervention to effect behavior change.

- The steps in an FBA and implementation of a behavior support plan are as follows:

  ➤ Defining the behavior of concern

  ➤ Gathering behavioral information

  ➤ Developing hypothesis statements

  ➤ Creating a behavior support plan

  ➤ Implementing intervention

  ➤ Monitoring implementation and outcomes

- When defining a behavior, the first step is to decide whether the behavior in question is a problem or merely an annoyance. Once this has been decided, it is important to describe the behavior in observable and measurable terms so that all involved are clear on what is being measured. Additionally, the behavior must be evaluated in terms of how often it occurs (frequency), how long it occurs (duration), and how strong it is (intensity).

- After the behavior has been defined, data or information about the behavior are gathered. Included in this information gathering is a quest to determine the function or cause of the behavior by examining the relationship between the behavior and conditions in the individual's life.

- Examining antecedents (what happens before the behavior) and consequences (what happens after the behavior) assists in determining what is maintaining the behavior.

- Antecedents fall into two types: *slow triggers* (setting events), which occur before the behavior but not immediately before the behavior, and *fast triggers*, which occur immediately before the behavior.

- Functional behavioral assessments must also take into account variables such as the history of the behavior, strengths of the student, reinforcement history, conditions under which the student does well, type of curriculum used and whether it is a match for the student, amount of structure in the student's day, types of instructional approaches used, occasions when the problem behavior is more likely to be exhibited, the apparent purpose served by the behavior, communication skills of the student, any medical/sleeping/nutritional concerns, and special conditions affecting the student outside the school setting.

- After information on the behavior has been collected, a hypothesis statement is developed about what may be the underlying causes for the behavior. This statement may be based on an underlying behavior pathway, in which setting events, immediate antecedents, behavior, and consequences are outlined about the behavior of concern.

- Behavior support plans using positive support approaches are written based on the hypothesis statements.

- Positive behavior support approaches focus on creating positive learning environments and teaching alternative ways of behaving.

- Curriculum considerations in implementing interventions focus on ensuring the curriculum matches student goals, skills, and needs, and include looking at teaching alternative and pro-social behaviors to replace those that may be problematic.

- Classroom management and instructional considerations focus on ensuring the classroom environment is structured in a positive way that creates opportunities for engagement, includes systematic instruction and clearly articulated expectations, allows for rehearsal, and supports student chances for success. Included are use of routines, consideration of the student's learning style, and teaching strategies for coping with the stresses of daily demands.

- Applied behavior analysis serves as the basis for positive behavior supports. Additionally, specific techniques within applied behavior analysis such as shaping of behavior, creating behavior chains, reinforcing successive approximations, prompting, extinction, and planned ignoring have been used successfully to effect behavior change in individuals with ASD.

- Monitoring and making changes in the plan are essential to ensure its effectiveness.

Chapter Review Questions

1. What is the definition of a crisis management approach and what are the advantages and disadvantages of using such an approach?

2. What are the shifting behavioral perspectives and the set of assumptions that accompany this shift in thinking?

3. Who are the members of the behavioral support team and what are their roles?

4. What are the components of a functional behavioral assessment?

5. What are the issues involved in defining behaviors of concern?

6. What is the goal of a functional behavioral assessment?

7. What are antecedents and consequences?

8. What types of questions must be asked in determining the true function of a behavior?

9. Why is collecting information an ongoing process in functional behavioral assessment and positive behavior support?

10. What are hypothesis statements and what are they based on?

11. Why are problem behavior pathways important in determining how to support appropriate behavior?

12. What is the focus of positive behavior support approaches?

13. List and describe curricular, classroom management, and instructional considerations involved in implementing interventions.

14. What is the role of applied behavior analysis in intervention?

15. Why are behavior support plans sometimes not successful?

16. Why is it important to monitor implementation and outcomes of support plans?

References

Carr, E. G. (2007). The expanding vision of positive behavior support: Research perspectives on happiness, helpfulness, hopefulness. *Journal of Positive Behavior Interventions, 9*(1), 3-14.

Durand, V. M., & Crimmins, D. B. (1988). Identifying the variables maintaining self-injurious behaviors. *Journal of Autism and Developmental Disorder, 18*, 99-117.

Frost, L. A., & Bondy, A. S. (1994). *The Picture Exchange Communication System (PECS): Training manual.* Cherry Hill, NJ: Pyramid Educational Consultants.

O'Neill, R. E., Horner, R. H., Albin, R. W., Sprague, J. R., Storey, K., & Newton, J. S. (1997). *Functional assessment and program development for problem behavior: A practical handbook.* Pacific Grove, CA: Brooks/Cole Thomson Learning.

Reichle, J., & Wacker, D. P. (1993). *Communicative alternative to challenging behaviors: Integrating functional assessment and intervention strategies.* Baltimore: Paul H. Brookes.

Touchette, P. E., MacDonald, R. F., & Langer, S. N. (1985). A scatter plot for identifying stimulus control of problem behavior. *Journal of Applied Behavior Analysis, 18*, 343-351.

Learner Objectives

After reading this chapter, the learner should be able to:

- Explain the importance of play and friendships for children's learning, development, and cultural participation

- Describe the challenges faced by children with ASD in terms of play behavior and the development of friendships

- Define "peer culture" and discuss the role it plays in involving children with ASD with peers

- Define "play culture"

- State the purpose of the Friend 2 Friend (F2F) model and discuss how it is implemented

- List and describe the four steps in the F2F teaching process

- State the five key learning goals of F2F

- Explain the F2F Seven Basic Friendship Tips

- Explain the purpose of the Integrated Play Groups (IPG) model

- Describe the environmental elements of IPG

- List and describe the elements included in observational assessment of play

- Explain the purpose and the components involved in intervention of play skills through guided participation

Chapter 8

Fostering Peer Play and Friendships: Creating a Culture of Inclusion

Pamela Wolfberg • Heather McCracken • Tara Tuchel

Richie is an intriguing boy who received a diagnosis of autism in early childhood. When he first entered kindergarten, he had little interaction with his classmates and had no friends. He mostly played by himself and occasionally watched his peers from a distance. At times he tolerated playing beside his peers, but when their play became loud, he would yell, "Would you pleeeeease shut up!" He didn't know how to initiate or maintain interactions with other children and had difficulty accepting invitations to play from his peers. Because he didn't have a wide repertoire of play schemes with which he was competent, he often rejected invitations to play because he didn't know what to do. Richie was able to play with toys in a functional way but used a lot of delayed echolalia, as he was re-enacting scenes from his favorite movies and cartoons.

At first, I thought, "wow ... he really is imaginative." However, after watching him closely over several sessions, I noticed that he was merely repeating and re-enacting his favorite movies and did not change his play at all. He was very rigid in his play. I realized that, for Richie, it was very difficult to let his peers into his play world because they were unpredictable and might change his carefully scripted, inflexible play routine. He was unable to handle that, so he rejected their attempts to interact and play.

Sean is a bright 27-year-old male, who was diagnosed with an autism spectrum disorder at the age of 5. Sean remained nonverbal until he was 9 years old. I met Sean at a university class on special education; he had been invited to speak to the class about his autism. Sean spoke openly and honestly about his school experiences, saying, "I hated school; it was the worst place. High school was a bit better but not much. I could not wait to get out of school; it was the most hostile environment I can imagine." During the question-and-answer portion of the class, a member of the class asked Sean, "I have a child with autism in my classroom. What could I do to help make school a better place for this child?" Sean replied, "Help him understand his autism, but just as important, help his classmates understand autism."

Wen observing children of diverse abilities in natural interactions with one another, it soon becomes apparent who is thriving and who is at risk in their development. Children with autism spectrum disorders (ASD) are among those at greatest risk, as they encounter significant challenges learning how to play, socialize, and form friendships with peers (Boucher & Wolfberg, 2003). Hallmarks of autism include a lack of varied and imaginative or imitative play as well as a failure to develop peer relationships appropriate to developmental level. Further, defining features of ASD are intricately tied to characteristic impairments in reciprocal social interaction, communication and imagination (American Psychiatric Association, 2000).

A common misconception regarding children diagnosed with ASD is that they consciously choose to isolate themselves and, thus, are incapable of play and friendships with peers. Yet, there is strong evidence to suggest that they share many of the same desires and capacities for play, companionship, and peer group acceptance as typically developing children (Bauminger & Kasari, 2000; Jordan, 2003). What differs is that they express their play interests and social overtures in ways that are uniquely their own and that often set them apart from their peer group. Without appropriate support, these children are highly vulnerable to being neglected, rejected, or even bullied by peers. This, in turn, deprives them of opportunities to learn how to socialize and play in more conventional and socially accepted ways and, ultimately, to form meaningful friendships.

From both a developmental and a socio-cultural perspective, the unique and complex difficulties children with ASD face in peer relations and play pose distinct challenges to educators, therapists, and family members seeking to help them. According to the National Research Council (2001), play and social instruction with peers are rated among the top interventions that should receive priority in educational programs for children with ASD. Recent advances in our understanding of ASD and social inclusion further underscore the need for high-quality interventions that explicitly value and support children's play and friendships (Wolfberg & Schuler, 2006).

The **Friend 2 Friend (F2F)** model (McCracken, 2004, 2005a, 2005b, 2005c, 2006) and **Integrated Play Groups (IPG)** model (Wolfberg, 1994, 1999, 2003, 2004; Wolfberg & Schuler, 1993, 2006) were created out of deep concern for the many children who are missing out on peer play and friendships as a vital part of their childhood experience. Drawing on current theory, empirical research, and evidence-based practices, these complementary models are designed to support children with ASD in play and friendships with typical peers in inclusive school, home, and community settings.

The F2F social facilitation model fosters mutual friendships for children with ASD by building awareness, understanding, acceptance, and empathy in their peers through demystification programs comprising specially designed puppet presentations and simulation games. The IPG model, in turn, focuses on guiding children on the autism spectrum as they interact in small groups with typically developing peers and/or siblings with an emphasis on stimulating, expanding, and scaffolding spontaneous social interaction, communication, play, and imagination.

This chapter aims to translate theory and research into effective and meaningful practice by presenting the principles and practices of the F2F and IPG models. By way of introduction, we will first describe the conceptual foundation for each of these models by addressing the role of play and friendships in childhood (as it impacts children's learning, development and social-cultural participation) and the challenges this presents for children with ASD. We will next describe and illustrate the key features of each model while drawing on first-hand experience with children of diverse ages, abilities, and backgrounds. The chapter concludes with a series of Tips for the Classroom related to demystifying autism while supporting peer play and friendships.

Importance of Play and Friendships

A prominent body of literature documents the importance of play and friendships for children's learning, development, and cultural participation. Thus, an abundant research base on play shows strong links to children's cognitive, language, literacy, social, emotional, creative, and sensory-motor development (for reviews, see Wolfberg, 1999, 2003).

Play

Vygotsky (1966, 1978) ascribed a most vital role to play as a primary social activity through which children develop social or interpersonal knowledge as well as symbolic capacities. In his writings he noted that play's significance is far reaching, extending beyond that of representing stages of development to actually leading development. Further, he emphasized the notion that play, like all learning and development, is mediated through social experiences with others.

When it comes to play, peers perform a distinct role in children's socialization and development by offering learning opportunities and experiences that cannot be duplicated by adults (Hartup, 1989, 1991). Thus, while playing together, children construct a peer culture that is uniquely their own (Corsaro, 1992, Wolfberg et al., 1999). It is based on active participation in the social activities that are most valued by the peer group.

"**Play culture**" more accurately describes that realm in which children create and live out their social and imaginary lives (Mouritsen, 1996; Wolfberg, 1994, 1999; Wolfberg et al., 1999). It is within the culture of play that children acquire many interrelated skills that are necessary for attaining social competence and, ultimately, establishing mutual friendships. Through jointly constructed activity, children refine their social communication strategies, learn to negotiate and compromise, resolve conflicts, build trust, and develop other foundation social skills. Play further provides opportunities to express intimacy and affection with peers, the core ingredients of friendship (Rubin, Fein, & Vandenberg, 1983).

Friendship

Friendships, like play, occupy a central place in children's social lives. Research suggests that friendship is not only associated with children's social, emotional, and cognitive development, but is also a determining factor for social adaptation and adjustment (Hartup, 1996; Ladd, 1990). Children with mutual friends are more socially competent and better adjusted than children without friends and tend to have higher self-esteem, be more sociable and cooperative, and better able to cope with change and manage interpersonal conflicts (Berndt, 2002; Gest, Graham-Bermann, & Hartup, 2001). Further, children with positive and stable friendships exhibit higher engagement, better adjustment, and greater achievement in school (Berndt, 1999).

In contrast, peer rejection, neglect, or bullying contributes to low aspiration in school performance (Bagwell, Schmidt, Newcomb, & Bukowski, 2001), increased problematic behaviors, withdrawn or isolative behaviors, depression, low self-esteem, and more negative expectations (Asher, Parkhurst, Hymel, & Williams, 1990; Boivin, Poulin, & Vitaro, 1994). Studies further reveal that children without close friends are decidedly lonelier than children with close friends (Parker & Asher, 1993). The presence of even one close friend has been associated with a child's happiness and sense of belonging.

Challenge of Play and Friendships for Children with ASD

Although children on the autism spectrum naturally differ from one another in distinct ways, as a group they face unique challenges in peer socialization and play. As compared to the highly interactive and creative play of typically developing children, the play of children with autism is markedly detached and impoverished. Without any direction, these children tend to fixate on a limited number of activities, which they often repeat and carry out for long periods while alone (Frith, 2003; Wing, Gould, Yeates, & Brierly, 1977). Many children with autism are attracted to toys, activities and themes that are conventional, consistent with play preferences of peers similar in development and age. Other children are attracted to unconventional activities that include preoccupations with objects or narrowly focused interests.

Research suggests that as compared to children of a similar developmental level, children with autism engage in higher rates of manipulation or sensory exploration of objects as opposed to **representational** forms of play (Libby, Powell, Messer, & Jordan, 1998; Sigman & Ungerer, 1984; Tilton & Ottinger, 1964). They are less inclined to spontaneously engage in functional play and rarely produce pretend play (Baron-Cohen, 1987; Jarrold, 2003; Libby et al., 1998; Williams, 2003). When they do show these capacities, their play is less diverse, flexible, and varied than that of other children. The play of children with autism often appears to be without direction or purpose as they pursue activities lacking in variations along a theme.

Socializing with peers in the context of play and other shared activities is particularly challenging for children with ASD (Jordan, 2003). Problems in both verbal and nonverbal communication (e.g., the use of eye gaze, eye contact, physical proximity, facial expression, pointing, and other conventional gestures) closely interface with underlying difficulties in joint attention, spontaneous imitation, and emotional responsiveness in social play (Baron-Cohen, 1989; Dawson & Adams, 1984; Mundy, Sigman, & Ruskin, 1999; Sigman, Ungerer, & Sherman, 1987).

With respect to social play, children with autism direct fewer obvious social initiations to peers and inconsistently respond to peers when they initiate with them. Less obvious attempts to interact with peers include initiations that may be characterized as subtle, obscure or poorly timed (Wolfberg & Schuler, 2006). Based on clinical observations, children with ASD present distinct social play styles that are consistent with Wing and Gould's (1979) early work. Some children appear "aloof," as they distance themselves from peers or act as though they are unaware of their presence. Others are "passive," as they follow along or watch what their peers are doing but rarely initiate interaction in obvious ways. Still others are "active and odd" in the sense that they attempt to engage peers, but do so in an idiosyncratic or one-sided manner, such as by talking excessively about one topic.

Addressing Peer Culture and the Social Void

The peer group, or **peer culture**, has a tremendous influence on the extent to which children with ASD are able to reap the benefits of play and friendships in childhood. Peer culture consists of those shared understandings, values, beliefs, and associated behaviors, activities, and relationship patterns that children construct out of their everyday experience with one another (Wolfberg et al., 1999). A common experience for many children with autism is that they are excluded from their peer culture because their behavior does not fit into peer perceptions of what is "normal." Consequently, a social void is likely to exist between children on the autism spectrum and typical peers when they are placed together in inclusive settings without carefully planned educational supports that demystify autism (McCracken, 2004). This social void arises in large part because typical peers lack a conceptual framework for understanding and appreciating the unique ways in which children with ASD communicate, relate, and play.

The unconventional or understated ways in which children with ASD initiate with peers are frequently mistaken for signs of deviance or limited social interest. As a result, children may be teased and taunted by intolerant peers or simply overlooked by well-meaning peers. In response, many children withdraw and cease to initiate further. Some children express feelings of alienation from their peer group. These feelings may lead to an increase in the child's anxiety and a breakdown in his or her ability to communicate. In some cases, increased anxiety manifests as negative and even aggressive behaviors. Peers seeing these behaviors are likely to continue avoiding or overtly dismissing the child with ASD, which in turn may lead to feelings of loneliness, decreased self-esteem, and the onset of depression (Bauminger & Kasari, 2000; Heinrichs, 2003). Thus, children with ASD may become caught in a cycle of exclusion, which deprives them of opportunities to learn how to socialize and play in more conventional and socially accepted ways, and ultimately to form friendships.

In order to break this cycle of exclusion, the social void must be addressed on both sides within the context of a shared peer culture. That is, effort should not only be placed on enhancing the skills and development of the children with autism, but also on educating typical peers by demystifying autism. Only by altering the skill, experience, and perceptions of all children is it possible to narrow the gap to eliminate the social void. This will allow a new peer culture to emerge, one that is open to neurodiversity and inclusive of children with unique ways of relating, communicating, and playing.

Friend 2 Friend Model

The Friend 2 Friend (F2F) model is designed to foster mutual friendships for children with ASD by building awareness, empathy, and understanding in their peers, siblings, and classmates (McCracken, 2004, 2005a 2005b, 2005c, 2006). This social facilitation model provides a framework for designing autism demystification programs for children ages 3 and up. F2F offers innovative educational programs that include puppet presentations targeting younger children (ages 3-8) and simulation games targeting older children (ages 9 and up).

Presented in an age-appropriate, sensitive, and inclusive manner, the approach allows all children (including those on the autism spectrum) access to information about characteristics commonly associated with autism. With an emphasis on supporting typically developing peers to understand, accept, and empathize with children on the spectrum, the programs set the stage for helping children develop prosocial skills (Eisenberg & Miller, 1987), which are the basis for becoming well-adjusted and caring adults (Hartup, 1989, 1991; Ladd, 1990). Promoting these pivotal prosocial skills in typical peers is an essential part of successfully supporting children on the autism spectrum in inclusive settings. Furthermore, these skills support all children in developing to the best of their abilities through the play and socialization that friendships provide.

Teaching Process

To support the ultimate goal of fostering mutual friendships between children with ASD and their peers, the F2F programs demystify autism using a four-step teaching process consisting of modeling, labeling, explaining, and normalizing.

Modeling. F2F programs support peers in understanding puzzling social, communicative, and self-regulating behaviors that they may see children on the autism spectrum exhibit. The first step in helping children understand the characteristics of autism is to provide a *visual model.* **Modeling** the characteristics of autism helps children formulate a concept of autism in their minds, which subsequently becomes the basis for fostering understanding, acceptance, and empathy for children on the autism spectrum they know and may come to know.

Labeling. The next step in the teaching process is to support children to accept the unusual social, communicative, or self-regulating behaviors that they may see children on the autism spectrum exhibit. After providing the visual model, we *label* the characteristics that have been modeled. **Labeling** provides the children with a name for what they do not understand and helps them accept the characteristics or behaviors as genuine and real.

Explaining. Once the characteristics of autism have been modeled and labeled, we *explain* the sometimes puzzling social, communicative, or self-regulating characteristics that peers may see children on the autism spectrum exhibit. Explaining the meaning or purpose behind the characteristics helps peers understand and accept children on the autism spectrum. Often typically developing peers have difficulty accepting the unique characteristics of autism because the child with autism looks "normal," making them conclude that the child "chooses" to behave in a manner that is unusual rather than realizing that the behaviors are symptoms of the autistic condition. Explaining the characteristics of autism provides children with the answers to the question, "Why does my friend do that?"

Normalizing. The final and most significant step in the F2F teaching process is to support peers in empathizing with children on the autism spectrum. Once we have modeled and labeled the characteristics of autism and explained their purpose, we link the otherwise puzzling characteristics with common characteristics that all children exhibit. Such *normalizing* of the characteristics of autism provides children with an opportunity for emotional perspective taking, which allows them to truly walk in the shoes of the child with autism. Identifying with children on the autism spectrum shifts typical peers past simply understanding and accepting to feelings of empathy. These feelings facilitate prosocial behaviors, which form the basis for fostering mutual friendships between children on the autism spectrum and their typically developing peers, siblings, and classmates (Eisenberg & Miller, 1987).

Key Learning Goals

As part of the F2F model, children are introduced to five key learning goals. These conceptual goals underline the learning and provide a basis for future learning when follow-up activities take place.

Five Key Learning Goals

- Recognize and accept differences in themselves and others
- Recognize individuals with autism and different kinds of minds as valuable friends
- Recognize that it is important to ask questions and express feelings
- Empathize with what it feels like to have autism and different kinds of minds
- Promote positive relationships with all peers

Seven Basic Friendship Tips

The F2F programs also introduce *Seven Basic Friendship Tips*. These include prosocial communication strategies that peers may use to interact successfully with children on the autism spectrum.

1. **Get Your Friend's Attention:** Say your friend's name and move closer to him to get his attention before you start to speak.

2. **Use Small Sentences and Gestures, and Wait:** Use small sentences when speaking to your friend because too many words can sound like blah, blah. Use gestures, like pointing, to help your friend understand what you are saying and wait to give your friend time to answer you.

3. **Watch Your Friend:** Watch your friend so you can learn the things that she is good at or likes to do.

4. **Give Your Friend Choices:** Ask your friend to play by giving him choices of the things that you know he is good at or likes to do.

5. **Ask Your Friend to Talk:** Try asking your friend questions like: What are you playing or pretending? Will you sit beside me? Everyone likes to be asked questions about themselves.

6. **Use Friendly Words:** What is the friendliest thing you can say to someone? "Hi" is sometimes the best way to make friends. How does it feel when people say hi to you?

7. **Accept Differences:** Everybody is different in his or her own way. Being a good friend means accepting differences.

Friend 2 Friend Puppet Presentations

The comprehensive F2F puppet program is designed to teach young children by tapping into their imagination. Using child-size puppets, humor, and interactive experiences, specially trained puppeteers (F2F Program

Guides) perform plays that are tailored to introduce characteristics associated with ASD. Presentations focus on modeling, labeling, explaining, and normalizing the characteristics of autism while never singling out the focus child or children on the autism spectrum. Each puppet presentation contains six learning opportunities to optimize learning for children with different learning styles or strengths. The various learning opportunities include the following.

Introduction (*opening ritual – assigned observers*). The introduction is designed to familiarize children with the program as well as to provide an overview of the presentation. The F2F Lead Program Guide begins by reviewing the steps in the lesson using specially designed picture communication symbols (PCS). The Lead Program Guide also assigns the children jobs to do. Assigning the children roles during the puppet play (*assigned observer*) increases their buy-in to what they will be learning.

Puppet play (*model or visual learning opportunity*). The puppet play provides children with a visual learning opportunity as they watch the puppets model, label, explain, and normalize the characteristics of autism. The puppets, representing a child with autism, two peers, and two teacher puppets, act out specifically designed skits that introduce children to the F2F Five Key Learning Goals and Seven Basic Friendship Tips. This provides children with a conceptual framework and language to promote further discussion and learning.

"What did Crystal learn?" (*auditory/visual learning style/performance feedback*). "What Did Crystal Learn?" is an auditory and visual review of the learning goals and friendship tips presented in the puppet play and accompanying story book. Directly following the puppet play, the Lead Program Guide reviews the learning goals and basic friendship tips with the children using the PCS as a visual support. This review offers a chance for children who are auditory and visual learners to gain additional insight into the program goals and tips. It also gives teachers an opportunity to evaluate which of the learning goals or friendship tips need to be emphasized during follow-up lessons or activities.

Pass-the-puppet circle (*role-playing and tactile learning opportunity*). The pass-the-puppet circle learning segment of the puppet presentations is a tactile learning opportunity where the children become the puppeteers while the Program Guides interact with them by role-playing with the puppets. This segment gives children an opportunity to review the learning goals and friendship tips through a tactile experience of holding and playing with the puppets.

Questions and answers (*open dialogue*). Once all the children have had an opportunity to interact with the puppets, the Program Guides collect the puppets and ask the children if they have any questions. Then they proceed to engage the children in open dialogue.

Sticker time (*closing ritual /transfer training*). Once all the children's questions have been answered, the puppet presentation concludes, and each child receives a sticker with the quote "I'm a Good Friend." The sticker serves to remind the children of the concepts introduced by the program and is a tangible reward for participating.

F2F follow-up guide and companion coloring story book. As part of the F2F puppet presentation program, each teacher/adult is given a F2F Follow-up Guide and a children's coloring story book. These resources provide educators and parents with activities, materials, and resources to continue the learning introduced during the puppet presentation. The *That's What's Different About Me* coloring story book is an adaptation of the puppet play that may be read and colored. These follow-up resources provide regular and continuous support in fostering mutual friendships for children on the autism spectrum.

Tim

After I had presented to two first-grade classes in a public school district, the classroom teacher approached me to tell me how much she liked the F2F program and how she felt that the typical peers had learned a great deal. She wondered if the focus child in this group (Tim) had gotten as much information or learning from the program as the other kids. She was pleased that Tim participated for the entire presentation, which is sometimes very difficult for him to do, but because Tim was nonverbal, she wondered if the messages modeled in the puppet presentation were lost on him.

As we talked, we watched Tim from the other side of the room playing with the computer prop during the pass-the-puppet circle. Tim did not want to play with any of the puppets but was fascinated by the computer. Then it was time for questions and answers, so the Program Guides began to collect the puppets. Tim's special education assistant asked him to "put the computer back" as she pointed to the puppet stage. Tim got up from the circle and went to the puppet stage. He took Min, the puppet representing the child with ASD in the puppet play, and placed him carefully on the stage. Then he put the computer in Min's lap. Tim's teacher smiled as we watched Tim arrange Min. But then Tim did the unexpected – he took Sherry (the puppet representing the typical peer in the puppet play) and sat her next to Min, leaned her over so she was looking at the computer, and placed one of her hands on the computer and the other around Min. At that point, Tim's teacher looked at me with tears in her eyes and said, "I guess he understands exactly what the puppet play was about."

Friend 2 Friend Simulation Game

This 50-minute educational presentation is designed to help children understand, in an engaging manner, what it feels like to have autism, while teaching the prosocial communication skills necessary to interact successfully with their peers with autism. Each simulation game presentation begins with a *Simon Says* game that targets the children's senses and their receptive communication in an effort to bring them to a state of confusion and frustration. The presenter gives instructions (e.g., "Simon Says touch your nose, stand up, sit down, turn around, jump up and down …") at an extremely rapid pace while a light machine is flashing colors of light, one volunteer is blowing a whistle, and another volunteer is touching the students' faces with a feather duster.

Directly following the simulation game, the F2F lead presenter reviews with the participants their sensory and communication experiences during the game, linking those experiences to what it feels like to have autism. Once the children have a basic understanding of autism, the presentation continues with a lively and open discussion, "I Have the Kind of Mind," in which students are encouraged to discuss what they are good at and what they are not so good at as a way to help them understand that "everybody is different in his or her own way." This discussion also introduces children to the concept of self-regulating behaviors.

Once the children have had an opportunity to empathize with what it feels like to have autism, the lead presenter introduces the *Seven Basic Friendship Tips*. These tips include prosocial communication strategies that may support social interaction between typical peers and children with ASD. The presentation ends by reading a poem about friendship written by a child with ASD and a discussion about friendships.

The entire F2F simulation-game presentation represents the perspective of a child with autism, making the concepts simple, easy-to-understand, and meaningful for all children by using sensitive language and encouraging the participation of all children. At no time during the presentation are references made to the focus child or to any other person with autism. The only exception is if the presenter has a personal connection to an individual with ASD who gives explicit permission to share his or her experiences.

Sam

Sam's parents and teachers were stumped. For the past six years, Sam, a sensitive and creative boy with Asperger Syndrome, had been fully integrated into his local school. These years had been happy and successful ones for Sam and his classmates. But suddenly in the fifth grade everything changed and, for no apparent reason, Sam began to have outbursts at school directed mostly at his peers.

I suggested to Sam's mother that perhaps it was time to implement an autism demystification program as a means of supporting Sam at school. Sam's mother agreed. As part of the demystification process, we implemented a series of interventions to help Sam understand his unique learning style, challenges, and gifts. For Sam's peers, we presented the F2F simulation game.

While presenting the F2F simulation game to Sam's class, I observed that only two students had ever heard the word autism *before, and none knew what the word meant even though most of them had been in school with Sam since kindergarten. At no time during the presentation did any of the students ask any specific questions about Sam or about autism. However, it was clear that many of the students did relate the information in the presentation to Sam, because when we were finished one student whispered to me, "I know someone with autism. His name is Sam; he is in my class."*

After this presentation to Sam's class, it was clear that Sam's anxiety about school, and in particular his classmates, was in direct correlation to his classmates' lack of understanding about autism and Sam's lack of knowledge about his challenges and gifts. In other words, Sam and his peers were experiencing the "social void." Sam's social situation at school continued to deteriorate to the point where he felt alienated from his classmates, which increased his anxiety and caused a breakdown in his ability to communicate. In turn, the increased anxiety and decreased communication caused Sam to exhibit aggressive behaviors. The change in Sam's behaviors caused his peers to avoid contact with him, which was exactly what Sam did not want.

Over the next few months, Sam worked very hard at home and at school to understand autism and his unique differences. At the beginning of Sam's sixth-grade year, Friend 2 Friend presented again at his school. Sam's mother felt that it might be best for Sam not to be present during the presentation, in hopes that Sam's peers might open up and begin to ask questions. When it was time for the class to come for the presentation, Sam decided he wanted to participate along with his class. Usually, Friend 2 Friend encourages the focus child with autism to be present and participate in the programs; however, the wishes of families are always respected. In this case Sam made up his own mind and participated along with his class.

When we came to the part in the presentation where I ask if anyone has ever heard the word autism, all the children raised their hands. Then I asked if anyone could tell me what the word meant. Now all the students' hands went down, except for Sam's. Sam put up his hand and said, "I know what autism means; it's a disability that is not really a disability but makes you think differently from other people; I should know because I AM AUTISTIC." For the first time, Sam spoke openly and honestly, sharing his perspective as an autistic individual, and in doing so he removed all the social barriers that had existed previously.

The F2F simulation-game presentation had helped Sam understand and accept his unique gifts and challenges and to feel safe enough to share his experience as an autistic individual. The F2F program also helped Sam's peers understand, accept, and empathize with Sam while introducing a shared vocabulary for further discussions and learning. Sam and his peers had taken the first step towards mutual friendships for Sam and all his classmates. Sam had a successful and happy sixth-grade year and continues to help others understand "I am autistic."

Integrated Play Groups Model

The following description of the Integrated Play Groups (IPG) model has been adapted from earlier work that offers more detailed accounts of its principles and practices (Wolfberg, 1999; 2003 and Wolfberg & Schuler, 2006). The IPG model is designed to support children of diverse ages and abilities on the autism spectrum in mutually enjoyed play experiences with typical peers/siblings as playmates (Wolfberg, 1994, 1999, 2003, 2004; Wolfberg & Schuler, 1993, 2006). Influenced by the work of Vygotsky (1966, 1978), the focus of IPGs is on guiding children's participation in culturally valued activities (i.e., play) with the guidance, support, and challenge of companions who vary in skill and status (Rogoff, 1990). Through a carefully tailored system of support, emphasis is placed on maximizing children's developmental potential as well as intrinsic desire to play, socialize, and form meaningful relationships with peers. Consistent with the Friend 2 Friend model, of equal importance is teaching peers to be empathetic, responsive, and accepting of children's differing social, communication, and play styles. A further intent is for the children to mediate their own play activities with minimal adult guidance.

Setting the Stage for Play: Program and Environmental Design

Integrated Play Groups are tailored for children (ages 3 to 11 years) as a part of an individualized educational or therapeutic program. Play groups are carried out by a trained adult facilitator referred to as a play guide. Small groups of children meet on a regular basis in school, home, and/or community settings (e.g., inclusive classrooms, after-school programs, recreation centers, or neighborhood parks). Play groups generally meet twice a week for 30- to 60-minute sessions over a 6- to 12-month period. Times may vary depending upon the age and developmental stage of the participating children.

Play group composition. Each group is composed of three to five children with a higher ratio of expert (typical peers and/or siblings) than novice players (children on the autism spectrum). Expert players include schoolmates, family friends, and neighbors who ordinarily have contact with the novice players. It is ideal when playmates are somewhat familiar and attracted to one another in order to foster the potential of a long-lasting friendship. There are different types of beneficial experiences when the composition of groups varies with respect to such variables as children's gender, ages, developmental status, and play interaction styles.

Prior to the first session, the players participate in the Friend 2 Friend program and an IPG orientation that offers an opportunity for the children to meet and ask questions while gaining information about what to expect when they begin their play groups. A major focus is on preparing the expert players to be accepting of and responsive to novice players' unique ways of relating, communicating, and playing.

Play space and materials. Size, density, organization, and thematic arrangements are all considerations with respect to the design of the play environment. A wide range of highly motivating sensory motor, exploratory, constructive, and socio-dramatic props with high potential for interactive and imaginative play are selected as play materials. These types of materials vary in degree of structure and complexity, which affords opportunities to support children who present diverse interests, learning styles, and developmental levels. The important point is to identify play materials that are intrinsically motivating, allowing for mutual enjoyment between novice and expert players.

Play session structure and supports. The play session follows a consistent schedule that incorporates routines and rituals while utilizing visual supports (consisting of words and/or pictures). These types of structures and supports are directed to fostering familiarity, predictability, and a cohesive group identity. From the beginning, the children are presented with basic rules that present guidelines for fair and respectful behavior and care of materials. To help children anticipate the meeting times and follow the progression of the play session, visual schedules are designed for both the individual and the group. Opening and closing rituals (e.g., greeting, song, and brief discussion of plans and strategies) begin and end each play session. Visual choice boards consist of a variety of preferred activities from which children may select to get started in play. Further, visual role tags may be worn by children to depict their different characters or roles, such as "cashier" or "customer" while playing restaurant. Story books are also created to help children review play activities and themes as well as to teach new play schemes. Finally, group membership is established by creating play group names and associated rituals, which also serve to provide the intrinsic motivation for true peer participation.

Observing Children at Play: Assessment Approach

The IPG model includes a comprehensive assessment approach which provides a basis for setting realistic and meaningful goals, identifying effective intervention strategies and documenting children's progress in a systematic fashion. These assessments include a focus on **symbolic** and **social dimensions of play**, social communication (communicative functions and means), play preferences, and diversity of play.

Symbolic dimension of play. This refers to a set of play characteristics (as opposed to mutually exclusive stages of development), which follow a relatively consistent developmental sequence. These include play acts that are directed to objects, self, or others and that signify events (adapted from McCune-Nicholich, 1981; Piaget, 1962; Smilansky, 1968). The symbolic dimension of play includes: *manipulation* play (exploring objects – e.g., spinning the wheels of a toy car); *functional play* (conventional object use and the association of two or more objects – e.g., rolling a toy car on the floor, placing a teacup on a saucer); and *symbolic-pretend play* (representing objects, people and events in imaginary ways – e.g., using a block as if it were an airplane, wiping the table as if holding an imaginary sponge, making the baby doll cry and soothing the baby doll while acting in the role of a mother).

Social dimension of play. This involves a focus on the child's distance to and involvement with one or more children (adapted from Parten, 1932). The social dimension includes: *isolate* (playing alone); *onlooker-orientation* (watching peers); *parallel-proximity* (playing beside peers); *common focus* (reciprocal play with peers); and *common goal* (collaborating with peers in a highly organized way).

Communicative functions and means. This focuses on the functions of communication (i.e., what the child intends to convey – e.g., requests for objects, peer interaction, affection, protests, declarations, and comments), which may be accomplished through a variety of verbal and non-verbal *communicative means* (e.g., facial expressions, eye gaze, physical proximity, touching, gestures, intonation, vocalization, echolalia, and simple or complex speech/sign/symbol/written word). Each child's communicative attempt (as expressed through any one or combination of communicative functions and means) is recognized as a potential initiation to play with someone or something, even when expressed in a subtle or obscure form (adapted from Peck, Schuler, Tomlinson, Theimer, & Haring, 1984).

Play preferences and diversity of play. This helps to identify the number and variety of play interests in an effort to help expand the child's play repertoire. In addition, documenting play preferences offers a means to match novice and expert players based on shared play interests. Children's play preferences may take various forms including fascinations with particular objects, actions, activities, themes and playmates. Examples include: object choices (e.g., prefers round objects, toys with moving parts, realistic replicas); action choices (e.g., prefers to spin toys, line up toys, uses toys according to function); activity choices (e.g., prefers rough-housing, quiet play, constructive play); theme choices (e.g., prefers familiar routines, invented stories, fantasy play); and playmate choices (e.g., prefers no one in particular, one or more peers).

Guided Participation in Play: Intervention Approach

The intervention approach (also referred to as **guided participation**) involves a system of support that is tailored to each child's unique profile of learning and development. The approach is especially responsive to the child's underlying core challenges while also offering a level of intensity that taps into the child's potential. Guided participation focuses on supporting opportunities that enable novice and expert players to incorporate preferred activities into socially coordinated play while also challenging novice players to practice new and progressively complex types of play. The play guide facilitates the play session in a methodical fashion, guiding novice and expert players to engage in mutually enjoyed activities that promote social interaction, communication, play and imagination – e.g., constructing, pretending, interactive games, art, music and movement. As the children demonstrate an increasing capacity to mediate play activities on their own, the adult gradually pulls out. The following practices represent the various layers that support the guided participation process.

Monitoring play initiations. This focuses on uncovering novice players' meaningful attempts to socialize and play by recognizing, interpreting, and responding to the subtle and idiosyncratic ways in which they express their intentions. Play initiations may include virtually any act or display that indicates a child's interest in or desire to play in the company of peers. They may be directed to objects (e.g., toys and props), others (e.g., peers and adults), or oneself. Also, play initiations may be conventional or unconventional and conveyed through overt, subtle, or obscure means. Even acts that reflect unusual fascinations, obsessions, rituals, or idiosyncratic language are recognized as play initiations.

Play initiations are the foundation on which to build the child's social and symbolic play repertoire. They are the springboards for novice and expert players to find common ground in mutually engaging activities. The adult's capacity to recognize, interpret, and respond to play initiations is essential for delivering support that is matched to the level of comprehension and ability – within the child's "zone of proximal development," defined by Vygotsky (1978) as

> the distance between the actual developmental level as determined by independent problem solving
> and the level of potential development as determined through problem solving under adult guidance,
> or in collaboration with more capable peers. (p. 86)

Scaffolding play. The process of scaffolding play involves systematically adjusting the amount and type of support provided so that it matches or slightly exceeds the child's ability to engage independently in play with peers (i.e., within the child's *zone of proximal development).*

From a facilitation standpoint, **scaffolding** involves moving in and moving out in response to observed social, communication and play behaviors at any given point in time. At a more intensive level, the play guide is much like a stage director who carefully directs and models the play by setting up the play scene with props and materials, delegating roles and play partners, performing actions and narrating lines. At a less intensive level, the play guide is much like a coach who redirects the children to one another to set the stage for their own play. This includes standing on the sidelines and posing questions, commenting, giving suggestions as well as offering subtle reminders using verbal and visual cues. At the least intensive level, the adult remains on the periphery and allows the children to practice the play on their own. By this point, the children exhibit a level of comfort and competency in exploring and trying out new activities. The play guide serves as a secure base, ready to step in and provide support whenever needed.

Social-communication guidance. The process of guiding social communication is ongoing with an emphasis on helping the children to elicit each other's attention and maintain interactions in reciprocal play. The focus is on promoting the use of verbal and nonverbal cues that are conventional with respect to children's development, age and peer culture. The strategies used to guide social communication are directed to both the novice and expert players. They include strategies to invite each other to play; persist in enlisting reluctant players to play; respond to each other's cues and initiations to play; and sustain and expand upon interactions in play. To a large extent the expert players learn how to interpret the cues of the novice players as having meaning and purpose. As complex social cues are broken down for the novice players, they in turn learn more conventional ways in which to initiate, respond and join peers for play.

A number of strategies are used for the purpose of guiding social communication in play. These include targeting relevant verbal and/or non-verbal social-communication cues that will serve to elicit and sustain mutual engagement in play. Visual supports have been developed for this purpose, which include posters and corresponding cue cards. The cue cards portray picture-word combinations that focus on What to Do (e.g., look, stand close, tap shoulder, take hand, point, give [toy], take turns, do what your playmate is doing) and What to Say (e.g., Say name of playmate, "Let's play," "What do you want to play?" "What are you doing?" "Can I have a turn?"). As relevant, the play guide provides instruction and practice on one or more cues, which are then supported in an incidental fashion as the need arises. The idea is for the children to incorporate these cues into their natural repertoire with the visual supports gradually faded out.

Play guidance. Play guidance comprises a progression of strategies that are specifically geared to novice players with consideration of both their present developmental level and experience in play with peers. These strategies are designed to scaffold full immersion in play experiences that slightly exceed the child's present level or capacity. This allows the child to participate with peers in more advanced play activities and themes, even if participation is initially minimal. For instance, a child who is predisposed to lining up objects might be eager to take on the task of lining up the grocery boxes on a shelf as a part of a larger play theme of shopping. With the assistance of more capable peers, the child may begin to explore and diversify existing play routines and eventually come to comprehend this role.

The progression of play guidance strategies includes ***orienting*** (watching peers and activities), ***mirroring*** (mimicking the actions of a peer), ***parallel play*** (playing side by side in the same play space with similar materials), and *joint focus* (active sharing and informal turn taking in the same activity) to socially coordinated activity involving ***joint action*** (formal turn taking), ***role enactment*** (portraying real-life activities through conventional actions), and *role-playing* (taking on pretend roles and creatively using objects while enacting complex scripts).

Richie

Richie had an opportunity to participate in Integrated Play Groups beginning in kindergarten. With careful scaffolding and guidance, he began to make progress in both the symbolic and social dimensions of play. The children were ready to be "coached." First, I tried to facilitate parallel play. I just wanted Richie to accept his peers playing with the same materials as he was. Rather than directly interact, I encouraged the kids to play near each other. Richie accepted this and continued to watch his peers from time to time to see what they were doing. This was important for Richie, because he has shown time and again that this is his way of learning most things: First he needs to sit back and watch for a while. Then he tends to start to understand and participate more directly.

One roadblock in the parallel play process was encountered when Richie was playing with the dollhouse and was hoarding all the dolls. He would come into the playroom, take all the dolls, and then start playing by himself. If another child asked for a doll, he would become upset and explode. I tried to coach Richie and help him understand sharing, but it was not working.

After play group was over, I brainstormed about what to do next. Do I take the dollhouse out of the playroom? Do I let Richie play alone, hoping that he'll start to share? Neither of those options seemed right. I decided that there was something Richie did not understand about sharing. That is when I thought of making visual supports for the situation. I took a digital picture of each doll from the dollhouse. Then I printed them off, laminated them, and Velcroed™ them to a small choice board. I brought the choice board to Richie's next play group and showed him that each child gets to take the picture of the doll they want to play with. It worked like magic. Richie chose first and picked his favorite doll. Next, he let his friends choose a doll. Something about the visual support helped him understand what he was supposed to do in a way that verbal language had not. Sharing the dolls was never a problem again.

Richie continued to expand his repertoire of play schemes over the course of his kindergarten year. He learned to play with a vet shop, trains, cars, dollhouse, restaurant, and other activities with his friends. He got out of the habit of coming into the playroom and playing with the exact same toys every time. This was partially due to a large choice board in the playroom showing pictures of several toys/items available. This helped Richie see all the choices available, so he didn't have to try to think of something new when he came in the playroom. During this time, Richie continued to play with toys in a functional manner (i.e., used a cup to represent a cup and a phone to represent a phone). He wasn't engaging in symbolic/pretend play at this time.

When Richie was in first grade, he became more interested in his peers. During this school year, I focused a bit less on the number of play schemes he used and more on his social interaction and emerging symbolic play. He was ready to accept guidance from me as well as his peers since he was more comfortable around them. Over the course of the year, we played vet shop during several play sessions, and I encouraged his friends to try to engage him a little more. Richie usually took the role of the vet and often worked on fixing one particular stuffed animal (the lemur). He didn't want the other kids to touch the lemur, so I helped him become more flexible with his play by expanding the play scheme. Since Richie did not want anyone else to "operate" on his lemur, I arranged for his peers to take other roles in the play scheme. One girl would use the phone to call the vet to let him know that other animals were coming into the emergency room (this expanded the number of animals he would pretend to fix), and another child would bring the animals to the "recovery center" after Richie was done fixing them.

This was the point at which the visual role tags were introduced, which subsequently helped Richie understand the different roles there are in play (in a more concrete way). He was usually able to accept his peers' roles and begin some common focus play. They started doing informal turn taking and actively sharing the materials. He still did his part, without much care for the role the others took, but he was able to accept their invitations and their play without rejecting them. He also began to accept that objects/toys may be used to represent something else. For example, when given a wooden block to represent a telephone, he was able to pretend to talk on it when one of his playmates pretended to call his vet office. These were all big advances in Richie's play during his first-grade year.

In second grade, Richie made even more advances in his play development. He still had his obstacles to overcome, one of which was sharing his favorite toys in the playroom, but he continued to improve. He loved to play with two small animal figurines (a tiger and a lion). These animals were named Shere Khan (from The Jungle Book*) and Jasper the lion. However, Richie didn't want anyone else to join him in his play with these two animals and definitely did not let anyone else touch them. Session after session, Richie grabbed the animals and had an elaborate "animal fight" between them. He controlled both the animals' actions and voices. He did not let others join him.*

This quickly changed when his playmate, Cameron, gathered all the other animal figurines in a semi-circle around Richie's animal fight. Richie was able to accept this from his friend, as it didn't interfere with his play scheme since the other animals were merely "watching." At this point, I facilitated the other kids in expanding the play scheme. They began to work on making tickets to the animal fight (Richie participated in this and made the best tiger drawing of all!). They also made a sign for the ticket booth and menus for the concession stand. After all of the visual supports were made, one last obstacle remained – would Richie let someone else directly participate in his play? I took a digital picture of the tiger and the lion and asked Richie to choose which one he wanted to be. He chose the tiger (his absolute favorite and always the "winner"). Next was the moment of truth – would he let his best bud, Cameron, be the lion? Again, the visual support worked like magic. Richie allowed Cameron to be the voice and to control the actions of the lion. Cameron, being a very intuitive friend, made sure that he kept the same name for the lion (Jasper) and made the same movements and noises as Richie used to do. Most important, he understood that Richie's tiger was ALWAYS the winner. Cameron was okay with that.

We were then ready for the official animal fight. There was an announcer, who made an announcement to "buy tickets now …," and a concession worker, who made an announcement that it was "last call for food." Next, the security guard announced to remain seated at all times during the fight, and finally Richie announced, "Ladies and gentlemen, welcome to the animal fight." Richie did it! He accepted Cameron's direct role in his beloved play scheme. All went off without a hitch, and Shere Khan won the fight. Then something really exciting happened: Richie tried to get his friends' attention by saying, "Hey guys, look!!! Shere Khan is sick from bubble gum!" Luckily, I was there to guide his friends in understanding that Richie was communicating to them that he wanted to change the play scheme from "animal fight" to "vet shop." Richie's peers quickly responded by pulling out the vet toys, and they all became engaged in another play scheme together. Two times in the same session, Richie engaged in common goal play with his peers. This hadn't happened in the previous two school years.

Now in third grade, Richie's growth continues to amaze me. Recently, Richie has expanded his play with the tiger and lion figurines by playing something other than the animal fight. He engages in what I call "free play," in which he doesn't rely on adult coaching or visual supports. Through the use of the visual supports in the past, he has developed the ability to understand the different roles and schemes that his animals can be involved in. He is more spontaneous and flexible. Just recently, Richie and Cameron were playing with the tiger and lion (of course, Richie still had the tiger), but the lion's name changed to Sparky. Cameron and Richie freely played with the animals, taking the dialogue and events as they unfolded. It was not scripted, and they based their play on back-and-forth interactions. Richie did not display the rigidity that he used to when he was unable to engage in play schemes other than his "movie scenarios." Over the course of this school year, Richie has also begun to play in more elaborate pretend roles with his peers without the use of toys. For example, there is an air cushion in the playroom that they pretend is a boat, and Richie likes for him and Cameron to be captains. The other two play group expert players have been "bad guys," "winter warlocks," and "crocodiles." Richie now accepts these ever-changing roles and is not upset or confused by the change. He is much more able to "go with the flow" of play rather than becoming upset by it and rejecting it.

Integrated Play Groups have made an invaluable impact on Richie's overall development. It has expanded his ability to be more flexible and has increased his social interactions and his self-confidence, which affects him throughout his entire school day. The benefits are enormous and have carried over into several other areas of development and education. Integrated Play Groups have given Richie the opportunity to make friends and become comfortable with his peers (and helped his peers to become comfortable with him just the way he is). He has generalized many of these skills into the mainstream classroom settings and can participate successfully in classroom plays and music concerts, which is something that used to be impossible for him.

Summary and Conclusions

The desire to play and make friends is an intrinsic need of all children. In light of their developmental differences as well as socio-cultural factors, children on the autism spectrum encounter unique obstacles in learning how to play and socialize with peers. In this chapter, we introduced the conceptual foundation, principles, and practices of the Friend 2 Friend and Integrated Play Groups models, which are designed to overcome these obstacles. These complementary models draw on current theory, empirical research, and evidence-based practices to foster children's peer play and friendships within school, home, and community settings. It is our hope to provide educators with some ideas for guiding children on the autism spectrum in mutual play and friendships with peers within a peer culture that embraces neurodiversity.

Tips for the Classroom

Demystifying Autism

Effective autism demystification programs provide information about the disorder in an age-appropriate, fun, and interactive manner. They are inclusive and respectful and model acceptance of diversity. The Friend 2 Friend model follows a set of guidelines to provide programs that foster understanding, acceptance and empathy. These guidelines include:

✓ **Focus on understanding and acceptance.** Autism demystification begins by supporting the child with ASD in understanding and accepting his or her own unique challenges and gifts. Supporting children in this way models a respect for individuality and diversity and empowers the child with autism. Autism demystification programs or activities should always include the focus child. This provides him with the same information made available to his peers and further models respect for diversity and a truly inclusive classroom, peer, and school culture.

✓ **Make it fun and educational.** Autism demystification should be delivered in a sensitive, age-appropriate, fun, and interactive way. Young children learn best through play and imagination; talking is often not as effective as games, story books, or fun activities. We all learn best when we are entertained and having fun.

✓ **Demystify, not identify.** Autism demystification should never single out the child with autism, nor should the child's name, diagnosis, or any personal information be discussed during the demystification process.

✓ **Model, label, explain, and normalize.** The key to demystifying autism is to provide a visual model of the characteristics of autism, label those characteristics, explain the reason behind them, and, most important, normalize the characteristics to support feelings of empathy.

✓ **Emphasize that we are all different.** Autism demystification should always include examples of various individuals with autism or role-playing to help generalize the characteristics of autism. This supports understanding and acceptance of autism as a spectrum disorder and the characteristics of autism as being real and genuine. Autism demystification should use sensitive language and encourage a shared vocabulary, such as "I have this kind of mind." "This is my stim, what's yours?" To promote an inclusive culture, avoid using references like "them" and "us." Instead, use "we" references such as, "We are all different in our own way."

✓ **Teach that autism is not a four-letter word.** Autism demystification should be direct and honest, while respecting individuality, diversity, and privacy. Using the word *autism* is fine. It is just a word, not a person, but it is not always necessary in providing autism demystification (especially with younger children).

Guiding Children with Autism in Peer Play

Effective peer play guidance is an art that requires a blend of knowledge, skill, experience, and intuition to refine and master. It requires adopting a flexible and holistic style involving many layers and levels of awareness and support. Therefore, play guides must draw on a number of different sources of knowledge and insight to accommodate children with diverse developmental levels, learning styles, interests, and experiences. The following tips were adapted from Wolfberg (2003).

✓ **Understand and appreciate play.** Recognize the importance of play for children's learning, development, and cultural participation and embrace play in the lives of all children. Be sure to devote special times for your students with ASD to play with their typical peers, siblings and classmates.

✓ **Hone your skills as a good observer.** Initially, spend time observing children of diverse ages and abilities at play in a variety of natural contexts. This will provide you with a framework for understanding typical play development. Next, observe the children in Integrated Play Groups without intervening. In doing so, you will become attuned to the unique qualities of play exhibited by the children with ASD and the dynamics of the group. This will offer a starting point for identifying meaningful goals and strategies for both the novice and expert players.

✓ **Expect to wear many hats.** Play guides invariably take on a variety of roles while facilitating Integrated Play Groups, including model, coach, spectator, interpreter, peacemaker, theater director, entertainer, and housekeeper. In other words, expect to wear many hats to effectively support the children.

✓ **Go with the flow.** Being neither too intrusive nor laissez-faire, play guides go with the flow when facilitating play groups. They must be extremely flexible and willing to follow the children's lead. This means being able to let go of control, as opposed to imposing a rigid agenda of prescribed activities.

✓ **Set the tone for the group.** Play guides can influence how the players treat one another without effectively taking over. It is important to set the tone for the group by modeling behavior that is respectful and inclusive of all the children. For instance, when giving an expert player a tip about a novice player, include the novice player in the discussion. Address the novice player even if she seems unable to comprehend. This will set a tone that emphasizes that all the children are competent and contributing members of the group.

✓ **Distribute attention among the players.** To ensure that every child is maximally included in the group, play guides must distribute their attention and support among all the children. At times, it may be appropriate to guide a pair of players. At other times, it may be appropriate to guide the entire group. Novice players do not always need to be at center stage to receive their due share of assistance. In certain instances, it may be beneficial for the novice player to be on the periphery as the play guide interacts with the expert players.

✓ **Grow into the role/find a personal style.** Play guides may initially feel awkward and frustrated in their roles. The best advice we can give is not to be too hard on yourself. Realize that this is a process that does get easier. Recognize that play guides grow into their roles, while gaining proficiency through extended and reflective practice. Each play guide must find his or her own personal style that is both effective and comfortable. Allow yourself the freedom to experiment through trial and error – to figure out not only what works best for the children, but also feels right for you.

✓ **Take hold of the moment.** It is important to recognize that we all have good days and bad days. If you feel you have reached an impasse, it can be immensely helpful to step back, breathe deeply, and take hold of the moment. You may be pleasantly surprised to discover that the situation resolves itself – that you must be doing something right after all! Keep in mind that all those little moments when things are going well add up over time.

✓ **Reflect on your practice.** To evaluate the fidelity of any intervention, it is important to engage in ongoing reflective practice. A part of the reflective process is introspection – contemplating your own experience and effectiveness as a play guide. Play guides may also engage in reflective practice with others by sharing experiences and evaluating one another in a constructive light. We have found videotapes to be especially useful for viewing oneself and others in action.

✓ **Enjoy the experience.** Perhaps one of the most vital things to keep in mind while facilitating play groups is to enjoy the experience and simply have fun. This is a lesson that we have learned from many practitioners and family members who have shared rich and amusing accounts of children's play and friendships.

Chapter Highlights

- Children with ASD encounter significant challenges learning how to play, socialize, and form friendships with peers due to impairments in reciprocal interactions, communication, and imagination.

- Evidence suggests that children with ASD share the same desires for play, companionship, and peer group acceptance as neurotypical peers.

- Play and social instruction with peers are viewed as a type of intervention that should receive priority in the design and delivery of educational programs for children with ASD.

- Play serves a vital role through which children develop symbolic capabilities, interpersonal skills, and social knowledge.

- Children playing together develop a peer group or "play culture" that is based on active participation in social activities leading to the development of foundational social skills.

- Friendship occupies a central place in children's social lives and serves as a determining factor for social adaptation and adjustment.

- Peer neglect, rejection, or bullying contributes to low aspiration in school performance, depression, withdrawn or isolative behaviors, low self-esteem, and loneliness.

- Many children with ASD demonstrate play that is detached and lacking in imagination.

- Children with ASD tend to stay with only a few activities that they may repeat over and over, with less inclination to engage in functional or pretend play than peers at a similar developmental age.

- While children with ASD vary in their social interaction skills, from seeming "aloof" to "passive" to "active and odd," they all demonstrate fewer interactions, inconsistency in initiating and responding, and difficulties in communication.

- Many children with ASD are excluded from their peer group or "peer culture" because their behavior lacks the culture's definition of "normal."

- Exclusion from the peer group/culture creates a social void caused by peers' lack of understanding of the behavior of children with ASD.

- Carefully planned activities and support are needed to help children with ASD and their peers develop reciprocal interaction skills.

- Friend 2 Friend (F2F) and Integrated Play Groups (IPG) are complementary models designed to support children with ASD in play and friendships with typical peers in inclusive school, home, and community settings.

- F2F is designed to provide a framework for demystifying autism for children aged 3 and up, including puppet programs for 3- to 8 year-olds and simulation games for ages 9 and up; these activities are intended to support typically developing peers in understanding, accepting, and empathizing with children on the spectrum.

- F2F uses a four-step teaching process consisting of modeling, labeling, explaining, and normalizing.

- Within F2F five key learning goals provide the basis for future learning:
  - ➢ Recognize and accept differences in self and others
  - ➢ Recognize individuals with autism and different kinds of minds as valuable friends
  - ➢ Recognize that it is important to ask questions and express feelings
  - ➢ Empathize with what it feels like to have autism and different kinds of minds
  - ➢ Promote positive relationships with all peers
- F2F introduces seven basic friendship tips involving prosocial communications strategies for peers to use to interact more successfully with children on the autism spectrum.
- F2F includes a puppet program designed to introduce young children to the characteristics associated with ASD. The four-step teaching process is used while never singling out the focus the child with ASD.
- For children aged 9 and above, F2F offers a 50-minute educational presentation in the form of a simulation game designed to help children understand what it feels like to have autism through an exploration of the senses and receptive communication. This is followed by discussion and introduction of the Seven Basic Friendship Tips.
- The Integrated Play Groups (IPG) model is designed to support children with ASD in play experiences with typical peers/siblings as playmates through a system of careful guidance and support.
- Program and environmental design in the IPG model include the group's composition, play space and materials, and play session structure and supports.
- Assessment within the IPG model focuses on systematic observation designed to analyze progress and setting realistic and meaningful goals, including evaluating the symbolic dimensions of play, the social dimensions of play, the communicative functions and means used by the children, and the play preferences and diversity of play exhibited.
- Intervention within the IPG model is based on assessment with guided participation used to implement a carefully tailored and intensive system of supports appropriate to each child's needs and abilities. The adult guides novice and expert players to engage in mutually enjoyed activities that encourage social interaction, communication, pretending, and interactive games.
- Support within the IPG model includes monitoring play initiations; scaffolding play; promoting the use of social communication; and play guidance, in which children are supported in experiences slightly beyond their capacity.
- Play guidance strategies range from orienting to mirroring to parallel play, joint focus, joint actions, role enactment, and role-playing.
- As children become more competent and independent in play skills, the adult lessens the intensity of support provided.

Chapter Review Questions

1. Why are play and friendships integral to children's learning, development, and cultural participation?

2. What are the challenges children with ASD face in terms of developing play skills and friendships?

3. What is "peer culture" and what role does it play in terms of children with ASD developing friendships?

4. What is meant by "play culture"?

5. What is the purpose of the Friend 2 Friend (F2F) model?

6. How is F2F implemented (include the four steps of the teaching process)?

7. What are the five key learning goals of F2F?

8. What are the F2F Seven Basic Friendship Tips and why are they important?

9. What is the purpose of the Integrated Play Groups (IPG) model?

10. How are environmental elements important to IPG implementation?

11. Which elements are included in the IPG observational assessment of play and why?

12. What is meant by guided participation in play (include discussion of the key components)?

References

American Psychiatric Association. (2000). *Diagnostic and statistical manual of mental disorders-IV (TR)*. Washington, DC: Author.

Asher, S. R., Parkhurst, J. T., Hymel, S., & Williams, G. A. (1990). Peer rejection and loneliness in childhood. *In Peer rejection in childhood* (pp. 253-273). New York: Cambridge University Press.

Bagwell, C., Schmidt, M., Newcomb, A., & Bukowski, W. (2001). Friendship and peer rejection as predictors of adult adjustment. *New Directions for Child and Adolescent Development, 91*, 25-50.

Baron-Cohen, S. (1987). Autism and symbolic play. *British Journal of Developmental Psychology, 5*(2), 139-148.

Baron-Cohen, S. (1989). Joint-attention deficits in autism: Towards a cognitive analysis. *Development and Psychopathology, 1*, 185-189.

Bauminger, N., & Kasari, C. (2000). Loneliness and friendship in high-functioning children with autism. *Child Development, 71*(2), 447-456.

Berndt, T. J. (1999). Friends' influence on students' adjustment to school. *Educational Psychologist, 34*, 15-28.

Berndt, T. J. (2002). Friendship quality and social development. *Current Directions in Psychological Science, 11*, 7-10.

Boivin, M., Poulin, F., & Vitaro, F. (1994). Depressed mood and peer rejection in childhood. *Development and Psychopathology, 6*, 483-498.

Boucher, J., & Wolfberg, P. J. (Eds.). (2003). Special issue on play. *Autism: The International Journal of Research and Practice, 7*(4), 339-346.

Corsaro, W. A. (1992). Interpretive reproduction in children's peer cultures. *Social Psychology Quarterly, 55*, 160-177.

Dawson, G., & Adams, A. (1984). Imitation and social responsiveness in autistic children. *Journal of Abnormal Child Psychology, 12*, 209-225.

Eisenberg, N., & Miller, P. A. (1987). Empathy and prosocial behavior. *Psychological Bulletin, 101*, 91-119.

Frith, U. (2003). *Autism: Explaining the enigma* (2nd ed.). Oxford, UK: Blackwell Publishers.

Gest, S. D., Graham-Bermann, S. A., & Hartup, W. W. (2001). Peer experience: Common and unique features of number of friendships, social network centrality, and sociometric status. *Social Development, 10*, 23-40.

Hartup, W. W. (1989). Social relationships and their developmental significance. *American Psychologist, 44*, 120-126.

Hartup, W. W. (1991). Having friends, making and keeping friends: Relationships as education contexts. *Early Report, 19*, 1-4.

Hartup, W. W. (1996). The company they keep: Friendships and their developmental significance. *Child Development, 67*, 1-13.

Heinrichs, R. (2003). *Perfect targets: Asperger Syndrome and bullying – Practical solutions for surviving the social world*. Shawnee Mission, KS: Autism Asperger Publishing Company.

Jarrold, C. (2003). A review of research into pretend play in autism. *Autism: The International Journal of Research and Practice, 7*(4), 379-390.

Jordan, R. (2003). Social play and autistic spectrum disorders. *Autism: The International Journal of Research and Practice, 7*(4), 347-360.

Ladd, G. W. (1990). Having friends, keeping friends, making friends, and being liked by peers in the classroom: Predictors of children's early school adjustment? *Child Development, 61*, 1081-1100.

Libby, S., Powell, S., Messer, D., & Jordan, R. (1998). Spontaneous play in children with autism: A reappraisal. *Journal of Autism and Developmental Disorders, 28*, 487-497.

McCracken, H. (2004). *Enhancing peer relations in children with ASD: Friend 2 Friend Model*. Presentation at the BC Association of Speech-Language Pathologists and Audiologists, Kelowna, BC, Canada.

McCracken, H. (2005a, Jan-Feb). Friend 2 Friend: Fostering mutual friendships for children with ASD. *Autism-Asperger Digest*, 6-15.

McCracken, H. (2005b). Friend 2 Friend programs help children with autism feel safe to say, "I'm autistic too." *Autism Spectrum Quarterly, 2*, 13.

McCracken, H. (2005c). *Fostering mutual friendships for children with ASD – The Friend 2 Friend Model*. Paper presented to the Autism Society of America national conference, Nashville, TN.

McCracken, H. (2006). *That's what's different about me – Helping children understand autism spectrum disorders*. Shawnee Mission, KS: Autism Asperger Publishing Company.

McCune-Nicolich, L. A. (1981). Toward symbolic functioning: Structure of early pretend games and potential parallels with language. *Child Development, 52*, 785-797.

Mouritsen, F. (1996). *Play culture: Essays on child culture, play and narratives*. Odense, Denmark: Odense University.

Mundy, P., Sigman, M., Ungerer, J., & Sherman, T. (1987). Non-verbal communication and play correlates of language development in autistic children. *Journal of Autism and Developmental Disorders, 17*, 349-364.

National Research Council. (2001). *Educating children with autism*. Committee on educational interventions for children with autism, Division of Behavioral and Social Sciences and Education. Washington, DC: National Academy Press.

Parker, J. G., & Asher, S. R. (1993). Beyond group acceptance: Friendship and friendship quality as distinct dimensions of peer adjustment. In W. H. Jones & D. Perlman (Eds.), *Advances in personal relationship* (Vol. 4, pp. 261-294). London: Jessica Kingsley.

Parten, M. B. (1932). Social participation among preschool children. *Journal of Abnormal and Social Psychology, 27*, 243-269.

Peck, C. A., Schuler, A. L., Tomlinson, C., Theimer, R. K., & Haring, T. (1984). *The social competence curriculum project: A guide to instructional communicative interactions*. Santa Barbara: University of California, Special Education Research Institute.

Piaget, J. (1962). *Play, dreams, and imitation in childhood*. New York: Norton.

Rogoff, B. (1990). *Apprenticeship in thinking*. New York: Oxford University Press.

Rubin, K. H., Fein, G., & Vandenberg, B. (1983). Play. In P. Mussen & E. M. Hetherington (Eds.), *Handbook of child psychology: Vol. 4, Socialization, personality, and social development* (pp. 693-774). New York: Wiley.

Sigman, M., & Ruskin, E. (1999). Continuity and change in the social competence of children with autism, Down syndrome, and developmental delays. *Monographs of the Society for Research in Child Development, 64*, 1-114.

Sigman, M., & Ungerer, J. A. (1984). Cognitive and language skills in autistic, mentally retarded and normal children. *Developmental Psychology, 20*, 293-302.

Smilansky, S. (1968). *The effects of sociodramatic play on disadvantaged preschool children*. New York: Wiley.

Tilton, J. R., & Ottinger, D. R. (1964). Comparison of toy play behavior of autistic, retarded and normal children. *Psychological Reports, 15*, 967-975.

Vygotsky, L. S. (1966). Play and its role in the mental development of the child (translation from 1933). *Soviet Psychology, 12*, 6-18.

Vygotsky, L. S. (1978). *Mind in society: The development of higher psychological processes* (translation from 1932). Cambridge, MA: Harvard University Press.

Williams, E. (2003). A comparative review of early forms of object-directed play and parent–infant play in typical infants and young children with autism. *Autism: The International Journal of Research and Practice, 7*(4), 361-377.

Wing, L., & Gould, J. (1979). Severe impairments of social interaction and associated abnormalities in children: Epidemiology and classification. *Journal of Autism and Developmental Disorders, 9*, 11-29.

Wing, L., Gould, J., Yeates, S. R., & Brierly, L. M. (1977). Symbolic play in severely mentally retarded and autistic children. *Journal of Child Psychology and Psychiatry, 18*, 167-178.

Wolfberg, P. J. (1994). Case illustrations of emerging social relations and symbolic activity in children with autism through supported peer play (Doctoral dissertation, University of California at Berkeley with San Francisco State University). *Dissertation Abstracts International, #9505068*.

Wolfberg, P. J. (1999). *Play and imagination in children with autism*. New York: Columbia University, Teachers College Press.

Wolfberg, P. J. (2003). *Peer play and the autism spectrum: The art of guiding children's socialization and imagination*. Shawnee Mission, KS: Autism Asperger Publishing Company.

Wolfberg, P. J. (2004). Guiding children on the autism spectrum in peer play: Translating theory and research into effective and meaningful practice. *The Journal of Developmental and Learning Disorders, 8*, 7-25.

Wolfberg, P. J., & Schuler, A. L. (1993). Integrated Play Groups: A model for promoting the social and cognitive dimensions of play in children with autism. *Journal of Autism and Developmental Disorders, 23*(3), 467-489.

Wolfberg, P. J., & Schuler, A. L. (2006). Promoting social reciprocity and symbolic representation in children with ASD: Designing quality peer play interventions. In T. Charman & W. Stone (Eds.), *Early social communication in autism spectrum disorders* (pp. 180-218). New York: Guilford Publications.

Wolfberg, P. J., Zercher, C., Lieber, J., Capell, K., Matias, S. G., Hanson, M., & Odom, S. (1999). "Can I play with you?" Peer culture in inclusive preschool programs. *Journal for the Association of Persons with Severe Handicaps, 24*(2), 69-84.

Learner Objectives

After reading this chapter, the learner should be able to:

- Explain what is meant by "multiple intelligences"

- List and describe the development of skills necessary for social cognition

- Explain general intervention/treatment options for assisting students with ASD in developing social skills

- State the potential problems in defining social skills

- Identify what is meant by the term "sharing space effectively" and provide examples of skills necessary to do so in various situations

- List and describe the four steps in perspective taking identified by the chapter author

- Explain the challenges students with ASD have related to sharing space

- List and describe the components of the ILAUGH acronym

- Explain how the components of ILAUGH contribute to understanding social thinking that goes beyond social interactions and affects academics

- Explain why the demand for effective social skills increases significantly starting in grade 3 and beyond

- Discuss the differences in teaching social skills to individuals with ASD depending on their social cognitive levels

- List key concepts for teaching social skills to students demonstrating "classical" or "moderate" autism

- Describe key concepts for teaching social thinking and related skills to students with high-functioning autism

- Discuss key concepts for teaching social thinking and related skills to students with Asperger Syndrome

- Explain how Social Stories™, Comic Strip Conversations™, Social Behavior Mapping, and the Incredible 5-Point Scale are used to teach social thinking and related skills concepts

Chapter 9

Social Thinking: Cognition to Enhance Communication and Learning

Michelle Garcia Winner

Doug was a cute 9-year-old boy when I first met him; he was fully included in a fourth-grade classroom with close support from his paraprofessional. He had been diagnosed with autism in his early preschool years along with his twin brother. Over the years, thanks to solid early intervention (including a discrete trial behavioral program), a focus on functional skill development, a consistent paraprofessional, and devoted parents, Doug was now referred to as having "high-functioning autism." His twin brother, Mark, when provided with the exact same treatment program, also developed some functional language skills, but has not become as capable as Doug.

In fourth grade, Doug was able to participate at the level of the mainstream class in most activities with consistent support from his paraprofessional, Kelly. Given Doug's normal IQ and near-average language skills, as determined through language testing, his educational team, including his mother, expected that Doug would be able to continue on the same path as his peers, as long as Kelly was there to support him. Doug did an excellent job recalling facts learned from the text and had a propensity for math. He read with good fluency (decoding), but could only answer the factual questions about what he read. Doug was a very nice child with a good sense of humor, and did not cause any problems in the class. He had difficulty learning from the teacher in the context of a large group, but Kelly helped him to stay focused and provided him with explicit instructions. He lacked eye contact and was not able to engage in the type of spontaneous communication necessary to engage with his peer group. His best friend was Kelly. At recess he preferred to sit under the slide on the playground and talk to himself.

Given Doug's ability to answer the teacher's questions and Kelly's ability to work with Doug to keep him productive in the classroom, his mainstream teacher reported at his IEP meeting that he was a "good participant" and a "very smart" one. At the end of the school year, it was recommended that he continue in the mainstream classroom program in fifth grade. His mother believed that the curriculum of the full inclusion classes would provide what Doug needed to excel during adolescence and into his adult years. After all, this is the method that is touted by the parent advocacy groups as well as from the educational community. In fact, when she began the discrete trials program with her two autistic twin boys, she was clearly told they would "outgrow" their autism by their teenage years.

I began to work with Doug and his mother when Doug was in fourth grade. I initially agreed to work with Doug only in individual sessions to help him learn more concretely about the abstract nature of social interaction and language meaning. Doug needed to learn that there were two codes of language, literal and figurative. The tricky part was (and continues to be) how to teach him to figure out what figurative and indirect language means. He also needed to learn to answer the "how" and "why" questions, which are at the heart of all real comprehension tasks.

From my vantage point, I saw a boy who had significant limitations in the development of social cognition, sensory integration, and executive function skills. A large part of his challenges stemmed from the fact that he could not understand what other people thought or felt. While he was always friendly, he had tremendous difficulty thinking about what someone else was thinking. Blessed with a lovely and compliant personality, he was happy to do what he was asked, but he did not try to interpret why he had to do it; he just did it. I began to help both his mother and his educators recognize that Doug's overall strengths and weaknesses would never be fully understood through a battery of tests, given that these tests would not be able to accurately assess the complexity of social cognition and its impact on not only his ability to develop a social understanding of the people who surrounded him, but also of the curriculum that required him to use these same sets of social thinking skills.

As I worked with Doug, he learned that eye contact was used to understand what other people are thinking; until then, he had never been able to interpret how or why one would look at another's eyes. Given his strong academic intelligence, he was fairly quick to understand that we "think with our eyes" by learning that the direction in which someone's eyeballs look often provides information about what that person is thinking about. This lesson made Doug realize that people have thoughts that are different from his own. We then began to explore what people might be thinking, based not only on what others were looking at but also on what they were doing with their bodies (e.g., if they were reaching for a cup of water, they were likely going to drink because they felt thirsty). We started to work heavily on making predictions based on what we were doing together in the therapy room, based on movie clips we watched, as well as on information from curriculum-based texts.

Given that Doug did not easily or quickly understand people's thoughts or that their thoughts were different from his, he had great difficulty interpreting what people meant by what they said. He could not read people's intentions or motives; he was not only incapable of doing this in his peer relations, but also when trying to interpret a literature passage from his classroom reading. Furthermore, he had great difficulty producing coherent written expression. His inability to read other people's minds also added to his writing challenges. Not only did he have difficulty with the task of handwriting itself, but he could not figure out what he was supposed to write, nor was he able to write paragraphs that one could easily interpret, since he was not able to write passages based on what other people needed to know. Given his social cognitive deficits, he was not able to figure out what people knew.

Doug's mother was amazed. As much as she had learned about autism, she did not understand what really made her child "act autistic." Her son was so friendly and compliant, yet he could not form friendships. As he aged, the classroom challenges of interpretation, group cooperation, and productivity became increasingly daunting to Doug. Kelly, Doug's paraprofessional, had to pull Doug from his classrooms with more frequency and for longer periods of time to provide him with extra lessons so he could keep trying to understand the basic lessons so many of his peers were learning intuitively. However, while school was clearly becoming more challenging academically, remarkably he was improving with his social understanding.

Doug's mother was delighted that in middle school her son was learning to distinguish between what someone thought and what someone knew. He was learning that not all people in school were his friends; he began to see that some people he did not know were "evil" and others were "nice." He was starting to make predictions and understand that some behaviors made people have "weird thoughts," including himself. When we compared Doug to who he had been a year earlier, we saw progress; when we compared Doug to his classroom peers, we saw that with each year of school he proved to be less and less academically capable.

Doug's mother realized that Doug was not intuitively learning the skills he needed to cope in the world. He was not learning how to shop in a store or manage money, even though he was tested as having excellent money math skills. He was not able to read people's intentions well enough to avoid being tricked or possibly cheated. He could not cross a street independently, because that required him to think about what each of the drivers was thinking (e.g., Does the driver see me? Even if the driver is driving in my direction, does he plan to stop?). By the last year of middle school, she agreed to have Doug move to a self-contained or special day class to help him focus on functional academic skills as well as home and community life skills. Upon entering this class, Doug made his first set of friends; he connected with people who thought more like he did. He also began to work with more independence, since the work assigned was at the level in which he could interpret on his own.

Doug now attends a similar class at the high school. Everyone who works with him adores him. He is gentle and patient with all of his teachers, even though they don't quite understand how he thinks about the world. He is willing to work hard, and he is learning to work through tasks independently and ask for help if he needs it. He is learning to joke around with people and follow clearly established directions. However, he gets easily overwhelmed, and when this happens, he tends to "space out" rather than seek assistance. To keep Doug motivated to work and learn all the small but complex steps of life that most people take for granted, he needs a positive behavior system.

Initially, his high school special day class teachers took Doug's positive attitude for granted and forgot to reward him for doing what he does best: follow routines. Doug started to show sadness and frustration; but with a positive reward system in place, he is now willing to work through the harder tasks. He is also learning to cope with the complex array of emotions and social and community skills that can overwhelm any teen, but specifically kids like Doug, who have relatively weak social cognition development. At the same time, he is included in mainstream academic classes, where he can perform with some level of independence.

Kelly, his paraprofessional who helped to teach him from the time he was 4 years old through middle school, was not able to transfer to the high school district with Doug. So Doug has had to deal with the challenges of training a new teacher and paraprofessional to understand him. Most professionals – medical, educational, and administrative – don't understand autism, because they fail to think more deeply about the impact of social thinking, sensory integration, and executive functioning skills across every moment of every day. They also fail to understand that simple testing is not going to get to the complex heart of this disability.

What has Doug's mom learned along the way? She has learned that at the center of autism lies a very inefficient system for interpreting the complex social information that surrounds us, even when we are not actively talking to another person. She has also learned that these same core interpretation skills are necessary to understand literature, express one's ideas on paper, and even participate as a member of a group in class. Doug's mom has also learned that many professionals don't understand the needs of students with autism.

A few weeks ago, when I was doing a rare lesson with Doug and his brother Mark, while both boys were struggling to figure out what each person knew or didn't know about a concealed picture at a table, their mom looked at me and whispered, "I thought they would be done with this by now!" I responded by saying, "Be done with what?" She said, "Be done with autism!" "Who told you that?" I asked. "The behavioral intervention team back when the boys were doing their discrete trial treatment. They told me the boys would be cured by the time they were teenagers!" She looked as if she was going to cry. Even with good interventions for all these years, in large part because Doug's mother learned she had to fight to get them, her boys still have a lot to learn to survive in the "real world."

Doug's mother has begun to trust that the most important thing to teach Doug and his brother is how to cope in the world outside of the classroom, since that is the real world that awaits her sons on the day that they graduate from high school. She understands that rather than keeping students tied to one curriculum in school, we need to figure out what each child needs to learn to help him be as productive and happy as possible in their adult years. This is the same wish all parents have for their child's elementary and secondary school years. Yet, Doug's mom had to learn that the path to making that wish come closer to being true was, in large part, based on learning about the complexity of social thinking and what we can all do to bolster it at home, at school, and in the community.

---

ypical social development is difficult to study given the intuitive pathways through which it develops. In this chapter, we will explore how **social learning** for people with autism spectrum disorders (ASD) tends to be a cognitive rather than an intuitive experience. Specifically, we will address the complex nature of social learning and factors that complicate social responses, such as understanding the unstated rules of social interaction and the perspectives of others. Since reading comprehension of literature, written expression, and organizational skills are often quite weak for students with ASD, the impact of social development on academic development will also be discussed. The **ILAUGH** model of social cognition will be reviewed to help illuminate specific social learning challenges that affect social and academic learning. In the last section of this chapter, current promising evidence-based practices will be introduced. This will help to provide a foundation on which to more deeply teach our students to become better social thinkers, while producing more accurately related social skills.

The Evolution of Social Development and Social Teaching

Teaching social skills is one of the primary goals of any treatment program for students with ASD. While this sounds fairly simple, its scope and complexity rival the most complicated of sciences. In fact, we ought to view it as if we were teaching our students "social algebra." Determining how to use our body, eyes, facial expressions, words, and so on, in synchrony at the right time and the right place requires a socially algebraic equation.

Multiple Intelligences

To respect the challenges of students with social skill challenges, it is helpful to consider the contribution of social cognition to our overall intelligence. Dr. Mel Levine (2002) describes eight types of cognition that can be explored to better understand how to evaluate and develop treatment programs for all types of students, including those with learning disabilities. While the validity of multiple intelligences (Gardner, 1993) may have sounded "funky" 20 years ago, it is now a popularly accepted part of our understanding of the whole child. That is, some students are predisposed to perform well in athletics, music, math, or social skills because, in large part, their neurological wiring provides stronger abilities in sports, music, math, or social skills. By the same token, students who do not do well in math, spelling, memorizing facts, or social skills likely have relative weaknesses in their cognitive abilities for these areas.

The importance of developing good social cognition, self-regulation, and problem-solving skills for promoting achievement, both academically and socially across our lifetime, was first explored in the research on early childhood development. Hirsh-Pasek, Golinkoff, and Eyer (2003) review a multitude of research studies to demonstrate the importance of developing social relations and problem solving to help students gain access to broader learning, while also tracking the early developmental milestones contributing to our social development.

Joint Attention

During the first days of life, babies start to imitate the faces of the people around them. By the end of their first year, neurotypical babies have evolved to the point where they can follow the direction of another person's eye gaze, anticipate what the other person is thinking about, and then seek more information about where the person is looking by looking there themselves. This critical skill is called joint attention – the ability to direct their attention to where someone else is looking. Ninety percent of infants who fail to develop this skill by 12 months of age are later diagnosed as being on the autism spectrum, most likely as having autism (Jones & Carr, 2004). Joint attention is one of the first abstract social skills we engage in that shows we are tracking the mind and perspective of others around us, even if we are not directly and actively communicating with them at the time. How often do you follow the eyes of strangers you see at a store? How many times has that led you to explore a product that you might not have thought about if it wasn't for this other person's interest in it?

Early Symbolic Communication

Shortly after babies start to establish joint attention with others, it is not surprising that they usually begin to use an index finger to point to objects or things that they are interested in, while looking from where they are pointing to the person they are trying to communicate with and then back to the object of their interest. This critical skill is the beginning of symbolic communication; that is, the baby uses the symbol (her index finger point) to encode her interest in a specific thing. While neurotypical babies are rapidly developing these skills of preverbal communication (looking, pointing, grunting and thinking about what other people are thinking about), they are simultaneously developing the ability to consider other people's intentions. For example, when a baby watches his mom walk to the refrigerator and open the refrigerator door, he anticipates that he is about to get food delivered. While this may seem relatively unimportant given all a baby has to learn (words, language, crawling, walking, feeding oneself, etc.), the ability to anticipate another's actions is at the core of social intelligence. This skill lays the foundation for much of the ability to "read" people's intentions, whether they are physically or linguistically based, as children grow into more sophisticated communicative patterns. Over the next few years, these babies will continue to develop their understanding of others. It is important for them to learn that people have different thoughts and preferences. As their ability to read people's intentions increase, children also start to get better at predicting what is happening in their environment and, eventually, they can even start to predict what people mean by what they say.

Imitation of Movement

It is also critical for the child to learn to imitate others' movements, first gross-motor and then fine-motor movements, to allow the brain to develop pathways to make learning more efficient. Imitation of others transitions into "parallel play," where children sit near each other and imitate different aspects of play that each engages in (Nadel & Aouka, 2006; Parten, 1932). Parallel play in turn evolves into cooperative play, where children begin to share a single concept and practice sharing, taking turns and working through basic problem solving. The simultaneous development of language allows for play to become more elaborate. More detailed ideas are expressed, and the children share a single imaginary concept that they can better manipulate and explore through actions, the use of toys, and language. By the fourth year of life, most children engage in complex interactions that allow them to anticipate the actions of others, read other people's thoughts and emotions, share an imagination, and initiate language – not only to get their needs met but to share their own thoughts and ideas about the world.

Continued Development of Social Cognition

This magnificent set of skills evolves without much notice. While these skills serve as the basis of social skills that will evolve in nuance and sophistication across much of our lives, they do not appear to be important since they are not "showy." Thus, as parents we celebrate the development of children's walking and talking, but we do not celebrate the more subtle development of social thinking. While neurotypical children's social cognition evolves seamlessly, the skills that get the notice and reward are ones that impress people such as a child who learns to count or read, build complex Lego towers, or play the piano at an unusually early age. Ironically, however, by adulthood, it is the social skills that are crucial for learning to live independently by forging solid relationships, solving personal problems, networking, organizing workload, and performing life's chores.

By 6 years old at the latest, neurotypical children are also learning that one person can try to deceive another by lying, cheating, stealing, and so on (Baron-Cohen, 1995). Children are learning that not all people's intentions are good at all times, thus becoming more sophisticated at trying to "read" people's plans encoded verbally and nonverbally. Therefore, it is critical that we are pervasively socially alert to who is around us, what they are doing, and why they are doing it. This is also part of our social thinking package.

Bronson (2000) explores this topic by suggesting that the development of social competence in the early elementary school years is positively correlated with higher levels of functioning in school and life as the child grows up. Thus, the children who we might think of as "intellectual stars" based on their precocious learning of patterns with regard to academics (science concepts, music, etc.), but who do not develop good play skills, may not be as "successful" as adults.

Unfortunately, from my clinical experience, this is often the pattern of those with Asperger Syndrome: They developed strong language and academic skills in the preschool years but are much weaker in their pre-adolescent and adolescent development of critical thinking, problem solving, and the subtle but significant skills that lead to social sophistication, making it much harder for them to cope in their adulthoods. The good news is that with new treatments available to persons with social cognitive learning challenges, we hope to lessen the impact of their neurological developmental challenges.

Cognitive Behavior Intervention

To help teach strategies related to fostering further social competence, **cognitive behavioral interventions** are showing great promise for higher-functioning students with ASD, those who have a language system and can use **metacognitive strategies** for exploring their own behavior (Simpson, 2005). Metacognition refers to the ability to think about thinking. Cognitive behavioral strategies are defined as strategies that encourage the student to think more deeply about the concept being explored and learn how we respond with our behavior to adapt to the situations we are thinking about. Teaching children to learn through suggestion, explanation, and reasoning rather than coercive controls such as external rewards, punishments, and so on, has been demonstrated to help children develop systems of internal controls (Hoffman, 1970) that can foster generalization of lessons learned across environments.

Generalization of skills learned by those who have ASD needs to be planned for in any treatment program (Klin, Volkmar, & Sparrow, 2000; Simpson, 2005). The lack of generalization of skills taught to students with autism is of concern (Gaylord-Ross, Haring, Breen, & Pitts-Conway, 1984; Ihrig & Wolchik, 1988), as many of our students tend to learn to use a specific skill in the environment where it is taught, but fail to "general-ize" it to other similar contexts or environments.

We are learning that we can do more to help during the critical preschool years and beyond (Wolfberg & Schuler, 2006); however, the exact same treatments are not appropriate for all students on the autistic spec-trum. All students with autism spectrum challenges, while sharing similar diagnostic labels, manifest their social needs and challenges in different ways. Therefore, based on what strengths and weaknesses they possess, treatment must be defined individually for each student. Nevertheless, we can make some global statements about treatment for students with autism spectrum challenges, as suggested below.

Treatment Options

1. Students with intellectual disability and autism who lack the strong development of language (many are minimally verbal or nonverbal) have difficulty learning new skills through a strongly language-based teaching program; thus, they will need to have a highly structured visual program. These visual and structured teaching skills are reviewed in Chapter 5 of this text. Developing a functional language system is also critical, along with determining the reason for the low language production (apraxia versus low theory of mind/low cognition); more may be found about this in Chapter 4.

2. Students with significant to severe verbal cognitive impairments, generally these are the students with verbal IQs below 70 and with autism, most likely do not benefit from a metacognitive teaching approach. Metacognition emerges across the early elementary school and is required for any student to be able to self-regulate or self-manage his behavior without strong extrinsic reward systems.

3. Students who tend to use sentences with immature language structures or who lack sophistication in their communication skills likely have limitations in their ability to predict others' motives, thoughts, and emotions quickly and efficiently. These students can benefit from concrete exploration of how the mind thinks about other people. They will also benefit from a program that develops a strong predictable struc-ture with activities clearly broken down into doable chunks. These students virtually always have great challenges interpreting language meaning (spoken or written) when it is not stated literally. Thus, their treatment program must be intensive in order for them to be able to cope with their classroom curriculum and to learn more sophistication in language meaning and use, while also learning to adapt to the skills required of their age group in the "real world."

4. Students who have strong cognitive and language skills often impress adults with their sophisticated use of language, but fail to impress their peers. These students tend to experience problems using language to relate to their peers while working as part of a group in the classroom or creating interactive play during free time that negotiates their peers' interests along with their own. They often demonstrate limited interpretations of their class work (e.g., social literature, written expression assignments) and balk at the "pointless" work assigned in the classroom curriculum, given their difficulties understanding their teacher's motives. These students benefit from stronger structures imposed in the classroom and on the playground; however, they

also need to learn to explore *how* everyone is thinking. For these students, most of whom are diagnosed with pervasive developmental disabilities-not otherwise specified (PDD-NOS) or Asperger Syndrome, teaching directly about social cognition and using the "social thinking approach" briefly described below is ideal.

What Does "Social" Mean Anyway?

With all this talk about social cognition, which I refer to more informally with teachers and students as "**social thinking**," it is important that we agree on what it means to be "social." When discussing what "effective social skills" means, the immediate response is that it is when "people interact in a reciprocal manner." When encouraged to continue offering ideas, people usually realize that it also means that one considers who is around and what types of behaviors one is to use in different contexts, and they realize that it includes conforming to societal expectations. In fact, the definition of effective social skills can go on and on, as we start to realize that being successfully socially is more often than not entirely removed from social interaction itself.

Sharing Space Effectively

As I write this paragraph, I am sitting on an airplane; one of the unwritten rules or hidden curriculum items (Myles, Trautman, & Schelvan, 2004) on an airplane is that you don't need to talk to the people around you unless they are your traveling companion(s) or the flight attendant. As I look around, I notice that even though relatively few people are interacting, everybody appears to be using appropriate social skills. It is critical to realize that having good social skills is not simply about effectively interacting socially. Instead, it is about how well we follow the hidden social rules in the environment. Most of the time when we are in the presence of others, we are simply adjusting our behavior to share our space effectively with them. To coexist well in an environment, demonstrating social competence and, ultimately, "good social skills" means that we adjust our behavior to help people continue to have "normal" or "good" thoughts about us, even though we may not be interacting with them. On an airplane, this means that we follow the hidden rules of sharing space in this environment. Some of the hidden rules of sitting on an airplane include:

- Sit in your chair; stare out the window or read books; do not look at the person who is sitting next to you unless you are talking to him.

- If sitting in a middle or in a window seat, avoid, as much as possible, getting up and walking in the aisle.

- Do not talk or sing to yourself.

- If the person next to you is busy reading or working on his laptop, avoid talking to him beyond a simple greeting.

- Do not touch the person next to you or lean on her if you fall asleep.

- Keep all your possessions within the confines of your seat or under the seat in front of you, unless the seat next to you is empty. Then you can put your possessions on this seat.

Thus, I define good social skills simply as "sharing space effectively" by considering a multitude of factors, such as the hidden rules or curriculum, who else is in the environmental context (e.g., we may react differently to males versus females, young versus old), and what each person's role is in this context. This is considered another element of the socially algebraic equation.

Social interaction happens every time you share space with another person, period. Consider when you are on an elevator. If you are by yourself and if there is a mirror, you might look at yourself, tuck your shirt in, fix your make-up, and so on, but as soon as another person comes on the elevator, you modify your behavior to just stare towards the elevator door, after perhaps acknowledging the person who got on. If you do this without anyone having a "weird thought" about you, you are successfully social; in this case, you have shared space well.

Sharing space with others requires you to be aware of others and what they are possibly thinking about you. Classrooms are ideal environments to study this, since children are gathered in a room with the intention to learn a specific subject (e.g., math, English, science). However, teachers intuitively realize that they cannot teach the curriculum of any of these topics if their students do not share space well. Thus, the challenge in a classroom is not the curriculum itself, but teaching the curriculum to 20 or 30 different students' brains, each of which has its own idea of how to relate in the classroom. Students whose teachers feel the calmest teaching are those who understand and abide by the hidden curriculum (Myles et al., 2004) or the hidden rules of this environment. All students in a classroom are expected to intuitively think about all the others in the class and then regulate their behavior around the group's need. When a student does this well, we say she is *taking perspective* of the others around her. Both fellow students and teachers notice. They may not say anything, since we often do not ac-knowledge when people are sharing space well, but they will almost immediately say something when a student does not do this well, since he or she disrupts the class by not being able to regulate his or her behaviors around the intentions of the group.

To better understand how we take perspective in a group environment, I developed the Four Steps of Perspective Taking to help all of us (adults and students) understand the process through which we share space effectively. Again, while you think of each of these four steps, imagine you are in an elevator by yourself and consider how your behavior changes as soon as somebody enters this space.

Four Steps of Perspective Taking

Step 1: When you come into my space, I have a little thought about you, and you have a little thought about me.

Step 2: I wonder "Why are you near me?" "What is your purpose for being near me?" "Is it because you are just sharing the space or do you intend to talk to me or do you intend to harm me?" I have to consider all these things in order to keep me safe around people as well as to predict what will happen next.

Step 3: Since we have thoughts about each other, I wonder what you are thinking about me.

Step 4: To keep you thinking about me the way I would like you to think about me, I monitor and possibly modify my behavior.

The "thoughts" we are having about each other are often tiny thoughts that are almost at the unconscious level. However, it is the always-present, very active thought processes of those around us, when we are neurotypical, that allow us to constantly regulate our behavior to make sure that most people have "normal" thoughts about us most of the time.

Many students with Asperger Syndrome have strong challenges related to sharing space. While many have a clear sense of some of the intuitive rules in the environment that they expect everyone else to follow (these students often get upset when others are not behaving appropriately), they often do not realize that this thinking is reciprocal. Thus, they don't understand that people have very strong social expectations of them as well. This is not only important to help us take perspective of how they process the world, it also helps us to learn that one of the first steps in teaching students with social cognitive deficits is to teach them that other people have social expectations for them. These students often don't share space or take perspective well.

In contrast, most students with classical autism are much more inefficient than students with Asperger Syndrome in even realizing Step 1 – that people are having thoughts about them and that they should also be forming thoughts about those around them.

Exploring the ILAUGH Model of Social Cognition: Social and Academic Ramifications

One of the greatest challenges of understanding which systems are weak in people with social cognitive learning disabilities stems from the fact that our social growth develops without significant notice. For example, parents don't celebrate the development of their children's "joint attention" skills; in fact, most have never heard of this skill before. Yet, unknowingly, they celebrate this skill every time they play peek-a-boo (a game that is fun because the child gets excited when she knows the person is thinking about her) with a baby. However, if a child doesn't want to play peek-a-boo, rarely do we run the child to the doctor with worry; we just think that the child is "shy" or has better things to think about than this silly game.

To understand social cognition and how we share space, we have to explore what factors help to create social thinking. How do educators of persons with social learning challenges begin to appreciate what we do unconsciously to help teach it to our students? Many have found that the best way to study what constitutes social thinking is to study people who were born with very limited or weak skills in this area: persons with autism, PDD-NOS, and Asperger Syndrome (Allman, 1994; Goleman, 2006). By carefully observing what children and adults on the autism spectrum don't do, we are able to slowly figure out what neurotypical social thinking actually is.

The ILAUGH Model of Social Cognition was born from studying both the research related to social development and real-life experiences with persons on the autism spectrum. For example, we observed that many of our students, even as they grow towards adulthood, fail to establish good patterns for social initiation or initiating communication when they need help. We also noticed that the majority of our students were weak listeners, failing to use eye contact to sustain active interaction when listening. Furthermore, the majority had difficulty taking the perspective of others. Not coincidentally, these same students had difficulty with interpreting something abstract and making inferences, while also having problems summarizing information and/or conceptualizing main ideas. Yet, in spite of these weaknesses, we also consistently observe that our students have a good sense of humor, which, if used appropriately when teaching, can help them stay calm and focused to work on these more challenging concepts.

The ILAUGH model serves as an acronym to represent six points to help further explain what constitutes social cognitive functioning. These components include (I) initiating communication, (L) listening actively with eyes and brain, (A) abstract and inferential thinking, (U) understanding perspective, (G) getting the big picture, and (H) humor. As you study these six components, you will start to realize that social thinking is not purely for the purpose of socializing, but also for helping us to share space effectively across the school setting as well as to interpret socially abstract concepts, which include personal problem solving, effective communication (asking for help, discussions around a topic in a class as well as more social conversational skills), and interpreting curriculum that requires us to think through socially abstract thoughts (e.g., reading comprehension of literature, social studies, history; written expression; working as part of a group).

As you explore the ILAUGH model, you realize that while all these skills are called on in the preschool years and continue to develop across our life spans, the demand placed on effective use of these concepts increases dramatically from third grade on, as children are expected to develop more socially abstract thinking in order to navigate their way towards developing independence in adulthood. Socially, by third grade, most students have moved into social "cliques." Cliques are groups that are defined by common thoughts and actions. As such, social cliques can lead to children teasing other children who are not perceived as fitting in because of the way they act or look. Thus, in early elementary school, many of our students do a reasonably good job with understanding and applying their skills as they pertain to the curriculum; they may even have some basic friendships. However, as they approach fourth and fifth grade, the demands evolve such that more abstract thinking is required, and our students often start to lose more and more footing, both academically and socially.

Academically, as students move up in the elementary and secondary school curriculum, the curriculum itself moves away from rote-based teaching to more socially abstract teachings. In kindergarten, first, and second grade, we often teach students the skills for learning by teaching them the alphabet, basic math, and penmanship. In third grade, however, we make a transition away from learning basic skills to applying what you have learned by using the basic skills. For example, now that students know how to decode a written passage (many call this reading), we begin to expect them to show that they are interpreting the reading by making more active predictions and interpretations. We also expect students to write longer and longer passages, explaining their personal point of view about the world or the text they read, but when they were younger, they were only required to copy the text to practice writing.

These increasingly abstract curriculum demands spiral higher and higher across middle school, high school, and postsecondary education, while at the same time the social environment becomes increasingly complex as students "leave the cocoon" where they had one teacher as their primary teacher on campus. In secondary schools they are expected to transition seamlessly between teachers with varying personalities, expectations, and applications of the school's rules, while also having to adjust to all the different students who share their space in each of their different classes. When recognizing all these changing demands, it is no surprise that many students with a social cognitive deficit do not outgrow their problems, but actually grow into them. Thus, it is common for students with Asperger Syndrome to appear to get worse as they age, both in their ability to stay with the curriculum demands and in their ability to navigate the social world, which is evolving steadily in nuance and sophistication.

Unfortunately, the age when our students need the most help is often when the least help is available. This is because most public funding goes into early intervention based on the mistaken belief that, with the right interventions, all young students should outgrow their problems prior to adolescence. There are also relatively few private practice service providers in education, mental health, speech and language, or occupational therapy who have the skills to understand the far more complex needs of the adolescent and adult.

We all have to do more to help students with social cognitive deficits face very real and, at times, extreme problems dealing with the challenges and abstract demands of the adult world. If school is to help students learn to develop into adults who can work collaboratively, contribute to society, problem solve, live independently, and develop meaningful relations, we must continue to explore how to infuse the teaching of social thinking and related skills into the curriculum, both within academic lessons and within the social curriculum.

The ILAUGH Model of Social Cognition helps us learn how to explore these challenges in students and offers ideas for how to help teach more socially abstract thinking. The ILAUGH acronym is described in a nutshell below. A more detailed description is offered in Winner (2000).

I = *Initiation of Language* (Krantz & McClannahan, 1993)

Initiation of language is the ability to use one's language and communication skills to seek assistance or information. A student's ability to talk about her own interests may be in sharp contrast to how she communicates when she needs assistance. Many of our students do not ask for help or clarification. While a student may talk a lot in class about his own knowledge and ideas, he is not proficient at using sizeable language skills to help him communicate effectively with others when he doesn't know the answer.

From my experience in working with adults, it is critical that we understand that people don't just outgrow these challenges once they become adults. It is also important to realize that if a student is planning to enter a junior college or a four-year university, these environments depend heavily on the student's ability to fend for himself (e.g., let people know when you have a question or clarification about an assignment). Further, social networking requires initiation of communication both to problem solve and to socialize.

L = *Listening with Eyes and Brain* (Baron-Cohen, 1995)

Most persons with social cognitive deficits have difficulty with **auditory comprehension**. However, listening requires more than just taking in the auditory information. It also requires the listener to integrate information he sees with what he hears to understand the deeper concept of the message, or to make an educated guess about what is being said when you cannot clearly hear it. This can also be referred to as "active listening" or "whole-body listening."

A = *Abstract and Inferential Language/Communication* (Minshew, Goldstein, Muenz, & Payton, 1992)

Communicative comprehension also depends on one's ability to recognize that most language or communication is not intended for literal interpretation. To interpret adequately, one must be flexible enough to make smart guesses about the intended meaning of the message. At times, one must analyze language or communication to seek the intended meaning. Abstract and inferential meaning is often conveyed subtly through verbal and nonverbal means of communication combined with the need to analyze the language in context.

This skill begins to develop in the preschool years and continues across the school years, as the messages we are to interpret, both socially and academically, become more abstract. Interpretation depends in part on our ability to "make a guess"; it also depends on the ability to take the perspective of another.

*U = **Understanding Perspective*** (Baron-Cohen, Jolliffe, Mortimore, & Robertson, 1997)
Understanding perspective refers to the ability to understand emotions, thoughts, beliefs, prior experiences, shared knowledge, motives, intentions, and personalities. Neurotypical babies are learning skills to think about other people's minds from infancy, with a critical phase in development occurring at 9-12 months when most children can look to a person's eyes and monitor where he is looking to figure out what he is thinking about. As mentioned before, this is referred to as "joint attention." As children develop joint attention, they are able to begin to make predictions about what people are going to do next. Most students have acquired a solid foundation in this ability between the ages of 4-6 years old. By 6 years old, most children understand how people can conceal the truth (e.g., lie), and with that comes manipulation to get their needs met.

As students evolve through the elementary and middle school years, great advances are made in the neurotypical child's ability to interpret other people's perspective at a level of increasing nuance and sophistication. This development continues throughout adulthood.

The ability to take perspective is key to participating in any type of group (social or academic) as well as to interpreting information that requires understanding other people's minds, such as reading comprehension, history, social studies, and so on. Weakness in perspective taking is a significant part of the diagnosis related to having social cognitive deficits.

*G = **Gestalt Processing**/Getting the Big Picture* (Fullerton, Stratton, Coyne, & Gray, 1996; McEvoy, Rogers, & Pennington, 1993; Shah & Frith 1993)
Information is conveyed through concepts, not just facts. For example, when having a conversation, participants intuitively determine the underlying concept being discussed. Similarly, when reading from a book, the reader has to follow the overall meaning (concept) rather than just collect a series of details. Conceptual processing is a key component in understanding social and academic information, given that relating to others, whether in person or through the curriculum, requires that we share common ideas.

Difficulty with organizational strategies is born from problems with conceptual processing, since organizational skills require us to "see the big picture" and assess what needs to be done and then plug in the details that will help us develop a process to accomplish our goals. Students with social cognitive deficits often have significant challenges with gaining access to the "main idea." In order to translate information from a level of detail to a main idea – whether relating to others, reading, or organizing information – one must use multiple processes of thinking all at once. This is called an "executive function skill" (e.g., multitasking); our students have tremendous difficulty with executive function skills.

H = Humor and Human Relatedness

Most of the clients I work with have a very good sense of humor, but they feel anxious since they miss many of the subtle cues that help them to understand how to participate successfully with others in a social context. It is important for educators and parents to work compassionately and with humor to help minimize the anxiety our students are experiencing. At the same time, many of our clients use humor inappropriately, so direct lessons about this topic are often mandated.

So Let's Just Teach These Kids Social Skills, Right? Wrong? Well, It Depends ...

Perhaps it is easiest to consider that the different "types" (autism, PDD-NOS, Asperger Syndrome) or the different levels of autism (e.g., classically autistic/low-functioning autism, moderate functioning autism and high-functioning autism) are mostly descriptions of the different levels of social cognition, general intelligence, and associated language levels that the typical student demonstrates by first or second grade. Given these different descriptions, if they are accurate for a child, we can make some general predictions about what a students needs to learn. At the same time, however, it is critical that educators and parents see each of these students as unique people first; people who have different moods, desires, joys, and skills. To teach any student effectively is to recognize what makes that person want to learn and to adapt strategies towards this end.

Below are some general ideas for how to approach developing the key lessons for students at different social cognitive levels on the autism spectrum.

Teaching Children with Classical or Moderate Autism

Given that students who tend towards "classical" and "moderate" autism usually have much more limited intuitive understanding of the social world, they have great difficulty using their metacognitive skills. Thus, we need to focus these students' learning on developing explicit functional communication systems (language-based, augmentative, or combined), along with understanding clear social behavioral expectations for school, home, and community. To teach these lessons, information has to be explicit and be consistently applied and expected. Typically, the students cannot engage in a discussion about why we have to develop specific communication skills; the goal is for them to apply these skills consistently to help them feel calm through transitions, as well as new and old experiences alike. The social teaching is often rote and explicit, using clear visual supports to encourage students to produce the responses more consistently.

The key concepts for any teacher or parent when helping these students acquire new skills include (a) establishing a **functional communication system** that helps them to communicate wants and needs and also to recognize their own emotions and, ultimately, some basic emotions of others; (b) using visual supports; (c) clearly listing expectations using explicit pictures or words; (d) consistently stating and adhering to expectations; (e) using positive praise and reinforcement; and (f) providing functional academic lessons that the student can use across environments (classroom, lunchroom, community, home, and playground).

Teaching Students Who Are Emerging in Their Awareness of Other People's Thoughts and Emotions

Students who function more at the level of "high-functioning autism" are often the students with a near-normal to above-normal academic intelligence, who have developed functional communication systems (language-based or augmentative), but have great difficulty figuring out the perspectives of those around them. They struggle with deciphering implied meaning from their classroom lessons, both within the text and from the group dynamics. They are often perceived as "friendly," but lack a strong friendship with many peers. They are perceived as "quirky," and their peer group immediately identifies that they are lacking in social understanding.

For these students, we can slowly introduce lessons about social thinking, helping them to understand that other people have thoughts and feelings, but we want to do much of the teaching described above as well. These students may require lengthy lessons to help them understand the motive behind a person's actions, which the neurotypical peer deciphers on the spot without any discussion or prompting.

Learning the lessons of social thinking can be a slow process. From our experience, it can take students one to two years to really think about how these lessons apply across environments, start to modify their behavior, and accommodate to the social needs of others. Just as with any type of learning, we all have to learn to think about or process information before we can react to it. Ultimately, these lessons are rewarding, as the student begins to understand people's thoughts and intentions in a way that more completely supports friendships, helps decipher lessons of the academic curriculum, and provides important information about people who may want to take advantage of them.

Doug in the opening vignette of this chapter is a student who functions at this level. When teaching students like Doug, and all students, it is critical that both educators and parents understand that they are working to facilitate new learning to promote increased social understanding and related social skills without having a goal to "fix" or "cure" the students' problems. Those working with these students feel the joy of helping teach concepts to students, but they will also experience the reality that these abstract social lessons move very slowly and will likely not be "mastered." Thus, the concrete, explicit lessons of clear expectations, consistently applied in a positive environment, along with academic lessons that the student can engage in without tremendous stress, are also critical.

Teaching Students Who Are Very Aware That Others Have Thoughts and Emotions, But Get Overwhelmed by the Information: Asperger Syndrome

If social cognition provides us with the ability to learn how to share an imagination and think about people's thoughts, emotions, motives, intentions, prior knowledge, and experiences, it also allows us to learn the social skills that are associated with each of these processes. For example, since a child intuitively learns to look to another person's eyes to see what that person is likely thinking about, the child learns to predict what the person might do next, which lays the groundwork for reading people's intentions. This intuitive ability for neurotypical children to establish joint attention also provides access to the social skill we define as "eye contact."

In contrast, students with Asperger Syndrome and related conditions, all of whom have weak social skill development and are lacking in social understanding, need to be explicitly taught about social understanding of the social world. Given that they typically have fair to strong academic, cognitive, and language skills, they can benefit from metacognitive exploration of social thinking. As we teach these students about how people think in different environments, we can also teach them what type of social skills are expected based on that teaching. As the student gains knowledge about why she would recognize the need for social skills, we can practice the social skills towards greater spontaneous use. Thus, our treatment model, used primarily for this group of students, is called Teaching Social Thinking and Related Skills.

The difference between teaching "social skills" and teaching "social thinking and related skills" can be enormous. Take the teaching of the skill of eye contact, for example. Students who lack consistent eye contact when interacting with others can be taught eye contact using a "social skills" approach. To do this, we simply cue the student to "look at me" or "look at the speaker" in teachable moments and then respond with praise or a token reward, as appropriate.

However, when teaching the child the skill of eye contact through teaching "social thinking and related skills," we assume that the student may not understand the intuitive purpose of eye contact (remember this is a skill that emerges intuitively for most people by 12 months old). Thus, we teach students that we all "think with our eyes," playing games to help them recognize that by looking at people's eyes they can figure out what others may be thinking about. As our lessons progress, we help students learn to be "social detectives" who can observe other people's thoughts even when they are not directly talking to a person, in large part by watching another person's eye gaze direction combined with his or her physical actions. We can cue students to use more eye contact by helping them to think not only about what they see, but about what we see from their eyes. For example, if we see a student who is distractedly looking away at a toy in the room, we can say to her, "I see you are looking at the toy, which means you are probably thinking about the toy, what do I expect you to think about?" The students usually respond by immediately looking at the person addressing them. Through this type of technique, we are helping students to see how social thinking is active throughout the day and not just a skill that is expected because someone said to do it. One of my teenaged students, Erin, when asked to reflect on what she had learned in our program said, "I learned what eyes are for. Prior to coming here, I was always just told to look at things but I never knew why I should."

One of the challenges in teaching social thinking is deciding where to begin, given the incredibly complex array of information that underlies all social cognitive activities. This author has found that a good starting place is by teaching students that interpersonal communication unfolds in a highly predictable manner. To speak to somebody in person means that one must first think about the person, then establish a physical presence, then use one's eyes to think about the person, and, finally, use language to relate to the other person.

This sequence of events, described as the "four steps of communication," teaches that communication is not one thing, but a synergistic, dynamic process. We first need to take students through the individual steps, then we can slowly increase the complexity of the lessons by combining steps and working towards more "social competence." More information about teaching social thinking and related skills may be gained from studying techniques such as those noted below.

***Social Stories*™** (Gray, 1994b). These provide concrete information about social expectations in specific contexts. A **Social Story**™ encourages us to concretely describe the expectations of a setting, the perspective of people who share space in that setting, and then the direct instructions to the student about what he or she can do to create a more positive or expected outcome in that setting. Carol Gray has developed, refined, and elaborated on this technique over the past couple of decades. For more information on her latest work, please go to her web site (www.thegraycenter.org).

Comic Strip Conversations™™. By using comic strip-type characters' thought bubbles and talking bubbles, we can help students to better understand why someone said or did something in a specific context. **Comic Strip Conversations**™™ help students to interpret social thinking. This technique has been discussed by a number of people over the years; for example, Carol Gray (1994a) has written a booklet that helps to understand how to use this tool.

Social Behavior Mapping (Winner, 2007). I created this social behavioral tool to help teachers and students explore how our behaviors, expected or unexpected, impact the feelings of people around us. It also teaches that people's reactions (natural consequences) to our behaviors are often based on how they feel about us in a given environment. We then realize that how we feel about ourselves is in part a byproduct of how people react to us. Therefore, our own production of social behaviors (expected or unexpected) can ultimately impact how we feel about ourselves.

The Incredible 5-Point Scale (Buron & Curtis, 2003). Buron and Curtis developed this tool to help students better understand social and emotional concepts. It is another social behavioral tool. One of the uses of the 5-Point Scale is to teach students to identify their own levels of anxiety. Numbers 1-3 would define their "in control" levels, whereas 4 and 5 would be used to describe out-of-control levels of anxiety. Strategies are then taught to help students self-manage their behaviors while building their self-awareness to assist in this process. The Incredible 5-Point Scale and Social Behavior Mapping can be used well in tandem.

Summary and Conclusions

Social cognition or social thinking underlies the interpretation of all social behavior and tasks that require social interpretation. Some of these tasks include reading comprehension of literature beyond understanding the facts, written expression to help people understand the writer's point of view, and working as part of a group in the classroom. Social cognitive development unfolds intuitively across our lifetimes, while it simultaneously increases in complexity. To better understand the complexity of social thinking, the ILAUGH Model of Social Cognition was described in the hope that it can provide a clearer lens through which to observe our students' strengths and weaknesses.

Our ability to use social skills with nuance and sophistication depends heavily upon our social cognition. Students on the autism spectrum have a clear learning disability in their development of social thinking and related skills. Differences in the functioning levels of persons on the autism spectrum have much to do with the level of social cognition to which each person has access.

As parents and educators, we can continue to facilitate the development of social thinking and related skills for all students; however, the way in which we apply these lessons will vary, depending on the student's initial functional level. The latter part of this chapter has provided a cursory glance at treatment options, ranging from rote teachings to help students establish functional basic communication and social skills, to helping students who are working more at the level of acquiring social nuance and sophistication by teaching them social thinking and related skills.

It is important to remember that while we have solid labels by which to better identify and learn about our students, as a field we are still in our infancy. There is still much that needs to be learned and explored to help our students gain critical information to support them throughout their adult years as productively and meaningfully as possible as members of our society.

Tips for the Classroom

The following strategies for working through issues relate to the ILAUGH Model of Social Cognition.

Sample of Strategies to Facilitate Initiation of Communication

✓ Define strategies the student can use to ask for help that may be more creative than raising his hand (e.g., showing the teacher an index card with "I need help" written on it or having the child establish physical proximity to the teacher's desk).

✓ Practice having the student ask for help; reward attempts at seeking information from others.

✓ Create an expectation. Work with all educators to encourage the child to ask for help, which means that the educators avoid offering unsolicited help.

✓ Work with the student to understand that asking for help or clarification is important for everybody, since no one can possibly know everything.

Sample of Strategies to Facilitate Listening with Eyes and Brain

✓ Work with students to learn the concept that we "listen with our eyes" by playing games that help them see that when we focus our eye gaze on someone, we are often seeking their attention or asking them to answer our questions.

✓ Help students recognize that they understand an auditory message better when they can interpret the related body language and facial expression.

✓ Work with younger students on "whole-body listening;" that is, helping them to understand explicitly that listening is far more than just hearing.

Sample of Strategies to Facilitate Abstracting and Inferencing

✓ Work with students on making "smart" or "educated" guesses. Teach students that a smart guess is when you know a part of the information and then make a small guess based on what you know. In early elementary school, we call this "prediction." We need to explicitly teach students that they are expected to make smart guesses at school and reward them for this more flexible (rather than literal/concrete) thinking.

✓ Help students learn to "code switch" more efficiently, making them recognize that the two codes of language are "literal" and "figurative." Once they have clearly understood that language can also be figurative, provide opportunities to practice switching between these two codes.

✓ Help students to explore that not only do we provide auditory messages, facial expressions, body language, tone of voice, and so on, but all of this is interpreted in a specific context.

✓ Help students learn to expand their abstract meaning of vocabulary words by encouraging them to explore semantic or word maps. These are graphic illustrations of how one word relates to other words and how these other words relate to even more words. This tool helps students develop more associations between words, thus interpreting meanings more easily.

✓ Encourage students to explore social scenario pictures, interpreting the meaning of these faces, gestures, and contexts when the information is "frozen" in the picture and can be studied. This level of interpretation explores meaning without having to involve language, since the pictures require only a visual interpretation.

Sample of Strategies to Facilitate Perspective Taking

✓ Continue the lessons offered in the "listening actively" section to help students learn to think with their eyes; this helps them learn more actively about the concept of joint attention.

✓ Work with children to learn that each person has different thoughts, and that when we are part of a group, our job is to try to think through other people's thoughts as well as our own. Only then can we begin to regulate ourselves around other people's desires or needs.

✓ Explore with students how we can predict what people will do next based on what they are looking at or on their physical movement through the environment. Also continue to explore language-based intentions.

✓ Explore how we think about people whom we just share space with, even if we are not directly interacting with them.

✓ Work with students on problem solving conflicts with others, based on understanding other people's intentions, thoughts, emotions, and so on.

✓ Explore with students their own emotions as well as those of others. Where do they come from? How predictably do people react emotionally to expected and unexpected behaviors produced by others? What do emotions look like on one's face or body? Can we control our emotions? Is it possible not to have emotions?

✓ Explore how we have to consider the motives, emotions, and intended language meaning of characters studied in the curriculum (literature, social studies, etc.).

Sample of Strategies to Facilitate Getting the Big Picture/Gestalt Processing

✓ Explore the difference between an idea or concept and a fact.

✓ Utilize graphic organizers or mind maps to help students explore how facts or details can help gain insight into a larger idea. They can "map" out information from a variety of sources, such as TV shows, movies, and pictures, in addition to reading material.

✓ Explore the presence of thinking about ideas or concepts in conversation, reading comprehension, and assignments where students must express themselves in writing.

✓ Help students explore organizing their ideas for written expression by using mind maps, outlining, stating an idea, and then exploring it with details or facts.

✓ Develop very explicit strategies to help students with organization of homework, their environment, and so on. Homework requires conceptualization at many levels: What is the homework assignment itself? How do I interpret it? How do I plan across time to get the project done? How do I budget time within a month, week, and day to meet multiple goals? How do I consider my assignment from my teacher's point of view? How do I lay out my ideas in a logical, coherent framework, and so on.

Sample of Strategies to Facilitate Learning About Humor

✓ Establish humor in your teaching environment. I use a rubber chicken as a prop to show that making mistakes is nothing more than a "rubber chicken moment." Students can choose to lightly tap themselves on their heads when they make a social error. Use the chicken on yourself as well. Every single person makes social errors on a regular basis. Social communication is so complex that we all mess it up.

✓ Explore relaxation and anxiety control techniques. Buron and Curtis' (2003) Incredible 5-Point Scale, and Social Stories™ (Gray, 1994b) are methods that help demystify stress, feelings, and expectations and promote the use of strategies for anxiety management.

✓ Strategies offered by occupational therapists can also help to calm the sensory system. The Alert Program (Williams & Shellenberger, 1996) helps to teach students to monitor their physical level of stress and attention.

✓ Recognize that students' social and emotional reactions to their often unsuccessful attempts at social interaction can create significant mental health problems that must be addressed as part of a treatment program. Do not treat these issues as if they are separate from the social issues.

✓ Many different types of professionals are developing strategies for anxiety management; keep an eye out for new ideas.

✓ Teach about the effectiveness of humor; not all perceived humor is humorous to others. Humor has a time and a place. People often laugh at jokes or odd behavior that they do not perceive as funny. The proof of successful humor is NOT that people laugh (we all laugh when we are nervous or uncomfortable); it is when people still want to be with us after they laugh. Thus, if people are laughing and leaving the person (meaning they don't want to stick around to socialize) who generated the humor, the humor did not work.

Explore the Four Steps of Communication

The Four Steps of Communication are described below and in further detail, along with activities to help encourage their development, in *Thinking About You Thinking About Me* (Winner, 2001, www.socialthinking.com).

✓ *Step 1: Thinking About Others and What They Are Thinking About Us*

We think about who we are near or who we want to talk to. If we are going to talk to others, we consider what information we may already know about them or what information we can infer based on the situation. For example, if you are in a school, you assume the other students there are fellow students. All forms of effective communication begin with thinking about the person you are about to talk to or share space with.

✓ *Step 2: Establishing a Physical Presence*

When we desire to communicate or "hang out" with someone, in addition to thinking about her, we have to establish a physical presence to show the person that we would like to talk to her or be with her. Our physical presence can include standing close (often about an arm's length away), having our shoulders turned towards the person and keeping our body relaxed to move easily to include other people, or to move away from the person, as needed. Our physical presence communicates intent, which helps to kick off communication. For example, if you are thinking about me and you want to hang out with me but you are standing about 4 feet away and looking around, wishing I would come to you, you have failed to establish a physical presence for me. That is, I would not be able to "read your intention" to communicate with me.

✓ *Step 3: "Thinking with Your Eyes"*

As we are thinking about the person we desire to communicate with and we establish physical presence, our intention to communicate is not explicitly clear until we have established eye contact with the other person. This is the third step, since it is possible to engage in the previous two steps without using eye contact. Communication or sharing space effectively is usually not functional without using our eyes, not only to show someone we are interested in talking but to also watch the physical movements and facial expressions of the other person in order to determine his intentions, feelings, and needs.

✓ *Step 4: Using Language to Relate to Others*

While language is indisputedly central to all language-based communication, it is often not effective or functional if the first three steps are not in place. For example, if a student comes up to you to tell you all the details about the *Titanic* and talks endlessly without considering what you are thinking about and without establishing eye contact, it is not true communication, even though it may be interesting to listen to (if you are an adult). It could better be described as "downloading" information. Language use in communication requires language users to constantly consider the thoughts, feelings, prior knowledge, experiences, intentions, and needs of the communicative partner. Each partner has to work to regulate his language to meet the needs of the listener while also conveying the message that helps to add his own thoughts to the interaction. Effective language-based communication requires students to ask questions about other people, produce supportive responses, and add their own thoughts by connecting their experiences or thoughts to what other people are saying, and so on.

Chapter Highlights

- "Multiple intelligences" refers to individuals having various types of cognition; social cognition is one of those types.

- Social cognition, self-regulation, and problem-solving skills are important for academic and social achievement.

- Early developmental milestones in social cognition include joint attention, early symbolic communication, imitation of movement, and the simultaneous development of language.

- Students with Asperger Syndrome often develop strong academic cognitive skills but lack social cognitive skills.

- Cognitive behavioral interventions seem to offer social skills learning opportunities for students with ASD who can use metacognitive strategies to explore their own behavior.

- Treatment options vary in terms of how and what to teach with regard to social skills/social cognitive development based on the strengths and needs of the individual on the spectrum.

- If social skills are considered in the context of sharing space effectively, the breadth and variety of skills becomes more apparent, including unwritten rules of behavior for different settings and contexts, adjusting behavior based on circumstances, and understanding what others may be thinking.

- Perspective taking involves understanding that others may have thoughts that are different from yours about your behavior and monitoring your behavior based on those thoughts.

- Many students with ASD lack skills in perspective taking.

- The ILAUGH Model of Social Cognition was developed both from research and from studying individuals with ASD.

- The ILAUGH model serves as an acronym to represent six points to help explain what constitutes social cognitive functioning:
  - (I) initiating communication
  - (L) listening actively with eyes and brain
  - (A) abstract and inferential thinking
  - (U) understanding perspective
  - (G) getting the big picture
  - (H) humor and human relatedness

- Social thinking is not only for the purposes of socializing but is also required in interpreting socially abstract concepts such as problem solving, effective communication, and interpreting curriculum that requires socially abstract thoughts.

- From grade 3 onwards, students are required to demonstrate more socially abstract thinking, both in terms of developing successful social interactions and relationships and in terms of successful academic achievement.

- It is not uncommon for students with Asperger Syndrome to appear to "get worse" as they become older. This reflects their difficulties in navigating an increasingly complex social and academic world.

- Different types and levels of ASD require different social skills interventions due to differences in social cognition, general intelligence, and associated language levels.

- When teaching students with "classical" or "moderate" autism, using metacognitive strategies is not effective. These students require a focus on developing functional communication and academic skills with a clear understanding of behavioral expectation. This should be taught through explicit instruction, consistency, and with the use of clear visual supports.

- Students with HFA are often near-normal or above-normal in academic intelligence and have developed functional communication systems, but have great difficulty in perspective taking, causing problems with understanding implied meaning both from text and from group dynamics.

- Students with Asperger Syndrome can benefit from a metacognitive approach to teaching social thinking and related skills.

- The "four steps of communication" for teaching social thinking are:

- Teach that interpersonal communication is predictable:

    ➢ First, think about the person before speaking to them

    ➢ Second, establish a physical presence

    ➢ Third, use your eyes to think about the person

    ➢ Fourth, use language to relate to the other person

- A variety of programs have been developed to teach students with ASD social thinking and related skills. These include:

    ➢ *Social Stories*™, which provide concrete information about social expectations in specific contexts

    ➢ *Comic Strip Conversations*™, which use character thought and speaking bubbles to help students understand why someone said or did something

    ➢ *Social Behavior Mapping*, which shows students how our behaviors impact the feelings of people around us and how others' perceived thoughts about us impact our behavior

    ➢ *The Incredible 5-Point Scale*, which is used to help students understand their level of anxiety and use strategies to manage it.

Chapter Review Questions

1. What is meant by "multiple intelligences"?
2. How do the skills necessary for social cognition develop?
3. What are general intervention/treatment options for assisting students with ASD in developing social skills?
4. Why are there problems in defining "social skills"?
5. What is meant by the term *sharing space effectively*?
6. Describe the four steps in perspective taking identified by the chapter author.
7. What are the challenges students with ASD face related to sharing space?
8. List and describe the components of the ILAUGH acronym.
9. Why does the demand for effective social skills increase significantly starting in grade 3?
10. How are the challenges in social thinking and related skills related to challenges in academics?
11. List key concepts for teaching social thinking and related skills to students demonstrating "classical" or "moderate" autism.
12. Describe key concepts for teaching social thinking and related skills to students demonstrating high-functioning autism.
13. Discuss key concepts for teaching social thinking and related skills to students with Asperger Syndrome.
14. What are Social Stories™, Comic Strip Conversations™, Social Behavior Mapping, and the Incredible 5-Point Scale and how are they used to teach social thinking and related skills concepts?

References

Allman, W. (1994). *The stone age present.* New York: Simon and Schuster.

Baron-Cohen, S. (1995). *Mindblindness: An essay on autism and theory of mind.* Cambridge, MA: The MIT Press.

Baron-Cohen, S., Jolliffe, T., Mortimore, C., & Robertson, M. (1997). Another advanced test of theory of mind: Evidence from very high functioning adults with autism or Asperger Syndrome. *Journal of Child Psychology and Psychiatry, 38*(7), 813-822.

Buron, K. D., & Curtis, M. (2003). *The incredible 5-point scale.* Shawnee Mission, KS: Autism Asperger Publishing Company.

Bronson, M. (2000). *Self-regulation in early childhood.* New York: The Guilford Press.

Fullerton, A., Stratton, J., Coyne, P., & Gray, S. (1996). *Higher functioning adolescents and young adults with autism.* Austin, TX: Pro-Ed.

Gaylord-Ross, R. J., Haring, T. G., Breen, C., & Pitts-Conway, V. (1984). The training and generalization of social interaction skills with autistic youth. *Journal of Applied Behavior Analysis, 17*(2), 229-247.

Gardner, H. (1993). *Multiple intelligences: The theory and practice.* New York: Basic Books.

Goleman, D. (2006). *Social intelligence: The new science of human relationships.* New York: Bantam Books.

Gray, C. (1994a). *Comic Strip Conversations™.* Arlington, TX: Future Horizons.

Gray, C. (1994b). *The original social story book and social stories ... all new stories teaching social skills.* Arlington, TX: Future Horizons.

Hirsh-Pasek, K., Golinkoff, R., & Eyer, D. (2003). *Einstein never used flashcards: How our children really learn – and how they need to play more and memorize less.* Emmaus, PA: Rodale.

Hoffman, M. L. (1970). Conscience, personality and socialization techniques. *Human Development, 13,* 90-126.

Ihrig, K., & Wolchik, S. A. (1988). Peer versus adult models and autistic children's learning: Acquisition, generalization, and maintenance. *Journal of Autism and Developmental Disorders, 18*(1), 67-79.

Jones, E., & Carr, E. G. (2004). Joint attention in children with autism: Theory and intervention. *Focus on Autism and Other Developmental Disabilities, 19*(1), 13-26.

Klin, A., Volkmar, F., & Sparrow, S. (Eds.). (2000). *Asperger Syndrome.* New York: The Guilford Press.

Krantz, P. J., & McClannahan, L. E. (1993). Teaching children with autism to initiate to peers: Effects of a script-fading procedure. *Journal of Applied Behavior Analysis, 26,* 121-132.

Levine, M. (2002). *A mind at a time.* New York: Simon and Schuster.

McEvoy, R., Rogers, S., & Pennington, B. (1993). Executive function and social communication deficits in young autistic children. *Journal of child Psychology and Psychiatry, 34*(4), 563-578.

Minshew, N., Goldstein, G., Muenz, L., & Payton, J. (1992). Neuropsychological functioning in non-mentally retarded autistic individuals. *Journal of Clinical and Experimental Neuropsychology, 14*(5), 749-761.

Myles, B. S., Trautman, M., & Schelvan, R. (2004). *The hidden curriculum: Practical solutions for understanding unstated rules in social situations.* Shawnee Mission, KS: Autism Asperger Publishing Company.

Nadel, J., & Aouka, N. (2006). Imitation: Some cues for intervention approaches in autism spectrum disorders. In T. Charman & W. Stone (Eds.), *Social communication development in autism spectrum disorders* (pp. 219-235). New York: Guilford Press.

Parten, M. B. (1932). Social participation among preschool children. *Journal Of Abnormal And Social Psychology, 27,* 243-269.

Shah, A., & Frith, U. (1993). Why do autistic individuals show superior performance on the block design task? *Journal of Child Psychology and Psychiatry, 34*(8), 1351-1364.

Simpson, R. (2005). *Autism spectrum disorders: Interventions and treatments for children and youth*. Thousand Oaks, CA: Corwin Press.

Williams, M., & Shellenberger, S. (1996). *How does your engine run? A leader's guide to the alert program for self-regulation*. Albuquerque, NM: Therapy Works.

Winner, M. G. (2000). *Inside out: What makes the person with social cognitive deficits tick?* San Jose, CA: Michelle G. Winner, Think Social Publishing, Inc. www.socialthinking.com

Winner, M. G. (2007). *Thinking about you thinking about me* (2nd ed.). San Jose, CA: Michelle G. Winner, Think Social Publishing, Inc. www.socialthinking.com

Wolfberg, P. J., & Schuler, A. L. (2006). Promoting social reciprocity and symbolic representation in children with ASD: Designing quality peer play interventions. In T. Charman & W. Stone (Eds.), *Early social communication in autism spectrum disorders* (pp. 180-218). New York: Guilford Publications.

Learner Objectives

After reading this chapter, the learner should be able to:

- List the skills needed to understand others' emotional and mental states

- Explain how difficulties in understanding mental states underlie the social interaction difficulties that are part of the ASD diagnosis

- Discuss what studies have shown regarding the ability of individuals with ASD to identify emotional states from visual, auditory, contextual, or multimodal examples

- Discuss what is meant by systemizing and how this skill in high-functioning individuals with ASD may be capitalized on when teaching individuals how to recognize emotions

- Explain how individuals with ASD are typically taught to recognize emotion

- State the advantages of using computers in teaching individuals with ASD

- Discuss how generalization difficulties related to ASD limit the effectiveness of intervention programs such as *Mind Reading* and how they are explained by the systemizing model

- Discuss what the program *Mind Reading* is and its value as a teaching tool for emotional recognition in individuals with ASD

Chapter 10

Systemizing Emotions: Using Interactive Multimedia as a Teaching Tool

Ofer Golan • Simon Baron-Cohen

During break time, Henry approached Matthew, who is 10 years old and diagnosed with Asperger Syndrome. Henry tried to make friends with Matthew and asked him about his favorite games. Matthew replied with a monologue about his favorite airplane models and the unique features of each. When Henry sarcastically commented, "That's sooo interesting!" and walked off in the middle of Matthew's monologue, Matthew couldn't understand why. If he found it so interesting, why had Henry walked away? Matthew couldn't interpret the look of boredom on Henry's face.

This description of one incident in the school life of a child with an autism spectrum disorder (ASD) demonstrates how many children and adults with ASD experience social interactions. The ability to use nonverbal information from **facial expressions**, **vocal intonation**, **body language**, and context to understand emotional and other mental states underlies social and communication skills (Baron-Cohen, 1995). Due to difficulties gathering, integrating, and interpreting such information, an individual with ASD can feel like a Martian on the playground (Sainsbury, 2000).

Difficulties with emotion and **mental-state recognition** (Baron-Cohen, 1995; Hobson, 1994), in turn, underlie the social difficulties that are part of the ASD diagnosis. Such difficulties have been found through cognitive, behavioral, and neuroimaging studies, and across different sensory modalities (visual and auditory) (Frith & Hill, 2004).

This chapter explores whether computer-based tailored interventions targeting emotion recognition and mental-state recognition difficulties are useful methods for helping people on the autism spectrum improve their emotion recognition skills.

Recognizing Emotions

Emotion recognition difficulties in ASD may be found in different sources of emotional information. Here we review research findings from each of these channels (**facial, vocal, contextual,** and **multimodal**).

Facial Emotion Recognition in Autism

The majority of studies of emotion recognition have focused on the face and have tested recognition of six emotions (happiness, sadness, fear, anger, surprise, and disgust). These "basic" emotions are expressed and recognized universally (Ekman, 1993; Ekman & Friesen, 1971). Some studies have revealed emotion recognition deficits among individuals with ASD compared to typically developing people matched on age and IQ, or individuals with learning difficulties (e.g., Down syndrome). These studies have used both still photos (Celani, Battacchi, & Arcidiacono, 1999; Deruelle, Rondan, Gepner, & Tardif, 2004; Macdonald et al., 1989) and dynamic videos of facial expressions (Hobson, 1986a, 1986b; Yirmiya, Sigman, Kasari, & Mundy, 1992).

Other studies have found that children and adults with high-functioning autism (HFA) or Asperger Syndrome (AS) have no difficulties in recognizing basic emotions from pictures (Adolphs, 2001; Grossman, Klin, Carter, & Volkmar, 2000) or films (Loveland et al., 1997), and that the deficit only becomes apparent when testing recognition of more "complex" emotions (such as embarrassment, insincerity, intimacy, etc.) (Baron-Cohen, Wheelwright, Hill, Raste, & Plumb, 2001; Baron-Cohen, Wheelwright, & Jolliffe, 1997; Baron-Cohen, Wheelwright, Spong, Scahill, & Lawson, 2001; Golan, Baron-Cohen, & Hill, 2006). Thus, these findings suggest that recognition of basic emotions is relatively preserved among high-functioning individuals with ASD and that they experience greater difficulties recognizing more complex emotional and mental states.

Neuroimaging studies of emotion recognition from faces reveal that people with ASD demonstrate less activation in brain regions central to face processing, such as the fusiform gyrus (Critchley et al., 2000; Pierce, Muller, Ambrose, Allen, & Courchesne, 2001; Schultz et al., 2003). Further, behavioral studies have shown that children and adults with ASD process faces differently than controls: Participants with ASD tend to process faces using a feature-based approach (i.e., attending to parts of the face, such as the mouth, nose, or the eyes), whereas typically developing individuals process faces as a whole (Hobson, Ouston, & Lee, 1988; Schultz et al., 2003; Teunisse & De Gelder, 1994; Young, 1998). Evidence has also been found of reduced activation in brain areas that play a major role in processing emotion, such as the amygdala, when individuals with ASD process social-emotional information (Ashwin, Baron-Cohen, Wheelwright, O'Riordan, & Bullmore, 2007; Baron-Cohen et al., 1999; Critchley et al., 2000).

Vocal Recognition of Emotion in Autism

Emotion recognition from voices has been studied less frequently than emotional recognition from facial recognition. As for facial recognition, the findings are inconclusive (Boucher, Lewis, & Collis, 2000; Loveland, Tunali Kotoski, Chen, & Brelsford, 1995; Loveland et al., 1997). Regarding recognition of complex emotions from voices, several studies have reported a deficit in performance of high-functioning adults with ASD compared to controls (Golan et al., 2006; Golan, Baron-Cohen, Hill, & Rutherford, 2007; Kleinman, Marciano, & Ault, 2001; Rutherford, Baron-Cohen, & Wheelwright, 2002). One study measured the brain activity of participants with ASD and matched typically developing controls while they were listening to stories that require understanding other people's mental states, taken from the **Strange Stories Test** (Happé, 1994) described below. Activation in the medial frontal area of the brain, an area used for judging others' mental states, was less intensive and extensive in the ASD group compared to controls (Nieminen-von Wendt et al., 2003). This finding suggests that the difficulties individuals with ASD show in eliciting emotional and mental information in the auditory channel are also reflected in a different pattern of brain activity.

Contextual Recognition of Emotion in Autism

Studies assessing the ability of individuals with ASD to identify emotions and mental states from context have also pointed to deficits in these areas relative to the general population or to other clinical control groups (Baron-Cohen, Leslie, & Frith, 1986; Fein, Lucci, Braverman, & Waterhouse, 1992). For example, adolescents and adults with ASD had difficulties answering questions on the *Strange Stories Test* (Happé, 1994; Jolliffe & Baron-Cohen, 1999), which assesses the ability to provide context-appropriate mental state explanations for nonliteral statements made by story characters. Stories include the use of irony, lies, white lies, or jokes, all requiring the ability to understand people's mental states.

For example, one story depicted a white lie. A child wanted a rabbit for Christmas. When she got a boring encyclopedia instead, she said that was exactly what she wanted. Participants with ASD were asked to explain why the child responded like that, and whether it was a true reflection of how she felt. To answer such questions assumes an understanding of the child's consideration of other people's feelings, which made her say the opposite of what she felt. Children and adults with ASD have difficulty with such tasks. When using this task in a neuroimaging study, reduced activation of the left medial prefrontal cortex was found in people with ASD compared to matched controls (Happé et al., 1996).

Multimodal Recognition of Emotion in Autism

A few studies have assessed the recognition of complex emotion and mental states from life like social situations (e.g., films). Such situations contain facial, vocal, body language, and contextual information, which the participant needs to process in parallel and integrate into a whole picture in order to understand what is going on. Individuals with ASD show a deficit compared to controls when performing such tasks (Golan, Baron-Cohen, Hill, & Golan, 2006; Heavey, Phillips, Baron-Cohen, & Rutter, 2000; Klin, Jones, Schultz, Volkmar, & Cohen, 2002). For example, a scene from the *Reading the Mind in Films* task (Golan, Baron-Cohen, Hill, & Golan, 2006), labeled *overcome* and shown in Figure 10.2, depicts a young woman complimenting an older woman on the way she educated the children. The older woman thanks her several times calmly, then runs towards her with tears in her eyes saying, "Oh Miss, I'm so glad you're here."

In order to tell how the older woman is feeling, information from her facial expression, tone of voice, and context must be integrated. Individuals with ASD score significantly lower on such tasks than controls. Their difficulties may be related to a failure to pick up the correct emotional cues and/or a failure to integrate them into a whole picture. The latter may stem from a cognitive style named weak central coherence, a major characteristic of ASD, and stress attention to detail instead of integration into a large, holistic, picture. At the neurobiological level, this difficulty may be manifested by under-connectivity between brain regions, which impedes integration of details in frontal brain areas (Belmonte, Allen et al., 2004; Belmonte, Cook et al., 2004; Critchley et al., 2000).

To summarize, although emotion recognition deficits in ASD are lifelong, some high-functioning individuals develop compensatory strategies that allow them to recognize basic emotions. However, when recognition of more complex emotions and mental states is required, either from faces, voices, context, or an integration of these, many individuals with ASD find them hard to interpret.

Systemizing in Autism

In contrast to these difficulties, individuals with ASD show good, and sometimes even superior, skills in systemizing (Baron-Cohen, 2003). "**Systemizing**" is the drive to analyze or build systems in order to understand and predict the behavior of rule-based events. Most individuals with ASD are hyper-attentive to detail and prefer predictable, rule-based environments, features that are intrinsic to systemizing. In addition, they are superior to controls on tasks that involve searching for detail, and analyzing and manipulating systems. This is reflected in improved performance on tasks such as visual scanning tasks (O'Riordan, Plaisted, Driver, & Baron-Cohen, 2001); the *Wechsler Intelligence Scale Block Design* task (Shah & Frith, 1993), which requires the ability to visualize a geometric gestalt as a combination of small constituent shapes; *Folk Physics* tasks (Baron-Cohen, Wheelwright, Spong et al., 2001; Lawson, Baron-Cohen, & Wheelwright, 2004), which include physics and mechanics questions that can be answered based on a lay person's everyday experience; and the *Embedded Figures Test* (Jolliffe & Baron-Cohen, 1997), which requires picking out a simple geometric shape from a complex pattern in which it is embedded. Individuals with ASD also report they are apt to pay more attention to and express more interest in systematic phenomena compared to the general population (Baron-Cohen, Richler, Bisarya, Gurunathan, & Wheelwright, 2003).

If high-functioning individuals with ASD possess good systemizing skills, it is possible that they will be able to use them to compensate for some of their empathizing difficulties, in this case, their difficulties recognizing emotions. This might be difficult, however, because the socio-emotional world is a context-related open system (Lawson, 2003) that is typically unpredictable and difficult to conceptualize using strict rules. Nevertheless, if provided with a *system* of emotions, it is plausible that their systemizing skills could be harnessed to help individuals with ASD learn to recognize emotions.

Next, we review past attempts to teach emotion recognition to individuals with ASD and describe a new systematic guide to emotions and its evaluation with adults with ASD.

Teaching Emotion Recognition

Past attempts to teach emotion recognition to adults and children with ASD have either focused on the basic emotions (Hadwin, Baron-Cohen, Howlin, & Hill, 1996; Howlin, Baron-Cohen, & Hadwin, 1999) or have been part of social skills training courses, usually run in groups (Barry et al., 2003; Howlin & Yates, 1999; Rydin, Drake, & Bratt, 1999). These training programs typically do not focus specifically on systematically teaching emotion recognition, but address other issues, such as conversation, reducing socially inappropriate behavior, personal hygiene, and so on. In such groups, it is difficult to target the individual's specific pace of learning. Finally, such groups are socially demanding and might, therefore, deter more socially anxious participants.

Using Computers to Teach Emotion Recognition

Other attempts to teach individuals with ASD to recognize emotions and mental states have used computer-based training (Bernard Opitz, Sriram, & Nakhoda Sapuan, 2001; Bolte et al., 2002; Hetzroni & Tannous, 2004; Rajendran & Mitchell, 2000; Silver & Oakes, 2001; Swettenham, 1996). The use of computer software has several advantages for individuals with ASD, including the following:

1. Individuals with ASD favor the computerized environment, since it is predictable, consistent, and free from social demands, which they often find stressful.

2. Users can work at their own pace and level of understanding.

3. Lessons can be repeated over and over again, until mastery is achieved.

4. Interest and motivation can be maintained through different and individually selected computerized rewards (Bishop, 2003; Moore, McGrath, & Thorpe, 2000; Parsons & Mitchell, 2002).

Previous studies have found that the use of computers can help individuals with ASD understand mental states (such as beliefs) and learn that mental states can differ from reality (such as in the case of false beliefs, when one believes something to be true, though in reality it is not) (Swettenham, 1996). Computer-based training programs have also taught individuals with ASD to recognize basic emotions from cartoons and still photographs (Bolte et al., 2002; Silver & Oakes, 2001) and to solve problems in illustrated social situations (Bernard Opitz et al., 2001). However, participants have found it difficult to generalize their knowledge from learned material to related tasks.

The computer-based interventions above used drawings or photographs for training rather than more life-like stimuli. This might have made generalization harder than if more ecologically valid or real-life stimuli had been used. In addition, the programs teaching emotion recognition have focused on basic emotions, and only on facial expressions.

No program reported to date has systematically trained complex emotion recognition in both visual and auditory channels with life-like faces and voices. In our research, summarized next, we have designed and evaluated such a program. The underlying question was: Can the good systemizing skills that individuals with ASD possess be used to teach them to improve their recognition of complex emotions?

Mind Reading – A Systematic Guide to Emotions

In the remainder of this chapter, we will focus on *Mind Reading* (Baron-Cohen, Golan, Wheelwright, & Hill, 2004), an interactive guide to emotions and mental states, and its value as a tailored teaching tool for emotion recognition for learners on the autism spectrum.

Mind Reading is based on a taxonomic system of 412 emotions and mental states, grouped into 24 emotion groups and 6 developmental levels (from age 4 to adulthood). The emotions and mental states are organized systematically, according to the emotion groups and developmental levels. Each emotion group is introduced and demonstrated by a short video clip giving some clues for later analysis of the emotions presented. Each emotion is defined and demonstrated by six silent films of faces, six voice recordings, and six written examples of situations that illustrate a given emotion. The resulting library of emotional "assets" (video clips, audio clips, or brief stories) comprise 412 x 18 = 7,416 units of emotion information to learn to recognize or understand, yielding a rich and systematically organized set of educational material. To facilitate generalization, the face videos and voice recordings comprise actors of both genders and of various ages and ethnicities.

Faces and voices are presented separately for each emotion (i.e., silent face films and faceless voice recordings) to encourage analysis of the emotion in each modality and to facilitate learning by avoiding overburdening the user perceptually as well as cognitively. All face video clips and voice recordings have been validated by a panel of 10 independent judges, and were included in *Mind Reading* if at least 8 judges agreed the emotional label given described the face/voice.

The Architecture of the Mind Reading *Software*

This emotions database is accessed using three applications.

The emotion library allows users to browse freely through the different emotions and emotion groups, play the faces, voices, and scenarios giving examples of the emotions, read stories, add their own notes, and compare different emotional expressions in the face and the voice using a scrapbook.

The learning center uses lessons, quizzes, and several reward collections to teach about emotions in a more structured and directive way. In addition to teaching about the 24 emotion groups, it also includes lessons and quizzes about the most common emotions, as well as a "build your own lesson/quiz" option. The various reward collections were chosen for their potential appeal to users with ASD, and were arranged systematically (e.g., pictures and information about space elements, clips of birds arranged by families, different types of trains to collect). A reward is given when a quiz question is answered correctly.

The game zone, comprised of five educational games, allows users to enjoy a game while studying about emotions. Games include a "pairs" game with emotional faces, matching thought and feeling bubbles to characters in a series of real-life situations, recognizing an emotion by gradually revealing different parts of a face, and others.

The software was created for use by children and adults of various levels of functioning. Vocal and animated helpers give instructions on every screen. Figure 10.1 shows screen shots from the software (www.jkp.com/mindreading).

A Study of Adults with ASD Using Mind Reading *over 10-15 Weeks*

We tested for any improvement in adults with AS and HFA in emotion recognition (ER) skills following independent use of the software, and the extent to which these users can generalize their acquired knowledge. The intervention took place over a period of 10-15 weeks to ensure a meaningful period for training, recognizing that a longer duration might lead to some participations dropping out.

Participants were tested before and after the intervention. A no-computer-intervention control group of adults with AS/HFA was matched to the intervention group. The AS/HFA control group was also tested before and

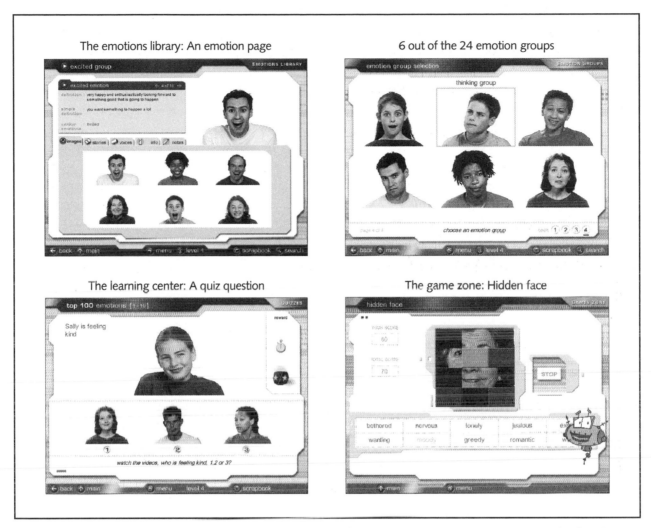

Figure 10.1. Screenshots from *Mind Reading*, the interactive guide to emotions. (Baron-Cohen, Golan, Wheelwright, & Hill, 2004). Used with permission.

after a similar period of time, but received no intervention. The no-intervention AS/HFA group was included to assess whether any improvement was related to the intervention or merely due to taking the tasks twice or to the passage of time. Finally, a third, typical, control group from the general population was matched to the intervention groups. This group was only tested once to obtain baseline measures.

In order to test whether software users could generalize their acquired knowledge to other situations, we compared the groups' performance at three different levels of generalization, using stimuli in two perceptual modalities (visual and auditory):

Close generalization. This level tested ER from stimuli that were included in *Mind Reading,* so that participants may have been exposed to them while using the software. This was tested by playing face video clips and voice recordings that were included in *Mind Reading* on a different computer program, with more answers to choose from and with no feedback or support, as provided in *Mind Reading.* The battery used to test facial and vocal

ER in this level, *The Cambridge Mindreading (CAM) Face-Voice Battery* (Golan, Baron-Cohen, & Hill, 2006), includes a face task and a voice task, with 50 items in each, to test recognition of 20 different complex emotions and mental states (e.g., intimate, insincere, nervous), all taken from *Mind Reading*.

In both tasks, four adjectives are presented after each stimulus has been played, and participants are asked which adjective best describes how the person feels. An example of the face task, showing one frame from one of the clips is shown in Figure 10. 2. The battery provides an overall facial and an overall vocal ER score, as well as individual scores for each of the 20 emotions assessed (pass/fail) and an overall number of the emotions correctly recognized. Individuals with ASD have been found to score significantly lower than controls on all three scores of the battery (Golan, Baron-Cohen, & Hill, 2006).

Feature-based distant generalization. This level tested the ability to transfer ER skills separately in faces and voices, using faces and voices that were not included in *Mind Reading*. This was tested in the visual channel using the *Reading the Mind in the Eyes* task (Revised, Adult version; Baron-Cohen et al., 2001).

The task includes 36 items. Participants are presented with a photograph of the eyes region of the face and must choose one of four adjectives or phrases to describe the mental state of the person pictured (see Figure 10.2 for an example). In the auditory channel, we used the *Reading the Mind in the Voice* task (Revised; Golan, Baron-Cohen et al., 2007), which includes 25 speech segments taken from BBC drama series. After each segment has been played, participants are asked to choose out of four adjectives the one that best describes how the speaker is feeling. Adult participants with ASD scored significantly lower than matched controls on both tasks.

Holistic distant generalization. This level comprised multimodal socio-emotional stimuli, including faces, voices, body language, and context. It used the *Reading the Mind in Films* task (Golan et al., 2006), which consisted of 22 short social scenes taken from feature films. Participants were presented with four adjectives and asked to choose the one that best describes the way a target character feels at the end of the scene. Figure 10.2 presents a screenshot from one of the task items. Participants with ASD performed significantly worse on this task compared to matched controls. This level was only tested at Time 2. Participants with AS/HFA were randomly allocated into the first two groups below.

Software home users. Nineteen participants (14 males and 5 females) were asked to use the software (provided free of charge) at home by themselves for 2 hours a week over a period of 10 weeks, for a total of 20 hours. Participants were included in the study if they completed a minimum of 10 hours of work with the software. If they did not complete this minimum, they were given an extension of up to 4 weeks to do more work with the software.

AS/HFA control group. Twenty-two participants (17 males and 5 females) attended the assessment meetings with a 10- to 15-week period between them, during which they did not take part in any intervention related to emotion recognition.

Typical control group. Twenty-eight participants were recruited for a control group from a local employment agency.

The three groups were matched on age, Verbal and Performance IQ, handedness, and gender. They spanned an equivalent range of employment and educational levels.

1. Close generalization: The CAM face task (Golan, Baron-Cohen & Hill, 2006).

2. Feature-based distant generalization: *Reading the Mind in the Eyes Test* (Baron-Cohen, Wheelwright, Hill, Raste, & Plumb, 2001).

3. Holistic distant generalization: *Reading the Mind In Films* task (Golan, Baron-Cohen, Hill, & Golan, 2006). Screenshot taken from *The Turn of the Screw* (1999). Courtesy of Granada International.

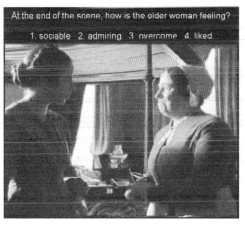

Figure 10.2. Examples of visual tasks from the three generalization levels. Used with permission.

Procedure of the Study

Participants in the AS/HFA control group were asked to come in for two assessments, separated by 10 to 15 weeks. *Mind Reading* was introduced to the participants of the intervention group in detail. This included a presentation of the emotion taxonomy and the different areas and a demonstration of a systematic analysis of an emotion, comparing different faces and voices to identify the unique facial/intonation features of the emotion. Participants were asked to use the emotions library and learning center as they wished, but not to use the game zone for more than a third of the usage time (to ensure they focused on systematic analysis of faces and voices).

Participants were encouraged to analyze the facial and vocal stimuli systematically. For example, systematically comparing all the facial expressions of *insincere* included in *Mind Reading* reveals a conflict between the smiling mouth and the avoiding eyes. Taken together, *insincere* could be distinguished from *interested* or *intimate*, which also involve smiles, as these genuine smiles involve the mouth as well as the eyes. Similarly, a systematic analysis of *insincere* in the voice showed a conflict between the content of the verbalization (e.g., "that is very interesting") and the intonation with which it is said, which breaks the sentence to suggest insincerity (e.g., "yes … that is very … interesting"). If participants studied the facial and vocal expressions systematically in the various emotions covered in *Mind Reading*, it was expected that they would not only be able to recognize these emotions when played to them using examples from the software (Example #1 in Figure 10.2), but also to use this knowledge to recognize visual and auditory stimuli not included in the software, like the *Reading the Mind in the Voice* task or the *Reading the Mind in the Eyes* task (Example #2 in Figure 10.2). In addition, if participants were able to integrate their knowledge of visual and auditory expression of emotion, it was expected they would be able to recognize emotions from holistic stimuli, such as the scenes presented in *Reading the Mind in Films* (Example #3 in Figure 10.2).

Does the Intervention Help?

After 10-20 hours of using the software over a period of 10-15 weeks, users significantly improved in their ability to recognize complex emotions and mental states from both faces and voices compared to their performance before the intervention, relative to the control group. This finding is encouraging, considering the short usage time, the large number of emotions included in the software, and the fact that participants were not asked to study these particular emotions. Since no differences were found between the two ASD groups at Time 1, any difference at Time 2 can be attributed to the intervention.

The intervention group also improved significantly on close generalization measures, including faces, voices, and the emotions with which individuals with AS/HFA had particular difficulties (Golan et al., 2006). In the case of *insincere*, described above, participants who used *Mind Reading* improved on their ability to recognize this emotion following systematic use of the software. Improvement in the ability to recognize deception, as well as other mental states such as *intimate* or *grave*, might have a positive effect on their confidence, willingness, and functioning in interpersonal situations. This, together with participants' reports of greater attention to faces and emotions and improved eye contact, suggests that analysis of emotions using *Mind Reading* allows people with ASD to improve emotion recognition skills from both faces and voices.

Generalization Issues

Improvement following the use of the software was limited to different presentations and variations on taught stimuli (i.e., to faces and voices taken from *Mind Reading*). Participants found it difficult to generalize their knowledge to other tasks of emotion recognition from voices and eyes, and did not perform better than controls on a task involving integration of facial, vocal, and contextual cues. Similar findings of poor generalization have been noted in studies teaching understanding of mental states, emotion recognition, and social skills to individuals with ASD (Bolte et al., 2002; Hadwin et al., 1996; Swettenham, 1996, 2000). However, software usage time was positively correlated with film task scores, suggesting that using the software for a longer period assists with generalization to holistic, life-like situations. Indeed, a followup a year later has shown that participants who continued to use *Mind Reading* reported having improved friendship skills.

Generalization difficulties have been reported to be characteristic of autism spectrum conditions (Rimland, 1965). A focus on small details at the expense of being able to see the larger picture (Frith, 1989), abstraction difficulties, and insistence on sameness may make generalization a challenge for individuals with ASD. Various models have been proposed to try to explain these generalization difficulties, including adherence to rule-based categorization while failing to use prototype-based categorizations (Klinger & Dawson, 1995); an inability to recognize the similarities between stimuli (Plaisted, 2001); or the inability to deal with open systems of the social world, instead focusing on closed-system, rule-based atomic physical phenomena (Klin, Jones, Schultz, & Volkmar, 2003; Lawson, 2003).

Weak Generalization or Strong Systemizing?

Our own view is that reduced generalization is not so much a reflection of a deficit as a reflection of the strong drive to systemize in people with ASD (Baron-Cohen, 2000). Good systemizing requires that one pays attention to the small details between variables in case they are important for understanding how the system works. As such, a good systemizer resists grouping variables together until there is reliable evidence to suggest that there are no functional differences between the variables. To group them together risks losing key information.

According to this view, the ability to generalize by individuals without ASD is a sign of reduced systemizing, whereas reduced ability to generalize by individuals with ASD is a sign of their talent at systemizing, as revealed on analytic tests (such as the *Embedded Figures Test* or the *Folk Physics* tasks described above). Because the socio-emotional world is flexible, context-dependent, and often unpredictable, it is difficult (if not impossible) to systemize. Thus, attempting to systematically teach about emotions to individuals with ASD may lead to rigid application of the system, and eventually to limited generalization.

Where Do We Go from Here?

Mind Reading was used as the intervention for adults with ASD to exploit their systemizing skills. As a systematic guide to emotions, *Mind Reading* trained recognition of faces and voices separately. Results showed that this was successful. Paradoxically, this way of teaching encouraged an atomized rather than an integrative learning style. Whereas it led to improved recognition of emotions and mental states from faces and voices separately, it did not promote integration of these features into a holistic picture, which limited generalization to holistic material. Hence, we recommend that *Mind Reading* be viewed as a first step in a training program.

In this first step, *Mind Reading* could be used (on an individual basis or in a classroom setting) to provide the user with examples. The next steps would deal with the systematic introduction of context and integration of different socio-emotional cues into one (flexible) picture. To ease generalization, each step must to be explicitly connected to previous ones, and the main features must be pointed out (Ozonoff, 1995). After acquiring sufficient understanding of how emotions look and sound, using *Mind Reading*, individuals with ASD should practice integrating these and adapting them according to contextual cues. This mediation between computer-based systematic training and real-life flexibility could be led by teachers in school settings, and/or by parents at home. Suggestions for such activities appear under Teacher Tips at the end of the chapter.

The use of computer-based tasks to evaluate learning and generalization in this study has its limitations. Though such tasks allow for controlled and structured assessment of emotion recognition skills, testing different modalities separately, they are quite different from real-life experience. Hence, the relevance of improvement among the software users in this study to real-life functioning should be considered with care. Indeed, some participants commented that they found recognizing emotions and mental states on the computer easier than doing this in real social situations, which requires cross-modal information processing and an immediate reaction in real time. This suggests that evaluation of emotion recognition abilities via computer tasks should be backed up by observations in real-life situations, as well as feedback from parents, teachers, and the individuals with ASD themselves.

Significant correlations were found between usage time and improvement scores on some tasks. Of particular interest were the positive correlation with the holistic film task and the results of our one-year followup, suggesting that the use of the software might be associated with distant generalization measures.

Research studies indicate that individuals with ASD have both developmental delays and long-lasting difficulties in mental state recognition (Baron-Cohen, 1995; Frith & Hill, 2004). Our results suggest that learning aspects of empathizing skills (such as the emotion recognition component) is possible by people with ASD even into adulthood and that improvement in such areas is achieved when the intervention harnesses their systemizing strengths. Even greater improvement may be achieved if intervention was started at a developmentally earlier point. We are currently investigating the effectiveness of this method with children with ASD (Golan & Baron-Cohen, submitted).

Summary and Conclusions

The results of this study, as well as the participants' reports of looking more at faces and engaging in more eye contact following the use of *Mind Reading,* call for neuroimaging studies to examine possible changes in the functioning of brain areas (in the amygdala, fusiform gyrus, or prefrontal cortex), and for gaze-tracking studies to examine subtle behavioral changes following the systematic study of emotions using *Mind Reading.* Such studies would help determine whether the observed cognitive changes reported here are arising from changes in those neural regions that are typically recruited by the non-autistic brain, or if they are due to compensatory strategies by other neural regions.

We conclude that the present experiment indicates that complex emotion-recognition can be improved over a relatively brief training period (10-15 weeks), when systematic methods such as *Mind Reading* are employed. Additional methods (possibly over a longer time period) are required to improve generalization.

Tips for the Classroom

✓ **Choose key emotions to work on that match the children's developmental stage**. With 412 different emotions and mental states included in *Mind Reading,* it is easy to lose track of the emotions and mental states that are appropriate for your students. The selected emotions should not be too challenging, but also not too easy for a given child. Use the level system of *Mind Reading* to determine which emotions are appropriate for the age group you work with.

✓ **Discuss emotion groups, emotion causes and consequences, and emotional valence and intensity with the children**. Ask questions such as the following: Which emotions belong to the same group? What are their common features? What makes some more basic than others? How does context distinguish different emotions in the same group (e.g., feeling *lonely* is feeling *sad* in the context of having no one to be with)? How do changes in the situation or in what other people say or do define the emotion we feel? Ask the children to provide their own examples of causes. Discuss consequences (e.g., what happens when I show my anger?). Sort emotions as either positive or negative. Discuss whether some of them could be positive at times and negative at other times (e.g., surprise). Could some emotions be positive to one person but negative to another? Sort different related emotions on a continuum from the most extreme to the most subtle (use the Famous Face game from *Mind Reading* as an example). Ask the student to come up with different emotion words to be placed on the continuum, with each child expressing a more extreme version of the emotions on her/his face (e.g., annoyed, angry, wild). Discuss how we can use different emotion words to describe different intensities of the same feeling.

✓ **Analyze facial expressions.** Using *Mind Reading*'s emotion library or a scrapbook, have students compare different examples of the same emotion. What are the common features in the face that tell us that different people express the same emotion? What do all (or most) people in the example do with their eyes/with the mouth? Do they move their heads or shoulders in a certain way? Can students mimic these faces? Can they guess the emotion from faces in *Mind Reading*'s quizzes or from the face of another child? Use the Hidden Face game from *Mind Reading* to emphasize the importance of certain areas in the face for emotion recognition. Can we tell how people are feeling by looking at their chin? their ears? or their eyes? Print and use worksheets available on the *Mind Reading* CD to provide the children with more opportunities to practice emotion recognition from faces.

✓ **Analyze vocal expressions of emotion with the children.** Emphasize the importance of intonation. Ask the children to listen to the "music" of speech. How is this music common to different vocal expressions of the same emotion? Use an oscilloscope to visualize sound waves to the children. Record some "sentences" in gibberish and ask the children to guess the emotion from them. Ask the children to make neutral sentences express certain emotions purely by using intonation.

✓ **Present body language to the children.** Present body language separately, as it is not covered in *Mind Reading*. A good place to do that is in the gym or outside, where different walking styles, postures, and hand gestures may be practiced and recognized.

✓ **Combine facial, vocal, and contextual expressions of emotion.** Discuss how these modalities complement each other. Use examples from electronic media to observe the different factors and how they contribute to our understanding of what a person is feeling. Ask the children to try to express contradicting emotions in their face and voice, and then to use the correct combination. Can other children tell how they are feeling in the first case/in the second?

✓ **Introduce display rules, insincerity, and mixed emotions.** After practicing emotion recognition in *Mind Reading*, discuss with the children how in real life we do not always show our emotions (e.g., why wouldn't someone show he is disgusted with the smell of his friend's new perfume?). Some emotions are not expected to be shown in certain contexts (e.g., happiness at a funeral). Ask the children to come up with examples of emotions that are hidden. Can we sometimes tell the hidden emotion by checking the different sources of information (face, voice, context)? For example, is someone who smiles happy, even though he just stepped into a puddle? Discuss how hiding one's emotions or presenting other emotions may be used to tease, lie, or conceal someone's real meaning. Analyze situations. Discuss the concept of mixed emotions. Demonstrate to students how different emotions may be felt at the same time, and how sometimes they create new emotions (e.g., *disappointment* mixes surprise over something that did not match one's expectation with sadness that it did not).

✓ **Teach degrees of emotion through the use of a system.** Use a scale, flow chart, or meter to introduce degrees of emotion to help students identify levels of emotion in themselves and others. Charting how various facial features, vocal tones, and body gestures might indicate the different levels of emotion may be added to increase understanding.

Chapter Highlights

- Individuals with ASD demonstrate difficulties gathering, integrating and interpreting the nonverbal information required to understand the emotional and mental states of others.

- The chapter offers a review of research studies regarding the abilities of individuals with ASD in terms of emotional recognition.

- Studies involving facial recognition of emotion indicate that, while some individuals with ASD who are high functioning are able to recognize basic emotions (happiness, sadness, fear, anger, surprise, and disgust), they still struggle with recognition of more complex emotions.

- Neuroimaging (fMRI) and behavioral studies of facial emotional recognition demonstrate that individuals with ASD process faces differently from neurotypicals, with parts of the brain showing less activation.

- While studied less frequently, emotional recognition from voices also demonstrates less brain activation occurring in individuals with ASD. As with visual recognition, individuals with ASD demonstrate difficulties in vocal recognition of emotion.

- Similar results of reduced brain activation and difficulties with emotional recognition have been shown in studies requiring individuals to use context and those requiring use of multimodalities (such as in real-life situations).

- Individuals with ASD have been shown to be attentive to detail and to prefer a predictable, rule-based environment.

- Given the good skills in systemizing shown by individuals with ASD, the chapter authors hypothesize that high-functioning individuals may be taught a system for understanding emotions/developing better emotional recognition across modalities and complexity.

- In reviewing attempts to teach emotional recognition to individuals with ASD, the authors point out that instruction has focused primarily on social skills development rather than emotional recognition and has taken place in group settings, which make it difficult to individualize pace.

- Computer-based training has also been used to teach emotional recognition with successful outcomes, but generalization of the learning has not occurred. Additionally, the computer-based programs focused on only basic emotions and on facial expressions.

- The benefits of using computers include less potential stress for the individual with ASD, working at one's own pace, the ability to repeat lessons, and the potential for increased interest and motivation.

- The majority of the chapter focuses on the use of a computerized program to teach emotional recognition, *Mind Reading*. This program is an interactive guide to emotions and mental states and was designed to systematically train basic and complex emotional recognition in both visual and auditory channels with life-like faces and voices.

- A study using the *Mind Reading* program over a period of 10-15 weeks with adults with Asperger Syndrome/high-functioning autism (HFA) was described. In the study, individuals used the software independently and were assessed both in terms of their improvement in emotional recognition and in their ability to generalize the newly acquired skills.

- Results from the study indicated the intervention was successful, with significant improvement in the ability to recognize complex emotions and emotional states from both faces and voices. However, generalization remained a problem.

- The chapter authors hypothesize that, by using a program that focused on the strong systemizing skills of individuals with high-functioning ASD, they were able to teach a system that improved emotional recognition but also created a limiting factor in that, by being so focused on the system or rules, individuals with ASD were unable to generalize to situations that lacked the rule-governed nature of the training tasks.

Chapter Review Questions

1. What abilities are needed in order to understand others' emotional states?

2. What did the authors mean by "an individual with ASD can feel like a Martian on the playground"?

3. What have studies shown regarding the ability of individuals with ASD to recognize emotion from visual, auditory, contextual, and multimodal examples? Why do such deficits appear to occur?

4. What is meant by the term "systemizing" in reference to individuals with ASD, and how might it be used to help teach individuals with ASD to understand emotions?

5. What are the advantages of using computers to teach individuals with ASD?

6. What is the *Mind Reading* program and how is it useful for teaching emotional recognition for individuals with ASD?

References

Adolphs, R. (2001). The neurobiology of social cognition. *Current Opinions in Neurobiology, 11*(2), 231-239.

Ashwin, C., Baron-Cohen, S., Wheelwright, S., O'Riordan, M., & Bullmore, E. T. (2007). Differential activation of the amygdala and the social brain during fearful face-processing in Asperger Syndrome. *Neuropsychologia, 45*(1), 2-14.

Baron-Cohen, S. (1995). *Mindblindness: An essay on autism and theory of mind.* Boston: MIT Press/Bradford Books.

Baron-Cohen, S. (2000). Is Asperger Syndrome/high-functioning autism necessarily a disability? *Development and Psychopathology, 12*(3), 489-500.

Baron-Cohen, S. (2003). *The essential difference: Men, women and the extreme male brain.* London: Penguin.

Baron-Cohen, S., Golan, O., Wheelwright, S., & Hill, J. J. (2004). *Mind reading: The interactive guide to emotions.* London: Jessica Kingsley Publishing.

Baron-Cohen, S., Leslie, A. M., & Frith, U. (1986). Mechanical, behavioural and intentional understanding of picture stories in autistic children. *British Journal of Developmental Psychology, 4*(2), 113-125.

Baron-Cohen, S., Richler, J., Bisarya, D., Gurunathan, N., & Wheelwright, S. (2003). The Systemising Quotient (SQ): An investigation of adults with Asperger Syndrome or high functioning autism and normal sex differences. *Philosophical Transactions of the Royal Society, Series B, Special Issue on Autism: Mind and Brain, 358,* 361-374.

Baron-Cohen, S., Ring, H. A., Wheelwright, S., Bullmore, E. T., Brammer, M. J., Simmons, A., & Williams, S. C. (1999). Social intelligence in the normal and autistic brain: An fMRI study. *European Journal of Neuroscience, 11,* 1891-1898.

Baron-Cohen, S., Wheelwright, S., Hill, J. J., Raste, Y., & Plumb, I. (2001). The Reading the Mind in the Eyes Test revised version: A study with normal adults, and adults with Asperger syndrome or high-functioning autism. *Journal of Child Psychology and Psychiatry, 42,* 241-251.

Baron-Cohen, S., Wheelwright, S., & Jolliffe, T. (1997). Is there a language of the eyes? Evidence from normal adults, and adults with autism or Asperger syndrome. *Visual Cognition, 4,* 311-331.

Baron-Cohen, S., Wheelwright, S., Spong, A., Scahill, V., & Lawson, J. (2001). Are intuitive physics and intuitive psychology independent? A test with children with Asperger Syndrome. *Journal of Developmental and Learning Disorders, 5,* 47-78.

Barry, T. D., Klinger, L. G., Lee, J. M., Palardy, N., Gilmore, T., & Bodin, S. D. (2003). Examining the effectiveness of an outpatient clinic-based social skills group for high-functioning children with autism. *Journal of Autism and Developmental Disorders, 33,* 685-701.

Belmonte, M. K., Allen, G., Beckel-Mitchener, A., Boulanger, L. M., Carper, R. A., & Webb, S. J. (2004). Autism and abnormal development of brain connectivity. *Journal of Neuroscience, 24,* 9228-9231.

Belmonte, M. K., Cook, E. H., Anderson, G. M., Rubenstein, J. L., Greenough, W. T., Beckel-Mitchener, A., Courchesne, E., Boulanger, L. M., Powell, S. B., Levitt, P. R., Perry, E. K., Jiang, Y. H., DeLorey, T. M., & Tierney, E. (2004). Autism as a disorder of neural information processing: directions for research and targets for therapy. *Molecular Psychiatry, 9,* 646-663.

Bernard Opitz, V., Sriram, N., & Nakhoda Sapuan, S. (2001). Enhancing social problem solving in children with autism and normal children through computer-assisted instruction. *Journal of Autism and Developmental Disorders, 31*(4), 377-398.

Bishop, J. (2003). The Internet for educating individuals with social impairments. *Journal of Computer Assisted Learning, 19,* 546-556.

Bolte, S., Feineis-Matthews, S., Leber, S., Dierks, T., Hubl, D., & Poustka, F. (2002). The development and evaluation of a computer-based program to test and to teach the recognition of facial affect. *International Journal of Circumpolar Health, 61* (Supplement 2*),* 61-68.

Boucher, J., Lewis, V., & Collis, G. M. (2000). Voice processing abilities in children with autism, children with specific language impairments, and young typically developing children. *Journal of Child Psychology and Psychiatry and Allied Disciplines, 41,* 847-857.

Celani, G., Battacchi, M. W., & Arcidiacono, L. (1999). The understanding of the emotional meaning of facial expressions in people with autism. *Journal Autism and Developmental Disorders, 29,* 57-66.

Critchley, H. D., Daly, E. M., Bullmore, E. T., Williams, S. C., Van Amelsvoort, T., Robertson, D. M., Rowe, A., Phillips, M., McAlonan, G., Howlin, P., & Murphy, D. G. (2000). The functional neuroanatomy of social behaviour: Changes in cerebral blood flow when people with autistic disorder process facial expressions. *Brain, 123* (Pt. 11), 2203-2212.

Deruelle, C., Rondan, C., Gepner, B., & Tardif, C. (2004). Spatial frequency and face processing in children with autism and Asperger syndrome. *Journal Autism and Developmental Disorders, 34,* 199-210.

Ekman, P. (1993). Facial expression and emotion. *American Psychologist, 48,* 384-392.

Ekman, P., & Friesen, W. (1971). Constants across cultures in the face and emotion. *Journal of Personality and Social Psychology, 17,* 124-129.

Fein, D., Lucci, D., Braverman, M., & Waterhouse, L. (1992). Comprehension of affect in context in children with pervasive developmental disorders. *Journal of Child Psychology and Psychiatry, 33,* 1157-1167.

Frith, U. (1989). *Autism: Explaining the enigma.* Oxford, UK: Blackwell.

Frith, U., & Hill, E. (2004). *Autism: Mind and brain.* Oxford, UK: Oxford University Press.

Golan, O., & Baron-Cohen, S. (submitted). *Teaching children with Asperger Syndrome and high functioning autism to recognize emotions using interactive multimedia.*

Golan, O., Baron-Cohen, S., & Hill, J. (2006). The Cambridge Mindreading (CAM) Face-Voice Battery: Testing complex emotion recognition in adults with and without Asperger Syndrome. *Journal of Autism and Developmental Disorders, 36,* 169-183.

Golan, O., Baron-Cohen, S., Hill, J. J., & Golan, Y. (2006). Reading the mind in films: Testing recognition of complex emotions and mental states in adults with and without autism spectrum conditions. *Social Neuroscience, 1*(2), 111-123.

Golan, O., Baron-Cohen, S., Hill, J. J., & Rutherford, M. D. (2007). Reading the Mind in the Voice-Revised. A study of adults with and without autism spectrum conditions. *Journal of Autism and Developmental Disorders, 37*(6), 1096-1106.

Grossman, J. B., Klin, A., Carter, A. S., & Volkmar, F. R. (2000). Verbal bias in recognition of facial emotions in children with Asperger syndrome. *Journal of Child Psychology and Psychiatry and Allied Disciplines, 41,* 369-379.

Hadwin, J., Baron-Cohen, S., Howlin, P., & Hill, K. (1996). Can we teach children with autism to understand emotions, belief, or pretence? *Development and Psychopathology, 8,* 345-365.

Happé, F. (1994). An advanced test of theory of mind: Understanding of story characters' thoughts and feelings by able autistic, mentally handicapped, and normal children and adults. *Journal of Autism and Developmental Disorders, 24*, 129-154.

Happé, F., Ehlers, S., Fletcher, P., Frith, U., Johansson, M., Gillberg, C., Dolan, R., Frackowiak, R., & Frith, C. (1996). Theory of mind in the brain. Evidence from a PET scan study of Asperger syndrome. *Neuroreport, 8*(1), 197-201.

Heavey, L., Phillips, W., Baron-Cohen, S., & Rutter, M. (2000). The Awkward Moments Test: A naturalistic measure of social understanding in autism. *Journal of Autism and Developmental Disorders, 30*, 225-236.

Hetzroni, O. E., & Tannous, J. (2004). Effects of a computer-based intervention program on the communicative functions of children with autism. *Journal of Autism and Developmental Disorders, 34*, 95-113.

Hobson, P. (1994). Understanding persons: The role of affect. In S. Baron-Cohen, H. Tager-Flusberg, & D. Cohen (Eds.), *Understanding other minds* (pp. 204-227). London: Oxford University Press.

Hobson, R. P. (1986a). The autistic child's appraisal of expressions of emotion. *Journal of Child Psychology and Psychiatry, 27*, 321-342.

Hobson, R. P. (1986b). The autistic child's appraisal of expressions of emotion: A further study. *Journal of Child Psychology and Psychiatry, 27*, 671-680.

Hobson, R. P., Ouston, J., & Lee, A. (1988). What's in a face? The case of autism. *British Journal of Psychology, 79*, 441-453.

Howlin, P., Baron-Cohen, S., & Hadwin, J. (1999). *Teaching children with autism to mind-read: A practical guide for teachers and parents.* Chichester, UK: B. J. Wiley.

Howlin, P., & Yates, P. (1999). The potential effectiveness of social skills groups for adults with autism. *Autism, 3*, 299-307.

Jolliffe, T., & Baron-Cohen, S. (1997). Are people with autism and Asperger Syndrome faster than normal on the Embedded Figures Test? *Journal of Child Psychology and Psychiatry and Allied Disciplines, 38*, 527-534.

Jolliffe, T., & Baron-Cohen, S. (1999). The Strange Stories Test: A replication with high-functioning adults with autism or Asperger Syndrome. *Journal of Autism and Developmental Disorders, 29*, 395-406.

Kleinman, J., Marciano, P. L., & Ault, R. L. (2001). Advanced theory of mind in high-functioning adults with autism. *Journal of Autism and Developmental Disorders, 31*, 29-36.

Klin, A., Jones, W., Schultz, R., & Volkmar, F. (2003). The enactive mind, or from actions to cognition: Lessons from autism. *Philosophical Transactions of the Royal Society, Series B, 358*, 345-360.

Klin, A., Jones, W., Schultz, R., Volkmar, F., & Cohen, D. (2002). Visual fixation patterns during viewing of naturalistic social situations as predictors of social competence in individuals with autism. *Archives of General Psychiatry, 59*, 809-816.

Klinger, L. G., & Dawson, G. (1995). A fresh look at categorization abilities in persons with autism. In E. Schopler & G. B. Mesibov (Eds.), *Learning and cognition in autism* (pp. 119-136). New York: Plenum Press.

Lawson, J. (2003). Depth accessibility difficulties: An alternative conceptualization of autism spectrum conditions. *Journal for the Theory of Social Behaviour, 33*, 189-202.

Lawson, J., Baron-Cohen, S., & Wheelwright, S. (2004). Empathizing and systemizing in adults with and without Asperger Syndrome. *Journal of Autism and Developmental Disorders, 34*, 301-310.

Loveland, K. A., Tunali Kotoski, B., Chen, R., & Brelsford, K. A. (1995). Intermodal perception of affect in persons with autism or Down syndrome. *Development and Psychopathology, 7*, 409-418.

Loveland, K. A., Tunali Kotoski, B., Chen, Y. R., Ortegon, J., Pearson, D. A., Brelsford, K. A., & Gibes, M. C. (1997). Emotion recognition in autism: Verbal and non-verbal information. *Development and Psychopathology, 9*, 579-593.

Macdonald, H., Rutter, M., Howlin, P., Rios, P., Le Conteur, A., Evered, C., & Folstein, S. (1989). Recognition and expression of emotional cues by autistic and normal adults. *Journal of Child Psychology and Psychiatry, 30*, 865-877.

Moore, D., McGrath, P., & Thorpe, J. (2000). Computer-aided learning for people with autism – A framework for research and development. *Innovations in Education and Training International, 37*, 218-228.

Nieminen-von Wendt, T., Metsahonkala, L., Kulomaki, T., Alto, S., Autti, T., Vanhala, R., & von Wendt, L. (2003). Changes in cerebral blood flow in Asperger syndrome during theory of mind tasks presented by the auditory route. *European Child and Adolescent Psychiatry, 12*, 178-189.

O'Riordan, M. A., Plaisted, K. C., Driver, J., & Baron-Cohen, S. (2001). Superior visual search in autism. *Journal of Experimental Psychology: Human Perception and Performance, 27*, 719-730.

Ozonoff, S. (1995). Executive functions in autism. In E. Schopler & G. B. Mesibov (Eds.), *Learning and cognition in autism* (pp. 199-219). New York: Plenum Press.

Parsons, S., & Mitchell, P. (2002). The potential of virtual reality in social skills training for people with autistic spectrum disorders. *Journal of Intellectual Disability Research, 46*, 430-443.

Pierce, K., Muller, R. A., Ambrose, J., Allen, G., & Courchesne, E. (2001). Face processing occurs outside the fusiform face area in autism: Evidence from functional MRI. *Brain, 124*(Pt 10), 2059-2073.

Plaisted, K. C. (2001). Reduced generalization in autism: An alternative to weak central coherence. In J. A. Burack (Ed.), *The development of autism: Perspectives from theory and research* (pp. 149-169). Mahwah, NJ: Lawrence Erlbaum Associates Publishers.

Rajendran, G., & Mitchell, P. (2000). Computer-mediated interaction in Asperger's syndrome: The Bubble Dialogue program. *Computers and Education, 35*, 189-207.

Rimland, B. (1965). *Infantile autism: The syndrome and its implications for a neural theory of behavior*. London: Methuen.

Rutherford, M. D., Baron-Cohen, S., & Wheelwright, S. (2002). Reading the mind in the voice: A study with normal adults and adults with Asperger syndrome and high functioning autism. *Journal Autism and Developmental Disorders, 32*, 189-194.

Rydin, O. T., Drake, J., & Bratt, A. (1999). The effects of training on emotion recognition skills for adults with an intellectual disability. *Journal of Applied Research in Intellectual Disabilities, 12*, 253-262.

Sainsbury, C. (2000). *Martian in the playground: Understanding the schoolchild with Asperger's Syndrome*. London: Lucky Duck Publishing.

Schultz, R. T., Grelotti, D. J., Klin, A., Kleinman, J., Van der Gaag, C., Marois, R., & Skudlarski, P. (2003). The role of the fusiform face area in social cognition: Implications for the pathobiology of autism. *Philosophical Transactions of the Royal Society, Series B, Biological Sciences, 358*, 415-427.

Shah, A., & Frith, U. (1993). Why do autistic individuals show superior performance on the block design task? *Journal of Child Psychology and Psychiatry and Allied Disciplines, 34*, 1351-1364.

Silver, M., & Oakes, P. (2001). Evaluation of a new computer intervention to teach people with autism or Asperger syndrome to recognize and predict emotions in others. *Autism, 5*, 299-316.

Swettenham, J. (1996). Can children with autism be taught to understand false belief using computers? *Journal of Child Psychology and Psychiatry, 37*, 157-165.

Swettenham, J. (2000). Teaching theory of mind to individuals with autism. In S. Baron-Cohen, H. Tager-Flusberg, & D. J. Cohen (Eds.), *Understanding other minds: Perspectives from developmental cognitive neuroscience* (2nd ed., pp. 442-456). Oxford, UK: Oxford University Press.

Teunisse, J. P., & De Gelder, B. (1994). Do autistics have a generalized face processing deficit? *International Journal of Neuroscience, 77*(1-2), 1-10.

Yirmiya, N., Sigman, M. D., Kasari, C., & Mundy, P. (1992). Empathy and cognition in high-functioning children with autism. *Child Development, 63*, 150-160.

Young, A. W. (1998). *Face and mind*. Oxford, UK: Oxford University Press.

Acknowledgments

Ofer Golan was supported by the National Alliance for Autism Research (NAAR), the Corob Charitable Trust, the Cambridge Overseas Trust and B'nai B'rith Leo Baeck scholarships. Simon Baron-Cohen was supported by the Shirley Foundation, the Medical Research Council, and the Three Guineas Trust. Parts of this chapter appear in Golan and Baron-Cohen (2006).

Learner Objectives

After reading this chapter, the learner should be able to:

- Explain what is meant by "transition planning"

- Discuss why planning the transition from school is a critical aspect of the IEP process in the middle and high school years

- Name the members of a typical transition team

- State what students with ASD should know about transition planning

- State the elements of a well-designed individual transition plan (ITP) and the federally mandated requirements of transition planning for persons with disabilities

- Explain why it is important to address career, self-advocacy, and independent living goals in the ITP

- Explain the use of the Underlying Characteristics Checklist in planning for individuals with ASD

- Discuss the types of assessment that may be used in transition planning

- List and describe the components of successful planning for and support of the transition process

- Discuss the considerations that affect job placement and retention for persons with ASD

- Explain why social skills aspects should be an important part of the ITP process

- State how services at the postsecondary level differ from those available to school-aged individuals

Chapter 11

Supporting the Transition Years

Brenda Smith Myles • Sheila M. Smith • Terri Cooper Swanson

Treat people as if they were what they ought to be,
and you help them become what they are capable of being. ~ Goethe

---

Joseph is a 19-year old student with Asperger Syndrome. He is working on an advanced diploma and has a GPA of 3.2. His career goal is to be a robotics engineer. His IEP team agreed that it would be in Joseph's best interest to extend his stay in high school to five years to give him more time to develop his independent living skills and social skills, and to "allow for maturation."

Joseph is outgoing, very bright, and has an excellent sense of humor. At times, his judgment and comments have caused difficulty in interpersonal interactions, however. He excels in science and math, but English and writing are more difficult for him. He has difficulty staying on task, unless it is something of interest to him (robotics, creating video games).

Doug is an 18-year-old enrolled in a self-contained class for students with autism. He is working towards a diploma that requires successful completion of IEP goals. Through a picture interest inventory, Doug indicated that he liked stock work and data entry jobs.

Doug is a strong young man who enjoys listening to the Oldies, watching the television show Stargate SG-1, *and playing video games. Although he is able to speak, he does not initiate communication. He has no sense of boundaries or of danger. He will not always stay with the group. Over the last year, he has begun touching others inappropriately.*

The **transition** to post-school options is a complex and critical part of any student's life. There are changes at many levels: environmentally, academically, and socially. During this time, students begin to focus on what they would like to do when they leave school and transition to life outside of school. They are beginning to learn their strengths, interests, and skills through their interactions with family, peers, and school personnel – an initial step in identifying future goals.

Students with autism spectrum disorders (ASD) are no different than their neurotypical peers in this aspect of their lives. However, their areas of skill deficit require support, not only in preparation for employment but also in preparation for success in all aspects of adult life. Regrettably, research indicates that individuals with ASD leave school programs ill equipped with the social and communication skills necessary for life success (Müller, Schuler, Burton, & Yates, 2003), despite legislation that mandates **transition planning** as part of the individualized education program (IEP) starting at age 16, or younger if determined by the IEP team (see Table 11.1). As a result, they have difficulties obtaining and sustaining employment as adults (Engström, Ekström, & Emilsson, 2003; Howlin, Alcock, & Burkin, 2005; Hurlbutt & Chalmers, 2004; Jennes-Coussens, Magill-Evans, & Koning, 2006).

Table 11.1
IDEA 2004 Transition Services Legislation

The Individuals with Disabilities Education Improvement Act (United States Department of Education [IDEA], 2004) defines transition services as follows:

A coordinated set of activities for a child with a disability that

- is designed to be within a results-oriented process that is focused on improving the academic and functional achievement of the child with a disability to facilitate the child's movement from school to post-school activities, including postsecondary education, vocational education, integrated employment (including supported employment), continuing and adult education, adult services, independent living, or community participation;

- is based upon the individual child's needs, taking into account the child's strengths, preferences, and interests;

- includes instruction, related services, community experiences, the development of employment and other post-school adult living objectives, and if appropriate, acquisition of daily living skills and functional vocational evaluation [Part A, Section 602(34)].

Transition planning is a critical component of each IEP for students with ASD. IDEA 2004 requires the following:

Beginning not later than the first IEP to be in effect when the child turns 16, or younger, if determined appropriate by the IEP Team, and updated annually thereafter, the IEP must include:

1. appropriate measurable postsecondary goals based upon age-appropriate transition assessments related to training, education, employment, and, where appropriate, independent living skills; and

2. the transition services (including courses of study) needed to assist the child in reaching these goals [Section 614(d)(1)(A)(VIII)].

In addition, IDEA 2004 requires that students be notified of their rights:

Beginning not later than one year before the child reaches the age of majority under state law, a statement that the child has been informed of the child's rights under IDEA, if any, that will transfer to the child on reaching the age of majority under Section 615(m).

Adapted from United States Department of Education. (2004). http://frwebgate.access.gpo.gov/cgi-bin/getdoc.cgi?dbname=108_cong_public_laws&docid=f:publ446.108

Planning students' transition from school to post-school is a critical part of the IEP process in the middle and high school years (Smith, 2001). Transition planning is ongoing and outcome-oriented, based on collaboration between students, their families, school and adult service personnel, and the community. Further, emphasis must be placed on acquisition of the skills necessary for **independent living** during these transition years. Research has shown that for students with disabilities opportunities for employment during their school years lead to increased success for employment after they leave school (Rogan, Banks, & Herbein, 2003). While job-related skills are typically identified as priorities for transition planning, preparing for successful employment is only one aspect of the transition to adult life. In addition to the focus on employment, schools must equip students with ASD with social skills, safety skills, and information on appropriate sexual behavior, if they are going to reach their potential as productive members of society.

This chapter offers an introduction to supporting individuals with ASD through the transition years. A major focus is on effectively preparing educators and related professionals, parents, as well as the individual with ASD him/herself, to navigate all the steps involved in a successful transition to postsecondary life. The chapter begins with an overview of transition services, touching on legal aspects that interface with the **individualized transition planning (ITP)** process. The importance of assessment in the ITP process is also addressed. The chapter concludes with a discussion of how to effectively support the transition process through implementation of the young adult's ITP.

Transition Services

When Should Transition Planning Begin?

According to the Individuals with Disabilities Education Act 2004 (IDEA 2004), an ITP, a required piece of an IEP designed to prepare a youth for adult success, must be in place by the student's 16th birthday. This is required practice; however, some professionals recommend that students start the transition process by the age of 14, if not earlier (Holtz, Owings, & Ziegert, 2006; Myles & Adreon, 2001; Schelvan, Swanson, & Smith, 2005). Planning should be results-oriented with a clear focus toward the future. Parents and professionals are responsible for collaborating on the most effective means of involving students in transition planning while taking into account their strengths and areas of challenge. Best practice is to involve the student in the process as early as possible.

Various state departments of education, local school districts, and community agencies have developed resources for parents and professionals working through the transition process. In many cases, specific personnel at a school or school district are designated as **transition coordinators/specialists**. Their role usually includes tasks such as recommending a timeline of activities during middle and high school to prepare for the transition beyond high school, connecting parents and school personnel to community agencies and resources, or working directly with students as they move through the transition process. Even if a transition specialist is not available, teachers and parents must ensure that the ITP focuses not only on the student's strengths and interests, but also includes opportunities to learn missing skills. In that connection, team members need to take responsibility to educate themselves with regard to the student's disability, as well as the transition process.

A typical transition planning team begins with the members of the student's IEP team and may include members from vocational options within the school system, agencies that focus on vocational support, and representatives from local universities, if appropriate. Holtz et al.(2006) identified the following as key members of the transition planning team:

- Parent and student/young adult with ASD and any other interested family member(s)
- Transition coordinator (or school personnel designated to assist with the transition planning process)
- General education teacher (may not be included in the entire process, but should be part of it)
- Special education teacher(s) working with the student/young adult
- Department of Vocational Rehabilitation (DVR) or other appropriate agency representative
- School-based administrator
- Psychologist

Other optional, helpful members may include:

- Advocacy organization representative
- Business education partnership representative
- Guidance counselor, when appropriate
- Residential services representative, when appropriate
- Mental health agency representative
- Postsecondary education representative, when applicable

As noted, the team should be tailored for each youth's specific needs, and students should be participating in their transition plan to the best of their ability (IDEA, 2004). Depending upon their needs, students may need extra time to learn about the transition process and what career options are available to them, and may need visuals to help them follow the process or communicate more effectively with others. Students should (a) know who are involved in their ITP, (b) know their rights as a student receiving services under IDEA, and (c) know what their rights are after graduation under Section 504 and the **Americans with Disabilities Act (ADA)**. Figure 11.1 outlines students' rights under IDEA as well as the rights of individuals over age 21 years under Section 504 and ADA.

Regardless of when planning starts or who comprises the transition team, certain activities should occur during the planning process. For individuals with ASD, priming students for upcoming activities has proven to be a successful strategy throughout their daily routine (Aspy & Grossman, 2007). Figure 11.2, adapted from the Virginia Department of Education's web site, provides a timeline of activities that students might engage in throughout their high school years and as they transition to postsecondary options. A more comprehensive form of this list may be found at http://www.fcps.edu. In its current version, this tool might be used as a checklist for developing the ITP or to discuss goals for students.

Americans With Disabilities Act (ADA), 1990	Individuals with Disabilities Education Act (IDEA), 1997/2004	Section 504 of the Rehabilitation Act, 1973
TYPE/PURPOSE		
Civil rights law to prohibit discrimination	An education act that guarantees free and appropriate public education	Civil rights law to prohibit discrimination
ELIGIBILITY REQUIREMENTS		
• Documented diagnosis of ASD • Qualified for the program, service, or job	• Documented diagnosis of ASD • Aged 3 to 21	• Documented diagnosis of ASD • Qualified for the program, service, or job
RESPONSIBILITY TO PROVIDE A FREE, APPROPRIATE PUBLIC EDUCATION (FAPE)		
• Not directly • Provides additional protection in combination with Section 504 and IDEA	• Yes	• Yes
PROTECTIONS PROVIDED		
• Details the administrative requirements, complaint procedures, and consequences for noncompliance related to both services and employment • Individuals discriminated against may file a complaint with the relevant federal agency or sue in federal court	• Provides for procedural safeguards and due process rights to parents in the identification, evaluation, and educational placement of their child • Disputes may be resolved through mediation, impartial due process hearings, appeal of hearing decisions, and/or civil action	• Requires notice to parents regarding identification, evaluation, placement, and before a "significant change" in placement • Local education agencies are required to provide impartial hearings for parents who disagree with the identification, evaluation, or placement of a student
STEPS/ACTIONS		
• Specifies provision of reasonable accommodations for eligible students across educational activities and settings • Reasonable accommodations may include, but are not limited to, redesigning equipment, assigning aides, providing written communication in alternative formats, modifying tests, reassigning services to accessible locations, altering existing facilities, and building new facilities	• With parental consent, an individualized evaluation must be conducted using a variety of technically sound, unbiased assessment tools • Reevaluations are conducted at least every 3 years • Results are used to develop an IEP that specifies the special education, related services, and supplemental aids and services to be provided to address the child's goals	• Provides for a placement evaluation that must involve multiple assessment tools tailored to assess specific areas of educational need • Placement decisions must be made by a tem of persons familiar with the student on the basis of his evaluation information and placement options • Provides for periodic reevaluation • Parental consent is not required for evaluation or placement
Condensed from Henderson, K. (2001, March). The ERIC Clearinghouse on Disability and Gifted Education (ERIC EC), ERIC EC Digest #E606. Available online at http://ericec.org/digests/e606/html		

Figure 11.1. Comparison of ADA, IDEA, and Section 504 legislation.

During the High School Years	High School to Postsecondary Transition
• Develop study skills and strategies that work for the individual across settings, including time management, stress management, and test-taking skills	• Identify ways that accommodations provided in high school will translate to postsecondary education, employment, and community settings
• Work to remediate deficit skills	• Meet with the transition specialist to identify appropriate and available career/vocational assessment options, and to make referrals as appropriate
• Identify accommodations and/or modifications that are required	
• Identify tentative postsecondary career and personal goals	• Work with transition planning specialists in the local district to make contact with vocational rehabilitative services and community service agencies to investigate support available during and after graduation
• Plan a course of study to meet graduation requirements, investigating diploma options	
• Explore special interests and try to develop schedule to support these interests	• Invite appropriate representatives from adult service agencies to the IEP meeting
• If students are able, they can meet with the case manager to plan the IEP meeting and decide on their role; if they are not able, staff should meet and decide for them, but include them as much as possible in the meeting	• Focus on matching interests and abilities to the appropriate postsecondary goals
	• Visit schools, colleges, or training programs early in the year
• Meet annually to develop ITP with case manager	• Evaluate the disability services, service provider, and staff of any schools in which the individual with ASD is interested
• Attend IEP meetings	
• Consider whether extending high school graduation by one to three years will help reach postsecondary goals	• Obtain copies of all school records that document the disability to obtain accommodations in the postsecondary environments
• If career plans will require a college degree, register and take the Preliminary Scholastic Aptitude Test (PSAT) in the fall of the sophomore year, considering test adjustments and auxiliary aids	• Take the SAT or ACT if appropriate
	• Make sure to investigate supports other than vocational – focus on social and independent living as well
• Explore opportunities for employment experiences, whether independently or with a job coach or mentor	
• During the junior year, if the career plan dictates, plan for participation in the SAT or ACT depending on which assessment best matches the chosen career path (remember to investigate all accommodations options with either instrument)	
• During the junior year, work with transition planning specialists in the local district to make contact with vocational rehabilitative services and community service agencies to investigate support available during and after graduation.	
• Invite appropriate representatives from adult service agencies to the IEP meeting	
• Meet with the transition specialist to identify appropriate and available career/vocational assessment options, and to make referrals as appropriate	
Adapted with permission from Fairfax County Public Schools, VA, Department of Special Services, Office of Special Education, Career and Transition Services section.	

Figure 11.2. Transition timeline for student activities.

What Does an Appropriate Transition Plan Address?

IDEA 2004 specifies that transition planning is a coordinated set of activities for a student with a disability that is:

- **Outcome-oriented** – a process with clear goals and measurable outcomes

- *Student-centered* – based on the specific skills that the student needs and reflective of the young adult's interests and preferences

- **Broad-based** – includes instruction and related services, community experiences, development of employment and post-school living objectives, and acquisition of daily living skills and vocational evaluation

- **A working document** – outlines current and future goals, along with specific strategies for achieving these goals, and changes over time. (United States Department of Education, 2004)

Although sustained employment is a goal for all, school prepares students for so much more. It prepares them to address social issues, to communicate and advocate for themselves, to become independent thinkers, and supports many other skills necessary for success in the adult world. Thus, when planning for individuals with ASD, ITPs should include (a) career goals, (b) **self-advocacy goals**, and (c) independent living goals, while keeping in mind the unique characteristics and strengths specific to individuals with ASD. Career goals might include academics, career awareness, career development, and work habits and behaviors. Self-advocacy goals might include decision making and self-awareness, while independent living goals might include taking care of personal needs, community participation, household responsibilities, leisure activities, and managing finances. Table 11.2 provides a list of goals that might be included in an ITP in each of these areas.

In their transition guide for individuals with ASD, the Organization for Autism Research (OAR) outlines information that might also be included in the ITP, such as vocational training and job sampling, employment goals with a timeline for achieving them, community participation goals including social and leisure skills, travel training, purchasing skills, and personal care, and goals relevant to postsecondary education. A young adult's transition plan will be customized based on his/her needs. In particular, a solid transition plan will include many of the following elements (Holtz et al., 2006):

- Assessment of young adult's needs, interests, and abilities

- Statement of preferences for education, employment, and adult living

- Steps to be taken to support achievement of these goals

- Specific methods and resources to meet these goals, including accommodations, services, and/or skills related to the transition goals

- Instruction on academic, vocational, and living skills

- Identification of community experiences and skills related to future goals

- Exploration of service organizations or agencies to provide services and support

- Methods for evaluating success of transition activities (e.g., a video portfolio)

Table 11.2
Examples of Career, Self-Advocacy, and Independence Goals

Academic	Career Awareness	Career Development	Work Habits and Behaviors
• Identify high school course offerings related to career goals	• Take part in vocational assessment activities	• Develop a resumé; obtain a work permit	• Identify appropriate action to take if late or absent from school
• Identify postsecondary schools that provide training in career field	• Identify several careers that match interests and abilities	• Participate in school-based work experiences	• Identify when assistance is needed and how to obtain it
• Explore support services available at postsecondary schools/programs of interest	• Observe/job shadow employee at business site	• Obtain a summer or after-school job	• Learn to respond to all types of directions or statements, including critical statements
• Learn about the wide variety of careers that exist	• Participate in on-the-job training opportunities	• Enroll in career-related courses	• Perform a series of tasks in response to instructions (both oral and written)
• Identify training needs and effective strategies to address deficits	• Explore interests through elective courses	• Participate in community-based work training program	• Identify appropriate dress code for a variety of work situations
• Enroll in test preparation courses if the career path necessitates taking the SAT or ACT	• Utilize the career supports available in the school building to investigate career options	• Attend seminars about college, employment, or other postsecondary services	• Use planner to organize school work and homework assignments

Adapted with permission from Fairfax County Public Schools, VA, Department of Special Services, Office of Special Education, Career and Transition Services section.

In addition to stating the goals for the young adult, the transition plan should include logistical information on how the plan will be implemented and monitored, such as a timeline for achieving goals, people or agencies responsible for helping with these goals, clarification of how roles will be coordinated, and a plan for identifying post-graduation services and supports and obtaining the necessary funding. In short, the ITP should address all aspects of the individual's life after high school.

Assessment

Services and supports preparing students with ASD for employment and adult life should match their characteristics. Aspy and Grossman (2007) have developed a tool that teams might utilize when planning for components of the ITP. The **Underlying Characteristics Checklist (UCC**; Aspy & Grossman, 2007) provides a framework for discussing and planning for the characteristics specific to this population, including (a) socialization differences, (b) restricted patterns of behavior, interests, and activities, (c) communication differences, (d) cognitive differences, (e) sensory differences, (f) motor differences, (g) emotional vulnerability, and (h) known medical or other biological factors. The UCC (see Figure 11.3) addresses each of the domains, providing a checklist format to facilitate team conversations and planning that thoroughly address all of the student's needs. When developing an IEP, ITP, or working with employers or institutes of higher education, the UCC provides a means for communication and assessment.

The UCC is just one informal assessment tool; other options are available. Assessments can range from simple questioning techniques to specific psychometric instruments. For example, Sitlington and Clark (2001) stress that the focus of the assessment should be on the "individual's current and future roles as a worker, lifelong learner, family member, community citizen, and participant in social and interpersonal networks" (p. 7). As adapted from Holtz et al. (2006), questions that parents, teachers, and community members might consider when conducting assessments for transition planning include the following:

- Are there topics or activities of particular interest to the student/young adult?

- Are there certain topics, activities, or environmental conditions that the student/young adult does not like or has difficulty tolerating?

- What are the student/young adult's current academic or related strengths or talents?

- To what extent does the student/young adult's current skill set match the demands of desirable activities or environments?

- What are the student/young adult's dreams?

- What kind of support will the student/young adult require to achieve his/her goals after graduation?

In order to develop an appropriate ITP for individuals with ASD, further questions need to be addressed:
- Where does the team see the student in 5, 10, and 20 years?

- What does the team (and the student) want the student's life to be like?

- What needs to be put in place to move from now to then?

These questions should be addressed keeping in mind the knowledge, skills, strengths, and challenges the student exhibits. Special interests are inherent in this population and should be taken into consideration during the assessment process. Each planning team should utilize assessment as part of the transition process from beginning to end.

UCC-CL
UNDERLYING CHARACTERISTICS CHECKLIST-CLASSIC

Ruth Aspy, Ph.D., and Barry G. Grossman, Ph.D.

NAME: _____ DATE: _____ COMPLETED BY: _____

FOLLOW-UP DATE: _____ COMPLETED BY: _____

DIRECTIONS: Place check beside all items that apply and describe behaviors observed.

Area	Item	✔	Notes	Follow-Up
SOCIAL	1. Has difficulty recognizing the feelings and thoughts of others (mindblindness)			
	2. Uses poor eye contact or fails to orient to others			
	3. Shows little interest in or response to praise			
	4. Does not seek others' attention in order to share an experience (e.g., bring an object to show, or point out an item or person)			
	5. Interacts with others as if they were objects (e.g., cause and effect)			
	6. Has difficulty maintaining personal space, physically intrudes on others			
	7. Has difficulty taking turns in social interactions or activities			
	8. Has difficulty imitating the actions or words of others			
	9. Fails to respond to the eye gaze or pointing of others – does not orient to the object or person			
	10. Has difficulty making or keeping friends			
	11. Has difficulty joining an activity			

From *The Ziggurat Model: A Framework for Designing Comprehensive Interventions for Individuals with High-Functioning Autism and Asperger Syndrome*, by R. Aspy and B. Grossman, 2007, Shawnee Mission, KS: Autism Asperger Publishing Company. Used with permission.

Figure 11.3. Underlying characteristics checklist.

Effectively Planning for and Supporting the Transition Process

The following section highlights some areas specific to ASD where support and guidance is particularly necessary for effectively implementing the ITP. References at the end of this chapter may be consulted for a more in-depth study of transition planning, employment supports, institutes of higher education that provide support for individuals with ASD, and life as an adult with ASD.

Self-Advocacy, Self-Determination, and Person-Centered Planning

Discussions of **self-determination** and self-advocacy for individuals with disabilities are prevalent in the literature (Field & Hoffman, 1999; Fullerton & Coyne, 1999; Izzo, Hertzfeld, & Aaron, 2001; Ward & Meyer, 1999; Wehman, 2002; Wehmeyer, 1999). Socialization, communication, and relationship building skills are vital to most work environments. According to the literature, individuals with ASD have significant difficulty with the social aspects of maintaining employment (Howlin et al., 2005; Hurlbutt & Chalmers, 2004). Indeed, challenges with communication and social deficits make the task of advocating and participating fully in the transition process particularly difficult for individuals with ASD.

Held, Thoma, and Thomas (2004) conducted a single-subject design study in which they wanted students to understand themselves and be able to speak up for themselves. "I want them to understand their disability and support needs. I want them to be able to use this information to make choices, decisions, problem solve, to write their own goals and to create their vision for the future, and to direct their own message" (p. 181).

The study was successful by implementating a combination of strategies, including **person-centered planning** methods, a self-determination curriculum, and technology, that enabled the student, who was nonverbal, to have a voice in the process. The advantage for all involved was that they got a chance to get to know this young man.

Resources such as **Making Action Plans (MAPS**; Falvey, Forest, Pearpoint, & Rosenberg, 2000) and **Planning Alternative Tomorrows with Hope (PATH**; Pearpoint, O'Brien, & Forest, 1998) were utilized to assist with the person-centered planning (see Figure 11.4). The PATH and MAPS provide a platform for team planning with the future in mind. Both are designed to assess where the student is, focus on strengths and challenges, develop goals for the future and prioritize them, and allow teams to plan for maximizing student involvement.

Strategies to increase self-determination skills must be specifically taught to individuals with ASD. Scripting dialogue, video modeling appropriate advocacy strategies, and printing out a list of needed accommodations or modifications are some solutions. Further, teaching students about their disability, strengths, and challenges empowers them to advocate. Some might require pictorial representations of where they are now, and where they are going. Various graphic organizers can offer support in developing these "webs" of pictures. Baker (2005) has produced a complete guide that includes lessons designed specifically for individuals with ASD. The key to increasing self-determination and self-advocacy is developing a person-centered plan, involving the individual with use of concrete terms, and discussions that are begun early.

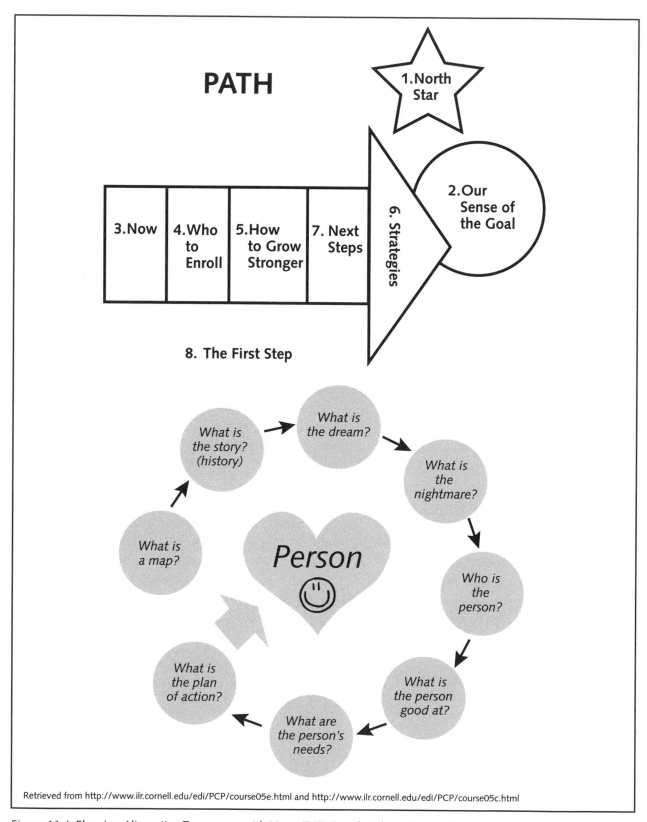

Retrieved from http://www.ilr.cornell.edu/edi/PCP/course05e.html and http://www.ilr.cornell.edu/edi/PCP/course05c.html

Figure 11.4. Planning Alternative Tomorrows with Hope (PATH) and Making Action Plans (MAPS).

Selecting Meaningful Coursework

The importance of involving students' special interests in planning for their future has already been mentioned. Having an open mind when approaching how a student can receive instruction at the secondary level is critical to individualizing the transition process. Incorporating special interests into career planning and coursework infuses motivation within the student's day.

The key to success is tailoring coursework that addresses skills in need of remediation and skills necessary to pursue future planning. The ITP should guide the course selection process. Course options are now more plentiful than ever before, offered with face-to-face components, in virtual environments, and in both large- and small-group settings. Course selection should begin with the end in mind and take into consideration such questions as:

- How will this course provide experiences that build on prior knowledge, remediate skill deficits, and provide opportunities for continued learning of new skills needed for life after high school?

- What types of accommodations or modifications are needed for the student to derive the most benefit from this course?

- What type of learning environment best enables the student to generalize learned skills for future use?

- How do special interests fit in with specific course requirements, so that the student is getting the most "bang for the buck" with his/her course experience?

Again, selecting coursework guided by the ITP and with the end in mind is key to success for individuals with ASD.

Increasing Job Placement Opportunities

Although IDEA mandates that students receive specific programs and services while they are in secondary school, no such mandate exists after they leave that environment (see Table 11.2). Teams need to take advantage of the resources available within school districts for student employment experiences prior to graduation. Employment is a central aspect of adult life. Finding a job that matches the individual's needs in terms of challenge, interests, comfort, camaraderie, status, hours, pay, and benefits is extremely important (Holtz et al., 2006).

Mawhood and Howlin (1999) found that a critical factor in maintaining long-term employment for individuals with ASD was assessing the job site for a match between skills and the abilities of the individual with ASD. Research on employment for individuals with ASD documents difficulties with

- sustaining employment
- social success
- appropriate job skills
- communicating with supervisors and colleagues
- level of income

(Garcia-Villamisar, Ross, & Wehman, 2000; Garcia-Villamisar, Wehman, & Navarro, 2002; Hagner & Cooney, 2005; Henn & Henn, 2005; Howlin et al., 2005; Hurlbutt & Chalmers, 2004; Mawhood & Howlin, 1999; Müller et al., 2003; Nesbitt, 2000; Unger, 1999, 2002). Providing appropriate experiences at the secondary level could help lessen these challenges as individuals transition to adult life.

Grandin and Duffy (2004) recommend that when looking at job placement opportunities and planning for future success, teams keep in mind that the individual with ASD should do what he does best. Thus, matching requirements with strengths, skills, and interests becomes important.

According to Grandin (1999), three types of thinking are unique to individuals with ASD and should be taken into consideration: (a) visual thinking, (b) music and higher math, and (c) verbal lists and language translator brains (see Table 11.3). Understanding which type of thinking relates to a specific student will help teams develop a job match.

Table 11.3
Job Ideas for Adults with Autism Spectrum Disorders

Jobs Ideas for Visual Thinkers	
• Architectural and engineering drafter • Photographer • Animal trainer • Graphic artist • Jewelry maker and other crafts • Web designer • Veterinarian technician	• Auto mechanic • Machine maintenance technician • Computer trouble shooter • Theater lighting director • Industrial automation programmer • Landscape designer • Biology teacher
Job Ideas for Music and Math Brains	
• Computer programmer • Engineer • Physicist • Musician/composer • Statistician	• Math teacher • Chemist • Electronics technician • Music teacher • Scientific researcher
Ideas for Nonvisual Thinkers with More Verbal Brains	
• Journalist • Translator • Librarian • Stock and bonds analyst • Copy editor • Accountant	• Budget analyst • Bookkeeper and record keeper • Special education teacher • Book indexer • Speech therapist • Inventory control specialist

From *Developing Talents – Careers for Individuals with Asperger Syndrome and High-Functioning Autism* by T. Grandin, & K. Duffy, 2004, Shawnee Mission, KS: Autism Asperger Publishing Company. Adapted with permission.

As for most of us, but even more so, the motivation of individuals with ASD to work is directly related to the extent to which they enjoy what they are doing. Holtz et al. (2006) recommend addressing the physical and social aspects of the job when determining an appropriate match. Components of the physical job match include:

- Hours of employment
- Acceptable noise levels at the job site
- Pay, leave, and other benefits

- Acceptable activity levels
- Physical requirements of the job (e.g., lifting)
- Acceptable margin of error (quality control)
- Production requirements

Components of the social job match include:
- Acceptable level of interaction with coworkers and supervisors
- Clear job expectations
- Grooming and hygiene requirements
- Demands on communication skills
- Personal space available
- Phone/vending machine/cafeteria
- Coworker training and support
- Community status

The ITP should guide the team in developing job experiences. Experiences, talents, and interests should match the plan for the future. Generally, jobs may be categorized as follows: **competitive employment, supported employment**, and **secured or segregated employment**. Much of the research related to employment of individuals with ASD focuses on supported and secured or segregated employment. Individuals with ASD have typically been placed within the more structured work settings. Current trends continue this pattern, and at this time only approximately 12% of higher functioning adults with ASD and approximately 6% of adults with more significant ASD characteristics are in paid employment situations (Howlin et al., 2005; Keel, Mesibov, & Woods, 1997; Mawhood & Howlin, 1999; Müller et al., 2003; Rogan et al., 2003; Rogan, Banks, & Howard, 2000; Unger, 1999). These are grim statistics, considering the considerable talents of this group of individuals.

Competitive employment is generally unsupported, and individuals suited for this kind of employment are usually skilled, such as a higher functioning individual with ASD. Competitive jobs include all types, from working in the computer industry to waiting tables, teaching, doing landscaping, and more.

Supported employment, on the other hand, allows individuals with disabilities to work alongside neurotypical coworkers while receiving ongoing support on the job. The amount of support may be reduced over time as the individual becomes familiar with the expectations of the position. Job environments within this sector often include hotels, restaurants, office buildings, and schools/universities.

Finally, secured or segregated employment provides a separate work environment that is usually self-contained, and where employees are not integrated with neurotypical workers. Typical tasks may include collating, packaging, and assembly. By the nature of their role requirements, such options are usually selected for individuals on the lower skilled end of the autism spectrum.

The team should take time to investigate the options that best match the needs and capabilities of the student. Concentrate on carving out a niche, possibly breaking larger, more complex jobs into smaller components. By careful planning and exploration, a range of jobs will likely emerge that meet the needs of the individual with ASD.

Preparing Employers

Employers' management practices, such as flexibility in adapting tasks and a willingness to provide accommodations, have been noted as being important to success for individuals with ASD in the workplace (Hagner & Cooney, 2005). Supervisors who establish an atmosphere of mutual support and develop a worker-friendly environment create a "win-win" situation that benefits both the employer and the individual with ASD (Rogan et al., 2000).

How do employers get the knowledge and skill to accommodate the needs of their employee with ASD? Transition teams must establish what information will be necessary to teach future employers and coworkers about each individual with ASD. They must also emphasize where the individual will need help and anticipate what training might have to be provided to the employer and coworkers, in addition to basic information on ASD. Providing a list of accommodations that the worker might need is beneficial (see Figure 11.5).

ADA guarantees that your young adult may request certain accommodations in the workplace. Your young adult may need others, depending on his needs and where he is working. These accommodations may include:

• Pictures or drawings of the task
• Templates of forms or documents
• A note taker
• A voice recorder
• Written instructions
• Daily checklists
• Written or verbal reminders
• Written or picture instructions next to machines, such as postage machine, copier, printer
• Minimal clutter in the work environment
• Minimal noise in the work environment (such as no radios or music)
• Large tasks broken down into small steps
• A "Where to" guide for resources or coworkers
• A timer or alarm as a reminder
• Additional hands-on training
• Headset for telephone or a speaker phone
• Multiple breaks
• Performance feedback presented visually (charts, diagrams)
• Mentor or job coach
• Information for coworkers about ASD
• His own desk or workspace
• Checklist for completing task
• Timelines for completion of task
• Assignment of one task at a time
• Training on appropriate workplace behaviors (e.g., interacting with customers)
• Notice before changes (such as rearranging supply closet or change in job-related work)
• Consistent supervision by one person
• Prioritization of tasks
• Regular feedback on performance (positive and constructive)

From *Life Journey Through Autism: A Transition Guide*, by K. D. Holtz, N. M. Owings, & A. K. Ziegart, 2006. Alexandria, VA: Organization for Autism Research. Adapted with permission.

Figure 11.5. List of reasonable and common job accommodations.

Hagner and Cooney (2005) interviewed the supervisors of 14 successfully employed individuals with ASD and found that some key supervisory strategies were utilized with this population. As suggested in Table 11.4, it might be helpful to share a list of strategies to supervisors of working adults with ASD.

Table 11.4
Key Supervision Strategies

Area	Strategy
Job modification	• Maintain a consistent schedule and job duties • Keep the social demands of the job manageable and predictable • Provide organizers to help structure and keep track of work • Add activities to reduce or eliminate unstructured time
Supervision	• Be direct and specific when giving directions • Verify that communications are correctly understood • Assist the employee in learning social rules and interpreting social cues encountered on the job • Explain and help the employee deal with changes on the job
Coworker relationships and social interactions	• Encourage coworkers to initiate interactions • Ensure that one or two coworkers play a role in helping to give job related suggestions and "keep an eye out" for the employee
Support services	• Provide a sense of familiarity and reassurance until the employee and company staff get to know one another • Transfer relationships and supports to company employees • Check in and remain on-call in case problems arise • Maintain a liaison role for nonwork issues that affect the job

From "'I Do That for Everybody': Supervising Employees with Autism," by D. Hagner & B. F. Cooney, 2005, *Focus on Autism and Other Developmental Disabilities, 20*(2), 91-97. Adapted with permission.

Developing a Social Network

In addition to life at work, the individual with ASD needs to achieve success at play/leisure. This has often been overlooked. Thus, research indicates that students with ASD leave school programs ill equipped with the social and communication skills necessary for life success (Müller, Schuler, Burton, & Yates, 2003). High school is the perfect time to address social issues and build social skills. Specific guides are available for teaching social skills, but teachers may need guidance regarding exactly what skills are important to teach at this age level. Although not all jobs or postsecondary experiences have high social demands, certain skills are vital for establishing a social network.

People make judgments about a person based on appearance and conduct in public. Therefore, it is important that individuals with ASD are taught skills in the areas of (a) general cleanliness and hygiene, (b) grooming, (c) age-appropriate clothing options, (d) social greetings, and (e) issues related to sexuality, including sexual orientation and safety.

Adults have lives outside of work where effective communication is required to express their wants, needs, likes, and dislikes. Transition planning must address the vast array of communication skills, from greetings to voice modulation to obtaining help when necessary. In addition, social behaviors, including table manners, personal space awareness, what to do on a break, the difference between private and public behavior, and so on, must be specifically taught. To ensure that is done, the ITP should address all of these social needs.

Further, individuals with ASD will need to gain experience in accessing community resources if they are effectively going to establish a social network for themselves. Therefore, community resources such as church, clubs, sports, transportation, and so on, should be addressed by the ITP team.

Planning for College/University Attendance

Depending on the ability and interests of the student with ASD, further education may also be something the ITP team will need to consider. For instance, the ITP should include activities that prepare the individual for completing the required paperwork and assessments necessary for acceptance in the school of his/her choice.

Choosing the right postsecondary program is key to success. Options include vocational schools, community colleges, technical schools, or liberal arts universities. Two-year programs or certificate programs are the best choice for many on the autism spectrum. Virtual colleges may be appropriate options for some individuals. The transition timeline provided in Figure 11.2 may be used as a resource as the team plans for further education.

If career plans include obtaining a college degree, once the student decides on a university, self-advocacy becomes vitally important. Colleges or universities offer different services, so the student should check ahead of time to make sure that the necessary services are available.

A main difference from high school is that at the postsecondary level students are responsible for requesting the help they need. Disability offices typically do not track down students to see what help they need, as they are now considered adults and must advocate for themselves. To qualify for services through a college's disability office, students generally must (a) present documentation of their disability prior to arranging accommodations and (b) meet with staff to arrange accommodations. In addition, students must talk with each of their professors to let them know what their specific needs for a given class are.

While services vary, below you will find a list and description of some basic services that may be provided to eligible students. Keep in mind that when the student qualifies for services, the official documentation will specifically state what accommodations he or she requires.

- **Tutoring services:** typically provided in a group setting at the disability service office for core requirement classes (e.g., English 101)

- **Test-taking:** for students who qualify to take tests in a quiet area, need a longer test time, or need the test to be given in a different format (e.g., oral instead of written)

- **Note-taking:** typically a note taker is solicited in class

- **Alternative print:** often needs to be requested one to two months prior to the start of the semester

- **Other resources:** may include large-screen computers, scanners, and audio or video recorders

At the postsecondary level, it is important to keep in mind that students must show proper documentation to receive services under ADA or Section 504. It is also very important that they talk with each of their professors about their needs and how the professor can best assist.

Summary and Conclusions

Planning students' transition from school to post-school settings is a critical part of the IEP process in the middle and high school years (Smith, 2001). To be effective, transition planning must be ongoing and outcome-oriented, based on collaboration between students and their families, school and adult service personnel, and the community. Research has shown that for students with disabilities, opportunities for employment during their school years lead to increased success for employment after they leave school (Rogan et al., 2003). Finally, while job-related skills are typically identified as priorities for transition planning, preparing for successful employment is only one aspect of transition to adult life. Emphasis must also be placed on acquisition of the skills necessary for independent living. Thus, schools must equip students with ASD with social skills, safety skills, information on appropriate sexual behavior, and so on, if they are going to reach their potential as satisfied and productive members of society.

Tips for the Classroom

✓ Consult some of the books that focus on the characteristics of individuals with ASD, such as *This Is Asperger Syndrome* by Gagnon and Myles (1999), which provides simple visuals depicting the unique characteristics of this population. Books such as these assist teams in developing an understanding of the student. They also assist students in understanding their own characteristics.

✓ Adapt forms and worksheets to promote independence and participation in the transition process. Mayer-Johnson's Boardmaker™ (Mayer-Johnson LLC, 1981-2005) may be utilized to adapt the ITP questions so that students who need extra visual supports can participate in the ITP planning process to their full potential.

✓ Some schools have developed units to teach students skills to increase their involvement in the transition process. Units might target developing a goals chart or checklist that includes (a) where they want to live, (b) how they want to get around, (c) where they would like to work, (d) what they would like to do in their leisure time, (e) and new skills they would like to learn. Units might also focus on identifying roadblocks to accomplishing goals and strategies to get around roadblocks, as well as identifying gifts and talents, and communicating those.

✓ Technology provides tools for transition planning. Web sites are available to assist professionals and families in extending questions and themes that this chapter discusses to specifically tailor planning for the needs of the individual students in your charge. An example is Mapping Your Future (http://www.mapping-your-future.org/).

✓ Develop relationships with school and community staff knowledgeable about and involved with transition early on. These resource personnel can help parents and professionals navigate the system. Relationships built with knowledgeable collaborators can make for a smooth transition.

✓ Utilize special interests when envisioning future employment opportunities or social situations for individuals with ASD. Remember it is their life the team is planning for.

✓ One of the primary obstacles to success in the workplace for individuals with ASD is a lack of social skills. Make social skill instruction a definite part of the curriculum and work with parents to provide opportunities for practice. Arm the individual with ASD with coping strategies for many social situations. Explore the *Hidden Curriculum* (Myles, Trautman, & Schelvan, 2004) of social skills that make or break a social situation.

Chapter Highlights

- Many individuals with ASD leave high school with inadequate social and communication skills for life success, often leading to difficulties in obtaining and sustaining employment as adults.

- IDEA 2004 mandates that transition services be implemented at age 16, or as early as age 14 if deemed necessary.

- Transition services include an individual transition plan (ITP) in which a coordinated set of activities is specified for the individual student. These activities are to be outcome-oriented; based on individual needs; and include instruction, community experiences, and the development of employment and other post-school living objectives.

- Transition teams include the individuals who are part of the IEP team but may also involve members of vocational services, agencies that focus on vocational support, representatives of postsecondary educational options and residential services, as well as others as appropriate.

- Students should be involved in the transition team to the best of their ability. Students should also be made aware of who transition team members are, as well as their rights under the law. Additionally, students need to be taught skills to enhance their participation in their own transition to post-school life.

- ITPs should be individualized and include assessment; the student's preferences; career goals such as academics, career awareness and development, as well as work habits and behaviors; self-advocacy goals such as decision making and self-awareness; and independent living goals, such as taking care of personal needs, community participation, household responsibilities, leisure activities, and managing finances; the steps, instructional methods, and resources to achieve these goals; and methods for evaluating success of transition activities.

- Services and supports for preparing students with ASD for employment and adult life should be based on an assessment of their characteristics and needs. The Underlying Characteristic Checklist (UCC) is an informal assessment tool designed to look at patterns of characteristics specific to individuals with ASD; it can be used to assess and then help in planning intervention based on the results.

- It is important to take into account the student's interests, strengths, skills, tolerance for various stimuli, and supports when creating transition plans.

- Effective planning for and support of the transition process needs to include self-advocacy, self-determination, and person-centered planning.

- Making Action Plans (MAPS) and Planning Alternative Tomorrows with Hope (PATH) are two resources that assist in person-centered planning by looking at hopes for the future as well as the student's current skill level related to those hopes and using that information to develop strategies that will lead to success.

- Strategies for self-determination and self-advocacy must be directly taught to students with ASD. This can be achieved through a variety of means, including scripting dialogue, video modeling, and teaching students about their disability.

- Using the ITP to assist in selecting meaningful coursework based on students' special interests, goals, skills and needs as related to those goals, and requirements for generalization is a critical use of the ITP.

- Students with ASD have documented difficulties in the area of employment, including issues with sustaining employment, social success, job skills, communication with employers and colleagues, and level of income.

- Increasing job placement opportunities for students with ASD should be addressed in secondary school through appropriate experiences; matching the student's interests, skills, and needs with job placement; and matching the type of job to the type of thinking unique to that individual.

- Physical and social aspects of the job need to be considered in matching the individual to a particular job.

- Jobs may be categorized as competitive employment, supported employment, and secured or segregated employment. Most research related to employment of individuals with ASD focuses on the latter two forms of employment.

- It is important to prepare employers to work with individuals with ASD. Such preparation may include strategies for job modification, supervision, coworker relationships, and support services.

- Teaching social behaviors necessary for work and for community involvement should be part of the ITP considerations.

- Students with ASD may consider pursuing postsecondary schooling as an option. If so, the ITP must include information about the student's strengths and needs in terms of self-advocacy and independency.

- Students with disabilities, including ASD, can obtain specialized services and accommodations at the postsecondary level. However, they are responsible for requesting the services and providing documentation of need.

Chapter Review Questions

1. What is meant by "transition planning"?

2. Why is planning the transition from school a critical aspect of the IEP process in the middle and high school years?

3. Who are the members of a typical transition team?

4. What should students with ASD know about transition planning?

5. What are the federally mandated requirements of transition planning for persons with disabilities?

6. Why is it important to address career, self-advocacy, and independent living goals in the ITP?

7. What are the elements of a well-designed ITP?

8. Why is the Underlying Characteristics Checklist (UCC) useful in planning for individuals with ASD?

9. What types of assessment might be used in transition planning?

10. What are the components of successful planning for and support of the transition process?

11. What are the considerations that affect job placement and retention for persons with ASD?

12. Why should social skills development be an important part of the ITP process?

13. How do services at the postsecondary level differ from those for school-aged individuals?

References

Americans with Disabilities Act, 42 U. S. C. §§ 12101-12213 (1990).

Aspy, R., & Grossman, B. (2007). *The ziggurat model: A framework for designing comprehensive interventions for individuals with high-functioning autism and Asperger Syndrome.* Shawnee Mission, KS: Autism Asperger Publishing Company.

Baker, J. (2005). *Preparing for life: The complete guide for transitioning to adulthood for those with autism and asperger syndrome.* Arlington, TX: Future Horizons.

Engström, I., Ekström, L., & Emilsson, B. (2003). Psychosocial functioning in a group of Swedish adults with asperger syndrome or high-functioning autism. *Autism: The International Journal of Research and Practice, 7*(1), 99-110.

Field, S., & Hoffman, A. (1999). The importance of family involvement for promoting self-determination in adolescents with autism and other developmental disabilities. *Focus on Autism and Other Developmental Disabilities, 14*(1), 36-41.

Falvey, M. A., Forest, M., Pearpoint, J., & Rosenberg, R. (2000). *All my life's a circle: Using the tools: Circles, MAPS, and PATH.* Toronto, Canada: Inclusion Press.

Fairfax County Public Schools. (2006). *Transition toolkit for parents.* Fairfax, VA: Fairfax County Public Schools, Department of Special Services, Office of Special Education, Career and Transition Services Section.

Fullerton, A., & Coyne, P. (1999). Developing skills and concepts for self-determination in young adults with autism. *Focus on Autism and Other Developmental Disabilities, 14*(1), 42-53, 63.

Gagnon, E., & Myles, B. S. (1999). *This is Asperger Syndrome.* Shawnee Mission, KS: Autism Asperger Publishing Company.

Garcia-Villamisar, D., Ross, D., & Wehman, P. (2000). Clinical differential analysis of persons with autism in a work setting: A follow-up study. *Journal of Vocational Rehabilitation, 14,* 183-185.

Garcia-Villamisar, D., Wehman, P., & Navarro, M. D. (2002). Changes in the quality of autistic people's life that work in supported and sheltered employment. A 5-year follow-up study. *Journal of Vocational Rehabilitation, 17,* 309-312.

Grandin, T. (1999). *Choosing the right job for people with autism and asperger's syndrome.* Center for Study of Autism. Retrieved August 20, 2006, from http://www.autism.org/temple/jobs.html

Grandin, T., & Duffy, K. (2004). *Developing talents: Careers for individuals with Asperger Syndrome and high-functioning autism.* Shawnee Mission, KS: Autism Asperger Publishing Company.

Hagner, D., & Cooney, B. F. (2005). "I do that for everybody": Supervising employees with autism. *Focus on Autism and Other Developmental Disabilities, 20*(2), 91-97.

Held, M. F., Thoma, C. A., & Thomas, K. (2004). "The John Jones show": How one teacher facilitated self-determined transition planning for a young man with autism. *Focus on Autism and Other Developmental Disabilities, 19*(3), 177-188.

Henn, J., & Henn, M. (2005). Defying the odds: You can't put a square peg in a round hole no matter how hard you try. *Journal of Vocational Rehabilitation, 22,* 129-130.

Holtz, K. D., Owings, N. M., & Ziegart, A. K. (2006). *Life journey through autism: A transition guide.* Alexandria, VA: Organization for Autism Research.

Howlin, P., Alcock, J., & Burkin, C. (2005). An eight-year follow-up of a specialist supported employment service for high-ability adults with autism or asperger syndrome. *Autism: The International Journal of Research and Practice, 9*(5), 533-549.

Hurlbutt, K., & Chalmers, L. (2004). Employment and adults with asperger syndrome. *Focus on Autism and Other Developmental Disabilities, 19*(4), 215-222.

Izzo, M. V., Hertzfeld, J. E., & Aaron, J. H. (2001). Raising the bar: Student self-determination + good teaching = success. *Journal for Vocational Special Needs Education, 24*(1), 26-36.

Jennes-Coussens, M., Magill-Evans, J., & Koning, C. (2006). The quality of life of young men with asperger syndrome: A brief report. *Autism: The International Journal of Research and Practice, 10*(4), 403-414.

Keel, J. H., Mesibov, G. B., & Woods, A. V. (1997). TEACCH-supported employment program. *Journal of Autism and Developmental Disorders, 27*(1), 3-9.

Mapping Your Future. (2002). *Welcome to mapping your future.* Retrieved July 30, 2007, from www.mapping-your-future.org. http://www.mapping-your-future.org/

Mawhood, L., & Howlin, P. (1999). The outcome of a supported employment scheme for high-functioning adults with autism or asperger syndrome. *Autism, 3*(3), 229-254.

Mayer-Johnson LLC. (1981-2005). *Boardmaker: The picture communication symbols.* Solana Beach, CA: Author.

Müller, E., Schuler, A., Burton, B. A., & Yates, G. B. (2003). Meeting the vocational support needs of individuals with asperger syndrome and other autism spectrum disabilities. *Journal of Vocational Rehabilitation, 18,* 163-175.

Myles, B. S., & Adreon, D. (2001). *Asperger Syndrome and adolescence: Practical solutions for school success.* Shawnee Mission, KS: Autism Asperger Publishing Company.

Myles, B. S., Trautman, M. L., & Schelvan, R. L. (2004). *The hidden curriculum: Practical solutions for understanding unstated rules in social situations.* Shawnee Mission, KS: Autism Asperger Publishing Company.

Nesbitt, S. (2000). Why and why not? Factors influencing employment for individuals with asperger syndrome. *Autism, 4*(4), 357-369.

Pearpoint, J., O'Brien, J., & Forest, M. (1998). *PATH: A workbook for planning alternative tomorrows and hope for schools, organizations, businesses and families.* Toronto, Canada: Inclusion Press.

Rogan, P., Banks, B., & Herbein, M. H. (2003). Supported employment and workplace supports: A qualitative study. *Journal of Vocational Rehabilitation, 19,* 5-18.

Rogan, P., Banks, B., & Howard, M. (2000). Workplace supports in practice: As little as possible, as much as necessary. *Focus on Autism and Other Developmental Disabilities, 15*(1), 2-11.

Schelvan, R. L., Swanson, T. C., & Smith, S. M. (2005). Making each year successful: Issues in transition. In B. S. Myles (Ed.), *Children and youth with Asperger Syndrome: Strategies for success in inclusive settings* (pp. 127-157). Thousand Oaks, CA: Corwin Press.

Sitlington, P. L., & Clark, G. M. (2001). Career/vocational assessment: A critical component of transition planning. *Assessment for Effective Intervention, 26*(4), 5-22.

Smith, T.E.C. (2001). Section 504, the ADA, and public schools: What educators need to know. *Remedial and Special Education, 22*(6), 335-343.

Unger, D. D. (1999). Workplace supports: A view from employers who have hired supported employees. *Focus on Autism and Other Developmental Disabilities, 14*(3), 167-169.

Unger, D. D. (2002). Employers' attitudes toward persons with disabilities in the workforce: Myths or realities? *Focus on Autism and Other Developmental Disabilities, 17*(1), 2-10.

United States Department of Education. (2004). *Individuals with disabilities education improvement act.* Retrieved October 29, 2006, from http://frwebgate.access.gpo.gov/cgi-bin/getdoc.cgi?dbname=108_cong_public_laws&docid=f:publ446.108

Ward, M., & Meyer, R. (1999). Self-determination for people with developmental disabilities and autism: Two self-advocates' perspectives. *Focus on Autism and Other Developmental Disabilities, 14*(3), 133-139.

Wehman, P. (2002). A new era: Revitalizing special education for children and their families. *Focus on Autism and Other Developmental Disabilities, 17*(4), 194-197.

Wehmeyer, M. (1999). A functional model of self-determination: Describing development and implementing instruction. *Focus on Autism and Other Developmental Disabilities, 14*(1), 53-61.

Learner Objectives

After reading this chapter, the learner should be able to:

- List the members involved in an educational support and intervention team

- Discuss the importance of collaboration among team members

- Differentiate between an IEP and a 504 Plan

- Discuss what is needed in terms of planning and preparation for effective team meetings

- Discuss the importance of preparing students for team meetings

- Discuss the factors that contribute to positive and effective collaboration

- Demonstrate an understanding of how students with ASD think and learn, based on the scenarios given in the chapter

Chapter 12

The Education Team: Positive, Effective Interdisciplinary Collaboration

Paula Jacobsen

Sam, now 10, was diagnosed with high-functioning autism (possibly Asperger's disorder) before he was 3. He could talk, but primarily repeated things he had memorized, such as parts of videos or educational TV programs. He did not use language for communication. He became easily overwhelmed by sensory stimuli, especially sounds, and demonstrated stimming behaviors (body movements), poor eye contact, and poor attention. From the age of 3, Sam received intensive speech and language therapy, behavior therapy, and occupational therapy through his public school district, as well as privately. As mandated by law, his IEP team met annually to determine continuing concerns and progress, and to write goals.

After several years, Sam had a larger vocabulary and used more eye contact (briefly stared, but did not use eye contact to regulate interactions to indicate meaningful attention). His gross-motor planning improved, but fine-motor continued to be poor. Sam had rote knowledge of some "appropriate" behaviors, such as sitting in a circle with his legs crossed and his hands in his lap. He had learned number facts so well that he scored above grade level when tested orally, but he did not grasp math concepts or even appear to understand number value beyond the number 3. He could attend to an adult who was working with him individually, but did not seem to follow the same basic communication and expectations in a small group (even when led by the same adult). He raised his hand and waited to be called on in class, but then made comments that were tangential or completely off topic. Medication reduced his anxiety and decreased his sensory overload somewhat, but it did not increase meaningful attention. By second grade, Sam had developed some skills but was unable to function adequately in school, even with an aide beside him.

Sam's parents invited all the specialists who had worked with him (from his public school and privately) to attend the next IEP, with the understanding and agreement of all that this would be an opportunity to share information and problem solve. Each participant spoke and was heard. Each described efforts, challenges, and concerns. Although the individual skills they worked on with Sam varied, there were similarities in their experience of Sam, and there were concerns about him that they all recognized. Each described instances in which they felt he could understand and learn, and then presented evidence that he could not apply what he seemed to know. The skills that were the focus of their goals and work seemed splintered, perhaps reflecting Sam's inability to integrate and use much of what he mastered.

As they spoke and listened, most recognized that Sam was not aware of his own behaviors or the point of their interventions, although he seemed to have a positive and comfortable relationship with each participant; most appreciated his efforts, regardless of how clueless he was about what he was doing. His math tutor had begun working with him on the most basic number concepts, utilizing concrete materials and verbal descriptions of concrete concepts, which he could understand and then express himself. This seemed like such a good idea that the school occupational therapist said she would begin describing concretely what he was doing or saying, using some of the specific language that was suggested by the language therapist. His teacher and aide would try to incorporate mirroring language, at least some of the time (pointing out the "obvious" that was occurring, not just redirecting), as would most of his school-based and private therapists.

This subsequently became an ongoing topic in formal team meetings and interim consultation between team members. Sam developed an awareness of and ability to describe what he and others were doing and sometimes why. Most team members saw this happening, as each recognized the effectiveness of articulating the obvious. As Sam became able to recognize what he was doing and what was expected, he did and continues to do more of what is expected.

At 10, Sam is close to grade level in many subjects, but he cannot learn in a classroom of 20 students. He is in a small special education class without an individual aide and, although he moves around a lot, he attends adequately for this setting (sometimes with reminders), participates on topic (with reminders), and is learning and producing grade-level work (with extra time and a reduced workload). He still has difficulty with pencil-paper tasks, but uses larger spaces for math problems and can now type his other written work. Over three years, there have been several meetings and many briefer collaborations between team members to address concerns as they arose. This team focus on understanding Sam, and then working with him in similar ways based on a mutual understanding, supports the work of team members and the tremendous growth that Sam has made.

Individuals with autism spectrum disorders (ASD), including Asperger Syndrome (AS), live in a world where most people around them think and communicate quite differently than they do. They often have specific strengths (some are gifted), and they also have cognitive, communication, and social challenges (Attwood, 1998; Klin, Volkmar, & Sparrow, 2000; Siegel, 1996). These students benefit from many therapies and supportive interventions (Bate, 2004; Leventhal-Belfer, 2004; Wiss, 2004). Each service may have a unique focus, such as language, gross- and fine-motor development, behavior modification, and assessing appropriate learning strategies, and services may be provided in a variety of locations. Yet, everyone's work with and on behalf of the child can be enriched, and the benefit to the child enhanced, when providers collaborate. In addition to each unique contribution, team members often develop a shared focus and a shared language that is meaningful to the individual child.

Once the student begins to receive special education services, teachers and classroom aides, administrators, other service providers at school and in the community, parents, and the students themselves, all become a part of an **educational support and intervention team**, as mandated by the law that provides access to education for students with disabilities. For those who work with these students, collaboration can be a supportive and a very rewarding aspect of that work (Jacobsen, 2003, 2005). Specifically, **collaboration** generally results in a better understanding of what students can and cannot understand, what they can and cannot be expected to do successfully, and what supports or scaffolding they require to learn and function at school.

This chapter addresses how knowledge of the factors that support **resiliency** can inform a collaborative team approach and the contributions each member on the student's team can make. Opportunities for collaboration, topics of importance or concern to the student's team, as well as how to prepare and plan for effective team meetings are explored. The final section clarifies and further explores the factors that contribute to positive, effective collaboration.

Understanding, Supporting, and Enhancing Resiliency Can Inform the Collaborative Process

Research has clearly demonstrated that children can succeed in school and in life if they feel that someone knows who they are (sees their challenges *and* their strengths), and if we have *appropriately* high (clear, manageable, and attainable) expectations for them. An interested, caring approach supports **school connectedness** (McNeely, Nonnemaker, & Blum, 2002; Noddings, 1992), and school success enhances resiliency and the likelihood of future success (Benard, 1991, 2004; Werner & Smith, 1992).

Students with ASD, even the most capable and high functioning, have very different ways of processing information, of understanding language, and of communicating, than typical students. As a result, knowing who they are (their challenges and their strengths) and determining appropriate, clear, manageable, and attainable expectations is not always easy. However, the likelihood of success is greater when team members work together with a shared desire to understand the student. Team members with varying degrees of knowledge about ASD can contribute and learn when they collaborate.

Education Team Members

Teachers

With the exception of parents, no adult spends more time with a student than his teacher(s) and classroom aide(s). General education teachers are responsible for many students, some with special needs and others with the range of abilities and learning styles that can occur in all classes. Special education teachers (including resource teachers) generally are responsible for fewer students, each with special needs and an individual plan. The challenge for the special education teacher is to know each student, his abilities, and special needs, and to provide a manageable environment in which he can function and learn.

Even teachers who are very familiar with ASD sometimes become frustrated or discouraged by their students' behavior and learning difficulties. Teachers' openness to knowing and supporting a manageable environment for their students is important. The power of a patient, positive, and collaborative relationship between teachers and their students with ASD, and the value of a supportive, collaborative relationship between the teacher and other team members, cannot be overstated. Such relationships can change situations in which challenges are something to avoid or eliminate to situations where challenges are to be expected and to be addressed as part of a problem-solving process.

Other School Professionals

School psychologists, speech-language therapists, and occupational therapists, administrators, behavior specialists, counselors, and others, may also be part of the student's team. They provide observations and assessments that determine eligibility for services, and they participate in planning goals. Finally, they may also provide direct interventions to students or consultation to teachers and each other. Often they have varying levels of experience and understanding about the behavior and learning style of a particular student.

For example, speech-language therapists generally work with pragmatic language, including translating and processing language issues as they occur. They may work with students individually, with small groups of students, and with classroom teachers. Occupational therapists (OTs) primarily address sensory needs. They can observe and explain certain behaviors (such as mouthing objects, covering ears, bouncing, pacing) as a student's attempt to manage internal and external sensory stimulation. They may recommend that such behaviors be allowed or suggest alternatives that better meet the student's need (such as sitting or kneeling on a special pillow or ball instead of a regular classroom chair, or chewing gum to calm).

When we identify a student's actions as "inappropriate," we focus on what we think must change. When we recognize that we do not understand the benefit of the student's actions or words, we can attend to who the student is and what he needs ... and we can recognize the necessity of meeting the student's needs as we try to bridge the gap between those needs and our own.

Outside Professionals

In addition to services provided by the school, parents may obtain private assessments and services, such as **neuropsychological** assessment, occupational therapy, speech-language therapy, social skills groups, individual **psychotherapy,** specific educational and/or behavioral therapies, and **psycho-pharmacological interventions** (medications). Collaboration between school personnel and outside professionals can benefit everyone's work with the student.

Outside professionals and school personnel can add to and learn from each other's understanding of the student when collaboration is informed by an effort to understand the student's perspective and make the school experience manageable for him. This is possible if the collaboration is one in which school and outside professionals listen to each other's concerns about and for the student … when all are open to seeing the positive contributions as well as the challenges of others, thus supporting the development of goals, plans, and specific interventions that support a student's success.

Parents

Parents have varying degrees of understanding of ASD. Some parents of higher-functioning children may have first learned of their child's issues through the school. Others may have had concerns about their child's development long before anyone else did, including their pediatrician. Often parents have had a range of experiences with professionals whom they have consulted before and after their child started school. These can vary in their usefulness. At worst, professionals who do not adequately understand ASD may be well meaning, but they may be reassuring that everything is fine (when intervention is needed) or critical of the parents' concerns (even when such concerns are realistic and relevant). Others may understand the child's challenges and offer direction that supports the parents and provides early intervention.

Parents sometimes develop responses that support their children that appear to others to be over-involvement or to foster dependence. For example, a parent may be facilitating and supporting a child with ASD by oversight, guidance, and direction that enables that child to function but that would be inappropriate for a more typical child. Just as it is most productive to understand the child's behavior as an attempt to master, it is most productive to attempt to understand what *is* supportive and effective about parents' behavior toward their child, as well as their understanding and interpretation of the child's needs and behavior. The support may be what is needed and, therefore, should be continued for as long as it is needed. In this kind of problem-solving atmosphere, it is also possible to consider and evaluate alternative or additional supports and interventions. Unfortunately, some parents have not had an opportunity to participate in a positive meeting in which they have felt heard. Indeed, many have even felt blamed and criticized by professionals and by family members.

Parents also can share information or provide support in very concrete ways, such as helping out in the classroom. For grade-school children, parents may be interested in talking to the class about ASD or AS. This can be very supportive to the student and to the entire class, and facilitates understanding and a more positive relationship between classmates (Jacobsen, 2005).

The Student

When a student with ASD is able to be a member of his team, he is more likely to know his strengths and be able to ask for and accept help. Maintaining positive, accepting, respectful, problem-solving relationships with adults engages the student as a member of his team. When it is difficult and energy-consuming for the team to understand the student's perspective, it can be instructive to remember how difficult and energy-consuming it is for the student to understand the rest of us.

Students are less likely to engage when they believe that adults are primarily interested in gaining compliance. By contrast, they view communication with and between adults as a support when they see adults as being interested in knowing them as well as wanting them to learn and to get along with others. Higher-functioning students can become aware of being part of a team when team members describe their work with the student as a team approach. Students can be informed about team meetings, and as they become older and more aware, students can develop lists of issues and concerns that they would like addressed and participate towards the end of the meeting or hear the team's responses later. Older students who can articulate their issues or concerns, perhaps with the prior help of a team member, and can listen as well as speak can be effective participants in team meetings.

Opportunities for Collaboration

Teachers and other professionals who work with students with ASD face many challenges. At times their work may not feel like part of a team effort, and remembering that they are part of a team may not be easy. In fact, collaborating with team members may not come to mind or may seem like an additional burden. The reality is that supportive, effective collaboration makes our work easier. Formal and informal collaboration, even if infrequent, can facilitate a team approach. Team members can share their perceptions and how each is responding to the student. The most helpful and meaningful collaboration addresses the student's perspective as well as the questions and dilemmas that perspective may present.

Formal and Informal Team Collaboration

Public schools must hold mandated team meetings as well as abide by district procedures for communicating about students of concern. School personnel must understand these procedures and requirements and inform parents about them when appropriate. Private schools, although not obligated by law, may also hold formal meetings. Understanding the differences between formal team meetings and informal collaboration can help team members remain aware of and better utilize the team, and thus support an effective team approach.

Formal Team Meetings

When parents, teachers, or other school personnel are concerned about a student who has not yet been evaluated or formally identified as having special education needs, they may request a team meeting, sometimes called a **student study team meeting (SST)**. Students who have been evaluated and identified as needing special services or support have an individualized education program (IEP) or a **504 Plan**.

Students who are eligible for an IEP receive services (such as special education placements, language therapy, occupational therapy, etc.), specific goals are developed and monitored, and accommodations and/or modifications are identified that may help meet their needs and support their abilities. A 504 Plan, on the other hand, is for students who can function adequately in the mainstream with accommodations, such as assistive technology for writing, reduced homework, longer time for tests and assignments, and so on.

Students with an IEP or a 504 Plan are assigned a team that is responsible for planning and monitoring progress. Other students may have a less formal team, which may include teachers, parents, the student, and outside tutors or therapists who work with and support them after school or through informal school support. Regardless of their specific purpose, teams meet to develop a shared understanding of the student and exchange ideas for supporting the student.

The perspective of the person who facilitates a team meeting can set the tone and greatly influence the effectiveness of the team. When there is a desire to know, to understand, and to support the student, this position of advocacy supports the efforts of all team members. Goals, benchmarks, accommodations, and modifications must be clearly stated so they make sense to the student and the adults. Recommendations should make it easier, not more complicated, for students to be successful.

Informal Collaboration

Whether or not a student has a formal team, informal collaboration between the teacher, the parents, and others who work with the student can facilitate understanding and enhance communication. Collaboration provides an opportunity for the teacher, other professionals, the parents, and the student to share information and address concerns and can be an opportunity to support strengths and respond to the student's needs and challenges. On occasion, when a student is experiencing difficulty with a particular situation or with an intervention, a telephone call or a brief meeting is enough to resolve the problem.

Andrew

Andrew is a fifth-grade student with AS. He was upset because he would not be able to complete his report on time. This was a major, long-term assignment, and he was convinced the report would not be accepted, because his teacher said that there would be no time extensions. Andrew knew that extra time was provided in his IEP but could not consider the possibility that the teacher did not mean him when she said to the class that there would be no extensions. He refused to ask her about it, because she had been perfectly clear.

Andrew's teacher and counselor discussed the situation, with Andrew listening quietly, but attentively. The teacher said that Andrew could have extra time if he needed it, as was always true, as stated in his IEP. When the teacher says "no exceptions," she does not mean him, she explained. Andrew does not understand why someone says "no exceptions" when there are exceptions. It is this inaccurate way of speaking that he has never been able to understand.

This brief collaboration between the teacher and the counselor meant the difference between Andrew accepting help and completing this assignment late or refusing to complete it and giving up. Andrew understood then that he was allowed more time, but he may never understand why someone would say "no exceptions" when there truly are exceptions.

The inexact communication of others can be difficult for students with ASD to understand and even difficult to accept when fully explained. This kind of overt clarification of assignments and other expectations often helps the student to move on, especially when he sees that he will be expected to do what he actually can do.

Addressing Areas of Importance or Concern

Language and Communication

Communication is an essential ingredient of every team function. Although the communication and comprehension difficulties of moderate and lower-functioning students with ASD are often apparent, even those who know them well sometimes misunderstand. This can occur when students understand something they are unable to convey, as well as when they make a rote statement that coincidentally fits a circumstance that they do not understand.

For high-functioning students, it is especially important for the team to remain aware of the pragmatic challenges that affect learning, communication, and relationships. Pragmatic language assumes shared meanings and recognition of what is relevant to others. Pragmatics cannot be easily taught. Keeping this in mind helps team members avoid setting unreasonable expectations for the student and other team members.

Joey

Joey is a sixth-grade student with AS. He recently began middle school. Joey's teachers saw him as bright, disorganized, inattentive, unmotivated, oblivious, and sometimes rude. His test grades were excellent, because he knew a great deal of the information already, yet he was failing. A student study team meeting was arranged. His English teacher told the team that Joey often did not listen when she explained an assignment to the class and subsequently asked her what to do. On one occasion he was to look up the definitions of the vocabulary and spelling list, write them down, and write a sentence using each word. "Well, that's a waste of time," Joey said, turning around and walking away, as though he were announcing this to the other students. His teacher saw this as an example of the very dismissive and rude way Joey sometimes speaks to her. From Joey's perspective, however, this was a statement of fact. He was talking aloud (not to the other students) as he turned away. This assignment was a waste of time for him: He knew the spelling and definitions of the words and was already using them. He intended to state a fact, and he did not understand why the teacher was upset when he gave her this factual information.

A brief follow-up: In this scenario, it would be important for the teacher to understand that Joey's language disorder impairs his ability to understand how his tone affects others. His teacher thought she would feel supported by a language clinician's recommendation that Joey's IEP include a goal related to nonverbal social communication skills.

Social-Emotional Issues

Social skills are dependent on understanding the experience of others, including our effect on them. When team members collaborate about social skills, even in schools in which social skill groups and Social Stories™ (Gray, 2000, 2002) are used to help the student anticipate and respond to a situation, it helps to remember that it is difficult to teach social skills that can be generalized. We can prepare a student for a specific situation or for many specific situations that occur regularly and are easily recognized, but even small changes in routine situations can be difficult for the student. Similarly, presented with a problem, the student may learn the expected answer, but in real-life situations, it is necessary to recognize what is relevant, to generate the questions, not just the answers, and that can prove problematic.

Collaboration can address social-emotional issues by considering the level of the student's awareness of himself and others, as well as his needs. For example, recess is a time to relax and play, because socializing for most students is often a break from structure and assigned work. If working on socialization is important, the team can plan structured, supervised instructional opportunities. If a break is important as an opportunity to relax, a school can allow alternatives to interactive playground recess in addition to opportunities to engage in interactive play with adult support (see Chapter 8 on peer play and friendships).

George

George, an 11-year-old fourth-grade student with high-functioning autism, did not like to miss anything that he saw as required, including school. The most difficult time for him was recess, which he understood as being a time when he was supposed to play with others. But there were too many people, too much activity, and too much noise for him. He walked around the periphery of the play area trying to keep away from others until he could return to the relative calm and predictability of the classroom. When George was informed that recess should be a break, a rest from class work, and a time to relax, he told his mother that he had decided to lie down on one of the benches after lunch. "What will you say if other kids ask you why you are doing that?" she asked. "I'll just tell them I'm resting," he answered. "They can rest their way. I'm going to rest my way."

George had participated in individual and group OT and speech-language therapy, as well as social skills groups, on and off since he was in preschool. He had gained a great deal, but it was hard work and could be exhausting for him. When George's team understood his perspective, they provided alternative choices instead of playground recess for him. They explained to him that this was to address his needs and ensure his comfort, not to manage his behavior or teach him to be different. He was relieved to have his perspective understood and his needs accepted.

Behavior

When team members collaborate to understand a student's behaviors, they have an opportunity to meet her needs as well as address the needs of others. Some behaviors, such as pacing, standing up to work, and so on, can be accepted. Standing or pacing may not distract the student or indicate avoidance of work. Instead, these behaviors may enable a particular student to attend longer to a task or to think more clearly and productively. At other times, a behavior may be acknowledged as meeting a need, but a substitute may be suggested, such as allowing the student to chew gum, use an object to fidget, sit on a special cushion, or take time-out.

Some students have little awareness of their emotional and behavioral escalation. They may not even recognize their loss of control when or after it occurs. Sometimes teams develop specific behavior plans for students with clearly stated expectations and prearranged cues. A team can ensure that the plan addresses the student's needs and abilities *as well as* the school environment. When collaboration focuses on developing awareness, recognizing the student's arousal state becomes more important than any expectation of teaching or compliance at that time (Buron & Curtis, 2004).

Teachable times are only those in which the student can maintain self-control. Cody (below) provides a vivid example of this. Some students, like Cody, become extremely angry or tantrum at more predictable times, such as when there is an expectation to work on a group project or to learn a new concept. When we know that, we can prepare for or avoid some of the situations that are particularly anxiety-producing for a student.

Cody

Cody, a student who had received special education services throughout his schooling, had academic strengths and challenges. He also had severe sensory and mood-regulation challenges. Cody understood and enjoyed math, but dreaded learning new concepts. He could learn from a computer lesson (when that was available), but did not expect to be able to learn from the teacher. He became frustrated, overwhelmed, and sometimes had a full-blown tantrum (screaming, crying, destroying papers, throwing things off his desk, etc.). Perhaps Cody anticipated more difficulty learning the new material than he would actually have encountered, but that was not relevant, given his inability to tolerate the process involved in learning new concepts or procedures. This was observed when he attended a self-contained special education day class for students with autism in kindergarten and first grade and also when he attended a higher-functioning special day class. He was also observed in mainstream classes (which he was able to attend for part of the day in fourth through sixth grade, after which he attended a special day school for students with ASD and other significant learning and behavior challenges).

Trying to force him to do what he was not ready for alienated Cody. Working to understand his needs let him know that the adults were trying to understand his experience and eventually engaged his cooperation in a problem-solving process. The team considered alternatives. Cody could observe the lesson without the expectation that he would demonstrate anything afterwards. He could observe the general education or resource teacher or another adult describe the concept and work on solving the problems (talking them through out loud), a first step in making him more comfortable. For Cody, that was somewhat like watching a video, but live, and it enabled him to watch without an expectation that he would participate or even fully understand. As a result, it reduced his anxiety and gave him a chance to recognize what he did understand – and later to do assignments based on what he had learned by observing.

Academics and Learning

"The problem with school," a middle school student with AS told his parents, teachers, and anyone else who would listen, "is that everything is either too easy or too hard." Schoolwork is supposed to support learning. Yet, the usual expectations for schoolwork may be a poor fit for a particular student's way of thinking and learning. Team members are often concerned about the discrepancy between students' ability and their performance.

Collaboration can support understanding and accepting what a student knows *and* how he learns. Modifying assignments or providing **accommodations** that reflect the student's needs and abilities makes school less overwhelming and learning more possible for more students. Discussing accommodations or **modifications** (what they are and why they are used) develops awareness in the teacher and the student.

Team members often worry that the student will not be prepared for the future ... the next grade, the next school experience, or independent adult life ... and, therefore, are resistant to changing their expectations. However, a stance that the student "must" learn to do what is expected of others can be overwhelming to everyone and, ultimately, be ineffective, or worse, detrimental to the student. The most effective way to prepare for the future is to keep the student from being too overwhelmed to function in the present. And the best way to help students in the present is to ask or require of them what they can do. While this sounds simple, knowing what the student can or cannot do is complicated by the appearance, at times, that a student is able to understand and do more than she can consistently sustain.

A collaborative process that begins with and addresses the student's subjective experience can allow the team the flexibility and creativity necessary to support the student's learning and management of academics. For example, students who have difficulty imagining what others mean often have difficulty understanding literature. They can be told in advance what is relevant (not be expected to discover it on their own), and then try to find it in the text. When writing fiction is difficult, students can write about a true event and, with help when needed, fictionalize it. Teams can address these issues, and many others, in a way that provides a more manageable school experience for the student.

Trevor

Trevor is a bright high school student whose social cognitive challenges were identified early. He had struggled in classrooms that were not a good match for his needs but responded more positively with formal and informal support. In addition to school support, he had benefited from early occupational therapy, language therapy (that addressed reading comprehension and paragraph composition), and individual psychotherapy that helped him learn about his own mind and the minds of others. When he started high school, Trevor had an IEP with goals that addressed organization and pragmatic language. The study skills teacher was helping him with organization (other teachers kept her informed when he was missing assignments), and he was given extra time when he needed it. However, even with this level of support, he was overwhelmed and depressed by the work required in high school.

Trevor had been interested in science for a long time. In addition to reading and watching educational TV programs on science, he had participated in hands-on enrichment programs at science museums, specialized summer school programs, and science camps. In his high school biology class, he was bored with the material and overwhelmed with the work. When Trevor was allowed to take several chapter tests (before reading the chapters), he scored from 80 to 90%. Because he had had adequate lab experience prior to high school, the team agreed that he could take a self-paced, teacher-supervised independent study using the textbook instead of doing the regular class work. After six weeks, Trevor was halfway through the book, because much of it was review for him. His school and his IEP team recognized how stressful and exhausting school could be for Trevor and wanted to support his success in the mainstream. He was trying to keep up on his assignments in many classes. Requiring less for a subject he knew well already (such as providing an alternative to the freshman biology class and allowing him to reduce his math homework when he clearly understood the concepts) was one way to support him.

Preparation and Planning for Effective Team Meetings

Formal meetings (including, but not limited to, IEP meetings) provide opportunities to develop meaningful goals and accommodations for students. Test assessments and observations of the student, as well as suggested goals and benchmarks, are usually prepared in advance by school personnel, sometimes in collaboration with outside consultants. These can be shared ahead of time so that team members can give thought to them (in light of their own observations) in preparation for a meaningful, problem-solving process. The student can also be prepared in advance to have his concerns addressed, or to participate actively when he is able to do this.

Formal Assessments

Test results may be used for determining eligibility and may also be helpful in assessing strengths and challenges. Results should be an accurate reflection of the student; they should be consistent with and help explain what team members experience with the student. If not, every effort should be made to understand the inconsistency. We know that some students do better on a test than in a classroom. Others who do well in the classroom may not do well in the test situation. This is as true of students with AS as it is for students with more severe autism. Some have difficulty answering if they are not sure of the answer, or if the tester does not tell them immediately whether their answer is correct (which is not possible in a formal assessment). Some students who have difficulty comprehending less concrete material may score well on some reading comprehension tests, because they attend to and remember factual details. Students who have had social skills or pragmatic language interventions may answer appropriately on a test of pragmatic language. They know the rules and the correct answers when presented with a situation, but may not recognize the relevant factors in real-life situations. On the other hand, a nonverbal student with autism may have learned a skill through a system using a visual cue, but cannot perform in a test situation, because the prompts are unfamiliar.

A neuropsychologist or skilled clinical child and adolescent psychologist, one who uses neuropsychological instruments, may understand and explain the way the student thinks and processes information. Specifically, he or she can explain the way that a child arrives at an answer, or the reason why the child is unable to generate an answer. Knowing these aspects of the child's thinking and processing can often result in meaningful recommendations about what is reasonable to expect and what methods to consider when working with and teaching the child.

Adam

Adam is a fifth-grade boy with AS who has difficulty knowing what to write even when he knows the information. He has difficulty summarizing, often does not understand what the teacher has in mind, and cannot generate ideas for an open-ended topic. Adam worked with an educational therapist and learned to write an acceptable three- or four-paragraph essay using a formula that sometimes worked. In a test situation, one of the stimulus pictures coincidentally reminded him of a topic he had previously written about, and he wrote an excellent short essay that was supposed to be based on the picture. Unfortunately, this rarely happened in schoolwork and homework situations, where he often spent hours unable to generate ideas, even with help. His educational therapist was at the team meeting, and she helped the team understand what had happened – Adam's testing seemed to demonstrate an ability that he had not really mastered.

Stephen

Stephen, a middle school student with AS, did poorly on math homework and standardized tests although he could answer word problems that required an understanding of concepts when they were presented one at a time. When asked about his poor performance, he said the work was too hard because there were too many problems and they were crowded on the page. The student felt overwhelmed when he saw the number of problems on the page and how little space was provided for the work.

Understanding this difficulty helped the team develop accommodations. Stephen needed math problems that were spread out on each page. He could demonstrate an ability to do each kind of problem, but not long assignments practicing similar problems over and over (something that may help other students become more proficient). Standardized testing seemed to demonstrate a math weakness that he does not have. Based on this understanding, his math teacher and resource specialist decided to provide less work in a format that enabled him to demonstrate his competence.

Formal and Informal Observations of the Student

Any team member may observe a student in the classroom, at lunch, or on the school grounds. All participants discuss their observations at a team meeting, but sometimes a written observation report is prepared, by itself or as part of a larger assessment. As with formal assessments, reported observations should be consistent with the observations and experience of other team members. Because it is natural to draw conclusions from our own perspectives, as well as our training and experience, our impressions may not be accurate for a student with ASD. However, even when impressions and conclusions are accurate, it serves the team better if the presentation develops in a way that team members can reconcile with their own experience of the student. The following is one way to organize written observations (or even those given orally) that facilitates this.

1. **Descriptions** are clearly stated (in a way that would have been observable to anyone present).

2. **Impressions** are an attempt to make sense of observations by considering what the observable behavior might mean about *and* mean to the student.

3. **Suggestions, recommendations, and questions** (for the team to address) follow in an understandable way from the descriptions and impressions.

It can be a challenge, even for an experienced observer, to differentiate objective observations from impressions of what observations mean. One strategy that can help when writing notes is to develop a list of what is observable and a separate column (perhaps even drawing a vertical line on the note paper) for thoughts, reactions, and impressions that occur to the observer at the time, such as these brief examples that were part of an hour-long observation of an 8-year-old, second-grade student with HFA.

Sample Observations (S=student, T=teacher)	Impressions
S reads at desk, chewing shirt. T tells class to take out workbooks and begin page 25. Class responds. S still reading. S reads for a couple of minutes. W/o looking up, S closes book, then takes out workbook and turns to correct page. Later: S sits outside group of students listening to T, who reads a story, stopping to show illustrations, make comments, or ask questions. S chews shirt, raises hand after some questions. S comments on a detail of a picture on the page three times. Once, the detail was relevant to the question, and the other two times it was not. T commented on what was relevant and repeated it for the class. T had questioning expression and called on another child w/o comment when S's response was not relevant.	S doesn't listen; does not respond to directions. Delayed, but correct response; no indication that S has heard and understood, although he has. S not willing to join group, not attending to meaning of story, responses to questions are inappropriate. S willing to participate but seems to need physical distance from other students (who are sitting close to each other). Seems to chew constantly when listening or concentrating. Wants to participate, but does not understand the main points of the story or T's questions. T does not correct S or direct to join group (perhaps understanding his need for physical distance, chewing). T responds in a positive way when S says something relevant, does not comment on tangential or incorrect responses. T shows that she is confused (other students may recognize this more easily than S) and moves on to another child's more relevant response, clarifying the correct response, and modeling a respectful handling of the inappropriate response for the other students.

Detailed observations enable us to better understand both the problematic and the successful aspects of the student's school experience. They should include examples of when the student is doing well and what the teacher may be doing to support that success. Noting when unusual behaviors, such as mouthing objects, kneeling when writing, or rocking, occur in conjunction with desired behaviors may help the team understand these as problem solving as opposed to problematic behaviors. Further, noting supports (cueing, direction, redirection, etc.) that are successful helps the team recognize what is effective. When we explore a breakdown in a student's school functioning, we sometimes find that supportive interventions used earlier have been withdrawn. The student may have been doing better, but only because the interventions, modifications, accommodations, or supports were in place.

Independent functioning is desirable when it is possible on a consistent basis, but sometimes supports are essential for a student to function adequately and should therefore be maintained. In addition, we can establish a goal, with and for the student, that he learns what helps him. Knowing his needs will eventually help him to advocate for himself, to ask for support that helps him succeed.

Goals and Benchmarks

There are specific legal requirements for writing IEPs, such as stating measurable goals and specifying benchmarks to work towards the success of those goals. The most meaningful and useful goals and benchmarks are based on an understanding of what the student does and does not understand – not just what he can or cannot do. For students who are capable of achieving them, academic goals and benchmarks must be aligned with **content standards** in general education. If benchmarks address the very smallest steps that come next (considering the student's current level of understanding), they address the possible. Just as with assessment reports and observation reports, when team members have an opportunity to look over suggested goals in advance, it allows for a more efficient and productive meeting.

Brandon

Brandon, an 8-year-old boy with AS, was well ahead of other students in his third-grade class in reading (decoding and comprehension of facts) and basic math, but he had significant difficulty participating in school and often read books unrelated to the lesson. He stood an open book on his desk in a way that formed a barrier between him and the class. At times, when attempts were made to engage him, he became so overwhelmed that he cried, pushed, or tried to withdraw, particularly when someone came close to him. He was unable to participate in any effort to resolve a problem that arose with a classmate, even with the assistance of an adult. At these times, he occasionally ran out of the class or even away from the school, resulting in concerns for his safety. Although he liked to listen to books that were read aloud, he was confused and upset when discussion questions were raised unless they were about specific details or concrete facts. Brandon was eligible for an IEP based on his poor pragmatic language skills. The following were suggested pragmatic language and abstract language goals that team members previewed prior to the meeting, along with the revised goals that the team adopted.

Suggested Goals (Previewed by team)	Revised Goals (Approved by team)
Social Pragmatics Goal. Increase awareness and use of strategies to assist with problem solving.	**Social Pragmatics Goal.** Increase awareness and use of strategies to assist with problem solving.
Given that a problem occurred, Brandon will accurately identify the cause of the problem with one prompt 50% of the time.	When an adult has identified a problematic situation, Brandon will be able to answer the question, "What has happened here?" descriptively from his point of view. If he cannot, the adult will describe her observation in the most specific, concrete language. Brandon will listen and say if he agrees 50% of the time.
Given that Brandon identified the cause of the problem, Brandon will generate two possible solutions and the consequences of each with minimal adult cueing 80% of the time.	Brandon will listen to the adult's view. If it is different from his own, Brandon will accept that it is a different perspective (tolerate hearing, and be able to stay with the class or go to an acceptable alternative place) 50% of the time. Brandon will be able to choose from solutions that are offered, solutions intended to meet his needs, and obey classroom and safety rules 80% of the time (e.g., Brandon may need a break. He does not want to stay with the class. The teacher says it is not safe or permitted to go outside, because there is no adult supervision. Brandon can go to a safe corner in the class or to another location in the school to rest, read, bounce).
Abstract Language Goal. Increase awareness of and use of abstract language and thought.	**Abstract Language Goal.** Brandon will differentiate questions of fact and opinion.
During discussion of a story, Brandon will answer questions such as "What might happen next?" "What do you think about ...?" with one prompt 50% of the time.	Brandon will identify questions of fact (Is it a who, what, where, or when question?) as questions about facts one out of three attempts.
Brandon will state if a question has a correct factual answer or if it asks for his thoughts or opinions with one cue 50% of the time.	Brandon will identify questions of opinion, possibility, or personal preference as questions that do not have a right or wrong answer, one out of four attempts.

It would be wonderful if Brandon were able to accomplish the suggested goals, but unfortunately, they were far beyond anything he could understand. Brandon did not know why his behavior was a problem for others. He rarely noticed other children, unless they were trying to engage him or interfered with what he was doing. He did not understand the consequences of his behavior. He did know when someone thought he was bad or angry, but not why. Also, Brandon did not understand questions that were not factual. To him, "What might [a character in a story] do next?" was a factual question with a right answer, and he did not know the answer. He did not fully understand this question because it required attention to the mind of others.

The revised goals addressed this student's needs in a way that matched the team members' experience of his functioning. The team agreed that if Brandon could recognize a situation (as an adult described it) and learn to describe what happened, that would be a good beginning. Knowing the difference between questions that have a right or wrong answer and questions that do not have a right or wrong answer would also be a good start. If Brandon could do that, he might begin to identify his preference for factual questions and difficulty answering opinion, possibility, or personal-preference questions, and eventually communicate that. The team members also felt they could adequately assess if this plan was working. If Brandon did not respond, it might be that the steps were too big and that new steps closer to his current abilities could be considered. It is the problem-solving process that is important, not a particular solution.

Long-Term Goals and Future Planning

At IEP meetings, parents are asked to state their long-term goals for their child. These are subsequently recorded, sometimes without discussion. To address long-term goals meaningfully and realistically, teams should examine them in the context of the student's current functioning, considering maladaptive functioning and missing skills. The small steps leading to improved skills and functioning can become the more short-term goals and benchmarks, meaningful benchmarks that consider current abilities and develop the foundation for functioning in school and in life. This also allows for re-evaluation and adjustment of meaningful short- and long-term goals as part of an ongoing team problem-solving process.

Tom, described below, is clearly engaged in a process that can lead to achieving his long-term goals. This was made possible because the team understands his strengths and his challenges and has set short-term goals and benchmarks that he can achieve and that develop the skills and help him to utilize supports that make the long-term goals possible.

Tom

Tom is a moderately functioning student with autism, who attended public school special education classes since preschool and recently graduated from high school. After many early interventions, step-by-step remediation, and therapies to address his language and other learning issues, attention, and behavior issues, the IEP team had a good understanding of Tom's ability to learn rote material and behavior, as well as his ability to use an interest in clear, straightforward computer games, computer programs, and other assistive technology. At the same time, team members understood his poor comprehension and his inability to solve or even identify problems accurately in the moment. Tom learned information and routines anew for each situation, even when the situation was similar to one he had mastered.

The transition-to-high-school IEP team addressed Tom's long-term goals. These were: to hold a job, to get himself safely to and from work, and to live as independently as possible, perhaps in a group home or apartment facility with a resident supervisor. Many aspects of his high school plan were structured to help him develop the skills he would need. For example, for two years, Tom participated in ROTC with mainstream students. This program did not require planning, problem solving, or much coordination. The rules were clear and exact, and the activities were repeated many times in the same way. The adult officer was understanding and appreciated Tom's enthusiasm and compliance with many repetitive drills. As a result, Tom did well.

In his junior and senior years, Tom attended a county-run, part-day vocational school for high school students. He took a school bus to the program with other high school students. One day he got on the wrong bus (one returning students to another high school). The driver kindly drove Tom to his school. After that Tom always checked the bus number and name (not only the spot where the bus was generally parked). This was important, because he now knew that the number and the words on the bus told him where it would take him. The location of the bus was also important, but it was not enough, and for this particular situation he had all the information he needed to successfully return to the school.

The first year he took the most basic course for office help. The second year he took managerial accounting, a computer-based bookkeeping course. He did not finish the course material, but his teacher created a special Introduction to Managerial Accounting certificate to give him. This was important to Tom. He saw getting a certificate at the end of the year (something he knew that the other students were earning) as meaning that a student had done what he was supposed to do, and not getting one would have meant he had not done the right thing. He was happy with his certificate, and his family was very appreciative of the teacher's understanding and sensitivity to Tom's way of seeing the world.

By his final high school IEP meeting, Tom's team members were very experienced at being flexible and open to creating or changing programs so that they would support Tom's best functioning. He could benefit from continuing the vocational school another year to finish the course and from attending a special education program at a community college that is designed to prepare students with developmental delays for work. He has started the college course. Although he is eligible for transportation, his family declined, so they could help him learn to use public transportation. After practicing with a family member several times, Tom takes a bus from the school to the light rail station, and then takes the light rail to meet his mother. Tom prepares his own lunch. He assembles and takes his school supplies, his cell phone, his wallet, and his bag lunch.

One day he forgot to make his lunch. He was very hungry when he met his mother outside the light rail station at 3 p.m., so she took him out for a late lunch. Another day Tom missed his bus stop and got off the bus on 2nd Street instead of 1st Street. He called his mother, told her the street names (by checking the sign at the corner) and a landmark, and she picked him up. She showed him that he could walk one block from 2nd to 1st Street if it happened again. (Everyone is quite confident that Tom will remember and follow his mother's suggestion if he gets out on 2nd Street again, but they are equally confident that he will call if he gets out on 3rd Street.)

Next year, Tom will return to the half-day vocational program to refresh his knowledge, complete the program, and begin a job or internship. After he is settled in a job, his family will work with community support services to find an appropriate supported, but more independent, living situation nearby. The collaboration of many people who were providing services and educational opportunities for Tom resulted in an understanding of the need for and benefit of adapting the programs and expectations to support as high a level of independence and functioning for Tom as he could manage. He will always need support and some supervision, but perhaps considerably less than he would have needed without the benefit of these ongoing efforts to understand him and the flexible problem-solving efforts of members of his team.

Preparing the Student

With all but very seriously challenged or very young children, someone can prepare for team meetings or conferences with the student, whether or not he attends the meeting in person. This may entail as little as making the student aware of the meeting and its purpose in making school a more comfortable place for him to be. It can include exploring issues of concern to him. Preparing with him in advance enables the student and the adult to clarify the student's perspective and articulate his concerns. It also allows them to examine together what has improved as well as what is still difficult or problematic. They can decide who will present the information, if the student attends all or part of the meeting.

Andrew

Andrew, described earlier, was preparing to enter sixth grade. He had learned to help his therapist, his mother, and his teacher prepare for his IEP meetings. He and an adult discussed what would be included. The list included any information that he felt the team should know, and was organized into positives and concerns.

Andrew's Preparation for the IEP Meeting
1. A list of positives and improvements:
   a. Does more work in class, cooperates more with what the teacher wants done, concentrates more during lecture and demonstration
   b. Still doesn't like how other kids act, but this does not bother him as much as it used to

c.   *Likes playground volunteer; sometimes plays in supervised team activities during recess; contact more O.K. in this situation (pushing with pressure, as part of a supervised game, is more comfortable than light touching)*

d.   *Has one friend who lives near him and also goes to the resource specialist's class (can't make more friends because you can't say "Hi" to be friendly, you have to say "Hey, dude" and Andrew does not want to do that)*

2. *Issues, concerns, and things that are hard:*

a.   *Homework:*

   • *Forgets or loses homework*

   • *Mom may tell him to do the assignment the wrong way (not the way the teacher wants)*

   • *The teacher said homework could be reduced to half plus one. For an odd number, that would be the "larger half" plus one. If there are five questions, the larger "half" is three (two and a half rounds up to three) plus one is four. Four out of five is too much.*

b.   *Math word problems: assignment is to solve, explain reasoning, and describe a three-step solution for each problem. Andrew can find the answer. He can generally explain how he gets it, although that is harder. He cannot find three steps and does not see that there are three steps for all the problems. That may be how the teacher solves the problem; it is not how he does it.*

c.   *Group project: Everyone loses 5 points if anyone forgets or loses work. Everyone is mad at him if he forgets. Answering comprehension questions can make up points, but he does not always know the answers. Other group members should not be punished; he is willing to take his punishment if he forgets his work.*

d.   *The teacher said that if there is cheating on tests, both the students whose work is copied and those who copy get a zero. Andrew cannot concentrate if he has to keep looking up to see if anyone is looking at his paper. (Andrew was asked if the teacher meant that students should not purposely show their work to someone. He was sure she meant more than this. "This teacher means exactly what she says," he explained. Even if he were unaware that someone was copying his work, he was sure he would get a zero.)*

The team considered Andrew's list. It was an excellent reminder of how Andrew thinks and why school is so exhausting for him. Everyone recognized how disturbed Andrew was by the results of his disorganization. His IEP had included organizational goals, which he did not achieve. It was modified to include organizational support. For now, an adult (the aide from the resource room) would check his backpack before he left school to be sure that he had his assignments and the materials he needed to complete them at home.

Andrew's list helped the team understand how overwhelmed he was by his need to do what he thought was "right." His teacher and mother agreed that he was to do assignments, as his mother understood them. Even if she were wrong, he would get full credit. The "half plus one" modification was changed to read: "If there were an odd number of problems, perhaps five, seven or nine, he could do the 'larger half' and not add one." The purpose was for him to do every kind of problem, but that was too difficult for him to deal with at this time. He needed a concrete formula. Although his teacher had thought that the students in the class were well aware of opportunities to make up points lost by a group, this was not clear to Andrew. He needed to know that the team would not be punished for anything he did wrong, and the teacher agreed to talk to his team about that. The teacher was surprised at his response to her rule about cheating. (It is easy to continue to be surprised by the thinking of students with ASD, even for those who know them well.) She did not want him to watch out for other students who were trying to cheat. She wanted him to concentrate on his test.

Although all Andrew's issues were not fully addressed (his difficulty explaining his reasons in math was acknowledged, but without time for discussion), the team was becoming much more aware of and accepting of the fact that Andrew often has his own way of understanding. His list was very clear evidence of that; it was also evidence that he cared and tried. Andrew saw that people were trying to understand his perspective. He was satisfied with the process, and the team members were pleased with his increasing ability to advocate for himself and with his level of participation.

Factors That Contribute to Positive, Effective Collaboration

It can be helpful to articulate the factors that support effective collaboration. This enables us to know what is working as well as what to address to improve team efforts. Utilizing the example of a specific student's team, we can examine some of the most important factors that contribute to functional and successful team collaboration.

Team members are open to hearing, reflecting on, and trying to understand each participant's observations and concerns.

Edward is mainstreamed with supports and accommodations. He has had an IEP since preschool, at which time he was unable to participate or attend without individual assistance, since he was unaware of what was expected or even what was happening around him. By third grade, Edward's team recognized significant improvement in his ability to respond to directions, complete many assignments, attend to the teacher, at least some of the time, and raise his hand to answer questions. These skills all corresponded to goals that had been articulated and agreed upon the year before. However, Edward continued to require and benefit from frequent cueing and redirection.

Some team members were concerned that Edward did not function independently, something that would be required in the higher grades. This could have developed into tension and polarization between those expressing "the need for support" and team members pressing for "expectations of independence." Instead, it led to agreement that the future was worrisome, but that providing what this student needed had slowly been resulting in less need. Perhaps more important, it was agreed that trying to make something happen before a student is ready can make it less likely to happen.

Team members make an effort to understand the student, to understand his strengths and challenges and how these impact his learning, as well as his responses to academic, social, and behavioral expectations at school.

Edward had an excellent memory. He wrote slowly, but learned vocabulary, spelling, and math facts easily. He had difficulty learning new math concepts (was overwhelmed by the new language, especially during class explanations and demonstrations), but could do new math problems once he understood the concepts. The team learned to recognize that Edward wanted to do well and often seemed stressed and exhausted by his efforts. At these and other times, sensory stimuli (internal and external) could be difficult or even overwhelming for him. He engaged in several behaviors (chewing, kneeling in his chair, standing up and pacing) that could have been seen as problematic, but the OT helped the team understand that many of Edward's physical movements were his way of managing his sensory overload, and in that sense were a solution rather than a problem. They enabled him to work or to stay in or near his seat, rather than distracting him from his work. Explaining this to him and the other students made him more aware and others more tolerant.

Many decisions were made based on an understanding of Edward's strengths and challenges. He was allowed to chew gum and take breaks. His teacher shortened his spelling assignments (since he knew most of the words or easily learned them). Edward was also allowed to pre-learn new math concepts with his tutor or his parents (utilizing concrete materials and vocabulary that was consistent with his own experiences and led to true comprehension of concepts). He was allowed more time for short-answer written work and to dictate longer writing assignments to his aide or parents.

Edward wanted to run around the field during recess, but the team wanted him to develop peer skills. It was decided that he could use his recess to run, but the language therapist facilitated a social/communication group for him and two peers once a week. In addition, his teacher placed him with a kind and supportive peer for small-group assignments. To make it easier for others to accept and support him, his mother explained Asperger Syndrome to the class, pointing out how it accounted for Edward's strengths and challenges.

Team members work to understand and show respect for the student's perspective (his view of his experience), whether or not it conforms to that of the team members or the student's classmates, and work to help the student learn about the perspectives of others.

Although Edward could be aware of and attentive to the teacher, he had appeared completely oblivious of other students until recently. Everyone was encouraged that Edward sometimes responded appropriately to a question or comment directed to him by a peer, although this was only likely to occur if the classmate was physically close and got his attention first (such as by saying his name or touching his shoulder, which is what the teacher or classroom aide sometimes did to get his attention).

More recently, some team members noted that Edward approached other children to engage them. He might start talking about something in great detail without determining interest or recognizing what the other child was doing. He might not give the other child enough information to make his reference clear. In addition, he sometimes moved in a kind of dancing motion, very close to another child. When the child backed away, Edward was likely to move closer and increase his motion. Team members were concerned for Edward and the other child. This was not the kind of peer interaction they wanted to see. Some children who had ignored or tolerated Edward before, and even some who were especially kind to him, now backed away from him. Explaining about personal space or providing redirection might be effective for the moment, but it did not have any real meaning to Edward and did not result in permanent change. That is, the pragmatic language/social skills group lessons did not carry over to these real-life situations. Several team members recognized that children like Edward often do not generalize, because they do not recognize the essential similarities in somewhat different situations.

Those who had observed Edward felt that in those situations he did recognize that the other child was near and did want to engage the child (have that child notice or respond to him). However, he was not aware enough of himself and others to understand what was happening. Strategies for heading off troublesome interactions were considered.

Explaining rules of engagement in a way that would make sense to Edward was not possible, considering his lack of understanding of other people. Raising Edward's awareness seemed to be a good first step. The prior year the team had developed a goal to raise Edward's awareness of the teacher's role in explaining and giving directions by directing his attention to what she said and what other students were doing as a result. He became more observant and responsive. The team decided to develop a response strategy that would raise Edward's awareness of his own behavior towards peers as well as their responses. Once or twice a day, when possible, an observing adult would tell Edward very concretely what she observed. (For example, she might note aloud: He is twisting and turning very close to a specific child. Does he want the other child to notice, to like what he is doing, and so on? The other child is backing away or telling him to stop. Does the other child want Edward to see that he is uncomfortable? Edward is moving even closer. He wants the child to play this way, and the other child does not. This is a dilemma.) Just articulating these observations can raise awareness and engage both children in a problem-solving process. If Edward continues, he might have to be separated, but what happened would be easier for all to understand as a dilemma. Edward, the other child, and the adult would be aware of Edward's intent (to be physically closer, to be watched, to be friends, to play with the other child), as well as the discomfort of the other child. This is a dilemma, and that can be articulated by or with the help of the adult.

Team members are interested and willing to provide support and develop expectations that the student can meet (a manageable environment).

In an ongoing collaborative process that includes relevant team members at various times, Edward's team continues to engage in problem solving. Team members try to understand Edward and to develop modifications, accommodations, and alternative learning options that support him at school. This, in turn, helps team members to understand and support each other's efforts on his behalf. The following are just a few of the supports and expectations that have served Edward's growth and mastery.

- *Since participating in class is such an effort for Edward, and he can relax and relieve his stress by pacing or running, he is allowed to run around the perimeter of the school yard and is not expected to participate in peer activities during recess.*

- *For unfamiliar assignments, he may not understand what is most relevant and has difficultly following multiple-step assignments when directions are given to the entire class. He is often given a sample or a list of sequential directions to keep beside him, even for familiar assignments. When the assignment is not familiar, he is given an opportunity to pre-learn or observe before participating.*

- *Edward is allowed to dictate, and later will be allowed to type. Students in Edward's school learn to type in a computer lab that utilizes a typing program that he has found very difficult and frustrating. It begins with the "home keys." Edward finds it easier to learn the location of the letters on the keyboard utilizing a program that teaches the letters in alphabetical order (King, 1986). He began at home during the summer and then was allowed to practice his own program during typing instruction class at school.*

If we truly are all here to understand and plan, in as meaningful a way as we can for the student, each participant in the education team both learns and contributes, and small steps for the immediate future can be achieved. As the team works to know a student, the plan can make sense in light of this knowledge, and team members often develop a common language. The shared language becomes familiar to the team and to the student.

Summary and Conclusions

Members of the most successful teams know that they have much to learn from the student – about the student's mind and his subjective experience. With greater understanding, meaningful long-term outcomes (competence, comfort, and independence) may be achieved. The student can see this as possible, because he sees that we value understanding his perspective as we try to meet his needs, as well as help him consider and respond to the reactions and expectations of others. It helps to keep in mind that "independence" does not have to mean doing something the way most other people do, or doing something without help. Independence may mean knowing our own strengths and challenges and asking for and accepting help when we need it. The objective is to problem solve and develop plans for cognitive, social, emotional, behavioral, and communication issues. Such plans must allow a student with ASD to be who he is, to experience an educational environment that he can manage, and (step by small step) to learn to live and function adequately in the world as it is.

Tips for the Classroom

✓ Recognize that each member of the team has something to contribute. There is no one answer to the questions faced by educational teams, and no one person is equipped to make all the decisions.

✓ Make an effort to include the student's perspective whenever possible. This may be done through direct interview or an interest survey or by gathering data about the student's preferences.

✓ Educate yourself about autism and Asperger Syndrome and the impact these disorders have on how the student thinks. Her thinking directly influences her ability to make good decisions.

✓ Reach out to other professionals involved with the student's life and invite them to the IEP meetings. These could include child care workers, extended family members, recreational supervisors, doctors, social workers, or therapists.

✓ Realize that parents can be terribly outnumbered and consequently overwhelmed at typical IEP meetings. Encourage parents to bring support people.

✓ Avoid falling into the "defensive" position. To work in the field of ASD, it helps to be humble. If people question your program ideas, accept the questions as opportunities to discuss the long-term goals and get added input for how to reach those goals.

✓ If there are obstacles to the process, address them. The teaming process should make life easier for everyone, not harder. When the team has difficulties, the focus should always return to the student's needs as identified in the evaluation, as well as previous goals and objectives and the levels of success.

✓ Keep in mind that futures planning involves identifying long-term life goals for the student and addressing any obstacles that may be keeping her from reaching those goals. Current levels of performance can be identified in each goal area, followed by a team discussion about how to systematically reach the goals.

✓ Task analyze goals when writing attainable objectives. For example, if team members have agreed that they would like the student to learn to do her own laundry, they can first break the task of doing laundry into steps (sorting colors, white and dark, measuring detergent, turning the knob, etc.). The team can then write objectives for each step, which provides a systematic way of addressing goals together.

Chapter Highlights

- It is important that all those working with a student with ASD communicate with one another and share information about what they know of how the student learns, the student's strengths and challenges, and how they meet the student's needs.

- Educational support and intervention teams are mandated by law. They are comprised of teachers, paraprofessionals, administrators, other service providers (such as speech and language therapists, occupational therapists, and behavior specialists), both in and outside of school, family members, and the student him/herself.

- Collaboration among team members can benefit all members of the team. When collaboration is based on a shared focus and shared knowledge of the student's challenges and strengths, the chances for student resiliency and school success are increased.

- Each team member brings different perspectives and knowledge to the collaboration, leading to opportunities for discussion that can result in greater opportunities for student success.

- Collaboration can be either formal or informal.

- The purpose of formal team meetings can be to initiate evaluations for a student not receiving services, to review progress for a student already being served, or to develop goals and objectives/benchmarks.

- Students can receive special educational services either through an individualized education program (IEP) if they meet eligibility requirements as a student with disabilities under federal law or through a 504 Plan if they are able to function adequately in the general education classroom with accommodations.

- Informal collaboration, which can occur at any time, gives all participants on the team the opportunity to address concerns and issues as they happen.

- Areas of importance or concern on behalf of a student may include language and communication, social-emotional issues, behavior, and academics and learning.

- Modifying assignments and providing accommodations can help keep the student from becoming too overwhelmed by school.

- Effective planning and preparation for team meetings may involve any and all of the following: formal assessments; observations of the student; developing goals and benchmarks; examining progress in terms of long-term, adult-outcome goals; future planning to reach long-term goals; and preparing the student to be actively involved in the meeting.

- Factors that contribute to positive and effective communication include (a) openness among team members as well as a desire for mutual understanding; (b) awareness of the student's strengths and challenges and how they impact learning; (c) respect for the student's perspective and a desire to help the student understand the perspectives of others; and (d) a desire to create a manageable environment for the student.

Chapter Review Questions

1. Who might be members of an educational support and intervention team?

2. Why is collaboration important?

3. What is an IEP? What is a 504 Plan? How do they differ?

4. What are some components necessary for successful team meetings?

5. Why might you want to plan with a student prior to a team meeting?

6. List some of the factors that contribute to effective collaboration.

7. Based on the scenarios in the chapter, give three examples of how individuals with ASD may think and learn.

References

Attwood, T. (1998). *Asperger's syndrome: A guide for parents and professionals.* London: Jessica Kingsley Publishers.

Bate, C. (2004). Enhancing relationships through speech and language intervention. In L. C. Levental-Belfer (Ed.), *Asperger's syndrome in young children* (pp. 190-210). London: Jessica Kingsley Publishers.

Benard, D. (1991, August). *Fostering resiliency in kids: Protective factors in the family, school, and community.* Portland, OR: Western Center for Drug Free Schools and Communities.

Benard, B. (2004). *Resiliency: What we have learned.* San Francisco: West Ed.

Buron, K. D., & Curtis, M. (2004). *The incredible 5-point scale.* Shawnee Mission, KS: Autism Asperger Publishing Company.

Gray, C. (2000). *The original social story™ book: Illustrated edition.* Arlington, TX: Future Horizons.

Gray, C. (2002). *The sixth sense II.* Arlington, TX: Future Horizons

Jacobsen, P. (2003). *Asperger syndrome & psychotherapy: Understanding asperger perspectives.* London: Jessica Kingsley Publishers.

Jacobsen, P. (2005). *Understanding how asperger children and adolescents think and learn: Creating manageable environments for AS students.* London: Jessica Kingsley Publishers.

King, D. H. (1986). *Keyboarding skills.* Cambridge, MA: Educators Publishing Service.

Klin, A., Volkmar, F. R., & Sparrow, S. S. (Ed.). (2000). *Asperger syndrome.* New York: Guilford Press.

Levental-Belfer, L.C. (2004). *Asperger's syndrome in young children: A developmental guide for parents and professionals.* London: Jessica Kingsley Publishers.

McNeely, C., Nonnemaker, J., & Blum, W. (2002). Promoting school connectedness: Evidence from the national longitudinal study of adolescent health. *Journal of School Health, 72*(4), 138-146.

Noddings, N. (1992). *The challenge to care in schools: An alternative approach to education.* New York: Teachers College Press.

Siegel, B. (1996). *The world of the autistic child: Understanding and treating autism spectrum disorders.* New York: Oxford University Press.

Werner, E. E., & Smith, R. S. (1992). *Overcoming the odds: High risk children from birth to adulthood.* London: Cornell University Press.

Wiss, T. (2004). Building connections through sensory and motor pathways: Occupational therapy. In L. C. Levental-Belfer (Ed.), *Asperger's syndrome in young children* (pp. 211-237). London: Jessica Kingsley Publishers.

Learner Objectives

After reading this chapter, the learner should be able to:

- Discuss the impact of early theories of autism on a family

- Discuss the options available for educating persons with disabilities prior to the passage of PL 94-142 (now known as IDEIA or IDEA 2004)

- Describe the educational experience of an individual with ASD through the eyes of a mother

- Discuss the impact of PL 94-142

- Discuss the importance of teacher acceptance of the unique strengths and needs of individuals with ASD

Chapter 13

Growing up with Autism: One Parent's Perspective

Julie A. Donnelly

Jean-Paul was in the same school from kindergarten to second grade. In 1975, he moved to a different state, a different home, and a different school. When he entered his new third-grade class, he felt overwhelmed, so he walked to the shelf of books at the back of the room. He began reading volume A of the encyclopedias and continued reading through the rest of the volumes for the next three days. He did not respond to requests that he go to his desk or participate in activities. Jean-Paul heard the call for lunch and the announcement to get on the bus to go home. Otherwise, he hid himself in the books.

On the third day, a letter was sent home telling me, his mother, that Jean-Paul was being placed in the class for the mentally retarded. There was no request for a meeting to discuss concerns. They did not require my signature for an evaluation. There was no evaluation or diagnosis. I was not asked my opinion about placement. There was no individualized education program (IEP) with goals and beginning and ending dates of services. I was not given a list of procedural rights. Jean-Paul and I apparently had no rights. The decision was made without us.

I cried for the rest of the day. However, the next morning, I went to the school and told the principal that they would not put my son in the special class. I then walked to the back of his third-grade room and told Jean-Paul to get to his desk and do what the teacher asked. He was on the final volume of the encyclopedias by then, but put it down and did what I asked.

*Today, as an over-25-year veteran of special education teaching under the **Individuals with Disabilities Education Act (IDEA)**, I complain about the paperwork load and the complexity of the ever-changing law. At the same time, I never stop giving thanks for the legislation that prevents the kind of injustice that happened before Public Law 94-142 – the first law to guarantee a free and appropriate education to children identified with special needs.*

During the first 20 years of my life, I was unaware of autism, but I heard the word pronounced over my son when he was 3 and I was 23. The year 1971 was not a good one to have autism. Bruno Bettelheim was still director of the Orthogenic School in Chicago and considered the leading theorist on autism. Bettelheim (1967) described mothers of children with autism as "rejecting mothers" and compared them to the "devouring witch" of *Hansel and Gretel* with destructive intents (p. 71). Bettelheim claimed that autism resulted from psychological damage to the child by cold, aloof parents, and referred to the mothers of children with autism as "refrigerator mothers."

It wasn't until after his death that the public became aware that Bettelheim had lied about his history, did not have a doctorate in psychology, was Freudian and psychoanalytic in his treatment methods without being trained in either, and was often cruel to and hit the children under his care. Bettelheim also falsified records about his experiences with children with autism and exaggerated the "cures" he supposedly effected (Pollack, 1997). Yet, most medical professionals of that period agreed with Bettelheim that autism was an emotional problem with no known cure.

In 1964, Bernard Rimland published *Infantile Autism,* the first work to present evidence for a physical, not psychological, cause for autism. But it took a long time for these ideas about autism to penetrate the medical establishment. Although Bettelheim's theories have been disproven, many are still misinformed about the cause of autism. Unfortunately for families of children with autism, many still do not understand that autism is a neurological difference. The people who blame the parents may be your neighbors or relatives, and their judgments can cause great personal misery.

This chapter gives a personal account of raising a child with autism at a time when little was known about the disorder. It reviews the early history of legal and educational services and how they affected the life of my son. Lessons are drawn from my experience as both a parent and an educational specialist in an effort to enhance parent-professional collaboration.

Early Childhood

In 1971, when my son, Jean-Paul, was first diagnosed, the medical recommendation was to put him in a mental hospital for an indefinite length of time. Instead, we chose to work with Jean-Paul in our home. In 1972, when my son was 4, I found a pamphlet from the National Society for Autistic Children (NSAC; later became the Autism Society of America). We were making progress with Jean-Paul in our home program, but were thrilled to know that there were others out there. We felt so alone and misunderstood by friends, family, and others, who had never heard of autism.

The pamphlet included a checklist entitled *Could Your Child Be Autistic?* As I read down the list, I noted that Jean-Paul met most of the criteria. He had been severely impaired in speech development, but after a year of work, he could communicate a little, although it was mostly echolalia. He was also impaired in his relatedness to others. While he was close to me, he mostly used me as an object to take care of his needs. He did not have difficulty with change; in fact, he seemed oblivious to it. He had no sense of himself and did not respond to his name when called. Further, he did not seem to have a feeling of ownership, and his belongings could all be taken from him with no protest.

The checklist also mentioned "Lack of intellectual development or retardation in certain areas, sometimes accompanied by normal or superior abilities in other areas." The schools tested Jean-Paul as retarded, but he knew his numbers and ABCs, and at 4 years of age was already reading. He showed no interest in other children or toys and chose to sit staring into space, listening to music or reading books. He often acted as if he was deaf. He did not seem to feel temperature or pain. He did not look at us, was poorly coordinated, and under- or hypoactive. The checklist from the National Society for Autistic Children was describing my son.

I was frustrated with doctors who said that autism was incurable by definition and then told me that I had caused it. Even if it had been true, it was not helpful. With no programs or books to guide us, Jean-Paul's stepdad, Mike Donnelly, and I devised a plan for him in our own home. Mike had some experience working in a residential placement with children with autism. He had ideas, and I was the chief implementer of the program. We had never heard of Lovaas or applied behavior analysis or any other model. However, we came up with some basic principles that turned out to be important aspects of autism programming.

Our home program was centered on communication, keeping Jean-Paul focused and engaged in our world, and teaching him to do age-appropriate self-care. We insisted that he try to use words instead of screaming to get his needs met. The first months were terrible, as Jean-Paul increased his screaming to try to get us to respond. We insisted he try to form words. He resisted, because this was difficult for him. His first communications were lines he had memorized from songs and a sound that resembled a yes and that we continuously shaped into a clear response. Jean-Paul loved to eat, so we used food reinforcement to encourage him to try these difficult skills. As Jean-Paul became used to the highly structured routine and expectations, he resisted less and began to make progress.

Jean-Paul did not like to move. Many years later we would find out that he had a neurological difference in the motor skill area of his brain that made it difficult for him to control his movements. In addition, he had an eye muscle problem that caused him to see double. Visual-motor coordination was a challenge. However, we insisted that he participate in family activities and chores. He was taught to take care of his body: brush his teeth, wash, dress, and make his bed. He screamed and resisted, so it sometimes took all morning to complete these basic activities.

Jean-Paul's love for music was obsessive. We had noticed as early as when he was 2 weeks old that when music was playing, he would stop crying and look entranced and happy. Since his father was a musician, and we were almost constantly surrounded by live or recorded music, this worked out well. By the time he was 3, we became aware that Jean-Paul's need for music was out of control. When there was an album on the record player, he would be watching the record spin around and be lost in a trance. When there was no music, he would scream. As we began trying to bring him back into our world, we decided that music took him too far away from us. We put away the record player and radio and only allowed live music that was participatory. This resulted in more screaming, but we endured.

His two sisters and brother were a tremendous help to Jean-Paul. They felt that he should play with them and they made him play by group force. They taught him to be a kid, often against his will. In addition, these three siblings kept him engaged in our world. Jean-Paul would have chosen to listen to music, read books, eat, or just space out. His siblings would not let him be off to himself. Sometimes it seemed cruel, but it was the greatest gift they could have given him. Jean-Paul gradually learned to focus and participate in the world of our family.

When he was 4-1/2, I took him to the University of Minnesota to see Dr. Uwe Stuecher and Sheila Merzer at the program for autistic-type children. Dr. Stuecher confirmed the diagnosis of early infantile autism. He was pleased with the progress that we had made in our home and agreed to advise us on our home program. When he left the University of Minnesota, Sheila Merzer became our advisor. Under Dr. Stuecher's advice and with a letter of explanation, we placed Jean-Paul in the rural community school at Orr, Minnesota, for his kindergarten year in 1973.

In 1974, the TEACCH (Treatment and Education of Autistic and related Communication-handicapped CHildren) program was started in North Carolina by Dr. Eric Schopler (Schopler, 1994). The program was remarkable for its acceptance of parents not as the problem, but as part of the solution. Schopler had studied under Bettelheim at the University of Chicago, but came to see him as a "negative role model." When I visited the TEACCH program, I found that they treated parents with respect. I was so moved by their willingness to listen and their considerate responses that I cried. It was a complete contrast to what I experienced with most professionals up to that point. For this alone, I am grateful to TEACCH.

Rather than being based on one technique or philosophy, the TEACCH center trained teachers and parents to support the individual with ASD in a wide variety of ways. They promoted structure and organization to help the individual with autism understand his environment and taught the use of visual schedules and supports. They also developed functional and community-based programming. Communication skills were stressed at TEACCH as were social and leisure skills. While the TEACCH program did not invent all these methods, it became a national and international model promoting what have now become standard aspects of good autism programming.

Elementary School Years

Orr is a very small community 50 miles south of International Falls, Minnesota, and the Canadian border. No one in Orr schools had heard of autism when we moved there. Although some special services were available, **Public Law 94-142** would not be in place for another three years. The public schools were not required to take a student with autism, but since two of our children already attended, they took their brother. The school attempted to give Jean-Paul an intelligence test and decided that he was "untestable" because of his lack of language. The speech therapist was able to give him a *Peabody Picture Vocabulary Test* (PPVT; Dunn, Dunn, Robertson, & Eisenberg, 1959), a test of receptive language. The test page shows four line drawings. The evaluator names one, and the child is asked to point at that picture out of the four. I am amazed that Jean-Paul scored at all on a test that required pointing, but his score was 2.8, which equated to an IQ of about 55 (average is 100).

Jean-Paul did not understand most of the social skills needed for kindergarten, but he was already reading and knew his numbers and letters well. I came in to assist his teacher every other day. The speech therapist recognized that Jean-Paul needed a lot of help and saw him an hour a day. His first speech/language goals included increasing attention span, reducing echolalic responses, improving eye contact, making communication a pleasant and necessary experience, using speech to make his needs known, using gesture and facial expression, responding to outside stimuli, and developing social skills.

In second grade, Jean-Paul received remedial reading instruction for comprehension and help completing his workbooks and ditto sheets. A note from the second-grade teacher said, "The main reason Jean-Paul's grades are low is that he loses his work, so I have no grades for him. I try to keep a watch on him so this won't happen, but it is just about impossible to do this constantly with all the other students I have to attend to." This is so typical for kids with autism that I can probably find the equivalent of this note in most students' files. In addition, we continued working with Jean-Paul at home, where our goals were adaptive and social rather than academic. Over his first three years of school, Jean-Paul made dramatic progress. When he was 7 years and 3 months old, he was retested with the PPVT. He now had a receptive language age level of 8-2, which equated to an intelligence score of 112. His tested receptive language ability had doubled.

Orr was a rural school with few resources; yet, they tried to make a difference with an unusual student. During his first-grade year, the school sent Jean-Paul to the Mayo Clinic for an in-depth evaluation. When the results said that Jean-Paul was retarded and his mother was hostile, the school ignored the results and went on working with the child they knew was bright but different. Were things perfect? Definitely not. After a good kindergarten teacher, his first-grade teacher was intolerant and tended to raise her voice at the students. Jean-Paul was unable to differentiate whom she was yelling at and always came home anxious. His second-grade teacher was kind, but I remember her saying, "What is it with Jean-Paul?" She never did have a clue about his autism, but a good teacher is a good teacher.

Public Law 94-142 was passed in 1975 and trickled down into the schools through 1976 and 1977. In my life, Public Law 94-142 and its reauthorizations as IDEA are THE LAW. According to this law, the public schools would provide an education for ALL students (no matter how severe their disability). Every child had a right to a free, appropriate public education. Orr School District took my son out of kindness, but many children with autism and other disabilities were turned away from their neighborhood schools. If they did not fit the classrooms the school had, if they were not toilet trained, if they could not communicate or had difficult behaviors, the school could turn them away. No longer!! The law promised all students the right to an education.

Years later, I had an experience while traveling in Asia that reminded me of the importance of THE LAW. I was presenting an autism workshop in Kuala Lumpur, the capital city of Malaysia. People had traveled from all over Asia to attend. On my first day in the huge city, I had visited their one and only special education class. I had also visited the American School, where people who could pay sent their children with disabilities. Needless to say, these two classes provided services for only a tiny percentage of students with disabilities. During my workshop, I told the attendees about our law, which says that our government is required to educate every child, no matter what their disability is. People gasped. One woman cried and asked, "How did you get your country to pass a law like that?" One mother was trying to educate her daughter with autism in her home because no school would take her. I had to admit to these people that our law is still a work in progress. It is an enormous commitment and is still not an actuality, but we are attempting to fulfill it.

I think many parents and professionals take the law for granted. They don't have a good sense of the past or a sense of our society compared to most of the world. They don't see what a new and different attitude this piece of legislation represents. It is also easy to lose sight of the enormity of the task. *All* children, no matter what their disability is, will have their educational needs met. Many of us know in the day to day that this is no small chore. And, certainly, some of our children with autism are major challenges.

By the time Jean-Paul entered third grade, he was what we would now call a child with high-functioning autism or Asperger Syndrome. But in 1976, I had never heard those terms; it was just autism. That year we moved out of the cold north woods to the south-central midwest. THE LAW was in effect, but it had not reached the schools in Winona, a small southern-Missouri town. As described in the opening vignette, Jean-Paul spent the first three days in his new school reading volume after volume of the encyclopedia while largely ignoring his teacher's directions.

Puzzled about their new student, the school sent a letter home with Jean-Paul, informing me that he was being put in the class for the mentally retarded (the catch-all special education class at the time. The only one they had.). There was no request that I come in and discuss concerns. There was no paper to sign for evaluation – and no evaluation. There was no permission for placement or individualized education program. Before IDEA was in effect, all decisions were made by the school, and parents did not even have to be informed.

At home, I progressed from a feeling of devastation to anger. I went to the school the next day to remedy the situation. I told the principal that my son was not going to the MR class. I told Jean-Paul to listen to his teacher and do what she said, which he tried to do. I talked to his teacher, a sweet person, who had never had a student like Jean-Paul and had no idea what to do. I gave her suggestions, and she was glad to keep him in her class and follow through with my ideas.

By the next year, 1977, THE LAW landed in Winona, and a teacher for students with learning disabilities (LD) was hired. Jean-Paul was served under LD, as autism was not put on the list of educational disabilities until 1990. He also continued to receive language services. In the rural schools, the speech-language pathologists (SLP) had more training than most of the staff members. They were the ones who had a clue about how to approach autism. I now realize that Jean-Paul desperately needed help from an occupational therapist for both fine- and gross-motor skills as well as sensory differences. However, he was out of high school before we even knew that such services existed. He might have benefited from additional adult support in the classroom, but we didn't realize that was possible. He received pullout language and LD support through his fifth-grade year.

During that period, his grades were poor. His handwriting was almost unreadable. He lost his worksheet ditto pages, did not complete his workbooks, and ignored a lot of his math class in favor of reading his own books on history and geography. He was "spaced out" and had no friends. His teachers had a sense that he was bright but did not have much hope that he would be able to graduate from high school. In the meantime, Jean-Paul was happy with his own interests and seemed unaware that he was different and friendless.

Sixth grade was a watershed year for my son in many ways. His sixth-grade teacher had taught for 40 years, many of them in special education. She asked if we could stop the pullouts for language and LD and just have Jean-Paul in her class full time. I was willing to let her try. She sat Jean-Paul front and center in her crowded classroom with his desk touching hers. When Jean-Paul was spacing out, she cracked her paddle across his desk, and he would jump and refocus on the classroom. Sometimes she would send Jean-Paul out of class on an errand and talk to the other students about how we all are different and how Jean-Paul was just different in more obvious ways. Most of the students were supportive. However, a few boys teased and tormented him. They picked on him verbally and physically in the bathroom and the hall when teachers were not around. Twice that year, they pulled his pants down in the hallway. Jean-Paul, who had begun to be aware of his differences, was humiliated by their actions and his inability to defend himself. For the next five years, he would continue to endure the torment of these bullies and become more and more depressed.

During his sixth-grade year, we also found out that Jean-Paul had an eye muscle problem that caused him to see double. His eyes had adapted and learned to work one at a time so he could read. However, other than for words, most of his vision was barely functional. He had never told us that he saw differently than others, because he did not know what typical vision was. With the prism glasses that were prescribed, his eyes slowly and painfully changed and began working together.

Secondary School Years

For seventh grade, in 1980, Jean-Paul was in the junior high/high school building and had to change classes every 50 minutes. We discussed the supports he would need with an educational resource teacher, who promised to talk to all his teachers and inform them about his differences and support needs. I assumed that she would do this before school started. When nothing had been done two weeks into the school year, I went in and talked to all Jean-Paul's teachers. I supplied them with pencils to give him, because he showed up without his materials. We got him a big backpack, and he carried all his books with him so that he would have what he needed. Some time in November, the educational resource teacher finally showed up, but did little or nothing to help.

Jean-Paul received virtually no services through junior high and high school. He only got the adaptations that I wrestled out of the school through my own advocacy. The only special education service available at the secondary level was a self-contained classroom. Students in that room were labeled MR and LD; however, they all worked as a group on the same materials and at the same level. The teacher was working on a master's thesis at a nearby university on individualized curriculum in special education. When I asked why she was not individualizing in this classroom, she laughed. That was only research to get her degree, she said; it was not possible to individualize in a real special education classroom.

With this person as the only special education resource, I realized there would be no support for my son, who was struggling through mainstream classes. Special education, despite what the law said, was an all-or-nothing business in most rural schools at the time. A push for inclusion and inclusive support practices would not come until the 1990s, and my son graduated in 1986.

There are some benefits to having a pushy mother. With his visual-motor problems, art was torture for Jean-Paul. After one particularly bad event where he destroyed his art project, I requested – no – insisted, that he be taken out of art class and allowed to substitute music class for that requirement. That removed a major source of stress.

Jean-Paul wanted to go on to college, but his handwriting was still barely legible. I knew he would have to learn to type, but I remembered speed-typing drills from my high school typing class. I could visualize Jean-Paul falling apart under the pressure to make his fingers move faster and faster. I demanded that he be graded only on accuracy, not speed. The business teacher said, "We have never done that before," to which I retorted, "There is always a first time for everything." Jean-Paul learned to type.

I did not rescue him from physical education (P.E.), and that is where the bullies antagonized him the most. I have now learned that it is O.K. to take some students out of typical physical education classes and allow them to earn P.E. credit in another way. Sometimes, they need this adaptation because of poor motor skills, poor social skills, emotional sensitivity, and/or vulnerability.

Another source of anxiety was algebra. Jean-Paul had learned basic math skills, but he could not understand abstract math. He had a particularly good teacher who got him through, just barely, and did not allow his algebra difficulties to keep him out of the Honor Society. Being chosen for Beta club (Honor Society) raised Jean-Paul's self-esteem, and was one of the first steps in pulling him out of a deep depression.

At age 14, everything began piling up on Jean-Paul: The bullies, his anger at his inability to deal with the bullies, his lack of friends or girlfriends – in contrast to his brother and sisters who had many – his inability to be an athlete – in contrast to his brother and sisters who were – the world situations (he took the nightly news personally); and then there was algebra, which he could not seem to understand. Jean-Paul talked of feeling that he would be better off dead, but despised himself for not having the courage to commit suicide. It was a frightening time.

At this point, the school tested his IQ, resulting in a verbal score of 145 and a performance score of 77. A neurologist found an unusual EEG reading in the motor area of his brain and said that Jean-Paul was not depressed; he was extremely frustrated. As we had always thought, he was a bright young man with difficulty showing all he knew.

Several factors helped to pull him out of the depression. Jean-Paul began receiving personal counseling. He took the neurologist's advice and gave up on his hope to play team sports and instead began competing against himself at long-distance running. He was also given the job of manager for the basketball team. Although this mainly consisted of carrying the balls and towels, he got to go on the bus with the team to games. He was such a loyal fan that one year he was allowed to dress in the tiger suit and be the team mascot. Despite his poor coordination, he developed a dance style that resembled break dancing, and he attended all the dances. People would circle around and clap for his unique and totally enthusiastic dance performances. Some of his teachers were so taken with his knowledge of the history and lyrics of rock music that they asked him to sing during class. This acceptance of his strengths by his teachers encouraged student acceptance, but it was all too unusual for the girls to choose him as a boyfriend. He had a shallow level of acceptance, but no true friends.

While many teachers were good to Jean-Paul, his history teacher realized that he had a prodigy on his hands. This teacher organized a history bowl team and invited Jean-Paul to be a member. There were five students on the team, including one of Jean-Paul's sisters. The other members just sat and watched while Jean-Paul answered the questions. The team won the district title and went on to compete at a university history bowl in a nearby city. When they defeated most of the big-city schools, Jean-Paul became a hometown hero. He ran for vice president of the student council against the principal's daughter, a popular cheerleader. While his opponent took victory for granted, Jean-Paul worked to win the vote, and when it was counted, he had won. He remained as vice president of the student council for his junior and senior years. He was captain of the history bowl team and won a history and a leadership scholarship to college.

Transition to College and Beyond

During his senior year, rather than special education classes, Jean-Paul was taking college courses and passing advanced placement tests for college. The month of his graduation, he was ready to tell his schoolmates and community about his disability. The newspaper in the nearby city interviewed Jean-Paul and our family and did a full-page Sunday special on this young man with autism who was graduating with honors and going on to college. It was something very new in 1986.

Was he ready for college? Was the university ready for him? Well, no; there was no special education support in college, and his struggles continued. Jean-Paul learned and grew, and after a B.A., two master's degrees, a job, and a marriage, I am sure he would say it was a hard road, but he would do it all again if he had to.

Summary and Conclusions

I frequently hear parents and professionals say there are so many choices of therapies and methods that they do not know which to select. It is unfortunate that we do not yet know which techniques work best for which profiles of children. However, we know so much more than we used to. And we actually have choices!

We know that our children function best in highly structured environments. We know that we have to ease their anxiety by creating patterns and routines and then teach them how to function more flexibly in real-life situations. We know that communication is extremely important, whether that means finding an alternative type of communication system or teaching pragmatic language in real-life situations. We know that play is the work of children, and we must help our children learn the many lessons of typical play in order to build a bridge to their peers. We know that our students should be included with typical peers at the level and amount that they can benefit from. We know how to help individuals with sensory and motor differences. We know that they need a wide range of services, varying from early intensive one-to-one teaching to support services for those in the mainstream with college as a goal. We know that social skills make the difference in a successful life for all the diverse individuals labeled with autism. We realize that many behavior differences have a function, and we can find positive supports that prevent difficult behaviors while we teach these individuals to understand the rules for functioning in the home, school, and community. We know that functioning in school is not an end in itself but a preparation for being an independent and interdependent human being.

The basic principles of good education for students on the autism spectrum are available on the Internet, in books, through conferences, and trainings. Universities are beginning to realize that autism is no longer a low-incidence disability and are starting to train teachers in these skills. The gap between our need for well-trained teachers and those ready to teach is huge, but the necessary skills are not rocket science. My first question to a prospective teacher is: Do you like individuals with autism? Are you interested in teaching and learning from the most unique individuals on the planet? None of Jean-Paul's teachers were trained in autism; yet, some were excellent, just because they were good teachers. I send them my heartfelt thanks.

When parents ask me, as they frequently do, where to move to get good educational services for their child with autism, I recommend that they stay in the area where they have the best personal support system. Don't move away from family, friends, church, or support groups expecting that being in a new location will solve the problem. Each child's needs are so unique that we cannot name one area that is excellent at every level for every student. It comes down to individuals, each particular administrator, teacher, parent, and child working out the best possible program in their own way.

It seems to me that we have come a long way, and yet I know that we have a long way to go. We parents and professionals still have the opportunity and the obligation to be trailblazers in autism education. Good educational services are not some lofty goal, but what we work at every day, as a team, together.

Tips for the Classroom

✓ It is important for professionals to understand the history of autism and its impact on the family. Although we know today that autism is a result of brain function, previous beliefs can still impact how the general public views autism and, as a result, affect the struggles a family may have to endure.

✓ An educational team must always include the child's parents. Parents have valuable input regarding their child's functioning at home and in the community and are the only members of the team who will go on to be lifelong advocates for that child.

✓ Formal testing has limitations in its ability to predict lifelong success for students with ASD. IQ scores can change over time and do not necessarily determine academic success.

✓ It is important for special educators to work in an advocacy role by training mainstream educators in the nature and implications of autism.

✓ Educators need to be aware of the impact of bullying and recognize that children with autism are likely targets for such behavior.

✓ A teacher's acceptance and appreciation of a student's unique strengths can influence the perspective of peers and lead to more acceptance.

✓ A good advocate for a mainstream student might be a teacher or mentor whose content area matches the special interest of the student with autism.

✓ Finding a role for a student with autism within the school setting, such as score keeper for an athletic team, can go a long way in alleviating depression and isolation in adolescence.

✓ It is crucial that educational teams determine the purpose of behaviors demonstrated by students with autism rather than dismissing them simply as noncompliance.

Chapter Highlights

- In the early 1970s doctors often told parents of children identified with ASD to institutionalize their children and that autism was incurable. At that time, the cause of autism was still seen as based on a reaction of children to cold, non-loving mothers.

- Siblings can be very important to the positive development of individuals with ASD.

- Pre-PL 94-142, options for schooling for individuals with ASD were limited, and the public schools did not have to even accept students with disabilities.

- PL 94-142 was essentially the civil rights law for individuals with disabilities.

- Families and teachers need to serve as advocates for children with ASD.

Chapter Review Questions

1. How did early theories of autism impact this family?

2. What were the choices for the family described in this chapter regarding educational options prior to the enactment of PL 94-142?

3. List and describe three things you learned about the educational experience of the child discussed in this chapter.

4. State why PL 94-142 was so important.

5. Why is it important that teachers and others within the school community accept and work with the strengths and need areas of individuals with ASD?

References

Bettelheim, B. (1967). *The empty fortress*, Toronto, CA: Collier-Macmillan.

Dunn, L. M., Dunn, L. M., Robertson, G. J., & Eisenberg, J. L. (1959). *Peabody Picture Vocabulary Test*. Circle Pines, MN: American Guidance Service.

Pollack, R. (1997). *The creation of Dr. B*. New York: Touchstone.

Rimland, B. (1964). *Infantile autism*. New York: Appleton-Century-Crofts.

Schopler, E. A. (1994). A statewide program for the Treatment and Education of Autistic and related Communication-handicapped CHildren (TEACCH). *Psychoses and Pervasive Developmental Disorders*, 3, 91-103.

Learner Objectives

After reading this chapter, the learner should be able to:

- Describe the experiences of one individual with Asperger's Disorder

- Explain what narration is and why the chapter author believes it is important

- Discuss the importance of understanding the "hidden curriculum"

- Discuss the importance of using special interests to engage students in learning

Chapter 14

Educational Experiences Across the Lifespan: A Personal Perspective

Stephen Shore

It may seem humorous now, but it wasn't when it happened ...

It's homeroom time in high school, and the secretary from the principal's office walks in the door. From my vantage point at the opposite corner of the room, I hear her mention to the homeroom teacher that "the principal has just lost his mother" and that she would like to have an announcement made to that effect. As the homeroom teacher started to tell the class about this unfortunate situation, my unflappable comments to my classmates went something like this: "Mr. Brown can probably find his mother in the last place he left her, and if he only concentrates on where he last saw his mother, he might just relocate her."

Well, the homeroom teacher heard my remarks, and the events that followed were not pretty.

Due to a lack of awareness of the hidden curriculum (Myles, Trautman, & Schelvan, 2004), I was unaware of the rules that everyone seemed to know, but that nobody ever talks about. As a result, like so many people with Asperger Syndrome and high-functioning autism, I became a social outcast. In addition to social challenges, there were many academic obstacles to overcome along the way.

This chapter will use an autobiographical framework to highlight some of the challenges in educating people on the autism spectrum, along with some practical suggestions for solutions from a personal standpoint.

Preparing for the Educational Experience

After typical development for the first 18 months, I suddenly lost functional communication, withdrew from my environment, got involved in self-stimulatory activities, and exhibited many other autistic behaviors. After spending a year seeking a diagnosis for my change in behavior, my parents were told by a team of professionals at a child clinic that they had never seen a child "so sick" and that an institution could take better care of me than my own family. Going against medical advice, my parents took me home to provide their own version of early intervention.

Many young children with autism demonstrate an inability to imitate others, and my parents' initial attempts to get me to imitate them failed as well. Despite having no formal schooling in psychology or child development, my parents figured out that imitating me would create a response from me. As a result of this approach, I became aware of their presence, and they could then begin the process of teaching me verbal interaction.

The important educational implication here is that before any significant teaching is to occur, a relationship must be developed with the learner. If that means getting on the floor and flapping with a child, that's where you start before you move on to teaching social, academic, and other skills.

Based on my experiences, ranging from teaching young nonverbal children with autism to adult students in doctoral programs, a personal connection must be made before any significant teaching will occur.

Another strategy my parents used during my nonverbal days was to talk through what I was doing in the style of an excited sportscaster. This technique, known as "**narration**," and used extensively in the Miller Method (Miller, 2007), sets the conditions for a child to attach meaning to words he hears. In my opinion, this technique is far superior to uttering "good job" every time a child succeeds on a task. For children who tend to live in the present, "good job" may be far too abstract to yield any useful meaning.

Preschool

By the time I entered the school that initially rejected me and was enrolled in a class with three other students, my speech was starting to return. The teacher often thought of the four of us as making up one whole child (Shore, 2003). One of us had verbal skills, another could emote and share feelings, the third child seemed to be more challenged than the rest of us, and I seemed to have the ability to engage in play.

Psychologically oriented, this school prohibited teachers from sharing the events in the classroom with the children's parents, based on the director's view that the teachers did not have the extensive psychological background necessary to be able to answer parental questions such as "Did my child eat lunch today?" This lack of communication with the parents was common in my early years. Parents were presumed to be part of the problem, and so were not often treated as "team members" like today. My teacher was and continues to be horrified by having been forced to deprive parents of vital information about their children and the lost opportunities for parent-school collaboration we see today.

In order to set the stage for interaction between the four of us, the teacher began by engaging us individually with our own train and set of tracks, all arranged as segments of a circle. Gradually, our tracks became longer and connected with the lengths from the other children. Connected tracks led into trains stopping at each other's stations, which led to social interaction. The teacher successfully engaged our interests and used them to encourage social interaction.

Elementary School

At age 6, I entered regular public school kindergarten. Even though my verbal skills were at least age-appropriate, school was a social and academic disaster for me. Unable to understand the hidden curriculum of interacting with others at school, I quickly became a social outcast (Myles et al., 2004) – with all the bullying and teasing that came along with it. Sometimes when the bullying got to be too much, there would be meltdowns – which I now suspect was what the bullies were looking for.

In those days, bullying was thought of as a developmental phase that all children went through. According to Heinrichs (2004), over 90% of children on the autism spectrum report having been bullied in grade school. Fortunately, we have authors such as Heinrichs to help us identify and eliminate this problem at the individual, classroom, and schoolwide levels.

Learning Mathematics and Other Subjects

Academically, things were difficult as well. All through my elementary days, I spent hours at my desk reading my favorite books on meteorology, geology, natural history, dinosaurs, cats, astronomy, and other interests. Although sometimes I wondered if there was more to school than just reading my favorite books, I was happy to continue to isolate myself.

Some time in first or second grade, as I was happily reading a book on astronomy, I remember a teacher telling me that I would never learn to do math. These days, an educator would probably have noticed the stack of astronomy books on my desk and built lessons around what was clearly a topic of interest for me. Just about everyone learns faster and better when they are interested in the content. The same holds true for those of us on the autism spectrum, maybe even more so.

This comment about not being able to do math stuck with me, which may be part of the reason why it was very hard for me to learn my multiplication tables. One day I noticed a slide ruler-like device called a multiplier pencil box and just knew it was the answer to my troubles. In those days, using this device might have been called cheating. These days it might be referred to as a low-tech assistive device.

The multiplier pencil box got a lot of use at school and at home as I spent hours in my bedroom using it for multiplication problems. While multiplication presented challenges, long division was even harder. But one day I figured out that by using this assistive device backwards, I could work out division. Slowly, and in the low-stress environment of my bedroom, I began to memorize the multiplication tables and no longer needed the multiplier pencil box.

An important implication of this experience is that it is often preferable to give people access to a skill using an assistive device if it is not possible to for them to do it on their own. For example, being able to perform arithmetic tasks with an assistive device (these days a calculator) is decidedly better than not having access to these skills because the operations cannot be done in one's head. There is another important lesson to be learned here. Eventually, I learned the multiplication and division tables as well as did my classmates. It just took longer. People with autism and other developmental delays do learn. Sometimes it takes more time. That is why conditions such as autism and intellectual disability are referred to as "delays." Assistive technology and accommodations are hand-ups, not hand-outs.

Later on, this teacher's remarks haunted me as I avoided all college majors that had a math requirement. Yet, I decided to add a bachelor's in accounting and information systems to my music education degree and had to face the math monster in a series of prerequisite math courses. Initially, the work was very hard, and I spent a lot of time trying the patience of the instructors as I received extra help in their offices. However, by the time I got to the statistics class, math had become a close friend and even a sort of special interest to me. At this time, one of my passions is teaching statistics at the college level and making sure that it is taught well.

Reading Comprehension and Literal Thinking

Reading comprehension was another challenge for me during my elementary school years. Catalogues of all kinds, the encyclopedia in our home, and the daily newspaper were fascinating reads for me. However, answering questions from reading assignments in class proved difficult. Many class periods would be spent reading a short passage in preparation for answering multiple-choice, fill-in-the-blank, and short-answer questions, usually with poor results.

I remember one time refusing to answer questions related to a passage containing an Indian legend on how the earth was formed. After learning from science books about the solar system and the formation of the planets, I was not about to accept that the ground was actually the carapace of a large turtle. Like many on the autism spectrum, I was literal-minded. If there had been mention that this passage was actually an Indian legend, I might have been able to get through the questions, even with the realization that American Indians had a lot more to learn about the science of nature – that is, until I learned more about other perspectives.

Social Interaction and Physical Education

As mentioned, appropriate social interaction and making friends did not come easily for me. I spent most of my social time at school trying to avoid and navigate around bullies. Fortunately, people are beginning to realize the damage bullying can have on victims, and tolerance for this activity is decreasing rapidly (Dubin, 2007; Heinrichs, 2004).

Most bullying takes place during times of less structure, such as on the school bus and during recess. My special interest in bicycles paid off handsomely in avoiding bullying situations on the school bus since I rode my bicycle to school most of the time. When I did take the bus, I would sit close to the front to be near the bus driver, who was trying to keep an eye on the other passengers. Recess, however, could not be avoided, and was a time of anxiety as I kept an eagle eye out for bullies and Velcroed™ myself to the "lunch ladies" for safety.

One day, one of these ladies suggested that if I just "did my own thing" and didn't look at the bullies, they would ignore me as well. I followed her advice, and much to my surprise, it worked! Nevertheless, knowing what I now know about bullies, I would rarely recommend a solution of essentially ignoring the presence of bullies in hopes they would go away, but instead would advocate for a more direct approach focused on the bullies themselves (Dubin, 2007; Heinrichs, 2004). It doesn't make sense to ask the person who is least empowered to take the most responsibility in these situations. However, perhaps in some very limited situations, if bullies know that you are not concerned about their presence, they may ignore you.

Sports was another challenge, made worse by the fact that engaging in and talking about sports plays a major role socially in our society, especially for males. Talking about science and other topics was much more interesting to me than talking about sports. Due to poor motor control and perception, baseball was a very scary activity. Catching a ball hit by a batter or even just tossed over by another person was impossible for me because it looked like the ball was going to hit me; so I'd run away out of fear of being hit.

One day, while at an overnight camp, my central nervous system must have matured to a point where I could hit a ball with a bat if it was tossed from close by. I caught my first ball at that same camp. Standing in the outfield, I noticed a fly ball headed my way. Unable to focus on the ball as it made its way to my glove, I focused on trees swaying in the breeze instead. The ball thumped into my glove, and the team switched sides. On the way from the field, a counselor remarked, "Steve, you made a great catch, but you really should keep your eye on the ball when you are catching it." What the counselor did not understand was that not looking at the ball was exactly what had enabled me to concentrate and catch it. Tracking the ball would have been overstimulating, resulting in my ducking from it. The implication is that, for people with autism, eye contact or looking at what one is attending to is not always necessary or even desirable for attending to a task or talking with another person.

Middle School

Middle school can be a very challenging time for students both on and off the autism spectrum. Schoolwork becomes more conceptual, and nightly homework becomes a reality. Additionally, there is a lot more physical transitioning between classes, and the entire social schema among the students begins to change. Finally, middle school is also a time of puberty with great changes taking place within the bodies of the students themselves. However, there are many positive things about middle school as well.

I was much more successful in social interactions and academics once I reached middle school. Below I take a look at how some of the elements of middle school can have a positive effect, based on the characteristics of children with Asperger Syndrome and high-functioning autism in terms of social interaction and academics.

Social Interaction and Academics

Possibly due to greater awareness of my impact on the environment and on others around me, middle school was actually easier for me than elementary school. First, interaction with my classmates became easier when I figured out that communicating using words rather than sound effects from the environment, as I had done in the elementary grades, went a long way towards making friends. Second, I began to realize what teachers wanted in order to properly evaluate my work. Since I was in general education classes from kindergarten, there was no thought of employing an aide or other person to help me understand the **hidden curriculum** (Myles et al., 2004) of the school classroom. Direct instruction, even as early as kindergarten, in proper interaction with my classmates and providing teachers what they needed would have helped ensure a more productive elementary school experience for me.

Between elementary and middle school, something must have "clicked," and teachers began to consider me better than average at mathematics and put me into an accelerated class. This worked well until we got to algebra and word problems. Navigating the differences between the letters and numbers, combined with having to keep two or more intermediary answers in mind while solving a problem, was too difficult for me. As a result, I was soon moved down to remedial math class – where the bullies were.

An administrator, who was also my math teacher, noticed the bullying and called me into his office for a discussion one day. He asked me if certain classmates were bothering me and whether I would like them to stop. I told him that, of course, I would like them to stop but that I was afraid of the repercussions from tattling on them. His plan was to bring each of the bullies into his office for a three-way discussion between them and me to inform them that their behavior was not acceptable and that it had to stop immediately. With much trepidation, I agreed to the process, and I am happy to say that it turned out well. Former bullies seemed much friendlier and would even talk with me.

The Role of Structure in Academic and Social Success

Another important reason why middle school was more successful than elementary school for me was that I was able to explore my special interests. Electronics was a passion of mine at that time, so I enrolled in an electronics shop class. I enjoyed making an electric motor as well as other devices run by electricity and finished the coursework about 3 weeks into a 15-week semester. However, in the school I attended, this and other shop classes, such as woodworking, drafting, and metalwork, were infested with bully-type students. Fortunately, the instructor saw the problem and, after finding out that I was a musician, had me transferred into band.

Socially, band was a much more successful experience for me for the following reasons. As with electronics, music was a special interest of mine. Further, in contrast to the electronics class, students in the fine arts were a bit different, making it easier for me to fit in. Finally, I had a structured activity that could be used to mediate my interactions with other students. In other words, there was predictability to the ensemble rehearsals, and there was always something about the band director or the music that I could use as the subject of conversation with my classmates. People on the autism spectrum need structure to be successful.

Social interaction is much more successful for individuals on the autism spectrum when gatherings are activity-based rather than socially oriented. Examples of activity-based gatherings include musical ensembles, computer clubs, bicycle clubs, and other events focused on a particular interest. Some socially oriented events include the senior prom, most class parties, and holiday dinners at a relative's house. However, non-structured events are a part of life, and it may be necessary to help a person with autism add structure to such situations. For example, a student with Asperger Syndrome could be helped in getting through a classroom holiday party by giving her a job arranging drinks, food, or other items related to the event.

Probably due to sensory challenges, along with differences in perception and thought processes (Myles et al., 2004), for children on the autism spectrum the world often seems to be a confusing and disorderly place with rules that do not make sense (Miller, 2007). Anything that can be done to make life more predictable will reduce anxiety and position the child better for academic and social success. In addition to helping all children plot how they will spend their time in school, it is important to use the schedule to announce changes in advance. For example, children may carry a text- or picture-based schedule in their notebooks. If it is known that a change is going to occur, the teacher and student can modify the schedule together in preparation for the new event. Failure to do so can result in a catastrophic meltdown, as seen below.

Lack of Structure Resulting in a Meltdown

Robert, who has high-functioning autism, asked his teacher when math class was later that day. Usually, this class was scheduled for 1:00 p.m., right after lunch, but today there was going to be a schoolwide assembly. Instead of telling Robert of the schedule change, the teacher thought she could put off the difficulty of dealing with the change of routine a little longer while she completed some work. Therefore, Robert's repeated queries were met with indefinite answers such as "later today" or "this afternoon."

Robert's anxiety continued to rise – his high voice became more and more strident, and he began to pace about the classroom. Soon his mother had to be called in because he had bitten a teacher and was in the throes of a full-scale meltdown.

Waiting quietly until Robert calmed down, his mother gently produced a 3 x 5 inch index card with the word "Oops" written on it and told her son how sorry she was that somebody had not told him of the change in plans. "Adults make mistakes, too," she added. Robert got up, and the two of them walked silently out of the room, went outside, and walked around the field as a way of calming Robert before returning to class.

What happened to Robert, and what was the significance of the "oops" card? Robert went through a rage cycle – he experienced increased anxiety to the point that he had a full-blown tantrum, followed by a period of calming down with his mother (Myles & Southwick, 2005; Shore & Rastelli, 2006). The "oops" card Robert's mother produced was part of a teaching tool she used to help her son deal with frustration in a systematic way. Because he has a very low tolerance for change and adult errors, his mother also wrote him a story about why these things might happen. She let him know that she understood how hard such things are for him and then introduced the oops card as a way to visually reassure him that she understood. The oops card can also remind Robert that changes sometimes happen and that adults sometimes make mistakes.

The Role of Sensory Issues

Although sensory challenges are not mentioned in the DSM IV-TR (*Diagnostic and Statistical Manual of Mental Disorders of the American Psychiatric Association* [APA], 2000) and most other definitions of autism at this time, I have never met a person on the autism spectrum who does not have challenges in sensory integration and modulation.

One way to conceive of sensory modulation is to think of a graphic equalizer with a slider representing each of the outer senses of sight, touch, taste, hearing, and sound, along with additional controls for the inner senses of proprioception and the vestibular and gustatory senses. Most people would have their sliders on or near 0 Db, close to the center. However, many people on the autism spectrum have some of these "sensory sliders" set too high, resulting in sensory overload due to hypersensitivity. For others, they are set too low, making those senses hyposensitive, thereby preventing sufficient data from being input to the brain. Additionally, data from the senses tend to be distorted. As a result, people on the autism spectrum depend on unreliable information from their senses as they attempt to make order out of what is often a confusing world.

Sensory issues were not taken into consideration throughout my time in grade school. However, that did not lessen their effect. Often I found unstructured time such as classroom parties, recess, and physical education overwhelming and causing me to withdraw from the environment. Sometimes even attending to my coursework in a room full of students was sensorially overwhelming, and I would have to leave the class. One teacher must have realized this intuitively, as she helped me tremendously by putting a three-part cardboard divider on my desk.

Sensory challenges may be responsible for the need of people with autism to prefer sameness of routine and careful attention to transitions. It is much harder to interact successfully with the environment using new information from the senses than it is to do something tried and true that allows you to predict the outcome.

Typical Asperger Relationships

In middle school, it suddenly occurred to me that all my friends were older than me. For example, I seemed to have more in common with my teachers than with my classmates. This fact did not trouble me, but I did find it curious. Upon graduation and entering the world of work, I found that all my friends were from other cultures. My sense is that the reason is cultural. People of a given culture intimately know how others are "supposed to behave." Those with differences often get bullied in grade school and shunned as adults. On the other hand, people of another culture may not perceive as many of those differences or may attribute them to local culture and, therefore, are more accepting. Finally, having their own challenges integrating into a new society, people from other countries may be more tolerant or even appreciative of differences from a societal norm.

As I continue to meet more and more people with Asperger Syndrome and high-functioning autism, I find that many of us have long-term relationships with individuals who also have "differences," be it racial, age, neurocognitive, physical, religious, or in other dimensions. The following are examples of my making friends with teachers and staff at school.

Shortly after my father had his first heart attack, I was called out of Spanish class to meet with a guidance counselor. The only thing I knew about these people was that they had a reputation among students in the school of being strange or weird. However, upon entering the guidance counselor's office, I found a friendly man who seemed interested in what I had to say. Later I found that he was always available for good conversation on short notice. We would trade stories of childhood experiences, and soon we became friends.

My time with him opened up a whole world of friendly counselors in the guidance office, as well as administrators. Having these relationships work properly was important to me, so upon finding malfunctioning fixtures around the school, I would be right in the principal's office making sure he was aware of what needed repair in the school. He was open-minded and interesting to be around as well.

My brother, Martin, two years my senior, was diagnosed with mild to moderate intellectual disability. I believe he has also some autistic characteristics. In contrast to me, almost all of his schooling took place in a special education room. When I realized my brother's classroom was just down the hall from my homeroom, I began to spend time in that classroom as well. There I found a teacher accepting of differences and students who seemed to know more about life than my general education classmates.

Physical Education

Physical education was always a difficult class for me. In elementary school, I was the last one chosen for any team sport, and my coordination (or lack of same) made me a liability to the team. Bombardment, sometimes referred to as dodgeball, was a particularly heinous game to me that violated the senses – you had to simultaneously avoid being smacked by a dozen or more balls while trying to hit someone on the other team. Middle school brought about more complexity in different team sports, and my participation continued to be poor.

However, just as the diversity in course and club options can be a boon to a person on the autism spectrum, so can carefully thought-out choices for physical education. My initial experiences in middle school physical education involved the challenges and anxiety of the boys' locker room and competitive team sports. One day, the gym teacher told our class to run around a track for 10 minutes. Having ridden my bicycle extensively the previous summer, I was in better shape than most of the other students for endurance activities. As I would do when bicycle racing, I stayed behind the lead people and then zoomed past them as we got close to the end. Upon seeing my performance, the coach invited me to join the track team; however, the ever-growing collection of negative experiences in gym kept me away.

In retrospect, joining the track team would have been good for me, since it was a sport that could be done individually as well as on a team. I have had good experiences with other similar sports, such as rock climbing and, of course, bicycling. Other people with Asperger Syndrome report success with similar types of sports.

What that experience of running around a track taught me was that walking or running could be fun, or at least not as onerous as standard gym class. I had noticed a poster listing the names of people who had joined the "100-mile club." A student's name was placed there if he or she completed 100 circuits around the field, to make up 100 miles. One day, I asked the gym teacher if I could join the club and if it might be possible to start right then, instead of joining my classmates for gym. Emboldened by his positive answer, I ventured further by asking if I could work on my goal in "civilian clothes." His consent solved two major problems I had with physical education. First, I could continue to get my exercise through alternative means instead of through team sports. Second, I bypassed the locker-room scene by not having to change clothes.

In today's educational world, such a modification would have required a team meeting and the signing of documents attesting that my being on the autism spectrum required an accommodation of alternate or adaptive physical education. In those days, all that was needed was a physical education instructor who perhaps intuitively sensed that walking or running around a track to reach a goal was better for me than engaging in standard gym activities. However, while the latter was less formal, it was by no means standard practice.

High School

Middle school was better than elementary for me, and high school was in some ways even better. One reason was that my special interests led me to meet some interesting teachers and administrators. Although I now got along better with most of my classmates, there was nobody, with the exception of a student from elementary school, whom I could really call my friend. Sometimes I would arrange to do something with a classmate, but most of my time outside of school was spent reading books, conducting experiments with my chemistry set, and feeding my bicycle interests by working as a bicycle mechanic and riding my bike.

Music

While mathematics remained a challenge, things were much better in the music room. Since music was a special interest of mine, I spent as much time in the band room as possible, practicing and learning new instruments. It became a passion of mine to learn as many of the band and orchestral instruments as possible. For example, I bartered trombone lessons for instruction in string bass from a student music teacher. In fact, one of the main reasons I chose music education as an undergraduate major was that learning all the instruments was a requirement.

Since I was interested in classical music, I made friends with a kindly older music teacher who conducted the orchestra. I also enjoyed his courses in music theory. Not many students seemed to like him, possibly because they thought he was old-fashioned. Music also made a good common interest with one of the guidance counselors at the high school. When he learned that I played the flute, he asked if I would be willing to teach him to play.

Counselors

My positive experiences with guidance counselors opened me to the possibility of making friends with the counselor mentioned above. In addition to learning how to play the flute, he was also interested in learning music theory. Perhaps this person saw my way of interacting through music as a way to address other issues. He was successful in doing this, as illustrated in the following.

Since I had good relationships with most of my teachers, I was puzzled about my difficulty in relating to my homeroom teacher. He seemed cold and distant and looked like a cat. I wanted to change my classroom so I could be with a friendlier teacher. Even if this meant that the teacher was boring, at least he or she would be friendly and comfortable to be with.

In responding to the counselor's queries about why I wanted to switch teachers, I mentioned that my current homeroom teacher was cold and unfriendly and that I had nothing in common with him. The counselor answered that he could change my homeroom assignment but that he wanted me to try something first. "See if you can strike up a conversation with your homeroom teacher about music. Maybe you could show him your flute."

I was willing to give it a try, and to my surprise it worked! The formerly cold, unfeeling homeroom teacher asked me to play my flute, and soon we were talking about music. We became friends, and I visited him at his home a number of times to fix his bicycles. Later on, I took a course from him, which I found enjoyable. As a result, I ended up adding him to the list of teachers that I kept in touch with after my graduation.

From this vantage point, I suspect that my counselor knew my homeroom teacher had an interest in music and saw that as a common point of interest. I am grateful to him for encouraging me to reach out and make the first step towards developing relationships with others. Without his suggestion, it might never have occurred to me to initiate contact in this manner.

Employment While in High School

Employment is usually something that takes place out of school. However, since many, if not most, students begin their work careers while in school, it merits some mention. First, it is important to make sure employment does not interfere with time needed for school, family life, and other important matters. When work can be fit into a student's schedule, many benefits can accrue, such as learning the value of money and gaining additional experience with social interaction. Common employment paths for young people, such as working in a restaurant, being a cashier, or other situations where there is high sensory input, are not suitable for people on the autism spectrum. As with education, it is important to take the person's interests into account.

My first two jobs in high school were serving as a busboy in a restaurant. Now that I understand more about sensory overload, I realize that my working slowly, even during busy times, was a form of shutdown due to overstimulation. Needless to say, I did not last long in those jobs. At that time, bicycles were a special interest, and with the help of a job counselor at school, I drafted a letter to managers of bicycle shops, introducing myself as a candidate for a bicycle mechanic position.

After sending the letter to local bike shops, I made followup calls, which netted me several interviews. I had a customized bike, which I rode to the interviews. My bicycle served as a sort of portfolio that could be used to start a conversation. After talking about the construction of my bicycle, right down to building the wheels, I would ask for a job. At that time, building a bicycle wheel from scratch was a valued skill. In fact, I got hired for one job by completing an assignment of building 10 bicycle wheels in short order. I stayed with this shop for four years, eventually rising to the role of shop manager.

This experience proved invaluable to me in college, as I ran my own bicycle repair shop to earn a good portion of my tuition. When asked by a financial aid officer why I did not use my work study funds, I told her that I could make much more money faster and be much happier fixing bicycles than serving as a security guard or working in the dining commons as part of the work study program.

Bicycle repair was much more suited to me than a standard job for the following reasons. First, it was an area of special interest, so I was motivated to do a good job. Second, it made use of my considerable mechanical ability. Third, fixing bicycles in the shop at the back of the store involved relatively low sensory input. As with teaching curriculum, it is important and often vital to match a student's interest and strengths with employment possibilities. Everyone learns better and faster the things he or she is interested in. For those on the autism spectrum, this fact is particularly true.

Learning Self-Advocacy Through Educational Planning

A topic that is getting more and more recognition is the importance of teaching children how to advocate for themselves, along with disclosure. Every person with a disability will arrive at a point when he or she has to advocate for him or herself in an effort to achieve better mutual understanding. For example, a person might need to ask for changes in the environment to help him focus or relax. It is important that the person be clear about the reason for the requested change so that others are able to empathize with the need (Shore, 2004).

These valuable skills can be taught by involving children in their own educational plan to the extent of their ability. For example, a more severely affected child who is nonverbal and hyperactive might be involved in an educational planning meeting by initially interacting with a couple of the IEP team members whom she already knows and then leave. In addition to introducing the child to the educational planning process, the team members – who may work with dozens of children – get a quick reminder of the specific child's strengths and needs.

Another child may be able to communicate through pictures, sign language, written words, or verbally that he likes and/or dislikes certain classes. Yet another child may state that she likes English class but the scratching of other students' pencils drives her to distraction. Students may get to a point where they can research different accommodations and lead portions of the IEP meeting under the watchful eye of the team leader.

For example, suppose a third grader with high-functioning autism or Asperger Syndrome needs to have an accommodation written into her IEP for a visual sensitivity to fluorescent lights. Like many people on the autism spectrum, this young student perceives fluorescent lights like most others see a strobe light – fun for holidays and special effects but a serious distraction while doing work in class. Possible accommodations include placing her near a window, allowing her to wear a baseball cap in class, unscrewing the fluorescent bulb above her head and using an incandescent lamp, or perhaps a combination of these suggestions. While it may be faster to just write these accommodations into the plan at a team meeting, it will be much more helpful to the student to bring her into the planning process.

Perhaps the first thing to do would be to have a discussion with the student to validate her feelings of frustration and anxiety in having to deal with this type of lighting in the first place. During this discussion, the teacher or other person supporting the student clearly indicates that together they will work to resolve the problem. By brainstorming and using familiar visual systems to review social situations, the student and supporting person develop a plan for resolving the challenge and meet with the IEP team, or even just the teacher of the class, in the advocacy effort.

Children with little or no experience in advocating for themselves may need to see the process modeled for them, whereas students with greater experience can take on more and more responsibility and may even learn to complete the entire advocacy effort entirely on their own (Sibley, 2004).

Perhaps later in life in a work situation, this same person is placed in an office illuminated with fluorescent light. The education in advocating for herself that she received in school will pay handsome dividends as she now has to request her supervisor for change in lighting and explain the reason why in a way the supervisor can understand and act on.

Summary and Conclusions

As for many children with different ways of learning and interacting with others, for me grade school was a time of anxiety, misunderstandings, and confusion. However, I was lucky for several reasons. First, the structure of the school day and my desire to learn new things attracted me to education in general. Second, I had some good teachers and school administrators along the way, who intuitively understood and accommodated for my needs. Even though there is now a special education law with the IEP as a vehicle of advocacy and provision of a free and appropriate public education, the best results occur when teachers combine an intuitive sense of the needs of a child with an educational background in providing for those needs. Third, no matter how difficult school was for me for academic and social reasons, my parents supported me in my efforts while at the same time working with the school to make sure I got the best education possible.

My wish is that this book allows readers to combine their desire and love for educating children who have differences with the plethora of easy-to-implement, practical solutions available today to address the educational and social needs of children with ASD in the school setting.

Tips for the Classroom

✓ Developing a relationship between you and the learner is vital to success in education. Sometimes this can be done with simple imitation.

✓ Narrate the activities of a child as he is doing them. This deposits the words into a sort of "bank," allowing for future retrieval to think about and describe what he is doing.

✓ Parents are the experts on their children. Seek to collaborate with them whenever possible.

✓ Engage a child through an interest as a launching pad for teaching social interaction skills and other areas.

✓ Bullying is a form of harassment and should not be tolerated.

✓ Assistive technology and accommodation are hand-ups and not hand-outs.

✓ Tell children what they *can* do; not what they can't.

✓ A common characteristic of people on the autism spectrum is literal-mindedness. It is important to be aware of this when using idioms or studying mythology, for example.

✓ Eye contact does not give people with autism the kind of information that those not on the autism spectrum receive. In fact, it may detract from paying attention. Just because we are looking away doesn't mean we are not listening, perceiving, or paying attention.

✓ Sensory challenges are a characteristic common to just about all children on the autism spectrum. Such challenges, if not addressed, can lead to challenging behavior.

✓ Direct instruction in the hidden curriculum of the classroom and school in general may mean the difference between failure and success for children on the autism spectrum during their school time.

✓ Many people on the autism spectrum desperately want to make friends. Unlike others, we may need direct instruction on how to do so.

✓ Involving students in their own educational planning will pay dividends after graduation, as adults with autism will have learned how to advocate and disclose for themselves at home, at work, in continuing education, in relationships, and in the community.

Chapter Highlights

- The chapter author describes experiences from pre-K through high school.

- Some of the areas the chapter author stresses as being of particular importance include:

  ➤ Developing a relationship between instructor and learner

  ➤ Engaging students through use of their special interests

  ➤ Teaching the "hidden curriculum"

  ➤ Realizing that individuals with ASD tend to be very literal in their thinking and taking this into account when teaching

  ➤ Making use of assistive technology as appropriate

  ➤ Understanding that many individuals with ASD are victims of bullying. It is important that school personnel are aware of this and take steps to deal with it.

  ➤ Being aware that structure is an important part of a comfortable environment for persons with ASD

  ➤ Understanding that persons with ASD have sensory integration and modulation challenges

  ➤ Involving students in educational planning so self-knowledge and self-advocacy skills are developed

Chapter Review Questions

1. List and describe three experiences discussed by the chapter author.

2. Define narration and explain why the chapter author believes it is important for children with ASD.

3. What is the "hidden curriculum" and why does the chapter author believe it is crucial to directly teach it to students with ASD?

4. How did using his special interests assist the chapter author in being successful?

References

American Psychiatric Association. (2000). *Diagnostic and statistical manual of mental disorders* (4th ed.; text revision). Washington, DC: Author.

Dubin, N. (2007). *Asperger Syndrome and bullying: Strategies and solutions.* London: Jessica Kingsley Publishers.

Heinrichs, R. (2004). *Perfect targets: Asperger Syndrome and bullying – Practical solutions for surviving the social world.* Shawnee Mission, KS: Autism Asperger Publishing Company.

Miller, M. (2007). *The Miller method: Developing the capacities of children on the autism spectrum.* London: Jessica Kingsley Publishers.

Myles, B. S., Trautman, M., & Schelvan, R. (2004). *The hidden curriculum: Practical solutions for understanding unstated rules in social situations.* Shawnee Mission, KS: Autism Asperger Publishing Company.

Myles, B. S., & Southwick, J. (2005). *Asperger Syndrome and difficult moments: Practical solutions for tantrums, rage, and meltdown* (rev. ed.). Shawnee Mission, KS: Autism Asperger Publishing Company.

Shore, S. (2003). *Beyond the wall: Personal experiences with autism and Asperger Syndrome* (2nd ed.). Shawnee Mission, KS: Autism Asperger Publishing Company.

Shore, S. (2004). Using the IEP to build skills in self-advocacy and disclosure. In S. Shore (Ed.), *Ask and tell: Self-advocacy and disclosure for people on the autism spectrum* (pp. 65-105). Shawnee Mission, KS: Autism Asperger Publishing Company.

Shore, S., & Rastelli, L. (2006). *Understanding autism for dummies.* New York: Wiley & Sons.

Sibley, K. (2004). Help me help myself: Teaching and learning. In S. Shore (Ed.), *Ask and tell: Self-advocacy and disclosure for people on the autism spectrum* (pp. 33-63). Shawnee Mission, KS: Autism Asperger Publishing Company.

Index

A

ABA. *See* Applied behavior analysis
Academic work
    accommodations, 289
    content standards, 293
    curriculum, 169, 174, 220
    elementary school, 321–322
    goals, 293
    homework, 125, 131, 228
    mathematics, 268, 321–322, 324
    middle school, 323–324
    modifications, 289
    reading comprehension, 322
    test-taking difficulties, 291, 292
Accommodations
    academic, 289
    in employment, 270
    physical education, 327
    test-taking, 292
ADA. *See* Americans with Disabilities Act
ADHD. *See* Attention deficit hyperactivity disorder
ADI-R. *See Autism Diagnostic Interview-Revised*
Administrators, school, 282, 324, 326–327
Adolescents with ASD
    brain studies, 47–48, 49, 54–55
    employment, 267, 329
    social skills training, 271–272
    See also High school; Transition planning
ADOS. *See Autism Diagnostic Observation Schedule*
Adults with ASD
    brain studies, 47–48, 49
    emotion recognition skills training, 240–244, 245–246
    independent living, 257, 261, 262
    See also Employment; Transition planning

AEPS. *See Assessment, Evaluation, and Programming System*
Affect sharing, 92, 93, 95, 97, 103
Alert Program, 228
American Psychiatric Association (APA), 20, 21, 23, 25, 69
Americans with Disabilities Act (ADA), 258, 259, 272
Amygdala, 30, 31
Antecedents, behavior, 167, 172
Anxiety
    in ASD children, 33
    causes, 187, 288
    cycles, 325
    5-point scale, 226, 228
    reducing with structure, 325
    relaxation techniques, 228
Applied behavior analysis (ABA), 71, 176
AS. *See* Asperger Syndrome
ASD. *See* Autism spectrum disorders
Asperger, Hans, 23
Asperger Syndrome (AS)
    behaviors, 25
    cognitive characteristics, 27
    common characteristics, 23
    diagnostic criteria, 23–24, 25
    distinction from high-functioning autism, 24–25
    emotion recognition skills, 236
    gender ratio, 34
    history, 23
    sensory processing patterns, 145, 146
    signs, 24–25
    social skills, 24, 215, 219, 224–225
    special interests, 27–28

    Structured Teaching application, 128–129, 130–131, 132–133
Aspy, R., 263
Assessment, Evaluation, and Programming System (AEPS), 76

Assessments
    curriculum-based, 76
    diagnosis of ASD, 70, 71
    by educational teams, 290–292
    intelligence, 238, 310
    language and communication, 101–103
    sensory perception, 139, 144
    situated pragmatics approach, 101
    standardized tests, 101
    test-taking difficulties, 291, 292
    transition planning, 263
Attention, joint. *See* Joint attention
Attention deficit disorder, 33
Attention deficit hyperactivity disorder (ADHD), 145
Auditory comprehension, 221
Auditory discrimination, 26
Auditory processing, 26
Augmentative communication devices, 74, 103
Autism
    culture of, 117–118
    definition, 20
    regressive or late-onset, 21
    See also Autism spectrum disorders
Autism Diagnostic Interview-Revised (ADI-R), 47
Autism Diagnostic Observation Schedule (ADOS), 47
Autism Society of America, 308
Autism spectrum
    cognitive dimension, 26–28, 58
    communication dimension, 26
    progression along, 28–29
    sensory dimension, 28
    social dimension, 25–26
Autism spectrum disorders (ASD)
    causes, 29–31, 56, 308
    co-occurring disorders, 33
    core deficit, 46

Appendix A: Chapter Review Answers

Chapter 1

1. Early-onset autism is characterized by sleep disturbances, feeding problems, inability to be comforted, withdrawal from social objects, lack of pointing to objects wanted, poor or no eye contact, fascination with sensory experiences, lack of imitation, limited language development, delayed self-care skills, lack of response to conversation or direction, and general developmental delay. Children who exhibit late-onset autism achieve the typical developmental milestones until late into their second year, demonstrate interaction skills and interest in others, and show early symbolic and imaginary play. However, over a short period of time, these skills begin to deteriorate and, by age 3, there may be no clear distinction between a child with early-onset and a child with late-onset autism.

2. ASD refers to a group of five disorders or syndromes associated with the autism spectrum and considered pervasive developmental disabilities or disorders.

3. Five subgroups under the umbrella term of ASD include:

   ✓ *Autism*: a child has a severe qualitative impairment in reciprocal social interaction and communication and a restricted range of activities and interests.

   ✓ *Rett's Disorder*: appears to occur primarily in girls and is a progressive neurological disorder. It is typified by loss of purposeful hand use, hand wringing, spasticity of lower extremities, microcephaly, seizures, and need for supports for daily living.

   ✓ *Childhood disintegrative disorder*: a rare condition in which a child develops typically on all milestones until between the ages of 3 and 5. The child then experiences rapid deterioration across all areas to the point where he demonstrates significant and severe difficulties across social, communication, and intellectual skills.

   ✓ *Pervasive developmental disorder-not otherwise specified*: a somewhat vague term generally used to refer to children who demonstrate some signs of autism but not the symptoms for a clear diagnosis. The author of the chapter describes PDD-NOS as "fragments of autism."

   ✓ *Asperger's Disorder/Asperger Syndrome*: includes lack of the significant early language and cognitive skills deficits that are commonly seen in autism, no clinically significant delay in self-help skills or adaptive behavior, and less likelihood of motor mannerisms than seen in classical autism. Asperger's Disorder may not be identified until individuals are school-aged.

4. The three areas in the diagnostic criteria for autism are:

   ✓ *Social interaction*: lack of understanding/use of nonverbal communication, difficulty with peer relationships, lack of reciprocity.

   ✓ *Communication*: delay or lack of spoken language; idiosyncratic language; lack of varied, spontaneous play; impairment in initiating and sustaining conversation.

   ✓ *Restricted patterns of behavior*: inflexibility, nonfunctional routines or rituals, preoccupation with parts of objects, repetitive motor mannerisms.

5. In Asperger Syndrome, there is not a significant delay in language and intellectual development, nor is there impairment in adaptive/self-help skills. Individuals with HFA demonstrate classic signs of autism in early childhood, but later testing in school indicates greater intellectual ability and self-help/adaptive behavior than is typical in classical autism.

   The controversy over the distinction is based on recent research that seems to show some of the APA diagnostic criteria may not accurately distinguish between the two.

6. The five dimensions of autism spectrum disorders are:

   ✓ *Social dimension*: including relating to others, social understanding, and social maturity.

   ✓ *Communication dimension*: including verbal and nonverbal language usage and understanding.

   ✓ *Cognitive dimension*: intellectual abilities, as well as organization, memory, and time management.

   ✓ *Special interests dimension*: demonstrating an extremely strong interest in an object or part of an object, collecting objects, acquiring large amounts of information on a particular topic.

   ✓ *Sensory dimension*: response to various things that affect the senses (e.g., sight, taste, smell, sound, touch, or body awareness).

7. Each dimension can be considered a continuum because an individual with ASD may demonstrate more or less ability, disability, or difference on a given dimension.

8. The term *refrigerator mother* was coined by Leo Kanner and used extensively by Bruno Bettelheim to refer to mothers of children with autistic disorder. Until the 1970s, the cause of autism was believed to be the response of children to mothers who lacked the ability to appropriately interact with their children and were seen as cold and unloving.

9. Currently, possible causes of autism include genetics, such as chromosomal abnormalities; neurological dysfunction; possible errors of metabolism; and infections in pregnancy.

10. Three psychological theories of autism are:

    ✓ *Theory of mind*: the ability to understand the mental states of others (e.g., beliefs, thoughts, desires, perceptions, and feelings) and apply this understanding to their actions. Theorists believe that individuals with ASD may lack abilities in this area, resulting in "mind blindness," or the inability to make sense of others' behavior.

✓ *Central coherence*: the ability to integrate information into a meaningful whole. Theorists believe individuals with ASD have weak central coherence in that they process information by tending to focus on the parts and lose sight of the whole.

✓ *Executive function*: the ability to properly use a group of mental processes, including organizational and planning abilities, working memory, inhibition and impulse control, time management and prioritizing, and using new strategies. It is believed that individuals with ASD have deficits in executive functioning.

11. The ratio for autism is 2:1 boys to girls; for Asperger's, it is 5:1.

12. There are several possible explanations. These include a broader definition of ASD, realization that ASD may co-occur with other disorders, and better diagnostic procedures.

Chapter 2

1. Core deficit refers to the concept that autism may be attributed to a single deficit that caused a cascade, resulting in a constellation of deficits. While a single core deficit is no longer regarded as the cause of autism, some theorists argue that there is, among all the other deficits displayed in autism, a primary impairment of earlier onset.

2. The most popular theories regarding primary impairment focus on lack of ability to shift attention, deficits in representational capacity, and deficits in social motivation, or ability to orient to social stimuli.

3. After performing several studies, the authors found that individuals with autism demonstrated differences not only in the neural systems underlying language, reasoning, and social development, but also showed impairments in memory and motor skills. Other studies have validated that autism appears to be a disorder characterized by a reduced capacity for information processing.

4. Based on several studies, it appears that individuals with autism/ASD have difficulty when task demands are high in terms of capacity to process information; for example, multitasking, in which individuals are required to hold multiple pieces of information at the same time.

5. Hidden information-processing demands refers to the fact that certain tasks require the brain to process meaning and retain it in working memory for a period of time in order to fully comprehend (or "process") information. An example is understanding information presented in spoken or written complex sentences involving phrases and clauses. Individuals with ASD have difficulty with material that requires these abilities, though they might fully comprehend each piece of material independently.

6. Helps with intervention and understanding of behavior and can be used as a guide for intervention. It helps to make clear the importance of conveying information succinctly to individuals with autism/ASD.

7. Complexity is a concept of evaluating material in terms of the demands made on the individual; for example, riding a bike requires a complex motor sequence that also involves integration of visual, vestibular, and position sense.

8. Central coherence describes the ability to integrate information into a meaningful whole. Individuals with autism/ASD display weak central coherence in that they tend to focus on details rather than on the whole.

9. Information processing for individuals with autism/ASD focuses on the fact that, across domains, higher-order abilities are impacted. In other words, simple information-processing demands appeared intact while complex information processing was impaired. This pattern of selective impact on more difficult information with intact simple information is unusual.

10. fMRI, or functional magnetic resonance imaging, is a technology that allows recording of brain activity during cognitive and language tasks. This technology has allowed researchers to observe differences in brain function in autism/ASD. Findings will aid in understanding compensatory strategies used by individuals with autism/ASD, leading to better interventions that will help individuals handle increasingly complex tasks.

11. Studies using fMRI have shown that the brains of individuals with autism/ASD demonstrate reduced connectivity and synchrony, indicating that regions of the brain are not working together as efficiently as in neurotypical individuals. Additionally, there appears to be less flexibility in managing tasks with changing demands.

12. Compensatory strategies refer to the fact that fMRI studies show individuals with autism/ASD use different cognitive approaches to tasks. Some of these strategies may interfere with acquisition, while others assist the individual. For example, focusing on the words rather than meaning in sentence comprehension may interfere with understanding language, whereas using visual strategies such as "thinking in pictures" may enable material to be understood.

13. Impairments in memory and learning are not included in the diagnostic criteria but have been documented in studies of neuropsychological functioning of individuals with autism/ASD. The chapter authors believe the diagnostic criteria need to be revisited to include this information.

14. Intellectual disability in autism is not a separate diagnosis because it reflects an information-processing impairment. As the severity of autism increases, so does the difficulty in information processing. The information-processing difficulty is part of the profile of cognitive impairment evident in all levels of autism/ASD; therefore, intellectual disability in autism is part of a profile of the disorder.

15. Implications of the brain basis of autism are:

   ✓ Immaturity should be expected as a consequence of the developmental disorder.

   ✓ Biological response may mean that students with autism/ASD do not always do what they are asked if it is something they don't like to do, as they may not have the executive function to override their tendency to resist doing a hard or unpleasant task.

   ✓ Individuals with autism/ASD do not exhibit the same level of common sense or problem-solving ability as their peers.

Chapter 3

1. A spectrum disorder is one in which children receiving the diagnosis can differ considerably in terms of abilities, needs, preferences, and areas of delay.

2. Early intervention is crucial for children diagnosed with ASD because research has unanimously demonstrated that the earlier the intervention, the better the potential outcomes in terms of independence, cognitive functioning, and communication.

3. Some of the major issues surrounding early identification of ASD include (a) a problem with early and accurate detection and diagnosis, particularly with regard to individuals who are culturally and linguistically diverse; (b) the fact that the diagnosis of ASD is complex and cannot be tied to any individual behavior at any age; (c) the need for improvement in the accuracy of screening and diagnostic tools; (d) the need for educating pediatricians and others about ASD; and (e) the need to influence policy and practice to ensure proper implementation of appropriate assessment tools.

4. The developmental red flags that may indicate ASD in infants and toddlers include:

   ✓ No big smiles, or other warm, joyous expressions by 6 months or thereafter

   ✓ No back-and-forth sharing of sounds, smiles, or other facial expressions by 9 months or thereafter

   ✓ No babbling by 12 months

   ✓ No back-and-forth gestures, such as pointing, showing, reaching, or waving by 12 months

   ✓ No words by 16 months

   ✓ No two-word meaningful phrases by 24 months

   ✓ A loss of speech or babbling or social skills at any age

5. It is important to provide families with information on intervention services and community supports because families are often left scared and confused by the diagnosis of an ASD. Helping families identify service providers, supplying information on the characteristics of effective intervention, resources such as books, websites and parent support groups, and providing families with temporary support until they can obtain support and assistance is crucial. Following up with a phone call or visit within two weeks to answer any additional questions is recommended.

6. The key elements of effective programs for young children with ASD include:

   ✓ Sufficient hours and intensity of services

   ✓ Comprehensible environments with access to typical peers

   ✓ Specialized curriculum with an appropriate scope and sequence

   ✓ Family involvement

   ✓ Problem-solving approach to challenging behaviors

   ✓ Appropriate evaluation tools for monitoring progress

7. The types of questions families should consider when selecting an intervention program include:

   ✓ What are the primary concerns for the child?

   ✓ Does the considered intervention(s) address those concerns?

   ✓ Are the procedures of the intervention acceptable?

   ✓ Are the interventions a good match for the child and family?

   ✓ What types of evidence of effectiveness of the intervention exist, and is it convincing?

   ✓ How will the interventionists communicate with the family and demonstrate the child's progress, and is that acceptable?

8. The term *outcome-oriented framework* refers to looking at desired outcomes for the child from the beginning and ensuring intervention strategies focus on achieving those outcomes.

9. In deciding on meaningful outcomes for their child, families need to look at the strengths and needs of the individual child, the family's priorities, and existing data.

10. Curriculum-based assessment (CBA) identifies functional skills across multiple domains (i.e., adaptive, social, cognitive, communication, and motor) that are common in early childhood. A CBA is useful by giving a starting point of where the child is functioning and what he or she needs to learn.

11. The five components of Project DATA are:

    ✓ Integrated early childhood experience

    ✓ Extended intensive instruction

    ✓ Technical and social support

    ✓ Collaboration and coordination of services

    ✓ Transition planning and support

12. The areas to which Project DATA preschool environments pay particular attention are:

    ✓ Structuring the classroom environment to promote independence, participation, and successful interactions with typically developing peers

    ✓ Developing a consistent schedule and following it

    ✓ Creating the need to communicate with adults and peers

    ✓ Using preferred materials and activities to promote engagement

    ✓ Providing embedded and explicit instruction on valued skills

    ✓ Providing frequent reinforcement and developing effective motivation systems

Chapter 4

1. Social communication involves the ability to use words to interact with others in order to affect their behavior and/or thoughts.

2. Theory of mind and social language learning are intertwined with the processes underlying language learning, including understanding what is in another person's mind.

3. Autism can be described as a deficit in communication because it leads to an inability to share feelings, beliefs, and knowledge with others. Individuals with autism may have the words but fail to understand how to use them based on others' perspectives.

4. A student with autism might have a large vocabulary but fail to understand how to use the words to communicate because he lacks knowledge of how to affect others, or even an awareness of the need to do so in order to communicate effectively.

5. The chapter authors describe ineffective language intervention with individuals with autism as being based on interventionists' lack of understanding of (a) the language learning process and (b) the effect of abnormalities in interpersonal relatedness and social cognition demonstrated by individuals with autism.

6. Interactive games assist infants in developing social communication because they provide opportunities for attention and affect sharing and social reciprocity, which helps the infant develop the interpersonal relatedness needed for later social communication.

7. Experiential learning is critical in brain development based on research showing an increase in brain activity when infants are actively involved, thus providing neuron development and increased brain connectivity.

8. Babies with autism do not engage in games as do their neurotypical peers and, therefore, miss out on opportunities for emotional regulation, attention sharing, anticipation, and reciprocity with their caregivers. Additionally, as infants with autism tend to engage in repetitive behaviors, their lack of opportunity to develop connectivity and the failure of neurons to be "pruned" may lead to less capacity for social-cognitive behaviors and brain development.

9. Joint attention refers to behaviors suggestive of an increasing understanding of the need to engage other minds, such as gaze following, pointing, and showing/offering gestures. It is important in the development of communication because social communication is based on a shared awareness and engagement, which is absent or less developed in children with autism. Additionally, research shows joint attention impacts both typically developing children and those with autism in a similar way in that the amount of joint attention engaged in is highly correlated with vocabulary development and sets the stage for intention reading.

10. Intention reading is central to social-pragmatic theory in that the development of language is based on an understanding of symbols and the development of social cognition. These are gained through the shared focus between the caregiver and infant in various pre-language activities.

11. Understanding social-pragmatic theory can provide a basis for understanding what goes wrong in the language acquisition process in autism; specifically, impairments in social cognition in terms of joint attention, affect sharing, and intention reading are seen as likely causes of the pragmatic deficits demonstrated by individuals with autism.

12. Pragmatics is important to the development of language because it is integral to the communication process, including understanding what others might be thinking (intention reading) and feeling, and using that knowledge to adequately convey thoughts and information.

13. Social-pragmatic theory might be considered the "rule" in typical language development as it seems to best account for why children develop words at certain times, the social-cognitive elements that underpin communication, and the way in which children typically learn language.

14. The statement that words have different pragmatic functions based on speaker intentions refers to the way a given word is used. For example, the same word can be used to summon, to attract or direct attention to something, or to make a declaration.

15. Presuppositional knowledge refers to having an understanding of the listener's needs in terms of information content and communication style. For example, one would probably recount an experience differently to a friend than to a policeman.

16. The four conversational maxims related to understanding the rules of spoken interactions are as follows:

    ✓ Quantity: using only what is needed to convey information

    ✓ Quality: understanding what is true and what is not

    ✓ Relevance: staying on topic

    ✓ Clarity: conveying information in a way that is clear to the listener

17. Research indicates that word learning depends on context, knowledge of the underlying concept, the communicative goal of the speaker, word class, and level of novelty.

18. The general considerations related to assessment of language for individuals with autism from a social-pragmatic perspective include (a) the use of situated pragmatics and naturalistic contexts, (b) evaluating conversational maxims and presuppositional knowledge, and (c) evaluating comprehension at both the literal and the discourse level.

19. The general principles include:

    a. Intervention must begin where the learner is

    b. Intervention should be experiential

    c. It is important to use augmentative means for communication

    d. Emphasis should be placed on comprehension

    e. Active student engagement is important

    f. Vocabulary targets should be within the individual's conceptual understanding

    g. Different classes of words need to be taught differently

    h. Intervention should take place in context in order to support learning of meaning

    i. Theory-of-mind activities should be included within language intervention

    j. Intervention that promotes generalization of language occurs in contextually relevant routines

Chapter 5

1. "Structure" as it relates to teaching refers to the teacher or caregiver deciding what the learning activities will be, where they will occur, and how long they will last.

2. TEACCH, the **T**reatment and **E**ducation of **A**utistic and related **C**ommunication-handicapped **CH**ildren, is a statewide autism service program used in North Carolina.

3. Structured Teaching refers to environmental strategies and environmental supports for individuals with ASD developed by the TEACCH program. A social-cognitive-behavioral approach, Structured Teaching can be used with all ages of individuals and in all settings. TEACCH focuses on organization of the environment, the way in which activities are presented, and the distinctive ways in which individuals with ASD perceive the world. Implications for students with ASD and their families include providing the learner with a comprehensible environment, teaching as many skills as possible, and providing support for and respect to families.

4. The chapter authors use the term *Culture of Autism* to refer to the patterns of thought and behavior characteristic of autism, such as preference for and strength in visual processing; difficulty combining or integrating ideas; communication problems, particularly in pragmatics; and strong interests and impulses to engage in favored activities.

5. The five questions Structured Teaching should answer by providing the learner with visual information and organization of the environment are:

   ✓ Where should I be?

   ✓ What work or activity will I do?

   ✓ How much work will I do/How long will the activity last?

   ✓ How will I know that I am making progress and when I have finished?

   ✓ What will I do next?

6. Structured Teaching makes use of schedules, task organization, activity/work systems, and routines to help students with ASD answer the five questions referred to in Question 5.

   ✓ Schedules are important by allowing individuals with ASD to know where they are supposed to be and what they are to be doing at a given time, as well as allowing for predictable environments with knowledge of what will come next. Schedules should be individualized, visual, accurate, and easy to alter should the need arise.

   ✓ Task organization and work/activity systems provide a visual representation for the student of what he is to do each step of the way during a task or activity.

   ✓ Routines are consistent daily activities. A student who has reached independence or mastery on an activity can be considered to have developed a routine (for example, placing completed work in a folder or washing hands before snack time).

7. Examples of strategies for each of the five questions of Structured Teaching include:

✓ For the first question, "Where should I be?" some strategies might be:

  o Providing a designated area such as a chair, carpet square, mark on floor, etc., so the student knows where to sit or stand

  o Defining space by using pillows, screens, pieces of furniture, etc.

  o Providing assigned seating

✓ For the second question, "What work or activity will I do?" some strategies might be:

  o Organizing materials so the student can see what he needs to do and for how long. The emphasis is on showing visually rather than telling, so use of pictures, concrete objects, written directions, and so on, is recommended.

  o Using office supplies to keep materials organized

  o Highlighting important parts of the visual or physical display of materials

✓ For the third and fourth questions, "How much work will I do/How long will this activity last?" and "How will I know I have finished?" some strategies include:

  o Organizing and counting out materials in advance so students can get the information by looking at the materials

  o Using visual timers such as hourglasses and timers

✓ For the fifth question, "What will I do next?" some strategies might be:

  o Providing an object or symbol to indicate what to do/where to go when work is completed

  o Showing the next item on a picture schedule

  o Providing written instructions as to what to do when finished

Chapter 6

1. Sensory processing is a person's way of noticing and responding to sensory events that occur during daily life.

2. Sensory processing systems include touch (somatosensory), body position (proprioceptive), sight (visual), hearing (auditory), smell (olfactory), taste (gustatory), and movement (vestibular).

3. Modulation is the balance of sensory input in the brain; thresholds are the point at which a particular sensory system responds (the level of input required).

4. Sensory systems transmit information to the brain to (a) generate awareness (arousal/alerting) and (b) gather information for brain mapping and discrimination.

5.

	Arousal/Alerting	Discrimination/Mapping
Somatosensory (touch)	**Light touch**: loose clothing on skin	**Touch pressure**: hugging
Vestibular (movement)	**Speed change**: person pushing wheelchair suddenly stops	**Repetitive head movement**: rocking
Proprioception (body position)	**Shifting muscle tension**: walking, lifting	**Sustained tension**: using heavy objects during play
Visual	**High intensity**: bright sunshine	**High similarity**: milk in a white cup
Auditory	**High intensity**: siren	**Rhythmic**: humming
Olfactory/gustatory (smell/taste)	**Strong intensity**: distinct taste/smell such as lemon	**Mild intensity**: taste/smell nondistinct such as plain noodles

6. It is useful to incorporate various sensory inputs into therapeutic programs to increase attention, establish awareness, increase arousal, increase comfort levels, and so on (see Table 6.2 for specifics).

7. Dunn's conceptual model for understanding patterns of sensory processing combines brain thresholds with self-regulation to create four patterns: registration, sensitivity, seeking, and avoiding.

   ✓ Registration: failing to notice stimuli that others notice

   ✓ Seeking: desiring movement, touch, sound, and visual stimuli

   ✓ Sensitivity: noticing things more than peers

   ✓ Avoiding: detecting and withdrawing from stimuli

8. In individuals with ASD, unlike in their neurotypical peers, arousal input often overpowers discrimination, which can create unusual behaviors as they try to manage distorted information. Additionally, children with ASD are more likely to be sensitive to touch, as well as auditory and oral sensory input. They also have significantly different scores on registration and avoiding, and have been found to display significant differences on virtually all areas of sensory processing.

9. A sensory processing framework is used for intervention to improve participation, not change the sensory processing patterns.

10. Examples of sensory processing interventions include:

    ✓ *Registration*: As students with low registration fail to notice things and, as a result, fail to focus on tasks, providing them with more intensity in sensory experiences can assist them in paying attention.

    ✓ *Seeking*: As students with a seeking pattern enjoy sensory experiences, providing more experiences as part of schoolwork can be helpful so they don't stop working to obtain the extra sensory input they desire.

    ✓ *Sensitivity*: As students with sensitivity tend to notice everything, it can interfere with schoolwork. Providing such students with more structured patterns of sensory experiences can be helpful.

    ✓ *Avoiding*: As students with an avoiding pattern notice and are bothered by things in the environment much more than peers, reducing sensory input is effective. Additionally, increased sensory experiences should be introduced gradually (see Tables 6.3, 6.4, 6.5, and 6.6 for specific interventions).

Chapter 7

1. Crisis management is designed to have an immediate impact on behavior, with the intention of diffusing or interrupting a potentially dangerous situation. While the approach may be effective in the short term, crisis management is not designed to effect sustained behavior change; additionally, in some cases, it may serve to be reinforcing to the individual.

2. Behavioral perspectives are shifting from focusing primarily on changing consequences in order to change behavior to designing support plans intended to teach prosocial ways of responding to situations. The set of assumptions that come with this shift in perspective include:

   ✓ Behavior is influenced by context.

   ✓ Behavior is functional, purposeful, and meaningful.

   ✓ Behavior is affected by external events, including emotional and biological conditions.

   ✓ Behavior is influenced by factors outside the immediate environment.

   ✓ Behaviors change as people mature and develop new competencies.

   ✓ Behavioral supports are guided by a strong base.

3. The members of the behavioral support team may include family members, educators, paraprofessionals, therapists, and the students themselves. Ideally, the team is composed of individuals from all environments in which the student interacts. The team's role is to problem-solve, support, and guide the process of the functional behavioral assessment.

4. The components of a functional behavioral assessment and intervention plan are:

   ✓ Defining the behavior

   ✓ Gathering behavioral information

   ✓ Developing hypothesis statements

   The information is then used in:

   ✓ Creating a behavior support plan

   ✓ Implementing intervention

   The final stage is:

   ✓ Monitoring implementation and outcomes

5. Major issues include the need for the behavior to be clearly specified so that it is observable and measurable.

6. The goal of a functional behavioral assessment is to identify the underlying causes of the behavior exhibited by the student.

7. *Antecedents* occur prior to the behavior being exhibited; they are sometimes referred to as triggers for the behavior. Typically, the focus has been on immediate antecedents (fast triggers); however, slow triggers or setting events (e.g., changes in health, schedule, how well the student slept) are also being considered as they may affect the student's ability to cope.

   Consequences are responses that occur after the behavior and can either serve to maintain the behavior or end it.

8. The types of questions that need to be asked include those related to the history of the behavior, strengths of the student, reinforcement history, conditions under which the student does well, type of curriculum and whether it is a match for the student, amount of structure in the student's day, types of instructional approaches, occasions when the problem behavior is more likely to be exhibited, the apparent purpose served by the behavior, communication skills of the student, any medical/sleeping/nutritional concerns, and special conditions affecting the student outside the school setting.

9. Collecting information is an ongoing process because as a student's life and educational circumstances change, conditions surrounding the behavior may also change.

10. Hypothesis statements are informed guesses about the potential underlying cause(s) of a behavior based on the information gathered in the functional assessment process.

11. Problem behavior pathways are important because they allow the interventionist to view the behavior in terms of antecedents (both slow and fast triggers) and consequences, which can lead to looking at various approaches to intervention, including antecedent control, changing consequences, and teaching alternative behaviors.

12. Positive behavior support approaches focus on creating positive learning environments and teaching students alternate ways of behaving.

13. Curriculum considerations in implementing interventions focus on ensuring the curriculum matches student goals, skills, and needs and include looking at teaching alternative and prosocial behaviors to replace those that may be problematic.

    Classroom management and instructional considerations focus on ensuring the classroom environment is structured in a positive way that creates opportunities for engagement, includes systematic instruction and clearly articulated expectations, allows for rehearsal, and supports student chances for success. Included are the use of routines, consideration of the student's learning style, and teaching strategies for coping with the stresses of daily demands.

14. Applied behavior analysis serves as the basis for positive behavior supports. Additionally, specific techniques within applied behavior analysis such as shaping of behavior, creating behavior chains, reinforcing successive approximations, prompting, extinction, and planned ignoring have been used successfully to effect behavior change in individuals with ASD.

15. Behavior support plans may be unsuccessful for several reasons, including lack of implementation across environments, lack of adequate information collecting in terms of monitoring (thus leading to either ending the plan early or continuing for too long), and inadequately planned interventions.

16. Implementation and outcomes of support plans must be monitored to determine if they are working and, if not, possible reasons why not. Additionally, even if the plan is effective, it is important to gain information as to why it works and how it might be changed or improved.

Chapter 8

1. Play is considered a primary social activity through which children develop symbolic capacities, interpersonal skills, and social knowledge. Learning and development are seen as being mediated through social experiences with others. Friendships, like play, occupy a central place in children's social lives and are considered to be associated with social, emotional, and cognitive development, as well as being a determining factor for social adaptation and adjustment.

2. Children with ASD face challenges in how they express play interests and how they make social overtures, leading often to isolation, bulling, neglect, and lack of friendships. Many children with ASD (a) demonstrate play skills that are detached, isolated, and repetitive; and (b) have unique fascinations or are attracted to toys, activities, or themes that reflect the preferences of younger children. In terms of developing friendships, children with ASD often have difficulties in both verbal and nonverbal communication and lack skills in joint attention and emotional responsiveness in social play.

3. Peer culture involves active participation in the social activities that are most valued by the peer group. It consists of shared understandings, values, beliefs, and associated behaviors, activities, and relationship patterns children construct out of their everyday experiences with one another. Many students with ASD are excluded from their peer culture because of behavior that does not fit perceptions of what is "normal. " As a result, a social void is likely to exist between children with ASD and their typically developing peers.

4. Play culture reflects the unique social and imaginary worlds that children create together, apart from adults. It refers to jointly constructed activity through which children acquire interrelated skills necessary for achieving social competence, mutual friendships, social communication strategies, resolving conflicts, problem solving, building trust, and developing other foundational social skills.

5. The F2F model fosters mutual friendships for children with ASD by demystifying ASD and by facilitating understanding, awareness, and empathy in neurotypical peers, siblings, and classmates.

6. F2F is implemented through a four-step teaching process of modeling, labeling, explaining, and normalizing.

   ✓ Modeling: a visual model of the characteristics of ASD is presented to help peers understand puzzling behaviors they may see in children on the spectrum.

   ✓ Labeling: after presenting the characteristics through modeling, children are helped in accepting them by giving each a name or label to make it easier to accept the characteristics or behaviors as real.

   ✓ Explaining: the meaning or purpose behind the behavior or characteristic is explained to help answer the question of "Why does my friend do that?"

   ✓ Normalizing: the characteristics and behaviors of children with ASD and their differences are linked to differences and commonalities all children exhibit, allowing typically developing peers to empathize with children on the spectrum.

   The program uses puppet programs for children aged 3-8 to teach characteristics associated with ASD through a six-step process; for children aged 9 and above, a simulation game is used for the same purposes.

7. The five key learning goals of F2F that provide the basis for future learning are:

   ✓ Recognize and accept differences in self and others

   ✓ Recognize individuals with autism and different kinds of minds as valuable friends

   ✓ Recognize that it is important to ask questions and express feelings

   ✓ Empathize with what it feels like to have autism and different kinds of minds

   ✓ Promote positive relationships with all peers

8. The Seven Basic Friendship Tips are important because they teach prosocial communication strategies that peers may use to interact successfully with children with ASD. Included are:

   ✓ Get your friend's attention

   ✓ Use small sentences, gestures, and wait

   ✓ Watch your friend

   ✓ Give your friend choices

   ✓ Ask your friend to talk

   ✓ Use friendly words

   ✓ Accept differences

9. The IPG model is designed to support children with ASD in play experiences with typical peers/siblings as playmates through a system of careful guidance and support.

10. Environmental elements are important because the IPG model focuses on supporting children with ASD in mutually enjoyed play experiences with peers. In order to do so, it is critical to set the stage by ensuring the program and environmental elements match students' needs. Included in these considerations are:

   ✓ Play group composition:

      o higher ratio of experts (typical peers/siblings) than novices (children with ASD)

      o playmates have some familiarity with one another

      o members participate in F2F program and orientation prior to beginning the group

   ✓ Play space and materials:

      o space and material choices vary based on the interests, learning styles, and developmental levels of the participating children

      o materials are highly motivating with the potential for interactive and imaginary play

   ✓ Play session structure and support:

      o structure is established through routines, schedules, and rituals

11. Assessments in the IPG model include evaluating the symbolic dimensions of play, the social dimensions of play, the communicative functions and means used by the children, and the play preferences and diversity of play exhibited.

   ✓ Symbolic dimensions of play: refer to play acts the child directs toward objects, self, or others to signify events, including manipulation, functional and symbolic-pretend play

   ✓ Social dimensions of play: involve a focus on the child's proximity and involvement with one or more peers, including isolate, onlooker-orientation, parallel, common focus and common goal

   ✓ Communicative functions and means used by the children: address both how and in what ways the child communicates within the play experience

   ✓ Play preferences and diversity of play exhibited: evaluate what the child and peers like to do to identify and match play interests

12. Guided participation refers to an adult guiding novice and expert players to engage in mutually enjoyed activities that encourage social interaction, communication, pretending, and interactive games. It is used to implement a carefully tailored and intensive system of supports appropriate to each child's needs and abilities. Key components include:

   ✓ Monitoring play initiations focuses on discovering and supporting novice players' meaningful attempts to socialize and play by recognizing, interpreting, and responding to the way they express their intentions.

✓ Scaffolding play involves building on the child's play initiations by systemically adjusting assistance to match or slightly exceed the level at which the child is independently able to engage in play with peers through support structures.

✓ Promoting the use of social communication involves using cues to guide social exchanges between children.

✓ Play guidance provides strategies to support children in engaging in experiences slightly beyond their capacity and include orienting, mirroring, parallel play, joint focus, joint actions, role enactment, and role playing.

Chapter 9

1. The term *multiple intelligences* refers to individuals having various types of cognition, including athletics, music, art, math, and social.

2. Skills necessary for social cognition, including joint attention, early symbolic communication, and imitation of movement, develop through interactions with caregivers and others.

3. Treatment options vary in terms of how and what to teach with regard to social skills/social cognitive development based on the strengths and needs of the individual on the spectrum. For students with intellectual disability who are minimally verbal or nonverbal, a highly structured visual program is needed. These students will not benefit from a metacognitive approach. For students who lack sophistication in their communication and ability to predict others' motives, thoughts, and emotions, a concrete exploration of how others think is recommended. For students with strong cognitive and language skills, a metacognitive approach teaching directly about social cognition and social thinking may be used.

4. Defining "social skills" can be problematic due to the breadth and variety of skills involved, including unwritten rules of behavior for different settings and contexts, adjusting behavior based on circumstances, and understanding what others may be thinking.

5. The term *sharing space effectively* refers to having the skills and abilities to understand the rules of behavior (verbal and nonverbal) in different settings and contexts.

6. The four steps in perspective taking described by the author are:

✓ When you come into my space, I think about you and you think about me.

✓ I wonder why you are there, what your intentions are, and what your purpose is, in order to predict what will happen next and to keep safe.

✓ I wonder what you are thinking about me.

✓ To keep you thinking about me in the way I would like, I monitor and possibly modify my behavior.

7. Students with ASD often have challenges in sharing space due to deficits in perspective taking, as well as failure to understand the rules of the environment.

8. The ILAUGH model serves as an acronym to represent six points to help explain what constitutes social cognitive functioning:

   a. (I) **initiating communication**: use language/communication to seek assistance

   b. (L) **listening with eyes and brain**: integrating information heard with what is seen to understand the concept of the message

   c. (A) **abstract and inferential thinking**: understanding that literal interpretation may not give the true meaning and having the flexibility to make smart guesses to interpret meaning

   d. (U) **understanding perspective**: comprehending that others have thoughts that may be different from ours and understanding others' minds

   e. (G) **getting the big picture**: Gestalt processing or getting the big picture or concept, rather than isolated facts to gain an understanding of overall meaning

   f. (H) **humor and human relatedness**: noticing subtle cues that indicate something is intended to be humorous and using humor appropriately

9. The demand for effective social skills increases significantly starting in grade 3 because from grade 3 onwards, students are required to demonstrate more socially abstract thinking, both in terms of developing successful social interactions and relationships and in terms of successful academic achievement.

10. Effective social skills are not only necessary for socializing but are also required in interpreting socially abstract concepts such as problem solving and effective communication, and in interpreting curriculum that requires socially abstract thoughts.

11. When teaching students with "classical" or "moderate" autism, using metacognitive strategies has not proved effective. These students require a focus on developing functional communication and academic skills with a clear understanding of behavioral expectation. This should be taught through explicit instruction, consistency, and with the use of clear visual supports.

12. Students with HFA are often near-normal or above-normal in academic intelligence and have developed functional communication systems, but have great difficulty in perspective taking, causing problems with understanding implied meaning both from text and group dynamics.

13. Students with Asperger Syndrome can benefit from a metacognitive approach to teaching social thinking and related skills.

14. These are programs developed to teach various types of social skills to individuals on the autism spectrum. While addressing different areas of social skills training, the programs share the use of concrete, consistent, and predictable elements.

Chapter 10

1. In order to understand others' emotional and mental states, one needs to be able to read nonverbal information from facial expressions, vocal intonation, and body language. One also needs to integrate information from all these channels in context in order to get a coherent picture of other people's emotions.

2. The authors were referring to the difficulties persons with ASD often face in gathering, integrating, and interpreting others' emotional states, which can leave them with no idea of what is going on socially.

3. Individuals with ASD demonstrate deficits in the ability to recognize emotion from examples. While findings related to determining a reason are inconclusive, theories link the problems to difficulties in empathy or theory of mind, to differences in how information is processed (feature by feature rather than holistically), also known as weak central coherence. Based on fMRI studies, there appears to be under-activity of brain regions in individuals with ASD compared to neurotypical peers.

4. Systemizing refers to the drive to analyze or build systems to understand and predict the behavior of rule-based events. Most individuals with ASD are hyper-attentive to detail and prefer predictable, rule-based environments, both of which assist in systemizing. As a result, it may be possible to teach high-functioning individuals with ASD a system for understanding emotions.

5. Individuals with ASD often prefer a computerized environment as it is predictable, consistent, and free from social demands. Additionally, one can work on computers at one's own pace and level of understanding, repeating lessons as necessary to reach mastery. Last, interest and motivation can be maintained through computerized rewards.

6. Capitalizing on the systemizing strengths exhibited by persons with ASD, *Mind Reading* is an interactive software program designed to systematically train complex emotional recognition in visual and auditory channels using life-like faces and voices. Early research has shown the program is successful in improving emotional recognition skills in isolation; however, generalization has proven problematic.

Chapter 11

1. Transition planning is a federally mandated part of the IEP of students with disablities and includes the skills necessary for success in postsecondary life. Starting at age 16 (or 14 if considered necessary), each student is required to have an individual transition plan (ITP), which is defined as a coordinated set of activities based on individual needs and designed to focus on improving academic and functional achievement to facilitate success in post-school activities.

2. Planning the transition from school is a critical aspect in the middle and high school years because it requires the team to focus on the skills necessary for independent living, including job-related skills, safety skills, social skills, self-advocacy, and so on.

3. The members of a transition team typically include the individuals who are part of the student's IEP team but may also involve members of vocational services, agencies that focus on vocational support, representatives of postsecondary educational options and residential services, as well as others as appropriate.

4. Students with ASD should know who is on the ITP team, as well as their rights both while in school and in the post-school world.

5. The federal mandate stipulates that the ITP must be a coordinated set of activities that are outcome-oriented, student-centered, and broad-based. Additionally, the ITP should be a working document that changes over time as needed and appropriate.

6. It is important to address career, self-advocacy, and independent living goals as part of the ITP because school is supposed to prepare students to function in the adult world and, for individuals with ASD, direct instruction in the areas noted is critical.

7. A well-designed ITP should include assessment; statements of individual preferences for education, employment, and adult living; specific steps, methods, and resources needed to meet goals; instruction in academic, vocational, and living skills; identification of community experiences and skills related to future goals; exploration of service organizations; and methods for evaluating the success of transition activities.

8. The UCC is useful because it is a framework for discussing and planning for the characteristics specific to individuals with ASD. A completed UCC yields an evaluation of an individual's specific characteristics in each of several domains that allows for team discussion and planning to meet that individual with ASD's specific and unique needs.

9. Types of assessments in transition planning can include everything from informal observation and checklists to formal assessment and asking questions. Regardless of the method used, it is important that the student's current and future roles in adult life be addressed.

10. The components of successful planning for and support of the transition process include (a) self-determination, self-advocacy, and person-centered planning; (b) selecting meaningful coursework; (c) increasing job placement opportunities; (d) preparing employers; (e) developing a social network; and (f) planning for college/university experiences.

11. Considerations affecting job placement and retention for persons with ASD include ensuring the job is a good match in terms of challenges and interests as well as in terms of a physical (hours, noise level, activity level, etc.) and a social match (e.g., communication demands, level of interaction required, coworker training and support, etc.); creating experiences at the secondary level in the areas of job skills, communication with employers, and social skills to help lessen the challenges that might be faced in adult life; matching the job with the type of thinking (visual, music and higher math, verbal) demonstrated by the individual with ASD; and category of employment (supported, segregated, or competitive).

12. Social skills development should be an important part of the ITP process because research shows that students with ASD often leave school with inadequate social and communication skills for life success. These skills include social behaviors such as table manners, personal space awareness, and so on, as well as grooming, hygiene, and issues related to sexuality, including sexual orientation and safety.

13. For school-aged individuals, IDEA mandates that services are received and students themselves are not responsible for requesting help. In post-school settings, individuals with disabilities can continue to receive assistance, but are responsible for requesting it and for providing documentation of their disabilities.

Chapter 12

1. Members of the educational support and intervention team include, at a minimum, the teachers who work with the student, the parents, the student, school administrators assigned to lead the teams, and various professionals both inside and outside of school (e.g., speech and language pathologists, occupational therapists, physical therapists, counselors, behavior specialists) who might work with the students with ASD.

2. Collaboration is important as it provides mutual support, usually results in better understanding of the student, ensures that everyone working with the student is focusing on the same outcomes using a consistent approach, and provides the opportunity to share perceptions and effective interventions.

3. An IEP, or individualized education program, is a federally mandated requirement for students found eligible for special education services. The IEP includes a statement of functioning, measurable goals, benchmarks or objectives to meet the goals, accommodations and modifications, persons responsible for services, and amount of services, among other requirements. 504 Plans, on the other hand, are used for students who may not meet eligibility requirements for special education services but who need accommodations or modifications to be successful in school. 504 Plans are also used in post-school settings as the IEP is only mandated for school-aged children.

4. Components necessary for successful team meetings may include:

   ✓ Discussion of findings from formal and informal assessments

   ✓ Development of goals and benchmarks and sharing them with team members for evaluation and modification

   ✓ Observation of the student and sharing among team members of the findings

5. Planning with a student prior to a meeting can serve a number of purposes, including gaining the student's perspective on goals and objectives; understanding the student's perception of challenges and strengths; exploring issues of concern to the student; and assisting the student in developing skills to work as a productive member of the team.

6. Factors that contribute to effective collaboration may include:

    ✓ Team members being willing to consider each other's perspectives, including the student's

    ✓ Team members working together to understand the student's strengths and challenges

    ✓ Team members who are willing to provide needed support

7. Three examples of how individuals with ASD may think and learn include:

    ✓ They may lack awareness of social situations.

    ✓ They may not be able to integrate information from various sources into a meaningful whole.

    ✓ They may need narration of their actions in order to develop an awareness of what they are doing and how that behavior affects others.

    ✓ They may be very literal in their thinking.

Chapter 13

1. The mother who authored this chapter describes being thought of as the cause of her child's autism and also writes about the fact that she was told autism was incurable. Both these aspects were hurtful and unhelpful.

2. Prior to the passage of PL 94-142, schools were not required to provide educational services for individuals with disabilities, including those on the autism spectrum. Therefore, placement options ranged from institutionalization to home teaching to the general education class with the hope that teachers would be supportive.

3. Three things related to the educational experience of the child:

    ✓ Formal testing has limitations: IQ scores can change over time.

    ✓ In many cases occupational therapy support is needed: Individuals with ASD have sensory and coordination difficulties.

    ✓ Lack of understanding and support can lead to frustration and depression; individuals with ASD may not interact socially as do other children, nor may they demonstrate the same level of academic and physical skills. Failure to understand these differences and support alternative ways of completing tasks can lead to frustration on the part of the individual with ASD.

4. PL 94-142 was important because it mandated public school services for all children with disabilities. Additionally, the law required that schools involve parents in all aspects of their child's schooling, from permission to conduct assessment, to placement decisions, to development of educational plans.

5. It is important not only because it can affect the educational experience and outcomes for the person with ASD, but also because it can affect the perception of and acceptance by peers.

Chapter 14

1. • Using a multiplier box to help in solving multiplication and division problems, essentially creating a low-tech assistive device.

   • Literal thinking, which led to misunderstanding and academic difficulties as the author experienced difficulty answering questions involving more abstract thinking.

2. Narration is the technique of someone talking through the actions of the person with ASD. This may help the individual with ASD to attach meaning to words as those words describe actions she/he is doing.

3. The "hidden curriculum" refers to the set of rules in school (and in the world) that are learned by neurotypical individuals without instruction but that need to be directly taught to individuals with ASD. Some examples include teacher-pleasing behaviors, the meaning of body language and personal space, and appropriate responses when asked questions (such as when a "white lie" is appropriate). It is crucial to teach these skills directly to individuals with ASD as doing so will allow for more successful social interactions.

4. The chapter author's special interests provided him with a vehicle for interacting with others (such as in band class) and also in job development (working at a bike shop).

Appendix B: Glossary

504 Plan. A formal plan for the school to provide appropriate accommodations to a student with a qualifying disability, as required by Section 504 of the federal Rehabilitation Act of 1973. (Does not include special education services.)

A

Accommodations. Alterations to the environment, equipment, or format of a curriculum to allow equal access to the content. Unlike modifications, accommodations do not alter the actual content of the material being taught.

Adaptive behavior. An individual's manner of dealing with the demands of daily life, including self-care skills, organizational skills, basic interpersonal skills, and conformance to community standards (obeying rules, taking responsibility, etc.).

Affect sharing. A mutual sharing of emotional states.

Americans with Disabilities Act (ADA). A federal law protecting the civil rights of individuals with disabilities.

Antecedent. An event that precedes a behavior.

Applied behavior analysis (ABA). An approach to intervention, rooted in behavioral psychology, that emphasizes a systematic approach of understanding, evaluating, and modifying behavior.

ASD (see autism spectrum disorder).

Asperger, Hans (1906-1980). Austrian pediatrician, whose 1944 paper "Autistic psychopathy in childhood" described four patients with severely impaired social skills, poor pragmatic speech, all-encompassing special interests, emotional immaturity, unusual use of language, sensory sensitivities, insistence on sameness, difficulty making friends, below-average self-help skills, and poor motor coordination. This set of characteristics later came to be called "Asperger Syndrome."

Asperger's Disorder (also known as Asperger Syndrome or Asperger's Syndrome). A high-functioning autism spectrum disorder characterized by average-to-high intelligence, significantly impaired social interaction, and repetitive behaviors or interests (most often, circumscribed interests about which they spend an inordinate amount of time gathering facts).

Attribution. Assignment of some characteristic or quality to a person or thing.

Auditory comprehension. Receptive language skills; understanding of spoken language.

Auditory discrimination. The ability to differentiate among similar sounds in words (e.g. "chair" and "share").

Auditory processing. How the brain processes and interprets what is heard through the ear.

Augmentative communication (also referred to as augmentative alternative communication, or AAC). Any communication system designed to supplement an individual's existing mode of communication.

Autism Diagnostic Interview-Revised (ADI-R). A standardized parent interview designed to identify children with autism.

Autism Diagnostic Observation Scale (ADOS). A standardized assessment tool that uses structured activities and materials to assess social interaction, communication, and play behaviors. The ADOS is considered the "gold standard" for assessing and diagnosing autism and pervasive developmental disorder (PDD) across ages, developmental levels, and language skills.

Autism spectrum disorder (ASD). A generic term referring to any of the five pervasive developmental disorders (autistic disorder, Asperger's disorder, Rett's disorder, childhood disintegrative disorder, or pervasive developmental disorder-not otherwise specified [PDD-NOS]). The term *autism spectrum* has become popular due to its emphasis on the wide range of characteristics exhibited by individuals with autism.

Autistic disorder. Previously known as "infantile autism" or "Kanner's syndrome." First described by Leo Kanner in 1943, autistic disorder is characterized by severe impairment in social interaction and communication, as well as restrictive, repetitive behaviors and/or interests. May include delay in or total lack of development of spoken language. Individuals with autistic disorder may or may not have comorbid mental retardation.

B

Behavior support plan. Based on a functional behavioral assessment, a written plan for changing a child's problem behavior(s), utilizing multiple intervention strategies to teach alternative behaviors and create a supportive learning environment.

Body language. Information about a person's thoughts or feelings that is unconsciously conveyed through physical mannerisms.

Brain connectivity. The rich array of neural pathways that carry signals to various areas of the brain.

Brain synchrony. Various regions of the brain increasing or decreasing their activity simultaneously.

Brain thresholds. The points at which the brain recognizes/responds to sensory input.

C

Central coherence. The brain's ability to process multiple chunks of information in a global way, connecting them and viewing them in context, in order to determine a higher level of meaning. Poor central coherence can make it difficult to generalize.

Chaining. A method of teaching in which a task is broken down into several smaller steps, which are then taught in order. The student must master a step before the next one in the sequence is added.

Childhood disintegrative disorder. A rare pervasive developmental disorder in which a child develops normally for at least two years and then experiences severe regression in two or more areas of previously acquired skills (language, social skills or adaptive behavior, bowel or bladder control, play, motor skills). Typically occurring between ages 3 and 4, the regression is more severe than the regression that is sometimes seen with autistic disorder.

Cognition. Conscious mental activity, including thinking, perceiving, reasoning, and learning.

Cognitive behavioral interventions. Interventions that change a child's behavior by altering or enhancing his understanding of a problem situation.

Cognitive delay. A deficit in intellectual abilities beyond typical variations for the child's age and background. Sometimes used synonymously with "mental retardation."

Collaboration. Individuals working together for a common goal.

Comic Strip Conversations™™. An intervention technique developed by Carol Gray that uses cartooning to help students interpret the reasons behind others' behavior.

Communication. The deliberate conveying of information to another person.

Communication deficit. A difficulty in expressing ideas or intentions (expressive communication deficit) and/or interpreting the language, thoughts, or intentions of others (receptive communication deficit).

Communicative function. The idea that a student is trying to convey through his behavior. For example, the communicative function of throwing a pencil on the floor may be that he doesn't want to work, that he wants a pen instead of a pencil, that he finds the process of handwriting physically painful, or a number of other possibilities.

Compensatory strategy. An unusual problem-solving tactic used to compensate for some sort of deficit.

Competitive employment. Employment in the community, at a competitive wage, without supports.

Complex language: Higher-level language, such as complex sentences, inferences, metaphors, or idioms.

Complex memory. Memory for complex material or for a large amount of similar material, such as word lists.

Complex motor abilities. Skilled motor abilities requiring coordination or precision, such as handwriting, typing, or skipping.

Complex sentences. Sentences consisting of multiple clauses.

Computerized axial tomography (CAT or CT) scan. A technique that uses a rotating x-ray machine and a computer to produce cross-sectional images of the body's internal structures.

Concept development/formation. Problem solving in the absence of set rules; understanding meaning/significance.

Concept identification. Recognizing a concept, although not necessarily understanding it. For example, a child might be able to read the word *cat* without understanding that the word represented the animal.

Connectivity. How well different regions are connected to one another, allowing signals/information to pass among them.

Consequence. The response (positive or negative) to a behavior.

Content standards. The state's expectations for what every student should know, understand, and be able to do at a given grade level.

Contextual recognition of emotion. The ability to infer another person's emotions and mind-set, based on situational clues.

Conversational maxims. The unspoken rules of conversation, relating to the quantity, quality, and relevance of a person's remarks.

Cooperative play. Interactive play involving sharing, turn taking, and basic problem solving.

Core deficit. A primary, underlying problem common to everyone with the same disorder. May result in a cascade of varying symptoms.

Crisis management. Finding a short-term solution to a dangerous or potentially dangerous situation.

Cueing. Providing prompts to indicate what a person should do next.

Culture of autism. Characteristic strengths, challenges, and patterns of thinking and behavior associated with ASD.

Curriculum-based assessment (CBA). An assessment of student performance in the local curriculum that is used to make instructional decisions.

D

Data collection. Any method of recording behavioral data for subsequent analysis.

Detroit Tests of Learning Aptitude (DTLA-2). A series of norm-referenced tests of specific mental abilities.

Developmental disorder. A disorder that typically develops during childhood.

Duration. The period of time from the beginning to the end of a single instance of a behavior.

E

Echolalia. The repetition of words or phrases used by another person.

Educational support and intervention team. Under IDEA, a mandated team for any student receiving special education services, consisting of teachers, paraprofessionals, administrators, service providers, parents, and the students themselves.

Electroencephalographic (EEG). A recording of electrical activity in the brain by means of electrodes attached to the scalp.

Elementary motor abilities. Simple motor skills requiring little coordination or precision.

Emotion recognition. The ability to recognize emotional states in another person or in oneself.

Emotional regulation. Control of emotions.

Empathy. The ability to understand how another person feels or what he/she may be thinking. Sometimes referred to as "putting yourself in another person's shoes."

Executive functions. Higher-order cognitive skills that include organization, planning, problem solving, self-regulation, and inhibitory control.

Experiential learning. Learning through experience. "Learning by doing."

Extinction. Weakening an undesirable behavior by withholding the reinforcer previously associated with it.

F

Facial emotion recognition. The ability to discern a person's emotional state based on their facial expression (e.g., a furrowed brow meaning that they are worried or a smile meaning that they are happy).

Facial expressions. Positioning of the facial muscles to convey emotions.

Fast triggers. One of two types of antecedents; also called "immediate antecedents."

First Signs. A national not-for-profit organization dedicated to teaching parents and pediatricians how to recognize the early signs of autism

Floor time. A play-based intervention emphasizing the child's interests and the affective interactions between the child and caregiver. The foundation of the Developmental, Individual-Difference, Relationship-Based Model Intervention Program (DIR) developed by Stanley Greenspan.

Frequency. Common way of measuring behavior (along with duration and intensity).

Friend 2 Friend model. Social facilitation model that fosters mutual friends for children with ASD by building awareness, understanding, acceptance, and empathy in their peers through demystification programs comprising specially designed puppet presentations and simulation games developed by Heather McCracken.

Functional behavioral assessment. A method of identifying the underlying cause of a behavior by analyzing the behavior's antecedents and consequences.

Functional communication system. A communication system that is meaningful to the student and helps him participate in his environment

Functional magnetic resonance imaging (fMRI). A relatively new procedure that uses MRI technology to map tiny metabolic changes in active areas of the brain.

Functional neuroimaging. Technology that measures brain function. It is often used to understand the activity in certain areas of the brain.

G

Generalization. Using a skill/behavior learned in one environment and/or with one person in other environments and with other persons.

Gestalt processing. The ability to understand overall concepts, rather than just a collection of individual facts.

Grandin, Temple (1947-). Considered one of the highest achieving adults with autism in the world. A professor at Colorado State University, international expert on livestock handling equipment and popular speaker/author on autism spectrum disorders.

Guided participation. A customized system of supports designed to help children with ASD learn how to play with their peers. See also Integrated Play Groups.

H

Hidden curriculum. Unspoken social rules or norms that are often missed by individuals with ASD.

High-functioning autism (HFA). Autistic disorder generally accompanied by an IQ above 70.

I

ICD-10. International Statistical Classification of Diseases and Related Health Problems, 10th Revision. The international coding system used to classify diseases and disorders.

IDEA (see Individuals with Disabilities Education Act).

Idiosyncratic language. Unique, unusual, personalized use of language.

ILAUGH. A model developed by Michelle Garcia Winner for understanding social thinking. The acronym stands for (I) initiating communication, (L) listening actively with the eyes and brain, (A) abstract and inferential thinking, (U) understanding perspective, (G) getting the big picture, and (H) humor.

Imitative learning. Learning by watching someone else perform an activity.

Incredible 5-Point Scale. A cognitive tool developed by Kari Dunn Buron and Mitzi Curtis for helping individuals with ASD better regulate their behavior by recognizing the stages of their particular behavioral challenges (e.g., stress).

Independent living. Being in charge of one's own life, including personal care, housing, community responsibility, and social relationships. Does not preclude the use of community resources, assistive technology, etc.

Individual family service plan (IFSP). A written plan specifying the services a child will receive through an infant-toddler (early intervention) program.

Individualized education program (IEP). A written plan specifying the services and accommodations the school will provide to a child with a disability, as well as related goals.

Individualized transition plan (ITP). A written plan addressing the post-secondary needs of a student receiving special education services. A required section of the IEP for students age 16 and over.

Individuals with Disabilities Education Act (IDEA). A federal law guaranteeing students with qualifying disabilities the right to a free appropriate public education.

Integrated Play Groups (IPG). A model developed by Pamela Wolfberg, in which children with ASD participate in mutually enjoyable, reciprocal play activities with neurotypical peers while being supported by an adult play group guide.

Intellectual disability. A disability characterized by a significantly below-average score on an intelligence test and limitations in functional abilities. Also referred to as mental retardation.

Intensity. Common way of measuring behavior (along with duration and frequency).

Intentional communication. The deliberate conveyance of information to another person.

Interpersonal relatedness. Interest in other people and skillfulness in interacting with them.

Intersubjective engagement. The ability to share the emotional states of others.

J

Joint action. Formal turn taking.

Joint attention. Consciously focusing one's attention on the same event or object as another person.

K

Kanner, Leo (1894-1981). Austrian-born child psychiatrist at Johns Hopkins Medical School, whose 1943 paper "Autistic disturbances of affective content" described the case histories of 11 children, all of whom exhibited extreme social isolation or withdrawal, ritualistic behaviors, and communication difficulties. These characteristics are now termed autism or autistic disorder.

L

Labeling. Giving a name to a characteristic.

Lexicon. Vocabulary; word bank.

Linguistic. Relating to language.

Lovaas model. An intensive early intervention ABA program emphasizing discrete trial training. Developed by UCLA clinical psychologist O. Ivaar Lovaas.

Low registration. High thresholds and passive self-regulation.

M

Magnetic resonance imaging (MRI). A noninvasive, painless medical procedure that uses magnetic fields, radio waves, and a computer to produce detailed pictures of organs, soft tissues, and bones.

Making Action Plans (MAP). A student-centered transition planning process.

Mental-state recognition. The ability to recognize others' intentions, emotions, desires, etc.

Metacognitive strategies. Intervention strategies that involve "thinking about thinking."

Microcephaly. Head circumference more than two standard deviations below the mean.

Mind reading. Empathy. Being able to tell what another person is thinking or feeling.

Mind Reading. A computer program for teaching recognition of emotions.

Mind blindness. Difficulty inferring another person's thoughts or feelings.

Mirroring. Mimicking the actions of another.

Modeling. Teaching a skill through demonstration.

Modifications. Changes to the curriculum and/or instruction to meet a student's needs. As opposed to accommodations, when using modifications students are not expected to master the same content as others in the classroom.

Motor skills. Purposeful movements of the body or limbs.

Multimodal recognition of emotion. Recognizing emotion based on a variety of clues, including facial expression, voice, body language, and context.

Multitasking. Doing several activities at once.

N

Narration. Verbally describing what a child is doing, in the manner of a sportscaster, to help him attach meaning to words.

Natural reinforcers. Reinforcers that are logically related to the task at hand. For example, if the student points at a book and says "book," handing him the book is the natural reinforcer.

Naturalistic context. A typical environment/typically occurring situation for the student.

Neurochemistry. The study of chemicals and chemical changes in the brain.

Neuro-developmental. Relating to brain development.

Neuroimaging. Advanced technologies that take x-ray-type pictures of the brain and nervous system, such as CT scans or MRIs.

Neurons. Cells of the brain/nervous system.

Neuropathology. Brain or nervous system abnormalities.

Neuropsychological. Related to how the structure and function of the brain affect cognitive processes and behaviors.

Neurotypical. A term to indicate that an individual does not have autism (i.e., the brain works in the "typical" way).

Nonverbal behaviors. Deliberate behaviors other than speech/vocalizing.

Normalizing. In the Friend 2 Friend model, explaining autism characteristics to peers by linking them to characteristics all children exhibit.

O

Orienting. Watching peers and activities.

Outcome-oriented framework. Identifying the desired results before intervention begins and then building in the methods or strategies that are most likely to produce those results.

P

Parallel play. Children playing similar games side-by-side, but not with each other.

Pathophysiology. Abnormalities in brain function.

Pedantic speech. Lecture-like or overly formal speech.

Peer culture. The unique set of values, beliefs, understandings, and relationship patterns that is shared by a group of peers, based on their common experience.

Person-centered planning. A process for planning for the future of a person with a disability based on their own desires/interests/dreams, rather than based on the systems and resources that may or may not be available to them.

Perspective taking. Looking at something from another person's point of view and, if necessary, changing one's behavior accordingly.

Pervasive developmental disorder-not otherwise specified (PDD NOS). An autism spectrum disorder characterized by severe impairment in social skills, plus impairment in communications skills *or* repetitive behaviors or interests, but that does not meet criteria for another more specific ASD.

Pervasive developmental disorders (PDDs). Also known as autism spectrum disorders. A category of disorders that are characterized by severe, pervasive impairments in several areas of development, including social interaction, communication, and repetitive behaviors or interests. Includes Autistic Disorder, Asperger's Disorder, Rett's Disorder, childhood disintegrative disorder, and pervasive developmental disorder-not otherwise specified (PDD-NOS).

Phenylketonuria (PKU). A genetic disorder that prevents the body from metabolizing phenylalanine, an amino acid found in meat and dairy products. Can lead to brain damage and intellectual disability.

Picture Exchange Communication System (PECS). A "low-tech" functional communication system utilizing picture symbols.

PL (Public Law) 94-142. The Education of All Handicapped Children Act of 1975, renamed the Individuals with Disabilities Education Act (IDEA) when it was reauthorized in 1990. The first law to guarantee a free and appropriate education to children with disabilities.

Planned ignoring. Deliberately ignoring a problem behavior that is reinforced by attention. A type of extinction.

Planning Alternative Tomorrows with Hope (PATH). An eight-step person-centered planning process.

Plasticity. The ability of the brain to adapt or change in response to experience.

Play culture. A central aspect of children's peer culture involving the co-creation of social and imaginary worlds apart from adults.

Positive behavior supports. Based on behavioral observations, strategies designed to change the student's problem behaviors by altering the environment and/or teaching alternative behaviors.

Positron emission tomography (PET) scan. A procedure in which a small amount of radioactive glucose is injected into a vein. An imaging scan then measures the activity level of the brain by measuring its use of glucose.

Pragmatics. The social aspects of language.

Presuppositional knowledge. In communication, the speaker's understanding of what his listeners already know, what they need to know in order to understand the information being communicated, and the style in which they would like the information to be communicated.

Problem behavior pathway. The sequence of events that typically precede and follow a problem behavior.

Proprioceptive. Relating to the sensory processes that inform the brain of body parts' movements and location.

Prosody. The intonation, rhythm, and pitch of spoken language.

Proto-declarative. Indicating an intent to communicate, share interest.

Proto-imperative. Communicating a desire to obtain something.

Psychogenic. Having a psychological, rather than physiological, cause.

Psycho-pharmacological interventions. Medications that affect the mind and behavior.

Psychotherapy. The treatment of emotional or behavioral problems through psychological counseling.

Q

Quality of life. Subjective well-being, including safety, health, happiness, autonomy, etc.

R

Reciprocity. Give-and-take.

Refrigerator mother. A theory, popular in the mid-20th century but later disproved, that autism was the result of a cold, unfeeling mother.

Reinforcement. Any response to an individual's behavior that maintains or increases the likelihood that they will perform that same behavior again.

Representational. Referring to something else; depicting something in another form. In children's play: pretend play.

Resiliency. Ability to overcome adversities and achieve success.

Rett's disorder. A pervasive developmental disorder, occurring primarily in females, that is characterized by normal development for at least 5 months, followed by sudden deceleration of head growth, loss of previously acquired hand skills and development of stereotyped "hand-wringing" movements, loss of social engagement, severely impaired receptive and expressive language development, and the appearance of poorly coordinated gait or trunk movements.

Role enactment. In play, imitating real-life activities such as making dinner or driving a car.

S

Savant. A person with an ability that far exceeds his overall level of development and may exceed those of most neurotypical individuals. Examples include photographic memory, ability to do complex math in the head, unusual calendar abilities, or perfect pitch.

Scaffolding play. In play interactions with peers, adjusting the level of support provided based on the child's level of comfort and competence.

Scatter plot. A simple two-dimensional chart used to track the occurrence of a behavior.

School connectedness. A student's belief that adults in the school care about his learning and about him as an individual.

Secured/segregated employment. A job in which individuals with disabilities work in a separate environment from neurotypical employees. Usually involves simple, repetitive work.

Seizure. A symptom of sudden, abnormal electrical activity in the brain. In *tonic-clonic seizures* (formerly referred to as "grand mal" seizures), the child loses consciousness and becomes rigid, then experiences convulsions with severe muscle spasms and jerking of the limbs. In *absence seizures* (formerly referred to as "petit mal" seizures), the child abruptly stops what he is doing, stares into space for a few seconds with his eyelids fluttering, unaware of his surroundings, then just as abruptly resumes normal activity, unaware that a seizure has occurred.

Self-advocacy. Speaking up for oneself; asking for what one needs.

Self-determination. Deciding one's own fate/future.

Self-regulation. In sensory processing, an individual's method of responding to sensory input.

Self-stimulatory (stimming) behaviors. Repetitive, apparently non-functional behaviors that provide some sensory input (e.g., finger flicking or rocking). Also know as "stereotypies."

Semantic. Relating to the meaning of a word or phrase.

Sensitivity. Level of reaction to sensory input.

Sensory meltdown. A tantrum in response to overwhelming, unavoidable sensory experiences (e.g., the noise and smells of a lunchroom).

Sensory needs. The necessary types/amounts of sensory input required for an individual to be comfortable.

Sensory perception. The brain's recognition and interpretation of sensory input.

Sensory processing. The brain's perception of and response to sensory input.

Sensory Profile. A norm-referenced questionnaire developed by Winnie Dunn for assessing an individual's sensory processing patterns.

Shaping. Teaching a new behavior by reinforcing successive approximations of it.

Shared focus. Two or more people paying attention to the same activity, object, or issue.

Simple memory. Basic memory for straightforward information.

Slow triggers (setting events). Situations that cause stress and make a student less able to cope with demands; indirect triggers.

Social Behavior Mapping. A cognitive behavioral strategy for teaching the connections among emotions, behaviors, others' perspectives, and consequences.

Social cognition. Social thinking. How a person processes and interprets information about other people and their interactions.

Social communication. Communication that has a deliberate effect on another person's concentration, thought processes, or emotions.

Social dimensions of play. The quality of a child's interactions with others during play.

Social interaction. Individuals modifying their behavior in response to one another.

Social learning. Learning to understand others' perspectives and to behave in ways that others will consider socially appropriate.

Social motivation. When the desire to have some interaction with others is an incentive.

Social referencing. Looking to others (especially parents) for clues as to how to behave, react, or interpret a situation.

Social stimuli. Stimuli involving human interaction.

Social Stories™. A cognitive intervention developed by Carol Gray that uses short, individualized narratives to explain social situations and appropriate behaviors.

Social thinking. (see Social Cognition).

Social-pragmatic theory. The theory that a child's language development is highly dependent on joint attention, affect and attention sharing, and intention reading.

Somatosensory. Relating to the sensory signals from the skin, muscles, and joints.

Speed of processing. The rate at which the brain is able to take in information, sort it, analyze it, and respond to it.

Standardized tests. Tests that are administered and scored in a uniform manner, after which an individual's results are compared to large group norms.

Strange Stories Test. A theory-of-mind assessment in which individuals are asked to interpret nonliteral statements (e.g., sarcasm) made by characters in stories developed by Francesca Happé.

Structured teaching. An educational approach to teaching children with autism that emphasizes physical organization of the environment, schedules, work systems, and visual structure. See also TEACCH.

Student study team (SST) meeting/Child study team (CST) meeting. A formal meeting of teachers, professionals, and parents, when there is concern about a child who has not yet been evaluated or formally identified as having special education needs.

Student-centered. Based on the individual student's needs, preferences, and interests.

Subjective states. The ability to share others' attitudes and feelings.

Successive approximations. In shaping, incremental changes in behavior that increasingly resemble the desired behavior.

Supported employment. Jobs in which individuals with disabilities work alongside neurotypical individuals but receive ongoing support.

Symbol. An abstract representation that communicates an idea. Symbols can range from pointing to pictures to written and spoken language.

Symbolic communication. Use of symbols of any sort to communicate meaning..

Symbolic currency. An abstract way of exchanging ideas — usually language.

Symbolic dimension of play (simple and advanced). Play acts directed by the child toward objects, self, or others to signify events, exploratory play, and/or conventional object use.

Syntactic. Relating to the grammatical arranging of words into sentences.

Systemizing. Creating and utilizing systems of rules to understand and predict events.

T

Tabula rasa. Latin term meaning "blank slate." Refers to the belief that an infant is born with no innate mental content, and that a person's entire resource of knowledge will be based on his or her experience of the world.

TEACCH (Treatment and Education of Autistic and related Communication handicapped CHildren). Statewide autism services program in North Carolina, where the Structured Teaching method was developed.